DOCUMENTS IN WORLD HISTORY

Volume 2

The Modern Centuries: From 1500 to the Present

SIXTH EDITION

Peter N. Stearns
George Mason University

Stephen S. Gosch
University of Wisconsin, Eau Claire

Erwin P. Grieshaber
Minnesota State University, Mankato

Allison Scardino Belzer
Armstrong Atlantic State University

PEARSON

Boston Columbus Indianapolis New York San Francisco Upper Saddle River
Amsterdam Cape Town Dubai London Madrid Milan Munich Paris Montreal Toronto
Delhi Mexico City Sao Paulo Sydney Hong Kong Seoul Singapore Taipei Tokyo

Executive Editor: Jeff Lasser
Editorial Project Manager: Rob DeGeorge
Editorial Assistant: Julia Feltus
Senior Marketing Manager: Maureen E. Prado Roberts
Senior Marketing Assistant: Samantha Bennett
Production Project Manager: Clara Bartunek
Cover Designer: Suzanne Behnke
Manager, Cover Visual Research & Permissions: Beth Brenzel
Cover Photo: © imagebroker.net / SuperStock
Full-Service Project Management: Hemalatha
Composition: Integra Software Services Pvt. Ltd.
Printer/Binder: STP/RRD/Harrisonburg
Text Font: 10/12 New Baskerville

Credits and acknowledgments borrowed from other sources and reproduced, with permission, in this textbook appear on the appropriate page within the text.

Library of Congress Cataloging-in-Publication Data
Documents in world history / Peter N. Stearns . . . [et al.]. – 6th ed.
p. cm.
ISBN-13: 978-0-205-05023-9
ISBN-10: 0-205-05023-9
ISBN-13: 978-0-205-05024-6
ISBN-10: 0-205-05024-7
1. World history–Sources. I. Stearns, Peter N.
D5.D623 2012
909–dc22

2011012490

10 9 8 7 6 5 4 3 2 —RRD VA—14 13

ISBN 13: 978-0-205-05023-9 (Volume 1)
ISBN 10: 0-205-05023-9 (Volume 1)
ISBN-13: 978-0-205-05024-6 (Volume 2)
ISBN-10: 0-205-05024-7 (Volume 2)

CONTENTS

SECTION THREE
The Twentieth and Early Twenty-first Centuries 209

Geographical Contents: The Major Societies

Europe

Africa

Latin America

Interregional Contacts

Topical Contents

States and Politics

Religion and Culture

Social Structure

Women and the Family

Economic Relations

Preface

This volume focuses on the major currents in the development of the modern world—not just the American or Western world but the wider world in which we live today. It deals with the interaction between established civilizations and new forces of change, including the acceleration in international commerce and the results of industrialization. It also deals with the impact of change on loyalties and beliefs; on social institutions and the conditions of various groups, such as workers and women; and on the role of the state.

The book examines the formation of the modern world through selected primary sources—that is, documents written at the time. Primary sources do convey elements of the flavor and tensions of history in the making that cannot be captured in any other way. The sources also challenge the reader to distill the meaning of these expressions.

The various documents offered illustrate characteristic features of key civilizations in the major modern stages of world history from about 1500 C.E. to the present. These documents were not written for posterity; some were not even intended for a wide audience at the time. They are collected here to raise issues of understanding and interpretation that can enliven and enrich the study of world history.

The book deals with several key facets of the human experience, again in various times and places, from war to politics to gender. Overall, the selections encourage discussion of how particular societies such as those in India or Latin America dealt with the modern forces that have encouraged economic, social, and political change. This new edition of *Documents in World History* has given us the chance to introduce a number of changes to what has already proved to be a successful and widely used collection.

NEW TO THIS EDITION

- We have changed more than a quarter of the readings. It seemed possible to improve the representation of some key priorities in world history.
- We've also reorganized readings, both new and old, particularly to highlight connections and contacts.
- We've restructured the twentieth- to twenty-first-century section to highlight major developments, including the world wars.
- Introductions to the readings have also been revised to place the developments in clearer global context.
- Other revisions to the introductions focus simply on greater clarity and explanatory power, and we have also reviewed all the analytical questions with clarity and global connections in mind.

- In response to helpful comments from users, we have streamlined coverage in several places to make room for new documents as well as to make the text more manageable for students.
- And for the sixth edition, the authors welcome Allison Scardino Belzer, who teaches a wide variety of courses at Armstrong Atlantic State University in Savannah, Georgia. In teaching both halves of World Civilization, she focuses on assigning texts that spark a positive response in students, texts that offer concrete knowledge while also inspiring questions. She developed her interest in history at Vassar College and received her Ph.D. at Emory University. Her book *Women and the Great War: Femininity under Fire in Italy* (2010) reflects her research interest in gender and cultural history and the history of war.

As editors, we think the results improved the collection in several ways. But it is important to stress that the basic purpose of the collection has not changed: we seek to diversify the experiences of world history learners, to raise issues and challenges different from conventional textbook coverage, and to develop skills of interpretation and argument building that can be carried into many venues besides the world history classroom. The ability to understand materials not deliberately written for classroom exercises, to assess nuances and points of view, applies to all sorts of activities in work and in citizenship. The capacity to do this on a global scale, to handle offerings from different cultures and from different stages in the evolution of societal contacts, obviously responds to the needs of an increasingly globalized human experience.

This book's organization facilitates relating it to a core textbook. Major civilizations—East Asia, the West, India, the Middle East, Eastern Europe, Africa, and Latin America—are represented with several readings. Thus, a course can trace elements of change and continuity within each civilization. The readings are divided into three modern periods: 1500 to 1750, during which the rise of the West and diverse reactions to it formed a central thread in world history; 1750 to 1914, a period dominated by new patterns of manufacturing, new international technologies for transportation and communication, and new cultural forces such as nationalism; and the twentieth and early twenty-first centuries, during which Western influence continued strong but the other major civilizations also began to find their own distinctive modern voices. Another principle of selection involves topics that can be coherently traced and compared both across different civilizations and across different time periods. A topical table of contents facilitates the identification of themes such as religion, the family, or politics, and the building of readings and analyses accordingly.

The goal of the book is not, however, maximum coverage. A host of interesting and significant documents are left out by necessity. Readings have been chosen that illustrate important features of an area or period, that raise challenging problems of interpretation, and that express some human drama. The readings also invite comparisons across cultures and over time. **Chapter introductions** not only identify the readings, but also raise some issues that can be explored. **Study Questions** and **Essay Suggestions** at the end of each chapter further facilitate an understanding of issues.

Dealing with documents in the world history context in fact involves several related exercises, and the study questions develop these exercises. First, of course, is what the document means—and meanings often have to be teased out of the literal words, as when a set of laws is "asked" about the nature of a social structure, which was not the explicit purpose of the document's author. Second is what relationship the document has to other features of the society or period in question—how representative it is and what quirks it has. Third—and the study questions in the revised edition pay increased attention to this point—what is the document's relationship to larger world history themes, whether they be comparative or focus on change and continuity over time. Study questions in this revised edition have been reworked to provide a clearer basis for all the desirable levels of document analysis.

This book was prepared by four world history teachers at work in several kinds of institutions. It is meant, correspondingly, to serve the needs of different kinds of students. It is motivated by two common purposes: first, a strong belief that some perspective on the world is both desirable and possible as a key element in contemporary American education, and second, that an understanding of world history can be greatly enhanced by exposure not just to an overall factual and interpretive framework but also to the kinds of challenges and insights raised by primary materials.

Dealing with primary sources is not an easy task. Precisely because the materials are not written with American college students in mind, they require some thought. They must be related to other elements we know about a particular society, they must be given meaning, and they must be evaluated more carefully than a secondary account or textbook designed deliberately to pinpoint what should be learned. By the same token, however, gaining ease with the meaning of primary sources is a skill that carries well beyond a survey history course into all sorts of research endeavors. Gaining such skill in the context of the civilizations that compose the world goes some distance toward understanding how our world has become what it is—which is, in essence, the central purpose of history.

Thanks go to the reviewers of this edition. They are Christopher Ely, Florida Atlantic University; Colum Leckey, Piedmont Virginia Community College; and Michael Proulx, North Georgia College and State University.

PETER N. STEARNS
STEPHEN S. GOSCH
ERWIN P. GRIESHABER
ALLISON SCARDINO BELZER

INTRODUCTION

John Barbot, an employee of a French slave-trading company, wrote of his trips to West Africa in the late seventeenth century. He claimed that after the harsh treatment by African traders, slaves were lucky to get on the ships. Their "fate is less deplorable than that of those who end their days in their native country." How could someone write this, given what we know about the brutalities of the slave ships? Was Barbot simply trying to camouflage the treatments? How can an account like this be used to help understand the slave trade and its consequences? Issues like this are what make using primary sources both challenging and revealing.

This book is a collection of selected primary sources, written materials and a few illustrations designed to enhance the study of world history. Primary sources in world history are the creations of various people at various times and places who were addressing their own audiences, not twenty-first-century students. Their work, as a result, requires an effort of interpretation, different from what is involved in reading a textbook.

There are two reasons for exploring these kinds of sources. First, the exploration offers fresh voices and analytical challenges, making world history more lively and varied than when textbooks are the only fare. Properly used, sources promote understanding of key issues in world history. But second, grappling with primary sources gives students experience in handling evidence and in dealing with some of the pitfalls involved. Interpreting primary sources, such as political speeches or laws or child-rearing manuals, is how historians build arguments about the past, but it's also what people do or should do in trying to understand evidence in the society around them. Deciphering evidence applies equally well to figuring out what today's political rhetoric means, or a foreign leader's comments on the United States, or a corporation's explanation of its environmental policies. Building skills and adding value: these are the goals in presenting a variety of source materials.

What are the skills needed to manage primary source materials? First, a sense of context is vital: When and where does the material come from? What audience was aimed at, and how might this help explain what the source says?

The skills also involve assessment of possible bias or point of view: might the author distort, intentionally or not, because of self-interest or simply the reigning preconceptions of his or her own day?

Testing assumptions is vital, to see how they differ from one's own values and how they might therefore require a special kind of evaluation. Few people today would write so openly about women's inferiority as Chinese writers did two thousand years ago or would try to justify the treatment of people on a slave ship. So how can we identify their different assumptions so we have a better chance of understanding what they are trying to say and what they reveal about their own society?

Besides trying to identify context and audience, point of view, and assumptions, using primary materials imposes at least two other tests.

First, it's often essential to ask questions that the authors or creators of the material did not intend to answer, but which improve our own understanding of what is going on. A law code thus unintentionally exposes the basic features of social inequality. A religious tract, designed to guide pious behavior, helps uncover aspects of women's lives, or a travel account lets us see how different parts of the world were connecting in new ways. Other sources may help explain *why* something was happening, even though the author was not explicitly aware of causation issues. Reading for implications and unintended insights, along with reading for intended meaning, is central to the strategy in using source materials.

Second, sources must be judged for what they don't say, either directly or indirectly—for where we need other types of evidence to round out the best possible understanding. A handbook on women may be great for identifying gender inequalities or the nature of women's roles but may say nothing about birth rates—yet these are at least as important in shaping actual women's lives. Knowing when to look for more is vital to the analysis of both historical and contemporary issues.

Sources, in sum, suggest a checklist of approaches, all aimed at identifying meaning and implications to the greatest extent possible. There's real detective work involved here. Specifying context and audience, probing bias, testing assumptions but also seeking implications beyond what the author intended, and defining the limits of the evidence, all aim at stimulating new levels of understanding.

Selections in this volume, covering the past five centuries, highlight the growing drama of confrontation between deeply rooted, highly valued, and often successful cultural forms and some common forces of change. Over the past five hundred years, all the major civilizations have encountered growing pressures from new ideas and institutions—many of them initially generated in Europe or the United States—and often brute force and commercial exploitation from the West as well. During the past century (and in some cases longer), these same civilizations have tried to take into account the new technologies springing from industrialization; new ways of thinking shaped by modern science and belief systems, such as nationalism and socialism; the need to reshape government functions and the contacts between government and citizens; and pressures to redefine the family to allow for children's formal education, new roles for women, and often a reduction in traditional birthrates. The modern drama, played out in different specific ways depending on region, has involved combining some of the common, worldwide pressures with retention of vital continuities from the past.

The varieties of response have been considerable because the variety of established cultures is great. Some societies, often after experimenting with other responses, copied Western technologies and organizations sufficiently to industrialize while maintaining their own identities in part. Other societies have faced greater problems in matching the West's industrial might. Some, such as Latin America, partially merged with cultural styles initially developed in the West; others have tried to remain aloof from Western art or popular culture. Some societies have widely embraced new belief systems, whereas in others—such as the Islamic Middle East—pressures to retain older religious values have maintained greater force. The point is clear: no civilization in the modern world has been able to stand pat, and all have responded to challenge in some similar ways—using nationalism, for example, or extending formal systems of education. At the same time, overall responses have been extremely varied because of continuities from diverse pasts and diverse modern experiences. Defining the tension between common directions of change and the variety that still distinguishes the major civilizations forms one of the major analytical tasks of modern world history.

Many readers of this collection will already have covered the traditional periods of world history before 1500. Volume 1 of *Documents in World History,* a companion reader organized similarly to this volume, offers source materials on important features of the traditional world and its major civilizations, including the great religions, durable political patterns, and aspects of social structure and family life. Such features should be compared with developments in the more modern centuries to obtain a full sense of the interplay between the continuity of civilizations' traditions and the general forces shaping the modern world.

Volume 2 focuses on three basic modern periods that took shape after the fourteenth century C.E. During the first period, which began to form around 1400 and extended to the mid-eighteenth century, the rise of the West and Western sponsorship of a new world economy provided one central theme for world history, although different societies were diversely affected. Other major forces included the capacity to form new empires—the territorial agglomerations developed by the Ottomans, Russians, and Mughals—and the impacts of contact with the Americas. Continued economic vitality in Asia was another important theme. The second period in modern world history opened in the middle of the eighteenth century and extended until about 1914. After 1750, Western influence intensified, becoming more literally international; during the nineteenth century, Western controls—through imperialism—extended over new sections of the world. The West itself underwent the Industrial Revolution, which heightened its economic advantage over the rest of the world while ushering in radically new technological, social, and cultural forms.

The third chronological section of this book is focuses on the twentieth and early twenty-first centuries. In part, this simply reflects the fact that twentieth-century developments, such as the Russian Revolution and feminism, are particularly important today because of their proximity in time. Readings from the twentieth century allow analysis of what has changed and what persists in the world's major societies. But the twentieth century also serves as the beginning of a new period in world history, marked by the relative decline of the West, the development of radically new forms of warfare, and the extension of at least partial industrialization and urbanization to most portions of the world. The twentieth and early twenty-first centuries are not only, then, close to us by definition; they also seem to harbor an unusual number of fundamental changes in world history. These transitions—and the various efforts to resist them in the name of older values, ranging from Islamic purity to yearnings for Western supremacy—provide some of the overriding themes for the selections in the final group of readings.

The selections in this volume, while in no sense offering a comprehensive survey, reflect different regional patterns as well as different time periods and interconnections. Materials range from East Asia to sub-Saharan Africa to Latin America. Finally, the selections touch on several different topics, for individual societies and contacts alike.

Politics is one topic area: First, every complex society must develop some government structure and political values. Second, each society must generate a culture, that is, a system of beliefs and artistic expressions that help explain how the world works. Among these, religion is often a cultural linchpin for a society, but science and art play crucial roles as well. Economic relationships—the nature of agriculture, the level of technology and openness to technological change, the position of merchants—form a third feature of a civilization. Fourth, social groupings, hierarchies, and family institutions—including gender relations—organize human relationships and provide for the training of children. Finally, attention to trade and other contacts captures a growing force in the modern world, influencing and provoking major regions and key topics alike. This book, then, aims at providing some of the flavors of several different regions, of three large time periods, and of several facets of the human experience. The collection is meant to help readers themselves breathe life into world history and grasp some of the ways that both great and ordinary people have lived, suffered, and created in various parts of the world at various points in our rich human past.

The documents presented in this volume, and the kinds of questions asked at the end of each chapter, encourage important exercises in analyzing change and continuity and major contacts and comparisons. But the documents require analysis in their own right: What do they reveal about societies that the authors did not explicitly intend but nevertheless convey? Who, in fact, are the authors, and what are their points of view? When are participants in a major event useful reporters, and when do they become part of the interpretive problem? How can modern readers best judge bias or representativeness in using documents to build arguments about significant aspects of the world's past? Learning to hone these interpretive skills helps in handling vital features of world history, and they can also be applied to the kinds of evidence that emerge from the world in the present day.

SECTION I

THE EARLY MODERN PERIOD, CENTURIES OF DRAMATIC CHANGE: 1400s–1700s

The early modern period focuses on developments between about 1450 and the mid-eighteenth century. A new range of global interconnections was the most important change in the period. Extensive new sea routes created worldwide linkages and a variety of novel exchanges. The inclusion of the Americas had huge impacts on both the "New" World and the Old.

While exchanges constituted the key themes of the early modern period, shifts within individual societies mattered as well.

Western Europe's emergence as an increasingly important actor on the world stage between 1300 and 1500 depended on several developments: new technologies, in part gained by previous contacts with Asia (such as explosive powder and the compass); acute international trade problems and fear of Muslim power, which prompted Europeans to seek new and direct routes to Asia; and changes within European society itself, including greater rivalries among monarchs, and the scientific revolution. Western Europe's power at the same time affected other societies, particularly those in the Americas, which were now open to growing European control. Elsewhere, the impact of Western contacts, higher levels of international trade, and the foodstuffs available from the Americas had diverse results, ranging from altered commercial patterns in Africa to deliberate imitation from Russia to controlled contact along with growing trade in East Asia. Other innovations shaped the early modern centuries as well, including the formation of vigorous new empires (the Ottoman and the Mughal) in the Middle East and India, both of which extended Muslim power. Renewed political and economic strength in China was another vital Asian development, as European influence and new global trading patterns had only selective impact on the largest continent during the early modern centuries.

1 THE NEW GLOBAL CONTACTS

A NEW MARITIME NETWORK

The establishment of new sea routes, including the Atlantic and Pacific Oceans, and the acceleration of maritime trade were hallmarks of the early modern period in world history. They resulted in new kinds of contacts between the Americas and other parts of the world. They created new trade relationships not only for the Americas but for Africa, Western Europe, and parts of Asia as well. The following three chapters all deal with major aspects of the new global system.

The authors of the new maritime network, as it took shape in the late fifteenth and sixteenth centuries, were primarily Europeans, although assistance from pilots and merchants from other societies played a role as well. A key question, obviously, involves the motivations that drew a few leading Europeans into this kind of innovation—for motivations not only help explain the causes of the new maritime system but suggest what some of the consequences would be as well in terms of the goals Europeans would pursue as they encountered different lands.

Materials in this chapter, from several writers and explorers in the fifteenth, sixteenth and early seventeenth centuries, suggest the mixture of knowledge/ignorance, materialism, and religion that helped spur the growing range of voyages. The challenge, in analyzing the documents, is threefold: first, to put together the combinations of motives and beliefs that the materials suggest, for they hardly point in one direction. And second, to ask about other factors—technology, for instance—that need to be built into any full explanation of why the Europeans moved out as they did. And third, to speculate about the kinds of policies that Europeans would pursue once they established the new maritime system, compared, for example, to the dominant interests of other societies at the time.

Selection I involves a mythical story about the mysterious Christian leader Prester John, the subject of a widely believed forged letter in France in the fifteenth century. The hope to find Prester John, and his wealth and religious leadership at a time of growing pressure from the Islamic world, motivated not only beliefs but actual policies; the Portuguese sent an expedition to Ethiopia (where there was indeed a Christian king but not Prester John), in 1493, to this end. Selection II is from a fifteenth-century geography

Selection I from *Prester John: The Letter and the Legend,* pp. 6–78, passim. Trans. Vsevolod Slessarev. Copyright © 1959 University of Minnesota. Renewed 1987 Helga Slessarev. Reprinted courtesy of the University of Minnesota Press. Selection II from Petrus Ailliacus: *Imago Mundi,* trans. E. F. Keever (Wilmington, N.C., 1948). Selection III from *The Diario of Christopher Columbus's First Voyage to America 1492–1493,* by Christopher Columbus, edited by Oliver Dunn and J. E. Kelley, Jr., pp. 109–129, passim. Copyright © 1989 University of Oklahoma Press, Norman, OK. Reprinted by permission. Selection IV from *The first voyage round the world, by Magellan,* by Antonia Pigafetta, translated by Lord Stanley of Alderley, 1874 (original is from 1522). Selection V from José de Acosta, *The Natural and Moral History of the Indies* [1590], trans. Edward Grimston (London, 1604). Book IV, Chs. 3–4. English modernized.

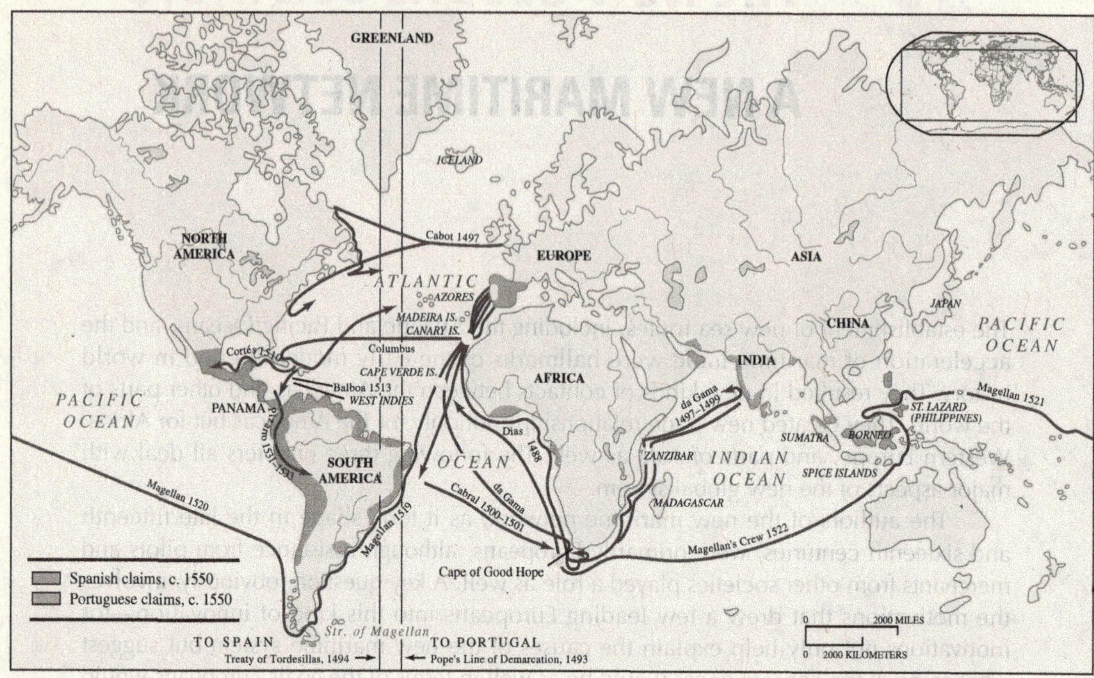

Spain and Portugal: Explorations and Colonies. In the early years of exploration, Spanish and Portuguese voyagers surveyed much of the coast of South America and some choice ports in Africa and Asia.

book by Petrus Ailliacus published in about 1414, summing up current understanding of classical geographical knowledge, from Aristotle, Ptolemy, and the Bible, and discussing the relationship between Europe and India. A selection from Columbus follows: in 1492, in the logbook of his first trip, he indicated where he thought he was in Asia, with obvious references to information gleaned from travel books such as Marco Polo's about the Mongol Khans, China, and Japan. A similar account of the first trip around the world, by Ferdinand Magellan (1480–1521) came from the pen of Antonio Pigafetta, an Italian scholar. Pigafetta kept detailed notes and was one of only eighteen people who survived the whole trip. This portion of his story deals with Magellan in the Philippines. Finally, a later comment, on what the Europeans had been finding in the New World, comes from José de Acosta's *Natural and Moral History of the Indies*, 1590.

COLUMBUS AND OTHERS

I. THE PRESTER JOHN STORY: FROM A LETTER FORGED IN FRANCE

Prester John, by the Grace of God most powerful king over all Christian kings, greetings to the Emperor of Rome and the King of France, our friends. We wish you to learn about us, our position, the government of our land, and our people and beasts.

And since you say that our Greeks, or men of Grecian race, do not pray to God the way you do in your country, we let you know that we worship and believe in Father, Son, and the Holy Ghost, three persons in one Deity and one true God only. We attest and inform you by our letter, sealed with our seal, of the condition and character of our land and men. And if you desire something that we can do for you, ask us, for we shall do it gladly. In case you wish to come hither to our country, we shall make you on account of your good reputation our successors and we shall grant you vast lands, manors, and mansions.

Let it be known to you that we have the highest crown on earth as well as gold, silver, precious stones and strong fortresses, cities, towns, castles, and boroughs. We have under our sway forty-two kings who all are mighty and good Christians. . . .

Our land is divided into four parts, for there are so many Indias. In Greater India lies the body of the Apostle Saint Thomas for whom our Lord has wrought more miracles than for the [other] saints who are in heaven. And this India is toward the East, for it is near the deserted Babylon and also near the tower called Babel. . . .

Know also that in our country there grows wild pepper amidst trees and serpents. When it becomes ripe, we send our people to gather it. They put the woods on fire and everything burns, but when the fire has died out, they make great heaps of pepper and serpents and they put the pepper together and carry it later to a barn, wash it in two or three waters, and let it dry in the sun. In this way it becomes black, hard, and biting. . . .

Let it be known to you that we have swift horses which can carry a knight in full armor for three or four days without taking food.

And whenever we go to war, we let fourteen kings, clad in garments of gold and silver, carry in front of us fourteen ensigns adorned with sundry precious stones. Other kings who come behind carry richly decorated banners of silk.

Know that in front of us there march forty thousand clerics and an equal number of knights, then come two hundred thousand men on foot, not counting the wagons with provisions or the elephants and camels which carry arms and ammunition. . . .

Know that I had been blessed before I was born, for God has sent an angel to my father who told him to build a palace full of God's grace and a chamber of paradise for the child to come, who was to be the greatest king on earth and to live for a long time. And whoever stays in the palace will never suffer hunger, thirst, or death. When my father had woke up from his slumber, he was overly joyful and he began to build the palace which you will see.

First of all, its walls are of crystal, the ceiling above is of precious stones and it is adorned with stars similar to those of the sky, and its floor is also of crystal. There are no windows or doors in this palace and inside it has twenty-four columns of gold and various precious stones. We stay there during the big holidays of the year and in the midst of it St. Thomas [an apostle of Christ who allegedly traveled to India] preaches to the people. And inside our palace there is [water] and the best wine on earth, and whoever drinks of it has no desire for worldly things, and nobody knows where the [water] goes or whence it comes.

There is still another great marvel in our palace, for no food is served in it except on a tray, grill, or trencher that hangs from a column, so that when we sit at the table and wish to eat, the food is placed before us by the grace of the Holy Spirit.

Know that all the scribes on earth could not report or describe the riches of our palace and our chapel. Everything we have written to you is as true as there is God, and for nothing in the world would we lie, since God and St. Thomas would confound us and deprive us of our title.

II. AILLIACUS, *IMAGO MUNDI*

The investigation into the quantity of the habitable earth demands that we should consider "habitability" from two angles. One has respect to the heaven; that is, how much of it can be inhabited on account of the Sun, and how much cannot. On this sufficient was said previously in a general way. From another angle it must be considered with respect to the water, i.e., how far the water is in the way. To this we now turn, and on it there are various opinions among the wise men. Ptolemy in his book *The Arrangement of the Sphere* (*Dispositione Spere*) would have almost a sixth part of the earth habitable because of the water. So also his *Algamestus,* in Book II, says that there is no known habitation except on one fourth of the earth, i.e., where we live; and that it extends lengthwise from east to west, the equator being in the middle. Its breadth is from the equator to the pole; and it is a fourth of the colurus [sphere]. Aristotle, however, in the close of his book on *The Heaven and the Earth* would have it that more than a fourth is inhabited. Averroes confirms this. Aristotle says that a small sea lies between the confines of Spain on the western side and the beginnings of India on the eastern side. He is not speaking of Hither Spain (*certeriori*) which in these times is commonly known as Spain, but of Farther Spain (*ulteriori*) which is now called Africa. On this topic certain authors have spoken, such as Pliny, Orosius, and Isidore. Moreover Seneca in the fifth book of the *Naturalium* holds that the sea is navigable in a few days if the wind is favorable. Pliny in the *Naturalibus* Book II informs us that it has been navigated from the Arabian Sea to the Pillars of Hercules in rather a short time. From these and many other reckonings, on which I shall expand when I speak of the ocean, some apparently conclude that the sea is not so great that it can cover three quarters of the earth. Add to this the judgment of Esdras in his IV Book [Bible] where he says that six parts of the earth are inhabited and the seventh is covered with water. The authority of this book the Saints have held in reverence and by it have established sacred truths. . . .

There ought to be an abundance of water toward the poles of the earth because those regions are cold on account of their distance from the sun; and the cold accumulates moisture. Therefore the water runs down from one pole toward the other into the body of the sea and spreads out between the confines of Spain and the beginning of India, of no great width, in such a way that the beginning of India can be beyond the middle of the equinoctial circle and approach beneath the earth quite close to the coast of Spain. Likewise Aristotle and his commentator came to the same conclusion because there are so many elephants in those regions. Says Pliny: "Around Mt. Atlas elephants abound." So also in India and even in ulterior Spain there are great herds of elephants. But, reasons Aristotle, the elephants in both those places ought to show similar characteristics; if widely separated they would not have the same characteristics. Therefore he concludes those countries are close neighbors and that a small sea intervenes; and moreover that the sea covers three-quarters of the earth; that the beginnings of the east and the west are near by, since a small sea separates them.

III. COLUMBUS'S LOGBOOK, 1492

Sunday 21 October

And afterwards I will leave for another very large island that I believe must be Cipango [Japan] according to the indications that these Indians that I have give me, and which they call Colba. In it they say there are many and very large ships and many traders. And from this island [I will go to] another which they call Bohío, which also they say is very big. And the others which are in between I will also see on the way; and, depending on whether I find a quantity of gold or spices, I will decide what I am to do. But I have already decided to go to the mainland and to the city of Quinsay [in Asia] and to give Your Highnesses' letters to the Grand Khan [Mongol ruler of China] and to ask for, and to come with, a reply.

Wednesday 24 October

Tonight at midnight I weighed anchors from the island of Isabela [Fortunate/Crooked Islands], from the Cabo del Isleo, which is in the northern part, where I was staying, to go to the island of Cuba, which I heard from these people was very large and of great commerce and that there were there gold and spices and great ships and merchants; and they showed me that [sailing] to the west-southwest I would go to it. And I believe so, because I believe that it is so according to the signs that all the Indians of these islands and those that I have with me make (because I do not understand them through speech) [and] that it is the island of Cipango of which marvelous things are told. And in the spheres that I saw and in world maps it is in this region.

Friday 26 October

He went from the southern part of the said islands five or six leagues. It was all shoal. He anchored there. The Indians that he brought said that from the islands to Cuba was a journey of a day and a half in their dugouts, which are small vessels made of a single timber which do not carry sails. These are canoes. He left from there for Cuba, because from the signs that the Indians gave him of its size and of its gold and pearls he thought it must be it, that is, Cipango.

Sunday 28 October

While he was going toward land with the ships, two dugouts or canoes came out. And when they saw that the sailors were getting into the launch and were rowing to go look at the depth of the river in order to know where they should anchor, the canoes fled. The Indians said that in that island there were gold mines and pearls, and the Admiral saw a likely place for pearls and clams, which are a sign of them. And the Admiral [Columbus] understood that large ships from the Grand Khan came there and that from there to *tierra firme* [the mainland] was a journey of ten days. The Admiral named that river and harbor San Salvador.

Tuesday 30 October

He went out of the Rio de Mares to the northwest and, after he had gone 15 leagues, saw a cape full of palms and named it Cabo de Palmas. The Indians in the caravel *Pinta* said that behind that cape there was a river and that from the river to Cuba was a four-day journey. And the captain of the *Pinta* said that he understood that this Cuba was a city and that that land was a very big landmass that went far to the north, and that the king of that land was at war with the Grand Khan, whom they call *cami,* and his land or city, Faba, and many other names. The Admiral decided to go to that river and to send a present to the king of the land and to send him the letter of the sovereigns. And for this purpose he had a sailor who had gone on the same kind of mission in Guinea, and certain Indians from Guanahani wished to go with him so that afterward they would be returned to their own land. In the opinion of the Admiral he was distant from the equinoctial line 42 degrees toward the northern side (if the text from which I took this is not corrupt). And he says that he must strive to go to the Grand Khan, whom he thought was somewhere around there, or to the city of Cathay [China], which belongs to the Grand Khan, for he says that it is very large, according to what he was told before he left Spain. All this land he says, is low and beautiful, and the sea deep.

IV. PIGAFETTA ON MAGELLAN

On the 6th of March, 1521, [Magellan and his crew] fetched two islands inhabited by many people, and they anchored at one of them, which is in twelve degrees north; and the inhabitants are people of little truth, and they did not take precautions against them until they saw that they were taking away the skiff of the flagship, and they cut the rope with which it was made fast, and took it ashore without their being able to prevent it. They gave this island the name of Thieves' Island.

Magellan seeing that the skiff was lost, set sail, as it was already night, tacking about until the next day; as soon as it was morning they anchored at the place where they had seen the skiff carried off to, and he ordered two boats to be got ready with a matter of fifty or sixty men, and he went ashore in person, and burned the whole village, and they killed seven or eight persons, between men and women, and recovered the skiff, and returned to the ships; and while they were there they saw forth or fifty [natives] come, which came from the same land, and brought much refreshments.

Magellan would not make any further stay, and at once set sail, and ordered the course to be steered west, and a quarter south-west; and so they made land . . . and they gave it the name of the island of Good Signs, because they found some gold in it. Whilst they were thus anchored at this island, there came to them two natives and brought them fowls and cocoa nuts. . . . [On yet another] island they were very well received, and they placed a cross in it. This king conducted them thence a matter of thirty leagues to another island named Cabo, and in this island Magellan did what he pleased with the consent of the country, and in one day eight hundred people became Christian, on which account Magellan desired that the other kings, neighbours to this one, should become subject to this one who had become Christian: and these did not choose to yield such obedience. Magellan, seeing that, got ready one night with his boats, and burned the villages of those who would not yield the said obedience; and a matter of ten or twelve days after this was done he sent to a village about half a league from that which he had burned, which is named Matam, and which is also an island, and ordered them to send him at once three goats, three pigs, three loads of rice, and three loads of millet for provisions for the ships; they replied that of each article which he sent to ask them three of, they would send to him by twos, and if he was satisfied with this they would at once comply, if not, it might be as he pleased, but that they would not give it. Because they did not choose to grant what he demanded of them, Magellan ordered three boats to be equipped with a matter of fifty or sixty men, and went against the said place; there they found many people, who might well be as many as three thousand or four thousand men, who fought with such a good will that the said Magellan was killed there, with six of his men, in the year 1521.

V. ACOSTA

Gold, silver, and metals grow naturally in land that is barren and unfruitful. And we see, that in lands of good temperature, which are fertile with grass and fruits, there are seldom found any mines; for that Nature is contented to give them vigor to bring forth fruits more necessary for the preservation and maintenance of the life of beasts and men. And contrariwise to lands that are very rough, dry, and barren (as in the highest mountains and inaccessible rocks of a rough temper) they find mines of silver, of quick-silver, and of gold; and all those riches (which come into Spain since the West Indies were discovered) have been drawn out of such places which are rough and full, bare and fruitless: yet the taste of this money makes these places pleasing and agreeable, well inhabited with numbers of people. . . .

We find not that the Indians in former times used gold, silver, or any other metal for money, and for the price of things, but only for ornament, . . . whereof there was great quantity in their temples, palaces, and tombs, with a thousand kinds of vessels of gold and silver, which they had. Coming therefore to our subject; at the Indies there is great abundance of this metal [gold], and it is well known by approved histories that the Incas of Peru did not content themselves with great and small vessels of gold, as pots, cups, goblets, and flagons; with bowls or great vessels, but they had chairs also and litters of massive gold, and in their temples they had set up many Images of pure gold, whereof they find some yet at Mexico, but not such store as when the first Conquerors came into the one and the other kingdom, who found great treasure, and without doubt there was much more hidden in the earth by the Indians. It would seem ridiculous to report that they have made their horse shoes of silver for want of iron, and that they have paid three hundred crowns for a bottle of wine, and other strange things; and yet in truth this has come to pass, yes and greater matters. They draw gold in those parts after three sorts, or at the least, I have seen all three used. For either they find gold in grains, in powder, or in stone. They refine powdered gold in basins, washing it in many waters until the sand falls from it, and the gold, as most heavy, remains in the bottom. They refine it likewise with quick-silver and strong water, for . . . this water has the virtue to separate gold from dross, or from other metals. After it is purified and molten, they make bricks or small bars to carry it to Spain for being in powder they cannot transport it from the Indies for they can neither custom it, mark it, nor take assay until it is melted down. . . .

Today the great treasure of Spain comes from the Indies, because God has appointed the one realm to serve the other by giving up its wealth so as to be under good governance, thus mutually enjoying one another's goods and privileges.

STUDY QUESTIONS

1. What kind of geographical knowledge helps explain the European expeditions that built the new maritime system?
2. How did religious belief and a hope for profit combine in motivating the new voyages?
3. How did Magellan's apparent motives compare with those of Columbus?
4. Why was European interest in Asia so high?
5. What other kinds of evidence would help assess the Europeans' ability to develop an unprecedented maritime system between the late fifteenth and the mid-sixteenth centuries?
6. What do the dominant European motives suggest about the impact Europeans' arrival would have on the areas touched by the early modern maritime system?
7. What might account for differences in local reception for Columbus in the West Indies and Magellan in the Philippines? Had Spanish Maritime experiences over thirty years led to changes in approach?

ESSAY SUGGESTIONS

A. Do the Europeans' motives associated with the new maritime system help explain why other societies could not or did not participate quickly in following the Europeans' lead?

B. Was it a distinctive European culture or other factors that best explain the new European surge in global commerce around 1500?

C. Discuss the various local reactions to the arrival of European explorers around 1500. Why was effective resistance limited?

2 GLOBAL CONTACTS: DRAMATIC CHANGES AFTER 1492

THE COLUMBIAN EXCHANGE IN THE EARLY MODERN PERIOD

Disseminated most widely by Alfred Crosby in *The Columbian Exchange: Biological and Cultural Consequences of 1492,* the term *Columbian exchange* refers to the worldwide transfer of pathogens, plants, and animals resulting from the expanded and intensified contact among civilizations after 1492. To America, Europeans brought diseases (smallpox and measles), animals (cattle, horses, sheep, and pigs), and plants (grapes, sugar, wheat, barley, and oats). From America, traders carried away not only precious metals but also corn (maize), potatoes, and sweet potatoes. These transfers contributed significantly to the formation of new civilizations in the Americas and altered the civilizations of Europe, Asia, and Africa.

In the Americas, smallpox and measles reduced the indigenous population of the Caribbean Islands almost to the vanishing point by 1540. In Central Mexico, the Indian population declined from about 18 million at the time of contact to approximately 1 million in 1605. Peru's native population declined from 11 million to about 700,000 by the early eighteenth century. Throughout the Americas, the indigenous population declined by about 90 percent.

In place of people, European animals claimed the land. This was especially true where open grasslands were available. To cite one example, in the Mesquital Valley north of Mexico City, sheep increased from 39,000 in 1539 to 4.4 million in 1589. As the number of sheep increased, the former corn-producing valley became scrub land.

Selection I from Bernadino de Sahagún, *Florentine Codex: General History of the Things of New Spain,* 2nd ed., translated by Arthur J. O. Anderson and Charles E. Dibble (Santa Fe, N.M.: The School of American Research and the University of Utah, 1975), part 13, p. 81. Reprinted courtesy of the University of Utah Press. Selection II from Antonio Vázquez de Espinosa, *Description of the Indies* (ca. 1620) (originally published as *Compendium and Description of the West Indies* in 1942), translated by Charles Upson Clark (Washington, D.C.: Smithsonian Institution Press, 1968), pp. 170–171, 173–175, 190–191, 731–733. Selection III from John Locke, *Locke's Travels in France, 1675–1679 as Related in His Journals, Correspondence and Other Papers,* edited by John Lough (New York: Cambridge University Press, 1953), p. 236. Reprinted with the permission of Cambridge University Press. Selection IVA from remarks by Robert Boyle in *Royal Society, 1662. Miscellaneous Papers of the Council,* etc., 20 March; Selection IVB from the gardener of Robert Boyle to Robert Boyle, *Royal Society Letter Book* (1663), Vol. 1, p. 83. The two quotes may be found in Redcliffe N. Salaman, *The History and Social Influence of the Potato* (New York: Cambridge University Press, 1949), pp. 228 and 238, respectively. Reprinted with the permission of Cambridge University Press. Selection V from Adam Smith, *An Inquiry into the Nature and Causes of the Wealth of Nations,* edited by Edwin Caanan (New York: Random House, 1937), pp. 160–161. Selection VI comes from *Fuzhou Fu Zhi.* Chapter 25: Products 1. Originally Published: Qing Qianlong 19 nian (1754), translated by Professor Tao Peng, Department of History, Minnesota State University, Mankato.

In other zones, now virtually empty of Indian farmers because of population loss, new crops of wheat, barley, and sugar became predominant.

In Europe and Asia, maize and potatoes became staple foods for the poor and in both areas contributed to population increases. Between 1650 and 1750, the population of Europe, including Asiatic Russia, increased from 103 million to 144 million; the population of Asia, excluding Russia, increased from 327 million to 475 million. As one of many factors, new crops bore a direct relationship to the population rise. Maize and potatoes increased the total food supply because they allowed previously uncultivated land, including fallow land, to be used.

The first selection describes a smallpox epidemic in the Aztec capital of Tenochtitlán, just months prior to the Spanish siege in August 1521. Written originally in Náhuatal, the Aztec language, in 1555 by native informants, the document was translated into Spanish in 1557 by Bernadino de Sahagún, a member of the Franciscan order. The selections on the spread of European plants and animals in Mexico and Chile were written in 1620 by a Carmelite friar, Antonio Vázquez de Espinoza. He not only identified the plants and animals but also described the native people's adjustment to their spread. Information on the importance of the sweet potato in China comes from a provincial gazetteer of the eighteenth century. European Enlightenment intellectuals wrote about maize and potatoes in Europe. As well, European artists depicted the social consequences of the new crops. Vincent Van Gogh's *The Potato Eaters* (1885) depicts the social and psychological circumstances of people who became dependent on potatoes.

THE MIGRATION OF FOOD AND DISEASES

I. DISEASE IN MEXICO

Twenty-ninth Chapter, in which it is told how there came a plague, of which the natives died. Its name was smallpox. It was at the time that the Spaniards set forth from Mexico.

But before the Spaniards had risen against us, first there came to be prevalent a great sickness, a plague. It was in Tepeilhuitl that it originated, that there spread over the people a great destruction of men. Some it indeed covered [with pustules]; they were spread everywhere, on one's face, on one's head, on one's breast, etc. There was indeed perishing; many indeed died of it. No longer could they walk; they only lay in their abodes, in their beds. No longer could they move, no longer could they bestir themselves, no longer could they raise themselves, no longer could they stretch themselves out on their sides, no longer could they stretch themselves out face down, no longer could they stretch themselves out on their backs. And when they bestirred themselves, much did they cry out. There was much perishing. Like a covering, covering-like, were the pustules. Indeed many people died of them, and many just died of hunger. There was death from hunger; there was no one to take care of another; there was no one to attend to another.

And on some, each pustule was placed on them only far apart; they did not cause much suffering, neither did many die of them. And many people were harmed by them on their faces; their faces were roughened. Of some, the eyes were injured; they were blinded.

At this time this plague prevailed indeed sixty days—sixty day-signs—when it ended, when it diminished; when it was realized, when there was reviving, the plague was already going toward Chalco.

II. EUROPEAN PLANTS AND ANIMALS IN MEXICO AND CHILE, 1620

Mexico: Mexico City

Of Other Features of the Archdiocese of Mexico, and of the Fruit Growing There.

- In the provinces of this district of the Archdiocese of Mexico described in the preceding chapters, there are over 250 Indian villages, with many cities among them; 100 [of them] are county seats (cabezas de partido). In these, and on over 6,000 establishments—corn and wheat farms, sugar plantations, cattle, sheep, and hog ranches—there are over 500,000 Indians paying tribute, and more than 150 convents of the Dominican, Franciscan, and Augustinian orders, and many curacies under priests, not to speak of the [many] Spanish towns in the district of the Archdiocese, and especially all the silver-mining towns, which are Spanish settlements.
- The city of Mexico is luxuriously provided with fruit, both of Spanish and native varieties: they all yield abundantly. There are excellent olive groves from which they gather quantities of eating olives. Grapes are brought in from Querétaro, and there are a few vines in the city, as well as peaches large and small, pippins, quinces, pomegranates, oranges, limes, grapefruit, citrons, and lemons; the gardens produce in abundance all varieties of Spanish garden stuff and vegetables; the lake provides delicious fish of different sorts, and the streams, bobos, which is an excellent fish, and others.

Mexico: Michoacán

The province has varieties of climate—cold, hot, and springlike—and famous valleys and meadowlands, with streams of crystal-clear water running through them; hot baths very beneficial for invalids; fertile fields which yield abundance of corn, wheat, and other cereals, both native and Spanish; there is plenty of pastureland, and in consequence large cattle ranches with constantly increasing product; sheep from Castile, from whose wool they weave in the mills fine and coarse woolen cloth, blankets, sombreros, etc.; they raise also many hogs.

At these villages they get two abundant harvests of wheat and corn each year, one in the rainy season and the other by irrigation; from them they supply many cities and towns in New Galicia, and San Luís de Potosí.

- In the northern part of this diocese, along their frontier with the Indian tribe of the Chichimecas, they gather wild cochineal [a plant that yields a red dye], very fine when worked up; there are large cattle, sheep, and hog ranches: they raise excellent horses and mules.

Mexico: Michoacán

- The town of La Concepción de Celaya was founded by the Viceroy Don Martin Enríquez in the year 1570 on the Zacatecas King's Highway to New Galicia and New Vizcaya, as a frontier post against the Chichimeca Indians. It has a springlike climate and fertile fields with wealth of pastureland, for which reason there are large cattle, sheep, and hog ranches, with good mules and horses; they harvest abundance of corn, wheat, and other cereals, (Marg.: for which there are large irrigation ditches); they raise many kinds of native fruit and all the Spanish ones. The town will contain 400 Spanish residents, with a parish church, Franciscan, Augustinian, and Barefoot Carmelite convents, with other hospitals, churches, and shrines; there are many Indian villages in the district. In this region there are other Spanish settlements with many farms full of cattle, (which I do not enumerate because it would be almost impossible). Celaya belongs to the Marqués de Villamayor.

Mexico: New Vizcaya

- The Diocese and State of New Vizcaya begins at the mines of Fresnillo, 12 leagues distant from Zacatecas; there will be 100 Spanish residents here, with a Franciscan convent; it has rich silver mines and veins. Twelve leagues farther on, as one travels toward Guadiana, like the mines of Los Plateros and Sombrerete and others, with rich silver veins and ore beds, and some establishments in which they smelt the metal. All this country has a good climate and is provided with plenty of supplies, for it is very fertile; they raise quantities of wheat, corn, and other cereals, with abundance of native and Spanish fruit and grapes, and much cattle, sheep, swine, mules, and horses.

Chile: City of Santiago

In the district of the city of Santiago there are 48 small Indian villages, assigned to 30 encomenderos. In the 48 villages in the year 1614 when they were inspected by Licentiate Machado, Justice of that Circuit Court, there were 2,345 Indians, 331 old people, etc. Tribute payers in the villages were 696; the others were away, some out on their work, others in the service of their encomenderos. In these villages of the district of this city and Diocese, and on the farms, there are 23 curacies, 21 administered by clerics and 2 by friars.

- At the above date there were 72 Indian men and 85 Indian women (?) slaves captured in the war after the slavery proclamation. There were likewise 501 Huarpes Indians from the Province of Cuyo residing in the country, of those who had come in for their mita, and 225 from Peru and Tucumán. There were likewise 481 of the Beliches tribe from these villages, who were artisans: Carpenters, 124; tanners, 100; tailors, 33; shoemakers, 81; silk weavers, 3; ropemakers for rigging, 2; masons, 30; blacksmiths, 7; water-jar makers, 19; stonecutters, 6; house painters, 4; they all lived and resided in the outer wards of the city of Santiago; the artisans alone numbered 409.

Round about the city there were 102 chacras, of wheat, corn, chick-peas, lentils, kidney beans, and other cereals and vegetables; there were some carts (carretas) which brought wood into the city and transported merchandise from the port and did all else necessary in the city service. In the city and on the chacras and ranches there are 41 tanneries in which every year they tan over 30,000 pieces of cordovan leather, and some hides for soles. On the river bank and on the chacras and ranches of the district there are 39 gristmills for wheat, and 3 woolen mills in which they work up and turn out every year over 14,000 varas of coarse cloth and grograms and more than 500 blankets.

Chapter IV

Continuing the Description of the Preceding Subject.

- Besides the above there were 354 farms—cattle ranches, corn, wheat, and other cereals; on them there were some Beliches Indians and 2,162 Yanaconas—part of them from the upcountry cities abandoned because of the rebellion of the Indians in that Kingdom, and others from elsewhere. These Indians are civilized (Ladinos); because their villages and natural surroundings are uncongenial, or because they are escaping from troubles they might have at home, or because they are wanderers, they bring themselves to enter the Spaniards' service. They are assigned (repartidos) to these farms, with their wives and children, 4, 6, or more to each, just as they would naturally settle: normally they live there and cultivate their own gardens and fields for their necessities, in addition to what the masters they serve give them in clothing, cash, or food.

  On the majority of the farms there are superintendents (mayor-domos), Spanish soldiers or mestizos, the sons of Spaniards and Indian women, or mulattoes or free Negroes. These keep track of the figures for the sowing and the harvest, and see that the people work and do all else necessary. On all the farms and ranches in the Indies, of any importance, they are to be found and have excellent salaries, according to the size of the establishment. In this Kingdom most are paid one-fourth of the products of the soil and of the stock bred; some are paid less, for there is every sort of system.
- In this Kingdom there are very large rivers, swollen in winter with water from the rains and in summer from the great freshets from the snow melting under the sun up on the Cordillera Nevada. These all run from E. to W., to the Pacific; with them they irrigate their property and fields. They are utilized for a distance of about 40 leagues, in which irrigation produces large amounts of wheat, corn, barley, chickpeas, lentils, peas (porotos), and other cereals and vegetables, which yield abundantly; they raise a few potatoes. The fanega of wheat is usually worth 8 reals; they normally ship large amounts to Lima when they need it there, and it is also taken for His Majesty's camp and army, for the soldiers' sustenance.

  There are quantities of vineyards around Santiago and on the farms; every year they get more than 200,000 jugs of wine from them; that was the figure in the year 1614, when they made the inspection of that Kingdom. In the 3 preceding years they had planted 498,500 vines, and many more have been set out since then; the land is very fertile and the vine grows thick, strong, and sturdy; they treat it with gypsum and ferment (cocido) as is done in many places. It is all consumed within the country; some is taken for His Majesty's army to the city of La Concepción.

- The residents of Santiago possessed in the district of the city 39,250 cattle, the yearly increase of which was 13,500; quantities are slaughtered every year for tallow; they raise oxen for plowing and for their carts. Every young steer is worth 4 8-real pesos; an ox broken to work, 8; when a herd is sold, it is at the rate of 12 reals a head. There were on the ranches in the district 4,278 mares, and their annual increase, 1,200; each is worth 4 reals. Riding horses are worth from 16 to 20 8-real pesos; sumpter horses, 8 to 10; choice fine steeds, from 100 to 200 pesos.

  They had in the district 323,956 goats, whose annual increase was 94,764; they slaughter quantities of gelded males and of females, and get over 2,500 quintals of tallow from them annually, worth 13 8-real pesos a quintal, and 25,100 pieces of cordovan leather, which they ship to Callao for Lima, since it is the best in the Kingdom. Before tanning, each sells for 16 reals; tanning each piece comes to 3½ reals. There were 623,825 sheep, whose annual increase was 223,944; they slaughter great numbers of them and get on the average 7,650 quintals of tallow from them every year. The usual price of a sheep is 2 reals, and a dressed mutton (carnero) the same, and in the city, 4. They are large, fat, and very good.

III. JOHN LOCKE ON MAIZE IN FRANCE

"MOND. SEPT. 12 from Petit Niort to Blay 6 (leagues). The country between Xantes & Blay is a mixture of corne, wine, wood, meadow, champaine inclosure, wall nuts & chestnuts, but that which I observd particularly in it was plots of Maize in severall parts, which the country people call bled d'Espagne, &, as they told me, serves poor people for bred. That which makes them sow it, is not only the great increase, but the convenience also which the blade & green about the stalke yeilds them, it being good nourishment for their cattle."

IV. POTATOES IN IRELAND AND ENGLAND

A. Robert Boyle on Potatoes in Ireland (1662)

[H]e knew that in a time of famine in Ireland, there were kept from starving, thousands of poor people by potatoes; and that this root would make good bread, mixed with wheaten meale; that it will yield good drink too, but of no long duration; that it feeds poultry and other animals well; that any refuge will keep them from frost; that the very stalks of them thrown into the ground, will produce good roots; that the planning of them doth not hinder poor people from other employment.

B. Robert Boyle's Gardener (1663)

I have according to your desire sent a box of Potato rootes; my care hath been to make choice of such, that are fit to set without cutting; for many, that have not small ones enough, are constrained to cut the great ones; but I doe not approve of that husbandry, neither do I make use of it, because when they are cut, the wormes doe feed on them, and so devouring the substance, the branch groweth the weaker, and the roote small: the ground which they thrive best in is a light sandy soyle, where ferns or briars do naturally grow. Their nature is not to grow fruitful in a rich soyle because they will spring forth many branches, and so encumber the ground, that they will have but small roots. You may cause them to be set a foot apart or something better, whole as they are, and there will be great encrease, and the branch will bring forth fruit which we call the Potato-apple, they are very good to pickle for winter and sallets, and also to preserve; I have tasted of many sorts of fruit, and have not eaten the like of that, they are to be gathered in September, before the first frost doth take them. If you are minded to have great store of small rootes which are fittest to set, you may cause them to lay down the branches; in the month before named, and cover them with earth three or four inches thick, and the branch of every joint will bring forth small rootes in so great number that the increase of one yard of ground will set twenty the next season, and it must be the care of the gardner to cover the ground where the rootes are with fearns or straw, halfe a foote thick and better at the beginning of the winter, otherwise the frost will destroy the rootes; and as they have occasion to dig out the great rootes, they may uncover the ground, and leave the small ones in the earth, and cover them as before and preserve the seed.

Now the season to dig the ground is April or May, but I hold it best the latter end of April, and when they dig the ground let them pick out as many as they can find small and great, and yet there will be enough for the next crop left; let the covering which they are covered withall be burried in the ground, and that is all the improvement that I doe bestow. I could speak in praise of the roote, what a good and profitable thing it is, and might be to a commonwealth, could it be generally experienced; as the inhabitants of your towne can manifest the truth of it, but I will be silent in speaking in the praise of them, knowing you are not ignorant of it.

V. ADAM SMITH ON POTATOES

[A]n acre of potatoes will still produce . . . three times the quanity [of food] produced by the acre of wheat . . . [and] is cultivated with less expence than an acre of wheat; the fallow, which generally precedes the sowing of wheat, more than compensating the hoeing and other extraordinary culture which is always given to potatoes. Should this root ever become in any part of Europe, like rice is in some rice countries, the common and favourite vegetable food of the people, so as to occupy the same proportion of the lands in tillage which wheat and other sorts of grain for human food do at present, the same quanity of cultivated land would maintain a much greater number of people, and the labourers being generally fed with potatoes, a greater surplus would remain after replacing all the stock and maintaining all the labour employed in cultivation. A greater share of this surplus too would belong to the landlord. Population would increase, and rents would rise much beyond what they are at present. . . .

It is difficult to preserve potatoes through the year, and impossible to store them like corn [refers to traditional grain crops such as wheat, oats, and barley; corn does not refer to maize] for two or three years together. The fear of not being able to sell them before they rot, discourages their cultivation, and is perhaps, the chief obstacle to their ever becoming in any great country, like bread, the principal vegetable food of all the different ranks of the people.

VI. AMERICAN CROPS IN CHINA

Sweet Potato in Fukien Province southeastern China, 1754

Fan-shu [Sweet Potato]

The Book of Min [Fujian]:

The skin is purple. The taste is sweeter than *shu-yu* [Chinese yam]. It is particularly easy to propagate. The prefecture initially did not have this species. In the *Jiawu* [one of the 60 Heavenly Stems and Earthly Branches] year of the Wanli reign of the Ming dynasty (1594), there was a yearly crop failure. Governor Jin Xue-zeng solicited the seeds back from the foreign barbarian country and instructed people to cultivate them as grain food. Famine did not evolve into a disaster.

Ji Han's *The Shape of Grass and Trees* [the full title is *Nafang Caomu Zhuang* (*The Shape of Southern Grass and Trees*), written in 304AD.] notes: There is *gan-shu* [sweet Chinese yam]. The shape is like *shu-yu.* The fruit is as big as a bowl. The skin is purple and the flesh is white. It could be steamed to eat.—Maybe this referred to sweet potato.

The Preface of the Sweet Potato Ode by He Qiao-yuan in the Ming dynasty:

There was the country of Lü-song [the Philippines] southward across the sea of Fujian. The Western Ocean was westward across the sea from the country. The country was abundant in gold and silver, using silver as China used copper. The gold and silver from the Western Ocean countries were all reshipped for trade from here. Therefore Fujian people did lots of business with Lü-song. The country had *zhu-shu* [red tuber], which covered wilderness and hills without waiting for cultivation. The barbarian people all took and ate it. Its stalks and leafs overgrew and, like such kinds as *gua-lou* [bitter melon], *huang-jing* [sealwort], *shan-yao* [Chinese yam], or *shan-yu* [mountain yam or Chinese yam], were smooth and eatable, either boiled or ground into powder. The root is like *shan-yao* or *shan-yu;* like *dun-chi* [taro], its skin is thin and red; it could be eaten with the skin removed, also cooked to eat, or brewed into wine too. Eating it raw is like eating kudzu vine; with cooked eating, its color is like honey and its taste is like eating water chestnut. Stored in the utensil, it had honeyed smell, and fragrance was smelled in the room. Although making neither calculation nor examination due to its overgrowth, the barbarian people were mean and did not give it to the Chinese. The Chinese cut off its vines about eight inches, carried them secretly in the small baskets and came, thus sweet potato had entered our Fujian over one decade. Although having withered, the vines, when cut, transplanted, and cultivated, would thrive in the fields in a few days. So they could be secretly carried to come. When the sweet potato was just introduced into our Fujian, our Fujian suffered a famine. Having the potato, people got full for one year. Its cultivation would not compete with five cereals [rice, millet, broomcorn millet, wheat and beans] for land. It could grow in any barren alkaline soil and sand hill. With manure applied, it would enlarge. With rain, the root would grow more vigorously; even in drought and without manure applied, it still would not lose one inch around in its diameter. The Quanzhou [Quanzhou was a prefecture in southeastern Fujian.] people sold it. One *jin* [half kg.] did not cost one penny, and two *jins* would get people full. So old men, children, street-walking venders and beggars all could use it as food. Hunger was then allayed. It was no hurt to take much of it. Even cocks and dogs all ate it.

STUDY QUESTIONS

1. Description of smallpox epidemic in Tenochtitlán: What statements in the document indicate that community cohesiveness broke down as a result of the disease? What are the military implications of such a breakdown?
2. Spread of animals and plants in Mexico and Chile: Identify the plants and animals introduced from Europe. Review the number of animals compared with people.
3. American crops in France, England, and Ireland: Who were Locke, Boyle, and Smith? In what way did they represent Enlightenment ideas? Why were they optimistic about cultivation of maize and potatoes? What were the advantages of cultivating these crops?
4. American crops in China: What advantages did the provincial governor see in the cultivation of sweet potatoes?
5. Compare the effects of the Columbian exchange in the Americas to its effects in Europe and China.

ESSAY SUGGESTIONS

A. Indians in the Americas who survived the epidemics were forced to adjust to new conditions. How did they adjust? What jobs did they perform? Who controlled the conditions under which they worked? What are the implications for social relations?

B. Based on the documents, indicate the major ways in which the Columbian exchange altered world history.

VISUAL SOURCE

The Potato Eaters

Dutch artist Vincent Van Gogh (1853–1890) began painting approximately ten years prior to his suicide at age 37. His short life was marked by strong humanitarian impulses toward the poor, especially miners, weavers, and peasants. Despite his intentions, the poor often ridiculed his efforts. Failures in his personal life and sickness led to despair. Unable to support himself regularly, he lived off his younger brother Theo. Bouts of epilepsy worsened his depression. Although tragic, these experiences enabled Van Gogh to depict the social circumstances and psychological moods of the people who interested him.

***The Potato Eaters* by Vincent Van Gogh, 1885.** Rijksmuseum Kroeller-Mueller, Otterlo, The Netherlands. (Erich Lessing / Art Resource, NY)

STUDY QUESTIONS

1. What features of the painting reveal the social circumstances of the people who became dependent on potatoes as their staple food? How do their circumstances compare with the views of thinkers who had earlier praised the potato?
2. How does the painting suggest the inner mood of the individuals depicted? How might Van Gogh define the purpose of this kind of art in industrial Europe?

3 AFRICA AND THE SLAVE TRADE

European contacts with sub-Saharan Africa increased from the fifteenth century onward, along all the coasts but particularly the Atlantic. Europeans hardly dominated African developments during the early modern period: they had little impact on African culture and only modest influence on the activities and expansion of the African kingdoms. Only in two areas—Angola and the Cape of Good Hope region—did they establish significant operations in the interior.

The European appetite for slaves, however, had huge consequences—for Africa, for the Americas, for European profit takers, and most of all for the slaves themselves. Along with the Columbian exchange, the slave trade was one of the vital new global contact operations in the early modern centuries. The rapidly growing trade reduced the population level of West Africa and distorted economic activity, although it did bring access to new earnings and products for some African merchants and leaders. The millions of Africans brought to the Americas and the Caribbean provided vital labor and important new cultural influences, amid great dislocation and suffering.

Most of our knowledge of the trade comes from the European side. The first of the documents that follows is, unusually, from East Africa, involving a French trading contract with a local ruler. The second document features an unusually expansive account by a French merchant, John Barbot, published in a travel collection in 1732. The third document is an African voice, from the famous autobiography of Olaudah Equiano, who was seized as a slave while still a boy in Nigeria, transported to the Americas, ultimately freed; he dedicated his later life to opposing the slave trade. Equiano's *Interesting Narrative* was first published in the United States in 1791. Collectively, the documents provide important information about the nature and experience of the slave trade, while raising key analytical issues about motivations and points of view.

Selection I from Monsier Morice, *A Slaving Treaty with the Sultan of Kilwa* (1776) from G. S. P. Freeman-Greenville, *The East African Coast* (Oxford University Press, 1962), pp. 47–48, 191, 196–197. Copyright owned by Bevil Master of Kinloss. Selection II from "A Description of the Coast of North and South Guinea, and of Ethopia Inferior, Vulgarly Angola, Being a New and Accurate Account of the Western Maritime Countries of Africa," by John Barbot, agent-general of the Royal Company of Africa and Islands of America, at Paris, in Awnsham and John Churchill, *Collection of Voyages and Travels* (1732), V. I–420. Selection III from *The Interesting Narrative of the Life of Olaudah Equiano*, ed., Robert J. Allison (Boston: Bedford Books, 1995), 46–58. (Follows the first American printing [New York, 1791]). Includes modernized spelling.

I. A SLAVE-TRADE AGREEMENT (1776)

A copy of M. Morice's Treaty with the King of Kilwa written in Arabic on the reverse side, with two identical octagonal seals inscribed in white in Arabic. On the front was the translation in these terms:

We the King of Kilwa, Sultan Hasan son of Sultan Ibrahim son of Sultan Yusuf the Shirazi of Kilwa, give our word to M. Morice, a French national, that we will give him a thousand slaves annually at twenty *piastres* each and that he [M. Morice] shall give the King a present of two *piastres* for each slave. No other but he shall be allowed to trade for slaves, whether French, Dutch, Portuguese, &c. until he shall have received his slaves and has no wish for more. This contract is made for one hundred years between him and us. To guarantee our word we give him the fortress in which he may put as many cannon as he likes and his Flag. The French, the Moors and the King of Kilwa will henceforth be one. Those who attack one of us we shall both attack. Made under our signs and seals the 14th X. 1776 signed Morice.

And further down is written:

> We the undersigned Captain and Officer of the ship Abyssinie, commissioned by M. Morice, certify to all whom it may concern that the present treaty was made in our presence at Kilwa on the 14th X. 1776 signed Pichard, Pigné,—Bririard.

II. JOHN BARBOT'S DESCRIPTION

Goods for Trade. The French import common red, blue, and scarlet cloth, silver and brass rings, or bracelets, chains, little bells, false crystal, ordinary and coarse hats; Dutch pointed knives, pewter dishes, silk sashes, with false gold and silver fringes; blue serges; French paper, steels to strike fire. . . .

Dutch cutlaces, strait and bow'd, clouts, galet, martosdes, two other sorts of beads, of which the Blacks made necklaces for women, white sugar, musket balls, iron nails, shot, white and red frize, looking-glasses in gilt and plain frames, cloves, cinnamon, scissors, needles, coarse thread of sundry colours, but chiefly red, yellow, and white, copper bars of a pound weight, ferrit; mens shirts, coarse and fine, . . . but above all, great quantities of brandy, and iron in bars.

The principal goods the French have in return for these commodities from the Moors and Blacks, are slaves, gold-dust, elephants teeth, bees-wax, dry and green hides, gum-arabick, ostrich feathers, and several other odd things. . . .

There they buy slaves in considerable numbers . . . which they convey down to their [ships] every year. . . .

Slaves. Those sold by the Blacks are for the most part prisoners of war, taken either in fight, or pursuit, or in the incursions they make into their enemies territories; others stolen away by their own country-men; and some there are, who will sell their own children, kindred, or neighbours. This has been often seen, and to compass it, they desire the person they intend to sell, to help them in carrying something to the factory by way of trade, and when there, the person so deluded, not understanding the language, is sold and deliver'd up as a slave, notwithstanding all his resistance, and exclaiming against the treachery. The kings are so absolute, that upon any slight pretence of offences committed by their subjects, they order them to be sold for slaves, without regard to rank, or possession. Thus a Marabout, or Priest, as I believe, was sold to me at Goeree, by the Alcaide of Rio Fresco, by special order of king Damel, for some misdemeanors.

Abundance of little Blacks of both sexes are also stolen away by their neighbours, when found abroad on the roads, or in the woods. . . .

[All these] slaves are severely and barbarously treated by their masters, who subsist them poorly, and beat them inhumanly, as may be seen by the scabs and wounds on the bodies of many of them when sold to us. They scarce allow them the least rag to cover their nakedness, which they also take off from them when sold to Europeans; and they always go bare-headed. This barbarous usage of those unfortunate wretches, makes it appear, that the fate of such as are bought, and transported from the coast to America, or other parts of the world, by Europeans, is less deplorable, than that of those who end their days in their native country; for aboard ships all possible care is taken to preserve and subsist them for the interest of the owners, and when sold in America, the same motive ought to prevail with their masters to use them well, that they may live the longer, and do them more service. Not to mention the inestimable advantage they may reap, of becoming christians, and saving their souls, if they make a true use of their condition. . . .

The Gold Coast, in times of war between the inland nations, and those nearer the sea, will furnish great numbers of slaves of all sexes and ages; sometimes at one place, and sometimes at another, as has been already observed, according to the nature of the war, and the situation of the countries between which it is waged. I remember, to this purpose, that in the year 1681, an English interloper at Commendo got three hundred good slaves, almost for nothing besides the trouble of receiving them at the beach in his boats, as the Commendo men brought them from the field of battle, having obtained a victory over a neighbouring nation, and taken a great number of prisoners.

I also remember, that I once, among my several runs along that coast, happened to have aboard a whole family, man, wife, three young boys, and a girl, bought one after another, at several places; and cannot but observe here, what mighty satisfaction those poor creatures expressed to be so come together again, tho' in bondage. For several days successively they could not forbear shedding tears of joy, and continually embracing and caressing one another; which moving me to compassion, I ordered they should be better treated aboard than commonly we can afford to do it, where there are four or five hundred in a ship; and at Martinico, I sold them all together to a considerable planter, at a cheaper rate than I might have expected, had they been disposed of severally; being informed of that gentleman's good-nature, and having taken his word, that he would use that family as well as their circumstances would permit, and settle them in some part by themselves.

Many of those slaves we transport from Guinea to America are prepossessed with the opinion, that they are carried like sheep to the slaughter, and that the Europeans are fond of their flesh; which notion so far prevails with some, as to make them fall into a deep melancholy and despair, and to refuse all sustenance, tho' never so much compelled and even beaten to oblige them to take some nourishment: notwithstanding all which, they will starve to death; whereof I have had several instances in my own slaves both aboard and at Guadalupe. And tho' I must say I am naturally compassionate, yet have I been necessitated sometimes to cause the teeth of those wretches to be broken, because they would not open their mouths, or be prevailed upon by any intreaties to feed themselves; and thus have forced some sustenance into their throats.

III. EQUIANO'S ACCOUNT

The first object which saluted my eyes when I arrived on the coast, was the sea, and a slave ship, which was then riding at anchor, and waiting for its cargo. These filled me with astonishment, which was soon converted into terror, when I was carried on board. I was immediately handled, and tossed up to see if I were sound, by some of the crew; and I was now persuaded that I had gotten into a world of bad spirits, and that they were going to kill me. Their complexions, too, differing so much from ours, their long hair, and the language they spoke (which was very different from any I had ever heard), united to confirm me in this belief. Indeed, such were the horrors of my views and fears at the moment, that, if ten thousand worlds had been my own, I would have freely parted with them all to have exchanged my condition with that of the meanest slave in my own country. When I looked round the ship too, and saw a large furnace of copper boiling, and a multitude of black people of every description chained together, every one of their countenances expressing dejection and sorrow, I no longer doubted of my fate; and, quite overpowered with horror and anguish, I fell motionless on the deck and fainted. When I recovered a little, I found some black people about me, who I believed were some of those who had brought me on board, and had been receiving their pay; they talked to me in order to cheer me, but all in vain. I asked them if we were not to be eaten by those white men with horrible looks, red faces, and long hair. They told me I was not, and one of the crew brought me a small portion of spirituous liquor in a wine glass; but being afraid of him, I would not take it out of his hand. One of the blacks therefore took it from him and gave it to me, and I took a little down my palate, which, instead of reviving me, as they thought it would, threw me into the greatest consternation at the strange feeling it produced, having never tasted any such liquor before. Soon after this, the blacks who brought me on board went off, and left me abandoned to despair.

I now saw myself deprived of all chance of returning to my native country, or even the least glimpse of hope of gaining the shore, which I now considered as friendly; and I even wished for my former slavery in preference to my present situation, which was filled with horrors of every kind, still heightened by my ignorance of what I was to undergo. I was not long suffered to indulge my grief; I was soon put down under the decks, and there I received such a salutation in my nostrils as I had never experienced in my life: so that, with the loathsomeness of the stench, and crying together, I became so sick and low that I was not able to eat, nor had I the least desire to taste anything. I now wished for the last friend, death, to relieve me; but soon, to my grief, two of the white men offered me eatables; and, on my refusing to eat, one of them held me fast by the hands, and laid me across, I think, the windlass, and tied my feet, while the other flogged me severely. I had never experienced anything of this kind before, and, although not being used to the water, I naturally feared that element the first time I saw it, yet, nevertheless, could I have got over the nettings, I would have jumped over the side, but I could not; and besides, the crew used to watch us very closely who were not chained down to the decks, lest we should leap into the water; and I have seen some of these poor African prisoners most severely cut, for attempting to do so, and hourly whipped for not eating. This indeed was often the case with myself.

In a little time after, amongst the poor chained men, I found some of my own nation, which in a small degree gave ease to my mind. I inquired of these what was to be done with us? They gave me to understand, we were to be carried to these white people's country to work for them. I then was a little revived, and thought, if it were no worse than working, my situation was not so desperate; but still I feared I should be put to death, the white people looked and acted, as I thought, in so savage a manner; for I had never seen among any people such instances of brutal cruelty; and this not only shown towards us blacks, but also to some of the whites themselves. One white man in particular I saw, when we were permitted to be on deck, flogged so unmercifully with a large rope near the foremast, that he died in consequence of it; and they tossed him over the side as they would have done a brute. This made me fear these people the more; and I expected nothing less than to be treated in the same manner. I could not help expressing my fears and apprehensions to some of my countrymen; I asked them if these people had no country, but lived in this hollow place (the ship)? They told me they did not, but came from a distant one. "Then," said I, "how comes it in all our country we never heard of them?" They told me because they lived so very far off.

At last we came in sight of the island of Barbados, at which the whites on board gave a great shout, and made many signs of joy to us. We did not know what to think of this; but as the vessel drew nearer, we plainly saw the harbor, and other ships of different kinds of sizes, and we soon anchored amongst them, off Bridge-town. Many merchants and planters now came on board, though it was in the evening. They put us in separate parcels, and examined us attentively. They also made us jump, and pointed to the land, signifying we were to go there. We thought by this, we should be eaten by these ugly men, as they appeared to us; and, when soon after we were all put down under the deck again, there was much dread and trembling among us, and nothing but bitter cries to be heard all the night from these apprehensions, insomuch, that at last the white people got some old slaves from the land to pacify us. They told us we were not to be eaten, but to work, and were soon to go on land, where we should see many of our country people. This report eased us much. And sure enough, soon after we were landed, there came to us Africans of all languages.

We were conducted immediately to the merchant's yard, where we were all pent up together, like so many sheep in a fold, without regard to sex or age. As every object was new to me, everything I saw filled me with surprise. What struck me first, was, that the houses were built with bricks and stories, and in every other respect different from those I had seen in Africa; but I was still more astonished on seeing people on horseback. I did not know what this could mean; and, indeed, I thought these people were full of nothing but magical arts. While I was in this astonishment, one of my fellow prisoners spoke to a countryman of his, about the horses, who said they were the same kind they had in their country. I understood them, though they were from a distant part of Africa; and I thought it odd I had not seen any horses there; but afterwards, when I came to converse with different Africans, I found they had many horses amongst them, and much larger than those I then saw.

We were not many days in the merchant's custody, before we were sold after their usual manner, which is this: On a signal given (as the beat of a drum), the buyers rush at once into the yard where the slaves are confined, and make choice of that parcel they like best. The noise and clamor with which this is attended, and the eagerness visible in the countenances of the buyers, serve not a little to increase the apprehension of terrified Africans, who may well be supposed to consider them as the ministers of that destruction to which they think themselves devoted. In this manner, without scruple, are relations and friends separated, most of them never to see each other again.

I remember, in the vessel in which I was brought over, in the men's apartment, there were several brothers, who, in the sale, were sold in different lots; and it was very moving on this occasion, to see and hear their cries at parting. O, ye nominal Christians! might not an African ask you—Learned you this from your God, who says unto you, Do unto all men as you would men should do unto you? Is it not enough that we are torn from our country and friends, to toil for your luxury and lust of gain? Must every tender feeling be likewise sacrificed to your avarice? Are the dearest friends and relations, now rendered more dear by their separation from their kindred, still to be parted from each other, and thus prevented from cheering the gloom of slavery, with the small comfort of being together, and mingling their sufferings and sorrows? Why are parents to lose their children, brothers their sisters, or husbands their wives? Surely, this is a new refinement in cruelty, which, while it has no advantage to atone for it, thus aggravates distress, and adds fresh horrors even to the wretchedness of slavery.

STUDY QUESTIONS

1. Why and how did African reactions to Europeans and to the slave trade vary?
2. How could Europeans justify their role in the slave trade?
3. Why did Africans participate in helping to conduct the slave trade?
4. What were the main results of the slave trade for the slaves themselves?
5. Are there any signs of embellishment in Equiano's account? Why might he have distorted his experiences?
6. What do the documents suggest about the impact of the slave trade on Africa and Africans in general during the early modern period?

ESSAY SUGGESTIONS

A. Discuss the combined effect of the Atlantic slave trade and the Columbian exchange on world population balances in the early modern period.

B. What were some of the leading complexities in the relationship between Christianity and the slave trade during the early modern period?

4 WESTERN CIVILIZATION AND EUROPE

THE EUROPEAN RENAISSANCE

The fourteenth century ushered in a new cultural movement known as the Renaissance ("rebirth"). Beginning in Italy and spreading northward over the next two centuries, this rebirth of interest in ancient Greco-Roman culture by the educated elite fostered a new worldview for Europeans. In their own minds, the values of this era contrasted greatly—in religious, stylistic, and philosophical terms—with the medieval culture that had preceded it in Western Europe. New literary and artistic styles; an increase in secular interests; and a major focus on classical models in writing, art, history, and philosophy mark the Renaissance era. A growing emphasis on individualism and individual achievement provided another unifying feature. In addition to cultural changes, this was an age of political change with city-states and regional kingdoms competing with one another for a share of the growing commercial economy.

In this competitive environment, a new round of theories sprung up offering advice about how best to govern. The following documents come from political essays written in the early sixteenth century. In *The Prince*, Niccolo Machiavelli described power politics: how could a prince gain and keep control? In presenting his observations as if he were an unbiased observer, Machiavelli set the stage for modern political science, the study of politics. According to the brief excerpts here (written around 1513), what are the key elements a ruler must have in order to succeed? Note how Machiavelli refrains from advising the prince on the type of society he should create.

In contrast, Sir Thomas More uses his book *Utopia* (published in 1516) as an opportunity to present a variety of ideas about good government. By writing in dialogue, More is able to present diverse ideas. The main character, Raphael, has allegedly just returned from a trip to Utopia, a nation in the New World. The character More is able to question Raphael about his travels. Of course, the whole discussion is a conceit, dreamed up by More to facilitate his critique of European society. Whereas Machiavelli focuses on gaining power, More philosophizes about a perfect society (a "utopia"), where politics and culture are completely removed from life in Renaissance Europe. In part, their approaches reflect their different origins. Machiavelli was from Florence, Italy; he lived in an unstable region divided into many city-states and prone to frequent invasion. More lived in England, which was united under one king. Both men worked as advisers in some form for rulers and wrote at almost the exact same time, but they present very different advice to those in charge.

From Niccolo Machiavelli, *The Prince*, ed. W. K. Marriott (London: J. M. Dent and Sons, 1908), selections from Chapters 15, 17, 18. Second selection from Thomas More, *Utopia*, translated with an introduction by Paul Turner (New York: Penguin, 2003), Book One, pages 35–38, 40–41.

MACHIAVELLI AND MORE

THE PRINCE BY NICCOLO MACHIAVELLI

I. Concerning Things for Which Men, and Especially Princes, are Praised or Blamed

It remains now to see what ought to be the rules of conduct for a prince towards subject and friends. And as I know that many have written on this point, I expect I shall be considered presumptuous in mentioning it again, especially as in discussing it I shall depart from the methods of other people. But, it being my intention to write a thing which shall be useful to him who apprehends it, it appears to me more appropriate to follow up the real truth of a matter than the imagination of it; for many have pictured republics and principalities which in fact have never been known or seen, because how one lives is so far distant from how one ought to live, that he who neglects what is done for what ought to be done, sooner effects his ruin than his preservation; for a man who wishes to act entirely up to his professions of virtue soon meets with what destroys him among so much that is evil.

II. Concerning Cruelty and Clemency, and Whether It Is Better to be Loved than Feared

Coming now to the other qualities mentioned above, I say that every prince ought to desire to be considered clement and not cruel. Nevertheless he ought to take care not to misuse this clemency. . . . A prince, so long as he keeps his subjects united and loyal, ought not to mind the reproach of cruelty; because with a few examples he will be more merciful than those who, through too much mercy, allow disorders to arise, from which follow murders or robberies; for these are wont to injure the whole people, whilst those executions which originate with a prince offend the individual only. . . .

Upon this a question arises: whether it be better to be loved than feared or feared than loved? It may be answered that one should wish to be both, but, because it is difficult to unite them in one person, is much safer to be feared than loved, when, of the two, either must be dispensed with. Because this is to be asserted in general of men, that they are ungrateful, fickle, false, cowardly, covetous, and as long as you succeed they are yours entirely; they will offer you their blood, property, life and children, as is said above, when the need is far distant; but when it approaches they turn against you. And that prince who, relying entirely on their promises, has neglected other precautions, is ruined; because friendships that are obtained by payments, and not by greatness or nobility of mind, may indeed be earned, but they are not secured, and in time of need cannot be relied upon; and men have less scruple in offending one who is beloved than one who is feared, for love is preserved by the link of obligation which, owing to the baseness of men, is broken at every opportunity for their advantage; but fear preserves you by a dread of punishment which never fails.

Nevertheless a prince ought to inspire fear in such a way that, if he does not win love, he avoids hatred; because he can endure very well being feared whilst he is not hated, which will always be as long as he abstains from the property of his citizens and subjects and from their women. But when it is necessary for him to proceed against the life of someone, he must do it on proper justification and for manifest cause, but above all things he must keep his hands off the property of others, because men more quickly forget the death of their father than the loss of their patrimony. Besides, pretexts for taking away the property are never wanting; for he who has once begun to live by robbery will always find pretexts for seizing what belongs to others; but reasons for taking life, on the contrary, are more difficult to find and sooner lapse. But when a prince is with his army, and has under control a multitude of soldiers, then it is quite necessary for him to disregard the reputation of cruelty, for without it he would never hold his army united or disposed to its duties.

III. Concerning the Way in Which Princes Should Keep Faith

Everyone admits how praiseworthy it is in a prince to keep faith, and to live with integrity and not with craft. Nevertheless our experience has been that those princes who have done great things have held good faith of little account, and have known how to circumvent the intellect of men by craft, and in the end have overcome those who have relied on their word. You must know there are two ways of contesting, the one by the law, the other by force; the first method is proper to men, the second to beasts; but because the first is frequently not sufficient, it is necessary to have recourse to the second. Therefore it is necessary for a prince to understand how to avail himself of the beast and the man. . . . A prince, therefore, being compelled knowingly to adopt the beast, ought to choose the fox and the lion; because the lion cannot defend himself against snares and the fox cannot defend himself against wolves. Therefore, it is necessary to be a fox to discover the snares and a lion to terrify the wolves. Those who rely simply on the lion do not understand what they are about. Therefore a wise lord cannot, nor ought he to, keep faith when such observance may be turned against him, and when the reasons that caused him to pledge it exist no longer. If men were entirely good this precept would not hold, but because they are bad, and will not keep faith with you, you too are not bound to observe it with them. A prince will always find legitimate reasons to excuse this nonobservance. Of this endless modern examples could be given, showing how many treaties and engagements have been made void and of no effect through the faithlessness of princes; and he who has known best how to employ the fox has succeeded best. . . .

For this reason a prince ought to take care that he never lets anything slip from his lips that is not replete with the above-named five qualities, that he may appear to him who sees and hears him altogether merciful, faithful, humane, upright, and religious. There is nothing more necessary to appear to have than this last quality. . . . Every one sees what you appear to be, few really know what you are, and those few dare not oppose themselves to the opinion of the many.

UTOPIA BY THOMAS MORE

More: My dear Raphael . . . there's so much wit and wisdom in everything you say. . . . But I still can't help feeling if you could only overcome your aversion to court life, your advice would be extremely useful to the public. Which means that it's your positive duty, as a good man, to give it. You know what your friend Plato says—that a happy state of society will never be achieved, until philosophers are kings, or kings take to studying philosophy. Well, just think how infinitely remote that happy state much remain, if philosophers won't even condescend to give kings a word of advice!

Raphael: Oh, philosophers aren't as bad as all that. They'd be only too glad to offer advice—in fact many of them have done so already in their published works—if only people in power would listen to them. . . . What do you suppose would happen if I started telling a king to make sensible laws, or trying to expel the deadly germs of bad ones from his mind? I'd be promptly thrown out, or merely treated as figure of fun.

For instance, just imagine me in France, at a top-secret meeting of the Cabinet. The King himself is in the chair, and round the table sit all his expert advisers, earnestly discussing ways and means of solving the following problems: how can His Majesty keep a grip on Milan, and get Naples back into his clutches? How can he conquer Venice, and complete the subjection of Italy? How can he then establish control over Flanders, Brabant, and finally the whole of Burgundy?—not to mention all the other countries that he has already invaded in his dreams.

One gentleman proposes a pact with the Venetians, to remain in force for just so long as the King shall find convenient. He should take them into his confidence, and even allow them a certain amount of the plunder—he can always demand it back later, when he has got what he wants. Another gentleman recommends the employment of German mercenaries, and a third is in favour of greasing the palms of the Swiss. A fourth advises His Majesty to propitiate the Holy Roman Empire with a sacrifice of gold. A fifth thinks it might be wise for him to improve relations with the King of Aragon, and as a peace-offering hand over the kingdom of Navarre—which doesn't belong to him anyway. Meanwhile a sixth is proposing that the Prince of Castile should be enticed into the French camp by promises of a marriage alliance, and that some of his courtiers should be paid a regular salary for their support.

And now for the knottiest problem of all—what's to be done about the English? . . .

At this point, while all these mighty forces are being set in motion, and all these worthy gentlemen are producing rival plans of campaign, up gets little Raphael, and proposes a complete reversal of policy. I advise the King to forget about Italy and stay at home. I tell him that France is already almost too big for one man to govern properly, so he really needn't worry about acquiring extra territory.

I then refer to an incident in the history of Nolandia, a country just south-east of Utopia. On the strength of some ancient marriage, the King of Nolandia thought he had a hereditary claim to another kingdom, so his people started a war to get it for him. Eventually they won, only to find that the kingdom in question was quite as much trouble to keep as it had been to acquire. There were constant threats of internal rebellion and external aggression. They were always having to fight either for their new subjects or against them. They never got a chance to demobilize, and in the meantime they were being ruined. All their money was going out of the country, and men were losing their lives to pay for someone else's petty ambition. Conditions at home were no safer than they'd been during the war, which had lowered moral standards, by encouraging people to kill and steal. There was no respect whatsoever for the law, because the King's attention was divided between the two kingdoms, so that he couldn't concentrate properly on either.

Seeing that this hopeless situation would continue indefinitely, if they didn't do something about it, the Nolandians finally decided on a course of action, which was to ask the King, quite politely, which kingdom he wanted to keep.

"You can't keep them both," they explained, "because there are too many of us to be governed by half a king. Why, even if we were a lot of mules, it would be a full-time job looking after us!"

So that exemplary monarch was forced to hand over the new kingdom to a friend of his—who was very soon thrown out—and to make do with the old one.

I also remind the French King that even if he does start all these wars and create chaos in all these different countries, he's still quite liable to find in the end that he has ruined himself and destroyed his people for nothing. I therefore advise him to concentrate on the kingdom that his ancestors handed down to him, and make it as beautiful and as prosperous as he can, to love his own subjects and deserve their love, to live among them and govern them kindly, and to give up all ideas of territorial expansion, because he has got more than enough to deal with already. . . .

[Raphael imagines a conversation with the King of France.]

Raphael: "Why do you suppose they made you king in the first place?" I ask him. "Not for your benefit, but for theirs. They meant you to devote your energies to making their lives more comfortable and protecting them from injustice. So your job is to see that they're all right, not that you are—just as a shepherd's job, strictly speaking, is to feed his sheep, not himself. As for the theory that peace is best preserved by keeping the people poor, it's completely contradicted by the facts. Beggars are far the most quarrelsome section of the community. Who is more likely to start a revolution than a man who's discontented with his present living conditions? . . .

"No, if a king is so hated or despised by his subjects that he can't keep them in order unless he reduces them to beggary by violence, extortion, and confiscation, he'd far better abdicate. Such methods of staying in power may preserve the title, but they destroy the majesty of a king. There's nothing majestic about ruling a nation of beggars—true majesty consists in governing the rich and prosperous. . . .

"In short, it's a pretty poor doctor who can't cure one disease without giving you another, and a king who can't suppress crime without lowering standards of living should admit that he just doesn't know how to govern free men. He should start by suppressing one of his own vices—either his pride or his laziness, for those are the faults most liable to make a king hated or despised. He should live on his own resources, without being a nuisance to others. He should adapt his expenditure to his income. He should prevent crime by sound administration rather than allowing it to develop and then start punishing it. He should hesitate to enforce any law which has long been disregarded—especially if people have got on perfectly well without it.

. . . Now there you have the type of king who's feared by bad men and loved by good ones—but if I said things like that to people who were quite determined to take the opposite view, do you think they'd listen to me?

More: Of course they wouldn't, and I can't say I'd blame them. Frankly, I don't see the point of saying things like that, or of giving advice that you know they'll never accept. What possible good could it do? . . .

Raphael: That's exactly what I was saying—there's no room at Court for philosophy.

STUDY QUESTIONS

1. During and long after the Renaissance, Machiavelli's name became synonymous with an evil, scheming, and unethical approach to gaining power. What ideas expressed here support that interpretation?
2. Is Machiavelli right that it is better for rulers to be feared than loved? Which other pieces of his advice ring true today? Which are implausible?
3. What does the excerpt from *Utopia* reveal about More's perception of European rulers and their priorities? Knowing that More himself became an adviser to Henry VIII of England and then was beheaded for disagreeing with the king's religious policies, what risks does he identify here for those who get involved with Renaissance politics?
4. How does Machiavelli view human nature? Does More agree?
5. What were the differences between Machiavelli and More as political theorists? What does their work suggest about the nature of Renaissance political theory?

ESSAY SUGGESTIONS

A. In what ways was Renaissance political theory a change from previous European standards?

B. How would Machiavelli's and More's interests and values be judged by intellectuals from another culture? How would a Confucianist assess the Renaissance spirit? A Muslim intellectual?

C. Did Renaissance values play a major role in causing new European global initiatives during the Age of Exploration? How do they compare to other major causes?

5 THE PROTESTANT REFORMATION

In 1517, a German monk, Martin Luther, issued 95 theses, or propositions, that condemned many practices of the Catholic Church. Luther particularly objected to the Church's practice of selling indulgences, or spiritual credits, by which people might gain credit toward salvation in heaven. In Luther's eyes, this practice reflected a corrupt church, headed by a venal papacy, but also a totally mistaken belief that people could gain salvation by specific practices rather than faith and divine predestination.

Luther's attacks were rejected by the Church, but he persisted in his protests against Catholicism—thus launching the Protestant version of Christianity and creating a permanent split in Western religion. Lutheranism itself spread widely in Germany and Scandinavia, while other versions of Protestantism gained ground elsewhere.

Protestantism most obviously generated significant changes in religious belief and practice, but it also had important implications for politics, the economy, and family life. In the document that follows, Luther explains many of his objections to Catholicism but also implicitly sketches an alternative vision for other aspects of Christian society. He also stakes out a variety of reasons that different kinds of people might be attracted to the new movement, in addition to simple agreement about religious doctrine. The following materials come from the "Letter to the German Nobility," written (in German rather than Latin), in 1520, early in Luther's career, seeking to rouse aristocratic support. In it, he explained many of his objections to Catholic practices and his growing opposition to the pope. He also implied the need for major changes in church government, in family life, in leisure, and in the economy that foreshadowed important developments in Protestant regions in the decades to come.

This document is an important statement in the early Reformation, but also a challenge to analysis, in figuring out some of the wider implications of Protestantism. Luther's letter also explains some of the diverse appeals offered through this new religious movement. Finally, the letter offers insight into Luther's own motivation, in what proved to be a determined but very difficult personal crusade.

From *Works of Martin Luther,* Vol. II (Philadelphia: A.J. Holman Company and The Castle Press, 1915), pp. 108–111, 114–115, 119, 127, 129, 134, 163–164.

WORKS OF MARTIN LUTHER

I. POPE AND EMPEROR

The pope should have no authority over the emperor, except that he anoints and crowns him at the altar, just as a bishop anoints and crowns a king; and we should not henceforth yield to that devilish pride which compels the emperor to kiss the pope's feet or sit at his feet, or, as they claim, hold his stirrup or the bridle of his mule when he mounts for a ride; still less should he do homage and swear faithful allegiance to the pope, as the popes have shamelessly ventured to demand as if they possessed that right. . . .

Such extravagant, over-presumptuous, and more than wicked doings of the pope have been devised by the devil, in order that under their cover he may in time bring in Antichrist, and raise the pope above God, as many are already doing and have done. It is not proper for the pope to exalt himself above the temporal authorities, save only in spiritual offices such as preaching and absolving. . . .

How can a man rule an empire and at the same time continue to preach, pray, study and care for the poor? Yet these are the duties which properly and peculiarly belong to the pope, and they were imposed by Christ in such earnest that He even forbade His disciples to take with them cloak or money, since these duties can scarcely be performed by one who has to rule even a single household. Yet the pope would rule an empire and continue to be pope! This is a device of the knaves who would like, under the pope's name, to be lords of the world, and by means of the pope and the name of Christ, to restore the Roman Empire to its former state. . . .

II. PAPAL HOMAGE

[By] pilgrimages men are led away into a false conceit and a misunderstanding of the divine commandments; for they think that this going on pilgrimage is a precious, good work, and this is not true. It is a very small good work, oftentimes an evil, delusive work, for God has not commanded it. But He has commanded that a man shall care for his wife and children, and look after such other duties as belong to the married state, and besides this, to serve and help his neighbor. Now it comes to pass that a man makes a pilgrimage to Rome when no one has commanded him to do so, spends fifty or a hundred gulden, more or less, and leaves his wife and child, or at least his neighbor, at home to suffer want. Yet the foolish fellow thinks to gloss over such disobedience and contempt of the divine commandments with his self-willed pilgriming, when it is really only curiosity or devilish delusion which leads him to it. So then we clearly learn from the Apostle that it should be the custom for every town to choose out of the congregation a learned and pious citizen, entrust to him the office of the ministry, and support him at the expense of the community, leaving him free choice to marry or not. He should have with him several priests or deacons, who might also be married or not, as they chose, to help him rule the people of the community by means of preaching and the sacraments, as is still the practice in the Greek Church. At a later time, when there were so many persecutions and controversies with heretics, there were many holy fathers who of their own accord abstained from matrimony, to the end that they might the better devote themselves to study and be prepared at any time for death or for controversy. Then the Roman See [papacy] interfered, out of sheer wantonness, and made a universal commandment forbidding priests to marry. This was done at the bidding of the devil. . . .

All festivals should be abolished, and Sunday alone retained. If it were desired, however, to retain the festivals of Our Lady and of the greater saints, they should be transferred to Sunday, or observed only by a morning mass, after which all the rest of the day should be a working-day. The reason is this: The feast-days are now abused by drinking, gaming, idleness and all manner of sins, so that on the holy days we anger God more than on other days, and have altogether turned things around; the holy days are not holy and the working days are holy, and not only is no service done to God and His saints by the many holy days, but rather great dishonor. There are, indeed, some mad prelates who think they are doing a good work if they make a festival in honor of St. Ottilia or St. Barbara or some other saint, according to the promptings of their blind devotion; but they would be doing a far better work if they honored the saint by turning a saint's-day into a working day. . . .

One of our greatest necessities is the abolition of all begging throughout Christendom. Among Christians no one ought to go begging! It would also be easy to make a law, if only we had the courage and the serious intention, to the effect that every city should provide for its own poor, and admit no foreign beggars by whatever name they might be called, whether pilgrims or mendicant monks. Every city could support its own poor, and if it were too small, the people in the surrounding villages also should be exhorted to contribute, since in any case they have to feed so many vagabonds and knaves in the guise of mendicants. In this way, too, it could be known who were really poor and who not.

There would have to be an overseer or warden who knew all the poor and informed the city council or the priests what they needed; or some other better arrangement might be made. In my judgment there is no other business in which so much knavery and deceit are practiced as in begging, and yet it could all be easily abolished. Moreover, this free and universal begging hurts the common people. . . .

I have many times offered my writings for investigation and judgment, but it has been of no use. To be sure, I know that if my cause is just, it must be condemned on earth, and approved only by Christ in heaven; for all the Scriptures show that the cause of Christians and of Christendom must be judged by God alone. Such a cause has never yet been approved by men on earth, but the opposition has always been too great and strong. It is my greatest care and fear that my cause may remain uncondemned, by which I should know for certain that it was not yet pleasing to God.

Therefore let them boldly go to work—pope, bishop, priest, monk and scholar! They are the right people to persecute the truth, as they have ever done.

God give us all a Christian mind, and especially to the Christian nobility of the German nation a right spiritual courage to do the best that can be done for the poor Church. Amen.

STUDY QUESTIONS

1. What aspects of the existing church-state relationship does Luther attack? What kinds of church-state relations might follow from his views?
2. What kind of political motivations might have prompted support for Lutheranism? What particular appeals did he offer to German nobles? .
3. What kinds of economic change does Luther imply? Would the spread of Protestantism affect the European economy?
4. What kinds of changes in family life does Luther imply?
5. What kinds of appeals does Luther offer, explicitly or implicitly, to the various groups in German society? What might motivate various groups to become Protestant? How does Luther relate to a sense of German identity?
6. How would you interpret Luther's own motivation? What caused him to take on one of the most powerful institutions in Western Europe?

ESSAY SUGGESTIONS

A. Compare the Renaissance and Reformation in their effects on European society: did they pull in different directions or were some of their impacts combined?

B. Compared to other factors, like expansion of trade and colonies, how important was Protestantism in changing the nature of early modern European societies?

6 WOMEN IN EARLY MODERN EUROPE

During the Renaissance and Reformation, the changes sweeping across Europe in the early modern era affected women as well as men. Although women as a group did not participate equally with men in either cultural movement, individual women did benefit from the new outlook that encouraged education and individuality. The most public role for women was as monarch, and this era saw a remarkable number of female rulers across Europe, including Elizabeth of England, Isabella of Spain, Mary Queen of Scots, and Catherine de Medici of France. Yet most women were not political leaders; they were married young, at which time their husbands took financial and legal control of them from their fathers. Women who did not marry (either by choice or fate) could join a convent or perhaps make a living as courtesans, basically acting as an escort and sexual partner for upper-class men. Although these options offered some independence from everyday patriarchy, they were certainly not solutions for everyone. It is rare to find women in the early modern era speaking and writing about female concerns. The following three excerpts from sixteenth-century Europe illustrate some of the different ways women talked about their roles in society.

Among monarchs of the era, Elizabeth I (1533–1603) stands out not only for her gender but also for her superb guidance through numerous internal and external threats during her almost fifty-year reign of England. The first document is a speech she gave in 1588 just after her small navy had defeated the larger Spanish Armada but before her people knew if Spain would invade the island. Note how she presents herself to her troops and how she both acknowledges and dismisses concerns about her sex.

The second selection is a poem by Anna Bijns (d. 1575) of Antwerp, one of the most famous women writers in the Low Countries. She worked closely with the Catholic hierarchy and published stinging critiques of Luther's Protestant Reformation. In this poem, she condemns marriage as an unworthy choice for women. What are her arguments?

The third selection is from a letter written by Veronica Franco (1546–1591) to a mother contemplating turning her daughter into a courtesan. Writing with firsthand knowledge of what it was like to serve the elite men of Venice, Franco frankly discourages the mother. Consider the variety of reasons she offers. Franco herself enjoyed a reputation for beauty and fierce wit; she was an educated woman, an accomplished poet, and a frequent guest at the most important salons in Venice. In her published poetry and letters, Franco speaks her mind, giving a voice to women in a time when not many spoke out publically, much less in print.

First selection from Katharina M. Wilson, ed., *Women Writers of the Renaissance and Reformation* (Athens: University of Georgia Press, 1987), 542–543. Second selection, Wilson, ed., *Women Writers*, 382–383. Third selection from Veronica Franco, *Poems and Selected Letters*, trans. and ed. by Ann Rosalind Jones and Margaret F. Rosenthal (Chicago: University of Chicago Press, 1998), 38–40.

WOMEN'S ROLES IN SOCIETY

I. THE TILBURY SPEECH, QUEEN ELIZABETH OF ENGLAND

My loving people: we have been persuaded by some that are careful of our safety to take heed how we commit ourselves to armed multitudes for fear of treachery, but I assure you I do not desire to live to distrust my faithful and loving people. Let tyrants fear. I have always so behaved myself that, under God, I have placed my chiefest strength and safeguard in the loyal hearts and goodwill of my subjects. And therefore I am come amongst you, as you see, at this time, not for my recreation and disport, but being resolved in the midst and heat of battle to live or die amongst you all, to lay down for my God, and for my kingdom, and for my people, my honor and my blood even in the dust. I know I have the body but of a weak and feeble woman, but I have the heart and stomach of a king—and of a king of England too—and think foul scorn that Parma, or Spain, or any prince of Europe should dare to invade the borders of my realm. To which, rather than any dishonor should grow by me, I myself will take up arms, I myself will be your general, judge, and rewarder of every one of your virtues in the field. I know already for your forwardness you have deserved rewards and crowns, and we do assure you, in the word of a prince, they shall be duly paid you.

II. UNYOKED IS BEST! HAPPY THE WOMAN WITHOUT A MAN, ANNA BIJNS

How good to be a woman, how much better to be a man!
Maidens and wenches, remember the lesson you're about to hear.
Don't hurtle yourself into marriage far too soon.
The saying goes: "Where's your spouse? Where's your honor?"
But one who earns her board and clothes
Shouldn't scurry to suffer a man's rod.
So much for my advice, because I suspect—
Nay, see it sadly proven day by day—
'T happens all the time!
However rich in goods a girl might be,
Her marriage ring will shackle her for life.
If however she stays single
With purity and spotlessness foremost,
Then she is lord as well as lady. Fantastic, not?
Though wedlock I do not decry:
Unyoked is best! Happy the woman without a man.

Fine girls turning into loathly hags—
'Tis true! Poor sluts! Poor tramps! Cruel marriage!
Which makes me deaf to wedding bells.
Huh! First they marry the guy, luckless dears,
Thinking their love just too hot to cool.

Well, they're sorry and sad within a single year.
Wedlock's burden is far too heavy.
They know best whom it harnessed.
So often is a wife distressed, afraid.
When after troubles hither and thither he goes
In search of dice and liquor, night and day,
She'll curse herself for that initial "yes."
So, beware ere you begin.
Just listen, don't get yourself into it.
Unyoked is best! Happy the woman without a man.

A man oft comes home all drunk and pissed
Just when his wife had worked her fingers to the bone
(So many chores to keep a decent house!),
But if she wants to get in a word or two,
She gets to taste his fist—no more.
And that besotted keg she is supposed to obey?
Why, yelling and scolding is all she gets,
Such are his ways—and hapless his victim.
And if the nymphs of Venus he chooses to frequent,
What hearty welcome will await him home.
Maidens, young ladies: learn from another's doom,
Ere you, too, end up in fetters and chains.
Please don't argue with me on this,
No matter who contradicts, I stick to it:
Unyoked is best! Happy the woman without a man.

A single lady has a single income,
But likewise, isn't bothered by another's whims.
And I think: that freedom is worth a lot.
Who'll scoff at her, regardless what she does,
And though every penny she makes herself,
Just think of how much less she spends!
An independent lady is an extraordinary prize—
All right, of a man's boon she is deprived,
But she's lord and lady of her very own hearth.
To do one's business and no explaining sure is lots of fun!
Go to bed when she list, rise when she list, all as she will,
And no one to comment! Grab tight your independence then.
Freedom is such a blessed thing.
To all girls: though the right Guy might come along:
Unyoked is best! Happy the woman without a man.

Prince,
Regardless of the fortune a woman might bring,
Many men consider her a slave, that's all.
Don't let a honeyed tongue catch you off guard,

Refrain from gulping it all down. Let them rave,
For, I guess, decent men resemble white ravens.
Abandon the airy castles they will build for you.
Once their tongue has limed a bird:
Bye by love—and love just flies away.
To women marriage comes to mean betrayal
And the condemnation to a very awful fate.
All her own is spent, her lord impossible to bear.
It's *peine forte et dure* instead of fun and games.
Oft it was the money, and not the man
Which goaded so many into their fate.
Unyoked is best! Happy the woman without a man.

III. LETTER TO A MOTHER, VERONICA FRANCO

I also fulfill a humane obligation by showing you a steep precipice hidden in the distance and by shouting out before you reach it, so that you'll have time to steer clear of it. Although it's mainly a question of your daughter's well-being, I'm talking about you, as well, for her ruin cannot be separated from yours. And because you're her mother, if she should become a prostitute, you'd become her go-between and deserve the harshest punishment, while her error wouldn't perhaps be entirely inexcusable because it would have been caused by your wrongdoing.

You know how often I've begged and warned you to protect her virginity. And since this world is so full of dangers and so uncertain, and the houses of poor mothers are never safe from the amorous maneuvers of lustful young men, I showed you how to shelter her from danger and to help her by teaching her about life in such a way that you can marry her decently. . . . Together we agreed on what needed to be done so that she'd be accepted there, and we were about to carry out our plan when you underwent I don't know what change of heart. Where once you made her appear simply clothed and with her hair arranged in a style suitable for a chaste girl, with veils covering her breasts and other signs of modesty, suddenly you encouraged her to be vain, to bleach her hair and paint her face. And all at once you let her show up with curls dangling around her brow and down her neck, with bare breasts spilling out of her dress, with a high uncovered forehead, and every other embellishment people use to make their merchandise measure up to the competition. . . .

Now, finally I wanted to be sure to write you these lines, urging you again to beware of what you're doing and not to slaughter in one stroke your soul and your reputation, along with your daughter's—who, considered from the purely carnal point of view, is really not very beautiful (to say the least, for my eyes don't deceive me) and has so little grace and wit in conversation that you'll break her neck expecting her to do well in the courtesan's profession, which is hard enough to succeed in even if a woman has beauty, style, good judgment, and proficiency in many skills. And just imagine a young woman who lacks many of these qualities or has them only to an average degree! . . .

I'll add that even if fate should be completely favorable and kind to her, this is a life that always turns out to be a misery. It's a most wretched thing, contrary to human reason, to subject one's body and labor to a slavery terrifying to even think of. To make oneself prey to so many men, at the risk of being stripped, robbed, even killed, so that one man, one day, may snatch away from you everything you've acquired from many over such a long time, along with so many other dangers of injury and dreadful contagious diseases; to eat with another's mouth, sleep with another's eyes, move according to another's will, obviously rushing toward the shipwreck of your mind and your body—what greater misery? What wealth, what luxuries, what delights can outweigh all this? Believe me, among all the world's calamities, this is the worst. And if to worldly concerns you add those of the soul, what greater doom and certainty of damnation could there be? . . .

Pay attention to what people say, and in matters crucial to life on earth and to the soul's salvation, don't follow examples set by others. Don't allow the flesh of your daughter not only to be cut into pieces and sold but you yourself to become her butcher. Consider the likely outcome; and if you want to observe other cases, look at what's happened and happens every day to the multitude of women in this occupation. If you can be convinced by reason, every argument about this world and all the more about heaven opposes you and urges you to avoid this fatal course.

STUDY QUESTIONS

1. What does Elizabeth's speech reveal about Renaissance monarchy? Compare how Elizabeth presents herself with the advice Machiavelli gives in *The Prince*. Did it matter which sex the ruler was? What obligations did all monarchs share?
2. Anna Bijns is skeptical about men's feelings toward women. What are her concerns? Why does she encourage women not to marry?
3. What does Veronica Franco's advice reveal about women's status in Venice and about the options available to women in this era?
4. Note that all three of these women were unmarried when they were participating in public discourse. What does that fact reveal about women's daily lives and the institution of marriage in this era? Could a married woman have written these documents? Why or why not?

ESSAY SUGGESTIONS

A. Although the Renaissance and Reformation stand out as times of growing individualism in European history, did women participate in and benefit from these changes? What new roles for women appeared? What older models of female identity persisted?

B. What do these three documents reveal about the roles of women in early modern Europe compared with men at the same time? How do they compare with women's gender roles during the classical or postclassical period?

7 THE SCIENTIFIC REVOLUTION AND THE ENLIGHTENMENT

Documents in this chapter come from one of the great cultural changes in world history: the redefinition of science and of the importance of science in overall intellectual endeavors in the sixteenth and seventeenth centuries. The Renaissance and Reformation generated important shifts, but the Scientific Revolution was clearly the great reorientation of intellectual life. Although resisted and debated, the principles of the Scientific Revolution, beginning with the idea that human reason could discover the clear-cut laws of nature, gained ground fairly steadily. By the eighteenth century, the implications or presumed implications of science were being pushed into other areas, including theories about society, in the movement known as the Enlightenment.

Galileo Galilei (1564–1642) was one of the early scientists in this great movement, with new experiments and statements about gravity and planetary motion. His work was part of a major recasting of earlier Western ideas, derived from the classical period, that Earth was the center of the universe, and it shocked those who believed it called Christian truth into question. Galileo's findings and methods, which included careful experimentation and measurement, combined with his delight at challenging authority; all these elements became part of the larger implications of the Scientific Revolution. How does Galileo defend his heliocentric theory? What arguments did critics make against him? Ultimately, his self-defense was unsuccessful; after a trial at the Inquisition, the Catholic Church in 1633 placed him under a mild house arrest.

Following on the heels of the discoveries of the Scientific Revolution, Enlightenment *philosophes* across Europe attempted to apply the same kind of rigorous thought to understanding human society as scientists had been applying to natural phenomena. Although the Enlightenment ideals of the eighteenth century flourished most of all in Paris, it was a European-wide phenomenon. Immanuel Kant (1724–1804) was a German philosopher and professor determined to articulate the uses and limitations of reason, a hallmark concept of the Enlightenment. In this selection, he explains the importance of seeking knowledge, gaining freedom, and endorsing religious tolerance.

Selection I excerpts from Galileo Galilei, *Discoveries and Opinions of Galileo,* trans. by Stillman Drake (NY: Anchor, 1957), pp. 175–95. Selection II excerpts from Immanuel Kant, *Foundations of the Metaphysics of Morals, 2/E,* trans. by Lewis White Beck (NY: Pearson, 1990), pp. 83–85.

GALILEO AND KANT

I. GALILEO GALILEI, IN A LETTER TO THE GRAND DUCHESS CHRISTINA (1615)

Some years ago, as Your Serene Highness well knows, I discovered in the heavens many things that had not been seen before our own age. The novelty of these things, as well as some consequences which followed from them in contradiction to the physical notions commonly held among academic philosophers, stirred up against me no small number of professors—as if I had placed these things in the sky with my own hands in order to upset nature and overturn the sciences. They seemed to forget that the increase of known truths stimulates the investigation, establishment, and growth of the arts; not their diminution or destruction.

Showing a greater fondness for their own opinions than for truth they sought to deny and disprove the new things which, if they had cared to look for themselves, their own senses would have demonstrated to them. To this end they hurled various charges and published numerous writings filled with vain arguments, and they made the grave mistake of sprinkling these with passages taken from places in the Bible which they had failed to understand properly, and which were ill-suited to their purposes. . . .

Persisting in their original resolve to destroy me and everything mine by any means they can think of, these men are aware of my views in astronomy and philosophy. They know that as to the arrangement of the parts of the universe, I hold the sun to be situated motionless in the center of the revolution of the celestial orbs while the earth revolves about the sun. They know also that I support this position not only by refuting the arguments of Ptolemy and Aristotle, but by producing many counter-arguments; in particular, some which relate to physical effects whose causes can perhaps be assigned in no other way. In addition there are astronomical arguments derived from many things in my new celestial discoveries that plainly confute the Ptolemaic system while admirably agreeing with and confirming the contrary hypothesis. Possibly because they are disturbed by the known truth of other propositions of mine which differ from those commonly held, and therefore mistrusting their defense so long as they confine themselves to the field of philosophy, these men have resolved to fabricate a shield for their fallacies out of the mantle of pretended religion and the authority of the Bible. These they apply with little judgment to the refutation of arguments that they do not understand and have not even listened to.

First they have endeavored to spread the opinion that such propositions in general are contrary to the Bible and are consequently damnable and heretical. . . . Next, becoming bolder, and hoping (though vainly) that this seed which first took root in their hypocritical minds would send out branches and ascend to heaven, they began scattering rumors among the people that before long this doctrine would be condemned by the supreme authority. . . .

In order to facilitate their designs, they seek so far as possible (at least among the common people) to make this opinion seem new and to belong to me alone. They pretend not to know that its author, or rather its restorer and confirmer, was

Nicholas Copernicus; and that he was not only a Catholic, but a priest and a canon. He was in fact so esteemed by the church that when the Lateran Council under Leo X took up the correction of the church calendar, Copernicus was called to Rome from the most remote parts of Germany to undertake its reform. . . . Since that time not only has the calendar been regulated by his teachings, but tables of all the motions of the planets have been calculated as well.

. . . I think in the first place that it is very pious to say and prudent to affirm that the holy Bible can never speak untruth—whenever its true meaning is understood. But I believe nobody will deny that it is often very abstruse, and may say things which are quite different from what its bare words signify. . . .

This being granted, I think that in discussions of physical problems we ought to begin not from the authority of scriptural passages but from sense-experiences and necessary demonstrations; for the holy Bible and the phenomena of nature proceed alike from the divine Word the former as the dictate of the Holy Ghost and the latter as the observant executrix of God's commands. It is necessary for the Bible, in order to be accommodated to the understanding of every man, to speak many things which appear to differ from the absolute truth so far as the bare meaning of the words is concerned. But Nature, on the other hand, is inexorable and immutable; she never transgresses the laws imposed upon her, or cares a whit whether her abstruse reasons and methods of operation are understandable to men. For that reason it appears that nothing physical which sense-experience sets before our eyes, or which necessary demonstrations prove to us, ought to be called in question (much less condemned) upon the testimony of biblical passages which may have some different meaning beneath their words. For the Bible is not chained in every expression to conditions as strict as those which govern all physical effects; nor is God any less excellently revealed in Nature's actions than in the sacred statements of the Bible. . . .

From this I do not mean to infer that we need not have an extraordinary esteem for the passages of holy Scripture. On the contrary, having arrived at any certainties in physics, we ought to utilize these as the most appropriate aids in the true exposition of the Bible and in the investigation of those meanings which are necessarily contained therein, for these must be concordant with demonstrated truths. I should judge that the authority of the Bible was designed to persuade men of those articles and propositions which, surpassing all human reasoning could not be made credible by science, or by any other means than through the very mouth of the Holy Spirit. . . .

But I do not feel obliged to believe that the same God who has endowed us with senses, reason and intellect has intended us to forgo their use and by some other means to give us knowledge which we can attain by them.

II. IMMANUEL KANT, WHAT IS ENLIGHTENMENT? (1784)

Enlightenment is man's release from his self-incurred tutelage. Tutelage is man's inability to make use of his understanding without direction from another. Self-incurred is this tutelage when its cause lies not in lack of reason but in lack of resolution and courage to use it without direction from another. Sapere aude! (Dare to know!) Have courage to use your own reason!—that is the motto of enlightenment.

Laziness and cowardice are the reasons why so great a portion of mankind, after nature has long since discharged them from external direction, nevertheless remains under lifelong tutelage, and why it is so easy for others to set themselves up as their guardians. It is so easy not to be of age. If I have a book which understands for me, a pastor who has a conscience for me, a physician who decides my diet, and so forth, I need not trouble myself. I need not think, if I can only pay—others will easily undertake the irksome work for me.

That the step to competence is held to be very dangerous by the far greater portion of mankind (and by the entire fair sex)—quite apart from its being arduous is seen to by those guardians who have so kindly assumed superintendence over them. After the guardians have first made their domestic cattle dumb and have made sure that these placid creatures will not dare take a single step without the harness of the cart to which they are tethered, the guardians then show them the danger which threatens if they try to go alone. Actually, however, this danger is not so great, for by falling a few times they would finally learn to walk alone. But an example of this failure makes them timid and ordinarily frightens them away from all further trials. . . .

But that the public should enlighten itself is more possible; indeed, if only freedom is granted enlightenment is almost sure to follow. For there will always be some independent thinkers, even among the established guardians of the great masses, who, after throwing off the yoke of tutelage from their own shoulders, will disseminate the spirit of the rational appreciation of both their own worth and every man's vocation for thinking for himself. But be it noted that the public, which has first been brought under this yoke by their guardians, forces the guardians themselves to remain bound when it is incited to do so by some of the guardians who are themselves capable of some enlightenment—so harmful is it to implant prejudices, for they later take vengeance on their cultivators or on their descendants. Thus the public can only slowly attain enlightenment. Perhaps a fall of personal despotism or of avaricious or tyrannical oppression may be accomplished by revolution, but never a true reform in ways of thinking. Farther, new prejudices will serve as well as old ones to harness the great unthinking masses.

For this enlightenment, however, nothing is required but freedom, and indeed the most harmless among all the things to which this term can properly be applied. It is the freedom to make public use of one's reason at every point. But I hear on all sides, "Do not argue!" The Officer says: "Do not argue but drill!" The tax collector: "Do not argue but pay!" The cleric: "Do not argue but believe!" Only one prince in the world says, "Argue as much as you will, and about what you will, but obey!" Everywhere there is restriction on freedom.

Which restriction is an obstacle to enlightenment, and which is not an obstacle but a promoter of it? I answer: The public use of one's reason must always be free, and it alone can bring about enlightenment among men. The private use of reason, on the other hand, may often be very narrowly restricted without particularly hindering the progress of enlightenment. . . . Thus it would be ruinous for an officer in service to debate about the suitability or utility of a command given to him by his superior; he must obey. But the right to make remarks on errors in the military service and to lay them before the public for judgment cannot equitably be refused him as a scholar. The citizen cannot refuse to pay the taxes imposed on him; indeed, an impudent complaint at those levied on him can be punished as a scandal (as it could occasion general refractoriness). But the same person nevertheless does not act contrary to his duty as a citizen, when, as a scholar, he publicly expresses his thoughts on the inappropriateness or even the injustices of these levies. . . .

If we are asked, "Do we now live in an enlightened age?" the answer is, "No," but we do live in an age of enlightenment. As things now stand, much is lacking which prevents men from being, or easily becoming, capable of correctly using their own reason in religious matters with assurance and free from outside direction. But on the other hand, we have clear indications that the field has now been opened wherein men may freely deal with these things and that the obstacles to general enlightenment or the release from self-imposed tutelage are gradually being reduced. In this respect, this is the age of enlightenment, or the century of Frederick.

A prince who does not find it unworthy of himself to say that he holds it to be his duty to prescribe nothing to men in religious matters but to give them complete freedom while renouncing the haughty name of tolerance, is himself enlightened and deserves to be esteemed by the grateful world and posterity as the first, at least from the side of government, who divested the human race of its tutelage and left each man free to make use of his reason in matters of conscience. . . .

I have placed the main point of enlightenment—the escape of men from their self-incurred tutelage—chiefly in matters of religion because our rulers have no interest in playing guardian with respect to the arts and sciences and also because religious incompetence is not only the most harmful but also the most degrading of all. But the manner of thinking of the head of a state who favors religious enlightenment goes further, and he sees that there is no danger to his lawgiving in allowing his subjects to make public use of their reason and to publish their thoughts on a better formulation of his legislation and even their open-minded criticisms of the laws already made. Of this we have a shining example wherein no monarch is superior to him we honor.

STUDY QUESTIONS

1. Why was the heliocentric theory of cosmology so hotly contested during the Scientific Revolution?
2. Galileo argues that the evidence produced through science is more reliable than that offered by the Catholic Church for understanding the universe. How does the scientific method work? What is his argument about the advantages of science? How does he reconcile his sincere belief in Christianity with his scientific discoveries?
3. Why is "Dare to know!" an excellent motto for the Enlightenment?
4. According to Kant, what are the key features of enlightenment? How does Kant view "freedom"?

5. What contributions did the Scientific Revolution and Enlightenment make concerning the importance of science, education, and knowledge? What kind of knowledge was increasingly valuable for Europeans?

ESSAY SUGGESTIONS

A. How did Galileo and Kant benefit from the legacies of the Renaissance and Reformation? Why do historians consider the Scientific Revolution a separate phase in European history?

B. How did the Scientific Revolution and Enlightenment affect the relationship between the West and other parts of the world over the next few centuries?

8 PETER THE GREAT REFORMS RUSSIA

During most of the early modern period, Russia was a rather different society from those of western and central Europe. Although it too gained a growing role in world history, it did so on separate bases. Russia emphasized rapid expansion over land rather than commerce or overseas empire. It did not experience movements such as the Reformation. Around 1700, however, Russia underwent a process of partial Westernization that developed new connections to other parts of Europe—while preserving or highlighting ongoing distinctions as well. Documents in this chapter deal with the reform process and some reactions to it.

Peter the Great ruled Russia as tsar from 1682 until 1725. Along with continued territorial expansion, Peter was eager to update Russia's administration and economy, which he saw as essential for military purposes and to establish Russian prestige and position in a wider European arena. The following selections show a number of Peter's initiatives to reform Russia and bring it in line with Western patterns. In these reforms, Peter set up an administrative council to improve the direction of the state bureaucracy and expand its functions. He worked to improve education, particularly of the nobility, and to facilitate manufacturing as well. These reforms, in sum, give a good picture of the directions in which the tsar was pushing his vast empire.

Peter's reforms also suggest important links with authoritarian political trends in Russia, including a willingness to regiment ordinary workers and peasants. Peter's vision of a Westernized Russia proved highly selective, as he found certain aspects of the Russian tradition eminently useful. A final document comes not from Peter but from a funeral sermon on his death by a court official, Feofan Prokopovich. The bias of the sermon, designed to please the royal family, is obvious: does the document nevertheless reveal something of the directions and limitations of Peter's efforts?

Peter the Great clearly illustrates a reform process from the top down. How do you think Russians at various levels would have reacted? From what you can judge by these documents, was Peter moving Russia in a useful direction?

Selections I, II, III, IV and V from Basil Dmytryshyn, *Imperial Russia: A Sourcebook, 1700–1917* (Gulf Breeze, FL: Academic International Press, 1999), pp. 14–16, 19, 21–22. Section VI excerpted from *Anthology of Russian Literature from the Earliest Period to the Present Time,* Leo Wiener, ed., and Tr. Pt. 1 (New York, 1902), pp. 214–218.

PETER THE GREAT

I. DECREES ON THE DUTIES OF THE GOVERNING SENATE

Each *gubernia* [region] is to send two officials to advise the Senate on judicial and legislative matters. . . .

In our absence the Senate is charged by this *ukaz* with the following:

1. To establish a just court, to deprive unjust judges of their offices and of all their property, and to administer the same treatment to all slanderers.
2. To supervise governmental expenditures throughout the country and cancel unnecessary and, above all, useless things.
3. To collect as much money as possible because money is the artery of war.
4. To recruit young noblemen for officer training, especially those who try to evade it; also to select about 1000 educated *boyars* for the same purpose.
5. To reform letters of exchange and keep these in one place.
6. To take inventory of goods leased to offices or *gubernias.*
7. To farm out the salt trade in an effort to receive some profit [for the state].
8. To organize a good company and assign to it the China trade.
9. To increase trade with Persia and by all possible means to attract in great numbers Armenians [to that trade]. To organize inspectors and inform them of their responsibilities.

II. DECREES ON COMPULSORY EDUCATION OF THE RUSSIAN NOBILITY (JANUARY 12 AND FEBRUARY 28, 1714)

Send to every *gubernia* [region] some persons from mathematical schools to teach the children of the nobility—except those of freeholders and government clerks—mathematics and geometry; as a penalty [for evasion] establish a rule that no one will be allowed to marry unless he learns these [subjects]. Inform all prelates to issue no marriage certificates to those who are ordered to go to schools. . . .

The Great Sovereign has decreed: in all *gubernias* children between the ages of ten and fifteen of the nobility, of government clerks, and of lesser officials, except those of freeholders, must be taught mathematics and some geometry. Toward that end, students should be sent from mathematical schools [as teachers], several into each *gubernia,* to prelates and to renowned monasteries to establish schools. During their instruction these teachers should be given food and financial remuneration of three *altyns* and two *dengas* per day from *gubernia* revenues set aside for that purpose by personal orders of His Imperial Majesty. No fees should be collected from students. When they have mastered the material, they should then be given certificates written in their own handwriting. When the students are released they ought to pay one ruble each for their training. Without these certificates they should not be allowed to marry nor receive marriage certificates.

III. AN INSTRUCTION TO RUSSIAN STUDENTS ABROAD STUDYING NAVIGATION

1. Learn [how to draw] plans and charts and how to use the compass and other naval indicators.
2. [Learn] how to navigate a vessel in battle as well as in a simple maneuver, and learn how to use all appropriate tools and instruments; namely, sails, ropes, and oars, and the like matters, on row boats and other vessels.
3. Discover as much as possible how to put ships to sea during a naval battle. Those who cannot succeed in this effort must diligently ascertain what action should be taken by the vessels that do and those that do not put to sea during such a situation [naval battle]. Obtain from [foreign] naval officers written statements, bearing their signatures and seals, of how adequately you [Russian students] are prepared for [naval] duties.
4. If, upon his return, anyone wishes to receive [from the Tsar] greater favors for himself, he should learn, in addition to the above enumerated instructions, how to construct those vessels aboard which he would like to demonstrate his skills.
5. Upon his return to Moscow, every [foreign-trained Russian] should bring with him at his own expense, for which he will later be reimbursed, at least two experienced masters of naval science. They [the returnees] will be assigned soldiers, one soldier per returnee, to teach them [what they have learned abroad]. And if they do not wish to accept soldiers they may teach their acquaintances or their own people. The treasury will pay for transportation and maintenance of soldiers. And if anyone other than soldiers learns [the art of navigation] the treasury will pay 100 rubles for the maintenance of every such individual. . . .

IV. A DECREE ON THE RIGHT OF FACTORIES TO BUY VILLAGES (JANUARY 18, 1721)

Previous decrees have denied merchants the right to obtain villages. This prohibition was instituted because those people, outside their business, did not have any establishments that could be of any use to the state. Nowadays, thanks to Our decrees, as every one can see, many merchants have companies and many have succeeded in establishing new enterprises for the benefit of the state; namely: silver, copper, iron, coal and the like, as well as silk, linen, and woolen industries, many of which have begun operations. As a result, by this Our *ukaz* aimed at the increase of factories. We permit the nobility as well as merchants to freely purchase villages for these factories, with the sanction of the Mining and Manufacturing College, under one condition: that these villages be always integral parts of these factories. Consequently, neither the nobility nor merchants may sell or mortgage these villages without the factories . . . and should someone decide to sell these villages with the factories because of pressing needs, it must be done with the permission of the Mining and Manufacturing College. And whoever violates this procedure will have his possessions confiscated.

And should someone try to establish a small factory for the sake of appearance in order to purchase a village, such an entrepreneur should not be allowed to purchase anything. The Mining and Manufacturing College should adhere to this rule very strictly. Should such a thing happen, those responsible for it should be deprived of all their movable and immovable property.

V. A DECREE ON THE FOUNDING OF THE ACADEMY (JANUARY 28, 1724)

His Imperial Majesty decreed the establishment of an academy, wherein languages as well as other sciences and important arts could be taught, and where books could be translated. On January 22 [1724], during his stay in the Winter Palace, His Majesty approved the project for the Academy, and with his own hand signed a decree that stipulates that the Academy's budget of 24,912 rubles annually should come from revenues from custom dues and export-import license fees collecting in the following cities: Narva, Dorpat, Pernov and Arensburg. . . .

> Now that an institution aimed at the cultivation of arts and sciences is to be chartered in Russia, there is no need to follow the practice that is accepted in other states. It is essential to take into account the existing circumstances of this state [Russia], consider [the quality of Russian] teachers and students, and organize such an institution that would not only immediately increase the glory of this [Russian] state through the development of sciences, but would also, through teaching and dissemination [of knowledge], benefit the people [of Russia] in the future.
>
> These two aims will not be realized if the Academy of Sciences alone is chartered, because while the Academy may try to promote and disseminate arts and sciences, these will not spread among the people. The establishment of a university will do even less, simply because there are no elementary schools, gymnasia or seminaries [in Russia] where young people could learn the fundamentals before studying more advanced subjects [at the University] to make themselves useful. It is therefore inconceivable that under these circumstances a university would be of some value [to Russia].
>
> Consequently what is needed most [in Russia] is the establishment of an institution that would consist of the most learned people, who, in turn, would be willing: (a) to promote and perfect the sciences while at the same time, wherever possible, be willing (b) to give public instruction to young people (if they feel the latter are qualified) and (c) instruct some people individually so that they in turn could train young people [of Russia] in the fundamental principles of all sciences.

VI. FEOFAN PROKOPOVICH'S FUNERAL SERMON ON PETER I

O Russia, this Samson of yours came to you when no one in the world had expected him, and when he appeared the whole world marvelled. He found you weak in power, and to conform with his name he made you of stone and adamant. He found an army dangerous at home, weak in the field and scorned by the foe, and he gave his country a useful army that is terrible to the enemy, and everywhere renowned and glorious. He defended his country, and at the same time returned to it the lands that had been taken away from it, and increased it by the acquisition of new provinces. When he crushed those who rose against us, he at the same time broke the strength of our ill-wishers and subdued their spirits, and, closing up the lips of envy, compelled the whole world to proclaim glorious things of himself.

O Russia, he was your first Japheth, who had accomplished a deed unheard of in your annals, having introduced the building and sailing of ships. He gave you a new fleet that, to the wonderment of the world and surpassing all expectation, was in no way inferior to much older fleets, and he opened for you a path to all the ends of the earth, and spread your power and glory to the extreme corners of the ocean, to the limits of your usefulness, to the limits which justice had placed; and the might of your dominion, which heretofore was firm on land, he has now made strong and permanent upon the sea.

O Russia, he is your Moses! Are not his laws like a firm protection of truth, and like unbreakable fetters of wrongdoing? And are not his statutes clear, a light upon your path? And are not the high ruling Senate and the many special institutions of his so many lights in the search of advantage, the warding off of harm, the safety of the peaceful, and the unmasking of the wrongdoers? He has verily left us in doubt whether he is more to be praised for being loved and cherished by the good and simple-hearted, or for being hated by unrepenting flatterers and rascals.

O Russia, he is your Solomon, who has received from the Lord his very great reason and wisdom. Have we not sufficient testimony thereof in the many philosophic arts, which he himself practised and many subjects introduced under his supervision, and in the many cunning industrial arts which have never before been heard of among us? And he also introduced the chins and degrees, and civil order, and decent manners in daily intercourse, and the rules of acceptable habits and customs, and now we see and admire the external appearance and internal worth of our country, which from within and without is far superior to what it was in former years. . . .

Let us not, O Russians, faint with sorrow and grief, for the great monarch and our father has not left us in a bad plight. He has left us, but not poor and necessitous: the immeasurable wealth of his power and glory, which has been realised by his above-mentioned deeds, is with us. Russia will be such as he has made it; he has made it an object of love to the good, and it will be loved; he has made it terrible to the enemy, and terrible it will remain; he has made it glorious throughout the whole world, and it will not cease to be glorious. He has left us religious, civil and military institutions. He has left us, and his body will decay, but his spirit will stay.

STUDY QUESTIONS

1. What were the main purposes of Peter's reforms?
2. What relationship between tsar and nobility did the reforms suggest?
3. What kind of economy was Peter seeking to build? For what reasons?
4. How did Peter's moves relate to changes occurring in Western European politics and culture around 1700? What major trends did Peter ignore?

5. In what ways did Russian reactions to the West differ from those of other parts of the world in the early modern period and why?
6. Did Prokopovich's oration capture Peter's major efforts? Was any area added and if so, why? Was the oration, despite the obvious hyperbole, on balance a fair assessment?

ESSAY SUGGESTIONS

A. What were the main emphases of Peter's "Westernization" efforts and the reasons behind them? What major aspects of Russian society were not subjected to a Westernization process?
B. What kinds of Russians might have objected to Peter the Great's efforts and on what bases?

9 ASIA: THE MIDDLE EAST, INDIA, AND EAST ASIA

THE RISE OF THE OTTOMAN EMPIRE

The formation of new empires, or renewed empires in China's case, was a crucial development in key parts of Asia during the early modern period. Japan was also the scene of significant political change, though without an imperial government of the same sort. The following chapters focus on political trends and values and invite comparisons of different Asian regions.

Between 1300 and 1450, the Ottoman Turks, initially one of many groups of Muslim warriors based on the eastern frontier of the Byzantine Empire, conquered much of western Anatolia and the Balkan Peninsula. Their most dramatic victory came in 1453 when Turkish forces broke through the massive walls surrounding the Byzantine capital of Constantinople (now Istanbul) and captured it.

A major turning point in world history, the conquest of Constantinople put the Ottomans in charge of the city that had symbolized Christian teachings and the legacy of the Roman Empire for more than a millennium. But more than symbols were at stake. Control of the choke point between the Black Sea and the Mediterranean boosted the fortunes of the Turks in two key arenas: long-distance trade and military deployments.

For about a century following 1453, Ottoman soldiers and sailors continued to push their borders outward. Meanwhile, the sultans (sovereigns) established a system of administrative rule that compared favorably with regimes elsewhere in the early modern period—in Europe, Russia, India, and China—and lasted until after World War I.

One feature of the Ottoman system of governance that made it distinctive was the reliance upon a type of slavery. In the Ottoman lands, slavery was based on religion rather than on skin color and on service in the imperial administration and army rather than labor on sugar plantations. Each year, the Turks conscripted Christian boys from Balkan villages and elsewhere, a practice known as *devshirme* (collection), and took them to the capital where they were trained to become administrators, soldiers in the elite Janissary corps, and, sometimes, palace officials.

The two selections provide clues to the reasons for the success of the Ottomans during the reign of the greatest of the sultans, Suleyman "the Lawgiver" (reigned 1520–1566), famous for his codification of Ottoman law, as well as other policies. In the first document, an inscription from a frontier garrison built by the Turks at Bender near the western border of Ukraine, Suleyman proclaims his vast power. The second document comes from letters written by Ogier Ghiselin de Busbecq, ambassador from the Holy Roman Empire (also known as the Habsburg Empire) to the Ottomans from 1554 to 1562. Busbecq's memory of the 1529 Ottoman siege and near conquest of Vienna, the Habsburg capital, forms the subtext of his letters. How do these documents help us see key features of the Ottoman regime? In what ways did the Ottoman state resemble other large polities during the early modern period?

THE REIGN OF SULEYMAN

I. SULEYMAN PROCLAIMS HIS POWER

I am God's slave and sultan of this world. By the grace of God I am head of Muhammad's community. God's might and Muhammad's miracles are my companions. I am Süleymân, in whose name the *hutbe* [Friday sermon] is read in Mecca and Medina. In Baghdad I am the shah, in Byzantine realms the Caesar, and in Egypt the sultan; who sends his fleets to the seas of Europe, the Maghrib [North Africa] and India. I am the sultan who took the crown and throne of Hungary and granted them to a humble slave. The voivoda [governor] Petru [in Romania] raised his head in revolt, but my horse's hoofs ground him into the dust, and I conquered the land of Moldavia [Romania].

II. FROM BUSBECQ'S LETTERS

A. The Turkish Army (1560)

The Sultan, when he sets out on a campaign, takes as many as 40,000 camels with him, and almost as many baggage-mules, most of whom, if his destination is Persia, are loaded with cereals of every kind, especially rice. Mules and camels are also employed to carry tents and arms and warlike machines and implements of every kind. The territories called Persia which are ruled by the Sophi, as we call him (the Turkish name being Kizilbash), are much less fertile than our country; and, further, it is the custom of the inhabitants, when their land is invaded, to lay waste and burn everything, and so force the enemy to retire through lack of food. The latter, therefore, are faced with serious peril, unless they bring an abundance of food with them. They are careful, however, to avoid touching the supplies which they carry with them as long as they are marching against their foes, but reserve them, as far as possible, for their return journey, when the moment for retirement comes and they are forced to retrace their steps through regions which the enemy has laid waste, or which the immense multitude of men and baggage animals has, as it were, scraped bare, like a swarm of locusts. It is only then that the Sultan's store of provisions is opened, and just enough food to sustain life is weighed out each day to the Janissaries and the other troops in attendance upon him. The other soldiers are badly off, if they have not provided food for their own use; most of them, having often experienced such difficulties during their campaigns—and this is particularly true of the cavalry—take a horse on a leading-rein loaded with many of the necessities of life. These include a small piece of canvas to use as a tent, which may protect them from the sun or a shower of rain, also some clothing and bedding and a private store of provisions, consisting of a leather sack or two of the finest flour, a small jar of butter, and some spices and salt; on these they support life when they are reduced to the extremes of hunger. They take a few spoonfuls of flour and place them in water, adding a little butter, and then flavour the mixture with salt and spices. This, when it is put on the fire, boils and swells up so as to fill a large bowl. They eat of it once or twice a day, according to the quantity, without any bread, unless they have with them some toasted bread or biscuit. They thus contrive to live on short rations for a month or even longer, if necessary. Some soldiers take with them a little sack full of beef dried and reduced to a powder, which they employ in the same manner as the flour, and which is of great benefit as a more solid form of nourishment. Sometimes, too, they have recourse to horseflesh; for in a great army a large number of horses necessarily dies, and any that die in good condition furnish a welcome meal to men who are starving. I may add that men whose horses have died, when the Sultan moves his camp, stand in a long row on the road by which he is to pass with their harness or saddles on their heads, as a sign that they have lost their horses, and implore his help to purchase others. The Sultan then assists them with whatever gift he thinks fit. . . .

I mentioned that baggage animals are employed on campaign to carry the arms and tents, which mainly belong to the Janissaries. The Turks take the utmost care to keep their soldiers in good health and protected from the inclemency of the weather; against the foe they must protect themselves, but their health is a matter for which the State must provide. Hence one sees the Turk better clothed than armed. He is particularly afraid of the cold, against which, even in the summer, he guards himself by wearing three garments, of which the innermost—call it shirt or what you will—is woven of coarse thread and provides much warmth. As a further protection against cold and rain tents are always carried, in which each man is given just enough space to lie down, so that one tent holds twenty-five or thirty Janissaries. The material for the garments to which I have referred is provided at the public expense. To prevent any disputes or suspicion of favour, it is distributed in the following manner. The soldiers are summoned by companies in the darkness to a place chosen for the purpose—the balloting station or whatever name you like to give it—where are laid out ready as many portions of cloth as there are soldiers in the company; they enter and take whatever chance offers them in the darkness, and they can only ascribe it to chance whether they get a good or a bad piece of cloth. For the same reason their pay is not counted out to them but weighed, so that no one can complain that he has received light or chipped coins. Also their pay is given them not on the day on which it falls due but on the day previous.

The armour which is carried is chiefly for the use of the household cavalry, for the Janissaries are lightly armed and do not usually fight at close quarters, but use muskets. When the enemy is at hand and a battle is expected, the armour is brought out, but it consists mostly of old pieces picked up in various battlefields, the spoil of former victories. These are distributed to the household cavalry, who are otherwise protected by only a light shield. You can image how badly the armour, thus hurriedly given out, fits its wearers. One man's breastplate is too small, another's helmet is too large, another's coat of mail is too heavy for him to bear. There is something wrong everywhere; but they bear it with equanimity and think that only a coward finds fault with his arms, and vow to distinguish themselves in the fight, whatever their equipment may be; such is the confidence inspired by repeated victories and constant experience of warfare. Hence also they do not hesitate to re-enlist a veteran infantryman in the cavalry, though he has never fought on horseback, since they are convinced that one who has warlike experience and long service will acquit himself well in any kind of fighting. . . .

B. Bows and Arrows and Other Matters (1560)

In many streets of Constantinople and at cross-roads there are shooting-grounds where not only boys and young men but even men of more advanced years congregate. An official is put in charge of the target and looks after it, watering the butt every day, since otherwise it would dry up and the arrows would not stick in it; for in

The Janissaries in European art. Woodcut by Melchior Lorich, 1576, British Museum, London, from "The World of Islam" ed. Bernard Lewis, (Thames & Hudson Ltd.)

The Janissaries in Ottoman art. (Sonia Halliday Photographs)

the shooting-grounds they only use blunt arrows. The custodian of the target is always present and extracts the arrows from the earth, and after cleaning them throws them back to the archers. This entitles him to a fixed payment from every one, which provides him with a livelihood. The front of the target looks like a small door, which may perhaps have given rise to the proverb about 'shooting against the door,' which the Greeks applied to any one who altogether missed the target. For I believe that the Greeks formerly used the same kind of target, and that the Turks adopted it from them. I know, of course, that the use of the bow by the Turks is very ancient, but there is no reason why, when they came as conquerors to the Greek cities, they should not have continued the use of the target and butt which they found there. For no nation has shown less reluctance to adopt the useful inventions of others; for example, they have appropriated to their own use large and small cannons and many other of our discoveries. They have, however, never been able to bring themselves to print books and set up public clocks. They hold that their scriptures, that is, their sacred books, would no longer be scriptures if they were printed; and if they established public clocks, they think that the authority of their muezzins and their ancient rites would suffer diminution. In other matters they pay great respect to the time-honoured customs of foreign nations, even to the detriment of their own religious scruples. This, however, is only true of the lower classes. Every one knows how far they are from sympathizing with the rites of the Christian Church. The Greek priests, however, have a custom of, as it were, opening the closed sea by blessing the waters at a fixed date in the spring, before which the sailors do not readily entrust themselves to the waves. This ceremony the Turks do not altogether disregard. And so, when their preparations for a voyage have been made, they come to the Greeks and ask whether the waters have been blessed; and if they say that they have not been blessed, they put off the sailing, but, if they are told that the ceremony has been performed, they embark and set sail. . . .

There is one point about Turkish military manoeuvers which I must not omit, namely, the old custom which goes back to the Parthians of pretending to flee on horseback and then shooting with their arms at the enemy when he rashly pursues. They practise the rapid execution of this device in the following manner. They fix a brazen ball on the top of a very high pole, or mast, erected on level ground, and urge their horses at full speed towards the mast; and then, when they have almost passed it, they suddenly turn round and, leaning back, discharge an arrow at the ball, while the horse continues its course. By frequent practice they become able without any difficulty to hit their enemy unawares by shooting backwards as they fly. . . .

C. Christian Slaves (1555)

After remaining about a fortnight at Constantinople in order to regain my strength, I started on my journey to Vienna, the beginning of which may be said to have been ill omened. Just as we were leaving the city, we were met by wagon-loads of boys and girls who were being brought from Hungary to be sold in Constantinople. There is no commoner kind of merchandise than this in Turkey; and, just as on the roads out of Antwerp one meets loads of various kinds of goods, so from time to time we were met by gangs of wretched Christian slaves of every kind who were being led to horrible servitude. Youths and men of advanced years were driven along in herds or else were tied together with chains, as horses with us are taken to market, and trailed along in a long line. At the sight I could scarcely restrain my tears in pity for the wretched plight of the Christian population.

STUDY QUESTIONS

1. What does the inscription reveal about Suleyman? For whom do you think it was intended?
2. What impressed Busbecq about the Ottoman army?
3. In what ways do the Ottomans seem to have been selective borrowers of cutting-edge technologies from Europe? How do you explain the selectivity?
4. What is Busbecq's reaction to the devshirme? Can you tell whether he is opposed to coerced labor in general or merely to the enslavement of Christians?

The Suleymaniye Mosque in Istanbul

After the Ottomans conquered Constantinople in 1453, they converted the famed Church of Saint Sophia into a mosque and then sponsored the construction of hundreds of new mosques and other religious buildings throughout their realm. Sinan the Great (1489–1588), the architect in charge of these projects from the 1530s onward, was a product of the *devshirme* system, having been born to a Christian family in central Anatolia.

Architectural historians consider the mosque Sinan designed for Suleyman to be one of his greatest triumphs. Featuring a massive central dome and many smaller ones, the mosque is surrounded by a complex of buildings *(kulliye)* that includes five madrasas (colleges), a medical school, a hospital, numerous courtyards and baths, and the mausoleums of Suleyman and his wife Haseki Hurrem.

The Suleymaniye Mosque complex with the Golden Horn in the background.
(Purepix / Alamy)

STUDY QUESTIONS

1. How does the mosque illustrate some of the teaching of Islam?
2. What aspects of the mosque suggest the openness of Sinan (and the Ottoman elite in general) to earlier traditions of Byzantine/Roman architecture?
3. In what sense is the Suleymaniye mosque a counterpart of the Bender inscription?

ESSAY SUGGESTIONS

A. What advice for the Habsburgs is suggested in Busbecq's observations?

B. Discuss the strengths and weaknesses of Busbecq's account as a source. How can the accuracy of an outside observer best be assessed?

C. Describe a typical day in the life of a Janissary during the reign of Suleyman.

10

CONQUERING AND RULING INDIA: BABUR AND AKBAR

Around 1500, a new Muslim military leader of Turkish and Mongol descent, Zahiruddin Muhammad Babur (1483–1530), emerged on the plains of Afghanistan. Babur captured Kabul, made this city his capital, and then began to attack the Muslim and Hindu warlords who controlled northern India. After winning a major victory at Panipat in 1526, Babur moved into Delhi and took over the surrounding region.

Babur's seizure of Delhi was a pivotal moment in the history of India. The regime he established was the seed of the Mughal dynasty (1526–1858), which brought political unity to most of South Asia for the first time in about a thousand years.

Within a few years of his victory at Panipat, Babur was dead. But before he died, he composed a remarkably revealing memoir, the *Baburnama.* In its pages, he tells us about his many battlefield successes (and defeats) but also about personal matters, such as his infatuation for a young boy he saw in a market, his fondness for Persian poetry, and his love for designing and planting gardens (actually, parks) wherever he went.

In the decades following Babur's death, the Mughals were nearly driven from power. Babur's grandson Akbar (reigned 1556–1605), however, was able to reestablish, consolidate, and expand the reach of the Mughal state by winning a series of battles. A Muslim (like all the Mughal emperors), Akbar was remarkably open minded to other religious traditions, including Christianity. As we shall see in the Visual Source, he was also a sponsor and collector of beautifully illustrated books.

The selections take us into the world of the two extraordinary founders of the Mughal dynasty. In the first document, Babur recalls the battle of Panipat. The second group of passages comes from the *Akbarnama,* the history of Akbar's reign compiled by one of his admiring court officials. What policies contributed to the success of Babur and Akbar? How does Mughal rule in India compare to Ottoman rule in the Middle East?

Selection I reprinted, with permission, from *The Baburnama: Memoirs of Babur, Prince and Emperor,* 323–326. Selection II from Abu-l Fazl, *Akbar-Nama* (Lahore, Pakistan: Sheikh Mubarak Ali Publishers and Booksellers, 1975), 30–31, 60, 72–73, 90–91. Originally published in 1875 in Lahore. No translator given.

MUGHAL DOCUMENTS

I. FROM THE *BABURNAMA*

Preparation for Battle [1526]

We marched from there, arrayed the right and left wings and center, and had a *dim* [a count of the soldiers]. We had fewer men than we had estimated. I ordered the whole army, in accordance with rank, to bring carts, which numbered about seven hundred altogether. Master Ali-Quli was told to tie them together with ox-harness ropes instead of chains, after the Anatolian manner, keeping a distance of six to seven large shields between every two carts. The matchlockmen could then stand behind the fortification to fire their guns. Five or six days were spent arranging it, and when it was ready I summoned to general council all the begs [lords] and great warriors who knew what they were talking about. We discussed the following: Panipat was a town with lots of suburbs and houses. The suburbs and houses would protect one side, but it was necessary to fortify our other sides with the carts and shields and to station matchlockmen and foot soldiers behind them. This having been decided, we marched, bivouacked, and then came to Panipat on Wednesday the last day of Jumada II [April 12].

To our right were the town and suburbs. Directly before us were the arranged shields. To the left and elsewhere were trenches and pylons. At every distance of an arrow shot, space was left for 100 to 150 cavalrymen to emerge. Some of the soldiers were hesitant, but their trepidation was baseless, for only what God has decreed from all eternity will happen. They cannot be blamed, however, for being afraid, even if God was on their side. They had traveled for two or three months from their homeland, and had had to deal with an unfamiliar people whose language we did not know and who did not know ours. . . .

Sultan Ibrahim's army was estimated at one hundred thousand. He and his commanders were said to have nearly a thousand elephants. Moreover, he possessed the treasury left over from two generations of his fathers. The custom in Hindustan is to hire liege men for money before major battles. Such people are called *badhandi.* If Sultan Ibrahim had had a mind to, he could have hired one hundred thousand to two hundred thousand troops. Thank God he was able neither to satisfy his warriors nor to part with his treasury. How was he to please his men when his nature was so overwhelmingly dominated by miserliness? He himself was an inexperienced young man who craved beyond all things the acquisition of money—neither his oncoming nor his stand was calculated to have a good end, and neither his march nor his fighting was energetic. . . .

The Battle of Panipat [1526]

On Friday the eighth of Rajab [April 20] news came at dawn from the scouts that the enemy was coming in battle array. We put on our armor, armed ourselves, and got to horse.

The enemy's troops appeared, headed toward the left wing. For this reason Abdul-Aziz, who had been assigned to the reserve, was dispatched as reinforcement to the left wing. Sultan Ibrahim's army could be seen nearby, coming quickly without stopping. However, as they came farther forward and our troops became visible to them, they broke the ranks they had maintained and, as though undecided whether to stand or proceed, were able to do neither.

The order was given for the men who had been assigned to the flank assault to circle around to the enemy's rear from left and right, shoot their arrows, and begin to fight, and for the right and left wings to advance and engage the enemy. The flank assaulters circled around and began to shoot. From the left wing Mahdi Khwaja had already reached the enemy; advancing upon him was a contingent with an elephant, but by shooting many arrows he drove them back.

Master Ali-Quli got off a few good gunshots from in front of the center. Mustafa the artilleryman also fired some good shots from the mortars mounted on carts to the left of the center. Right wing, left wing, center, and flank assault shot arrows into the enemy from all sides and fought in all seriousness. Once or twice the enemy tried halfhearted assaults in the direction of our right and left wings, but our men pushed them into their own center by shooting. The enemy's right and left flanks were so crowded into one spot that they were not able to go forward or to find a way to escape.

The sun was one lance high when battle was enjoined. The fighting continued until midday. At noon the enemy was overcome and vanquished to the delight of our friends. By God's grace and generosity such a difficult action was made easy for us, and such a numerous army was ground into the dust in half a day. Five or six thousand men were killed in one place near Ibrahim. All told, the dead of this battle were estimated at between fifteen and sixteen thousand. Later, when we came to Agra, we learned from reports by the people of Hindustan that forty to fifty thousand men had died in the battle. With the enemy defeated and felled, we proceeded. Along the way the men began to capture the fallen commanders and Afghans and bring them in. Droves of elephants were caught and presented by the elephant keepers. . . .

II. FROM THE AKBARNAMA

Remission of the Tax on Hindu Pilgrims (1564)

It was an old standing custom for the rulers of Hindustan [India] to exact contributions, according to their respective means, from the [Hindu] pilgrims who visited the holy shrines. This tax was called *karmi.* His Majesty's judgment and equity condemned this exaction, and he remitted it, although it amounted to *krors* [millions] of rupees. An order was accordingly issued abolishing it throughout his dominions. . . . He was pleased to say that although this was a tax on the vain superstitions of the multitude, and the devotees did not pay it except when they travelled abroad, still the course they adopted was their mode of worshipping the Almighty, and the throwing of a stumbling-block and obstacle in their way could never be acceptable in the sight of God.

Remission of the Poll Tax on Non-Muslims (1565)

One of the munificent acts of the Emperor at the beginning of this the ninth year of his reign was the remission of the *jizya* (poll-tax upon infidels), which, in a country so extensive as Hindustan, amounted to an immense sum.

European Novelties (1578)

Haji Habib had been sent to the port of Goa [a Portuguese colony], with a large sum of money and intelligent artisans, to examine and bring to the Emperor's knowledge the various productions of art and skill to be found in that town. He now returned to Court, having with him a number of men clad in Christian garb, and beating drums and playing European instruments. He presented fabrics which he had selected. The artisans who had gone there to acquire knowledge exhibited their skill, and received applause. Musicians of that country played upon various instruments, especially upon the organ, and gave great delight to all who heard them.

Burning of Widows (1584)

In the interior of Hindustan it is the custom, when a husband dies, for his widow willingly and cheerfully to cast herself into the flames (of the funeral pile), although she may not have lived happily with him. Occasionally love of life holds her back, and then the husband's relations assemble, light the pile, and place her upon it, thinking that they thereby preserve the honour and character of the family. But since the country had come under the rule of his gracious Majesty, inspectors had been appointed in every city and district, who were to watch carefully over these two cases, to discriminate between them, and to prevent any woman being forcibly burnt. About this time, Jai Mal (son of Mal Deo), who had been sent with his forces to join the *amirs* in Bengal, died of sunstroke in the vicinity of Chaunsa. His wife, the daughter of Muna Raja, was unwilling to burn; but her son Udi Singh, with a party of his bigoted friends, resolved upon the sacrifice. The matter came to the Emperor's knowledge, and his feeling of justice and humanity made him fear that if he sent messengers to stop the proceedings, some delay might occur, so he mounted his horse, and rode with all speed to the place. As the facts were not fully known, some of these men, in their thoughtlessness, were disposed to resist and make disturbances. . . . But when His Majesty arrived, Jagganath and Rai Sal came forward to meet him, and brought the leader of these foolish men to him. He accepted their assurance of repentance, and only placed them in confinement.

Europeans at Court (1591)

At this time, Padre Farmaliun [a Roman Catholic priest] arrived at the Imperial Court from Goa, and was received with much distinction. He was a man of much learning, and eloquence. A few intelligent young men were placed under him for instruction, so that provision might be made for securing translations of Greek books and of extending knowledge. With him came a number of Europeans and Armenians, who brought silks of China and goods of other countries which were deemed worthy of his Majesty's inspection.

STUDY QUESTIONS

1. How did Babur prepare for the battle?
2. How did he explain his victory at Panipat? Do you find his explanation plausible?
3. What aspects of Akbar's character and policies are evident in the Akbarnama?
4. In that Abul Fazl was a member of Akbar's court, can his history be trusted? In general, what are the strengths and weaknesses of "court history"? How does this example seem to measure up?

VISUAL SOURCE

Portrait of Babur

Babur is shown reading in his garden, probably the one he designed in Kabul that contains his tomb. The portrait is likely one of many sponsored by Akbar to illustrate the sumptuous hand-copied books produced at his court. He had Babur's memoir translated from its original Turkish to Persian, the language of higher learning for the Mughals. It was issued in numerous editions, in part to promote the authority of the newly established dynasty.

Although Akbar could not read (he may have been dyslexic), he enjoyed being read to and established a huge palace workshop—which included calligraphers, illustrators, and bookbinders—for the production of fine books. The illustrators worked in teams, fusing Persian, Indian, and European styles of painting. Their efforts resulted in a distinctive style of Mughal art.

Babur Reading in His Garden, Sixteenth Century. Babur (r.1526–30) Reading, Mughal (w/c on paper), Das, Bishn (fl.1613–19) / British Library, London, UK. (Bridgeman Art Library)

STUDY QUESTIONS

1. How does the painting illustrate important aspects of Babur's life?
2. For whom was the portrait intended? How does it illustrate a goal of Akbar?
3. Why did Akbar not adopt printing?

ESSAY SUGGESTIONS

A. Compare Mughal rule in India to the Ottoman regime in the Middle East.

B. "Akbar was the most enlightened ruler in the early modern world." Discuss this proposition, taking a position for or against.

C. "During the sixteenth century, the most powerful states in the world were Muslim." Discuss this proposition, taking a position for or against.

11 CONFUCIANISM IN MING AND QING CHINA

Emperors in the Han dynasty (206 B.C.E.–220 C.E.) were the first Chinese rulers to select some of their officials based on their mastery of Confucian teaching, hoping that this procedure would yield administrators who were both learned and loyal. The Han rulers also began the practice of promoting Confucianism more widely, sometimes by having brief passages carved on polished stones (steles) for display in prominent locations.

Later emperors continued these practices and expanded them. By the time of the Song dynasty (960–1279), every candidate for a position in the imperial administration—the dream job for all Chinese males—spent many years preparing for rigorous examinations on Confucian teachings; there was no other way to become an official. The Song emperors also accelerated the effort to promote the Confucian canon among ordinary people. They sponsored the publication of numerous handbooks, printed by the woodblock method, for wide distribution on the theme of "how to be a good Confucian."

The selections in this chapter help us see how the promulgation of Confucianism continued and even intensified during the Ming (1368–1644) and Qing (pronounced ching; 1644–1912) dynasties. In the first document, dating from the late Ming period, Confucian ideas are illustrated in a set of instructions issued by the leaders of a lineage group in southern China. Lineage groups, also known as clans or common-descent groups, were alliances of extended families joined together for mutual support. The members met regularly to celebrate the memory of their ancestors and to manage their common interests, which often included the joint ownership of land. Lineages were important social institutions in China from the Ming period onward, especially in the south.

The second document is one of the most famous expressions of Confucian teaching in early modern China. Seeking to consolidate the power of the newly established Qing dynasty, Emperor Kangxi (pronounced kahng shee; reigned 1654–1722) prepared a brief set of Confucian maxims or slogans for wide distribution. They were displayed throughout China in the rough equivalent of roadside billboards. Officials read the maxims aloud at public meetings and on various ceremonial occasions.

How do the documents help us identify key Confucian teachings and assess their importance in early modern China? Were similar teachings promulgated in other world regions or was China alone in this regard?

CONFUCIAN DOCUMENTS

I. LINEAGE INSTRUCTIONS

Work Hard at One of the Principal Occupations

1. To be filial to one's parents, to be loving to one's brothers, to be diligent and frugal—these are the first tenets of a person of good character. They must be thoroughly understood and faithfully carried out.

One's conscience should be followed like a strict teacher and insight should be sought through introspection. One should study the words and deeds of the ancients to find out their ultimate meanings. One should always remember the principles followed by the ancients, and should not become overwhelmed by current customs. For if one gives in to cruelty, pride, or extravagance, all virtues will be undermined, and nothing will be achieved.

Parents have special responsibilities. The *Book of Changes* says: "The members of a family have strict sovereigns." These "sovereigns" are the parents. Their position in a family is one of unique authority, and they should utilize their authority to dictate matters to maintain order, and to inspire respect, so that the members of the family will all be obedient. If the parents are lenient and indulgent, there will be many troubles which in turn will give rise to even more troubles. Who is to blame for all this? The elders in a family must demand discipline of themselves, following all rules and regulations to the letter, so that the younger members emulate their good behavior and exhort each other to abide by the teachings of the ancient sages. Only in this way can the family hope to last for generations. . . .

2. Those youngsters who have taken Confucian scholarship as their hereditary occupation should be sincere and hard-working, and try to achieve learning naturally while studying under a teacher. Confucianism is the only thing to follow if they wish to bring glory to their family. Those who know how to keep what they have but do not study are as useless as puppets made of clay or wood. Those who study, even if they do not succeed in the examinations, can hope to become teachers or to gain personal benefit. However, there are people who study not for learning's sake, but as a vulgar means of gaining profit. These people are better off doing nothing.

Youngsters who are incapable of concentrating on studying should devote themselves to farming; they should personally grasp the ploughs and eat the fruit of their own labor. In this way they will be able to support their families. If they fold their hands and do nothing, they will soon have to worry about hunger and cold. If, however, they realize that their forefathers also worked hard and that farming is a difficult way of life, they will not be inferior to anyone. In earlier dynasties, officials were all selected because they were filial sons, loving brothers, and diligent farmers. This was to set an example for all people to devote themselves to their professions, and to ensure that the officials were familiar with the hardships of the common people, thereby preventing them from exploiting the commoners for their own profit.

3. Farmers should personally attend to the inspection, measurement, and management of the fields, noting the soil as well as the terrain. The early harvest as well as the grain taxes and the labor service obligations should be carefully calculated.

Anyone who indulges in indolence and entrusts these matters to others will not be able to distinguish one kind of crop from another and will certainly be cheated by others. I do not believe such a person could escape bankruptcy.

4. The usual occupations of the people are farming and commerce. If one tries by every possible means to make a great profit from these occupations, it usually leads to loss of capital. Therefore it is more profitable to put one's energy into farming the land; only when the fields are too far away to be tilled by oneself should they be leased to others. One should solicit advice from old farmers as to one's own capacity in farming.

Those who do not follow the usual occupations of farming or business should be taught a skill. Being an artisan is a good way of life and will also shelter a person from hunger and cold. All in all, it is important to remember that one should work hard when young, for when youth expires one can no longer achieve anything. Many people learn this lesson only after it is too late. We should guard against this mistake. . . .

5. Housewives should take full charge of the kitchen. They should make sure that the store of firewood is sufficient, so that even if it rains several days in succession, they will not be forced to use silver or rice to pay for firewood, thereby impoverishing the family. Housewives should also closely calculate the daily grocery expenses, and make sure there is no undue extravagance. Those who simply sit and wait to be fed not only are treating themselves like pigs and dogs, but also are leading their whole households to ruin. . . .

Observe the Rituals and Proprieties

1. Capping and wedding ceremonies should be carried out according to one's means. Funerals and burials, being important matters, should be more elaborate, but one should still be mindful of financial considerations. Any other petty formalities not found in the *Book of Rites* should be abolished.

2. Marriage arrangements should not be made final by the presenting of betrothal gifts until the boy and girl have both reached thirteen; otherwise, time might bring about changes which cause regrets.

3. For the seasonal sacrifices, the ancestral temple should be prepared in advance and the ceremonies performed at dawn in accordance with [Zhu Xi's] *Family Rituals* and our own ancestral temple regulations.

4. For burials one should make an effort to acquire solid and long-lasting objects to be placed in the coffin; but one need not worry as much about the tomb itself, which can be constructed according to one's means. The ancients entrusted their bodies to the hills and mountains, indifferent to whether their names would be remembered by posterity; their thinking was indeed profound.

5. Sacrifices at the graves should be made on Tomb Sweeping Day and at the Autumn Festival. Because the distances to different mountains vary, it is difficult to reach every grave on those days. Therefore, all branch families should be notified in advance of the order of priority: first, the founding father of our lineage; then ancestors earlier than great-great-grandfather; next, ancestors down to each person's grandfather. Established customs should be followed in deciding how

much wine and meat should be used, how many different kinds of sacrificial offerings should be presented, and how much of the yearly budget should be spent on the sacrifices. All of these should be recorded in a special "sacrifice book" in order to set standards.

6. Not celebrating one's birthday has since ancient times been regarded as an exemplary virtue. An exception is the birthdays of those who are beyond their sixty-first year, which should be celebrated by their sons and grandsons drinking to their health. But under no circumstances should birthdays become pretexts for heavy drinking. If either of one's parents has died, it is an especially unfilial act to forget him or her and indulge in drinking and feasting. Furthermore, to drink until dead-drunk not only affects one's mind but also harms one's health. The numbers of people who have been ruined by drinking should serve as a warning. . . .

Exercise Restraint

1. Our young people should know their place and observe correct manners. They are not permitted to gamble, to fight, to engage in lawsuits, or to deal in salt privately. Such unlawful acts will only lead to their own downfall.

2. If land or property is not obtained by righteous means, descendants will not be able to enjoy it. When the ancients invented characters, they put gold next to two spears to mean "money," indicating that the danger of plunder or robbery is associated with it. If money is not accumulated by good means, it will disperse like overflowing water; how could it be put to any good? The result is misfortune for oneself as well as for one's posterity. This is the meaning of the saying: "The way of Heaven detests fullness, and only the humble gain." Therefore, accumulation of great wealth inevitably leads to great loss. How true are the words of Laozi!

A person's fortune and rank are predestined. One can only do one's best according to propriety and one's own ability; the rest is up to Heaven. If one is easily contented, then a diet of vegetables and soups provides a lifetime of joy. If one does not know one's limitations and tries to accumulate wealth by immoral and dishonest means, how can one avoid disaster? To be able to support oneself through life and not leave one's sons and grandsons in hunger and cold is enough; why should one toil so much?

3. Pride is a dangerous trait. Those who pride themselves on wealth, rank, or learning are inviting evil consequences. Even if one's accomplishments are indeed unique, there is no need to press them on anyone else. "The way of Heaven detests fullness, and only the humble gain." I have seen the truth of this saying many times. . . .

8. Young family members who deliberately violate family regulations should be taken to the family temple, have their offenses reported to the ancestors, and be severely punished. They should then be taught to improve themselves. Those who do not accept punishment or persist in their wrongdoings will bring harm to themselves.

9. As a preventive measure against the unpredictable, the gates should be closed at dusk, and no one should be allowed to go out. Even when there are visitors, dinner parties should end early, so that there will be no need for lighting lamps and candles. On very hot or very cold days, one should be especially considerate of the kitchen servants.

10. For generations this family has dwelt in the country, and everyone has had a set profession; therefore, our descendants should not be allowed to change their place of residence. After living in the city for three years, a person forgets everything about farming; after ten years, he does not even know his lineage. Extravagance and leisure transform people, and it is hard for anyone to remain unaffected. I once remarked that the only legitimate excuse to live in a city temporarily is to flee from bandits. . . .

13. On the tenth and twenty-fifth days of every month, all the members of this branch, from the honored aged members to the youngsters, should gather at dusk for a meeting. Each will give an account of what he has learned, by either calling attention to examples of good and evil, or encouraging diligence, or expounding his obligations, or pointing out tasks to be completed. Each member will take turns presenting his own opinions and listening attentively to others. He should examine himself in the matters being discussed and make efforts to improve himself. The purpose of these meetings is to encourage one another in virtue and to correct each other's mistakes.

The members of the family will take turns being the chairman of these meetings, according to schedule. If someone is unable to chair a meeting on a certain day, he should ask the next person in line to take his place. The chairman should provide tea, but never wine. The meetings may be canceled on days of ancestor worship, parties, or other such occasions, or if the weather is severe. Those who are absent from these meetings for no reason are only doing themselves harm.

There are no set rules for where the meeting should be held, but the place should be convenient for group discussions. The time of the meeting should always be early evening, for this is when people have free time. As a general precaution the meeting should never last until late at night. . . .

Preserve the Family Property

1. The houses, fields, and ponds that have been accumulated by the family should not be divided or sold. Violators of this rule will be severely admonished and barred from the ancestral temple.

II. EMPEROR KANGXI'S MAXIMS, 1670

1. Strengthen filial piety and brotherly affection to emphasize human relations.
2. Strengthen clan relations to illustrate harmony.
3. Pacify relations between local groups to put an end to quarrels and litigation.
4. Stress agriculture and sericulture so that there may be sufficient food and clothing.
5. Prize frugality so as to make careful use of wealth.
6. Promote education to improve the habits of scholars.
7. Extirpate heresy to exalt orthodoxy.
8. Speak of the law to give warning to the stupid and stubborn.

9. Clarify rites and manners to improve customs.
10. Let each work at his own occupation so that the people's minds will be settled.
11. Instruct young people to prevent them from doing wrong.
12. Prevent false accusations to shield the law-abiding.
13. Prohibit sheltering of runaways to avoid being implicated in their crime.
14. Pay taxes to avoid being pressed for payment.
15. Unite the *baojia* system [the five-family system of mutual surveillance and responsibility] to eliminate theft and armed robbery.
16. Resolve hatred and quarrels to respect life.

STUDY QUESTIONS

1. What is good character for a Confucian? What roles are prescribed for men, women, parents, and young people?
2. How are the lineage rules enforced?
3. What can you infer about the likely age, sex, and social class of the author of the instructions?
4. How do Kangxi's maxims compare with the lineage instructions? Do you see any differences?
5. Why did lineage groups become important in much of southern China? What needs did they fill? Why are they no longer significant?

Confucian Architecture

One of the most influential books in China, ca. 1200–1900, was Zhu Xi's *Family Rituals,* a work first published around 1170 and frequently reprinted in later centuries. Zhu Xi (pronounced joo shee) was the leading Confucian philosopher of his time. He wrote the *Family Rituals* to provide people with instructions on the correct way to practice the Confucian rites required at births, weddings, funerals, and other ceremonial occasions.

The first chapter of *Family Rituals* focuses on the importance of the offering hall, the ritual center in the ideal Chinese home. In the offering hall, the family worshipped the spirits of its ancestors from the past four generations. (The spirits of earlier forebears were worshipped in communal offering halls.) Small wooden tablets that bore the names of the deceased—arranged according to generation and sex—stood on a shrine in the center of the hall.

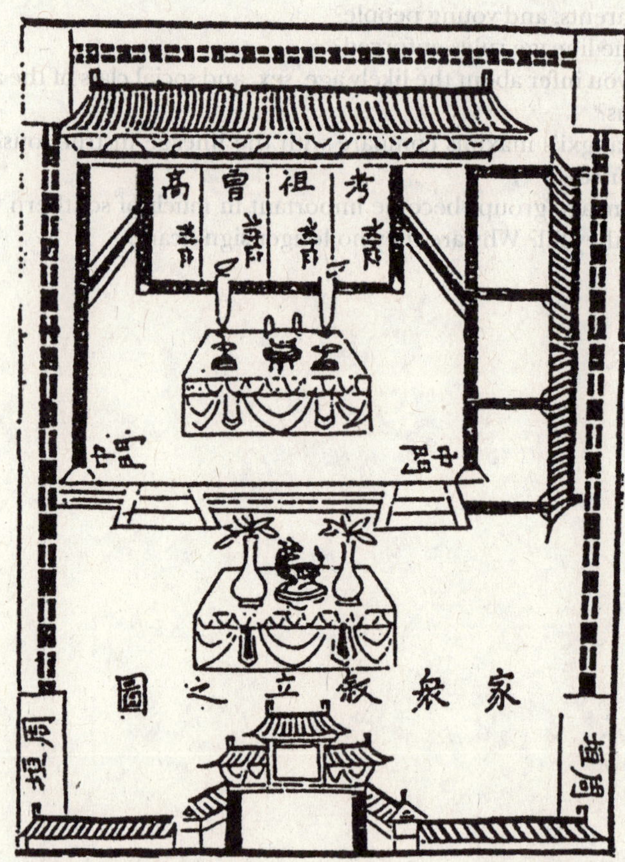

Family Offering Hall, China. Woodblock print, 1602. (Public Domain)

Although no ancestor tablets appear in the woodcut shown here, many of the features of a typical offering hall are clearly illustrated. The hall, which was to face south when possible, is located at the rear of a walled courtyard. A large and decorative gate provides access. Two small stairways lead from the courtyard to the shrine, one on the east for the eldest male and one on the west for the eldest female. Behind the shrine, the characters on a four-part screen indicate the order in which the ancestral tablets are to be arranged.

Illustrated guidebooks on ancestor worship circulated widely during the Ming and Qing periods.

STUDY QUESTIONS

1. How does the print demonstrate the importance of Confucian teachings?
2. What does the publication of illustrated guidebooks suggest about the extent of printing and literacy in China during the Ming and Qing dynasties?

ESSAY SUGGESTIONS

A. Why was Confucianism such a durable feature of Chinese society and culture, from the classical period to the twentieth century?

B. In what ways do Confucian teachings seem to both promote and discourage the development of a modern industrial society?

12 EARLY MODERN JAPAN

The key event in early modern Japan occurred in 1600 when Tokugawa Ieyasu, the greatest of the Japanese warlords, ended a century of ferocious civil war and reunified the country. Faithful to established practice, Tokugawa did not use his power to challenge the largely symbolic authority of the emperor in Kyoto. Instead, he assumed the title of shogun (supreme military commander), established his own "alternate" dynasty, and built a new capital in the small coastal village of Edo (now Tokyo). Although the emperors continued to reign in theory, in practice the shoguns now held the reins of power and continued to do so until they were overthrown in 1868.

From their immense palace complex in Edo, the shoguns issued a steady stream of decrees intended to control their subjects in the most thoroughgoing way. One of Tokugawa Ieyasu's last edicts, the first selection, laid out the rules for the warrior class. Other decrees regulated the lives of the peasants, the vast majority of the population. The use of wheeled vehicles was banned. So also was travel on the main roads, except with special permission from the authorities. Christianity, which had spread widely in southern Japan beginning in the 1550s, was banned and driven underground. One of the most significant decrees, the second selection, all but severed Japanese ties with the wider world for more than two centuries. Only some strictly regulated trade by Chinese merchants and an annual visit of Dutch ships to Nagasaki kept Japan from total isolation during the Tokugawa period.

Despite the policy of "closed country" and the harsh controls, there was much vibrancy in Japanese life. Agricultural output increased significantly. Commerce in rice, sake, soy sauce, silk, cotton, and tea flourished. Cities such as Edo, Osaka, and Kyoto grew into major population centers. A prosperous merchant class, with its own sense of collective identity, became increasingly important (see the third and fourth selections).

The Visual Source highlights another aspect of the dynamism in Japan during the early modern period, namely the growth of a lively and popular urban "counterculture"—one that appealed mainly to merchants and other city people rather than to samurai and peasants.

How do the selections illustrate the mix of repression and change during the Tokugawa centuries? Did the policy of isolation benefit Japan in any way?

Selections I–III from John David Lu, ed. *Japan: A Documentary History* (Armonk, NY: M. E. Sharpe, 1997), 206–208, 221–222, 229. Selection IV from E. S. Crawcour, "Some Observations on Merchants: A Translation of Mitsui Takafusa's *Chonin Koken Roku*," *Transactions of the Asiatic Society of Japan*. 3rd series, Vol. 8 (1962), 31–32, 38–39.

TOKUGÁWA DOCUMENTS

I. LAWS FOR THE WARRIOR CLASS (1615)

[Shortly before his death, Tokugawa Ieyasu issued the following decree to the members of the warrior class (daimyō, lesser lords, and samurai).]

1. The study of literature and the practice of the military arts, including archery and horsemanship, must be cultivated diligently.

"On the left hand literature, on the right hand use of arms" was the rule of the ancients. Both must be pursued concurrently. Archery and horsemanship are essential skills for military men. It is said that war is a curse. However, it is resorted to only when it is inevitable. In time of peace, do not forget the possibility of disturbances. Train yourselves and be prepared.

2. Avoid group drinking and wild parties.

The existing codes strictly forbid these matters. Especially when one indulges in licentious sex, or becomes addicted to gambling, it creates a cause for the destruction of one's own domain.

3. Anyone who violates the law must not be harbored in any domain [landed estate]. Law is the foundation of social order. Reason may be violated in the name of law, but law may not be violated in the name of reason. Anyone who violates the law must be severely punished.

4. The *daimyō*, the lesser lords (*shōmyō*), and those who hold land under them (*kyunin*) must at once expel from their domains any of their own retainers or soldiers who are charged with treason or murder.

Anyone who entertains a treasonous design can become an instrument for destroying the nation and a deadly sword to annihilate the people. How can this be tolerated?

5. Hereafter, do not allow people from other domains to mingle or reside in your own domain. This ban does not apply to people from your own domain.

Each domain has its own customs different from others. If someone wishes to divulge his own domain's secrets to people of another domain, or to report the secrets of another domain to people of his own domain, he is showing a sign of his intent to curry favors.

6. The castles in various domains may be repaired, provided the matter is reported without fail. New construction of any kind is strictly forbidden.

A castle with a parapet exceeding ten feet in height and 3,000 feet in length is injurious to the domain. Steep breastworks and deep moats are causes of a great rebellion.

7. If innovations are being made or factions are being formed in a neighboring domain, it must be reported immediately.

Men have a proclivity toward forming factions, but seldom do they attain their goals. There are some who [on account of their factions] disobey their masters and fathers, and feud with their neighboring villages. Why must one engage in [meaningless] innovations, instead of obeying old examples?

8. Marriage must not be contracted in private [without approval from the *bakufu* (shogunate)].

Marriage is the union symbolizing the harmony of *yin* and *yang*, and it cannot be entered into lightly. The thirty-eighth hexagram *kui* [in the *Book of Changes*], says "Marriage is not to be contracted to create disturbance. Let the longing of male and female for each other be satisfied. If disturbance is to take hold, then the proper time will slip by." The "Peach young" poem of the *Book of Odes* says "When men and women observe what is correct, and marry at the proper time, there will be no unattached women in the land." To form a factional alliance through marriage is the root of treason.

9. The *daimyō*'s visits (*sankin*) to Edo [which became compulsory in alternate years after 1635] must follow the following regulations:

The *Shoku Nihongi* (*Chronicles of Japan, Continued*) contains a regulation saying that "Unless entrusted with some official duty, no one is permitted to assemble his clansmen at his own pleasure. Furthermore no one is to have more than twenty horseman as his escort within the limits of the capital. . . . " Hence it is not permissible to be accompanied by a large force of soldiers. For the *daimyō* whose revenues range from 1,000,000 *koku* [1 *koku* = 5 bushels] down to 200,000 *koku* of rice, not more than twenty horseman may accompany them. For those whose revenues are 100,000 *koku* or less, the number is to be proportionate to their incomes. On official business, however, the number of persons accompanying him can be proportionate to the rank of each *daimyō*.

10. The regulations with regard to dress materials must not be breached.

Lords and vassals, superiors and inferiors, must observe what is proper within their positions in life. Without authorization, no retainer may indiscriminately wear fine white damask, white wadded silk garments, purple silk kimono, purple silk linings, and kimono sleeves which bear no family crest. Lately retainers and soldiers have taken to wearing rich damask and silk brocade. This was not sanctioned by the old laws, and must now be kept within bounds.

11. Persons without rank are not to ride in palanquins.

Traditionally there have been certain families entitled to ride palanquins without permission, and there have been others receiving such permission. Lately ordinary retainers and soldiers have taken to riding in palanquins, which is a wanton act. Hereafter, the *daimyō* of various domains, their close relatives, and their distinguished officials may ride palanquins without special permission. In addition, briefly, doctors and astrologers, persons over sixty years of age, and those who are sick or invalid may ride palanquins after securing necessary permission. If retainers and soldiers wantonly ride palanquins, their masters shall be held responsible. The above restrictions do not apply to court nobles, Buddhist prelates, and those who have taken the tonsure.

12. The samurai of all domains must practice frugality. When the rich proudly display their wealth, the poor are ashamed of not being on a par with them. There is nothing which will corrupt public morality more than this, and therefore it must be severely restricted.

13. The lords of the domains must select as their officials men of administrative ability.

The way of governing a country is to get the right men. If the lord clearly discerns between the merits and faults of his retainers, he can administer due rewards and punishments. If the domain has good men, it flourishes more than ever. If it has no good men, it is doomed to perish. This is an admonition which the wise men of old bequeathed to us.

Take heed and observe the purport of the foregoing rules.

First year of Genna [1615], seventh month.

II. THE EDICT OF 1635 ORDERING THE CLOSING OF JAPAN

1. Japanese ships are strictly forbidden to leave for foreign countries.

2. No Japanese is permitted to go abroad. If there is anyone who attempts to do so secretly, he must be executed. The ship so involved must be impounded and its owner arrested, and the matter must be reported to the higher authority.

3. If any Japanese returns from overseas after residing there, he must be put to death.

4. If there is any place where the teachings of padres (Christianity) is practiced, the two of you must order a thorough investigation.

5. Any informer revealing the whereabouts of the followers of padres (Christians) must be rewarded accordingly. If anyone reveals the whereabouts of a high ranking padre, he must be given one hundred pieces of silver. For those of lower ranks, depending on the deed, the reward must be set accordingly.

6. If a foreign ship has an objection [to the measures adopted] and it becomes necessary to report the matter to Edo, you may ask the Omura domain to provide ships to guard the foreign ship, as was done previously.

7. If there are any Southern Barbarians (Westerners) who propagate the teachings of padres, or otherwise commit crimes, they may be incarcerated in the prison maintained by the Ōmura domain, as was done previously.

8. All incoming ships must be carefully searched for the followers of padres.

9. No single trading city [see 12 below] shall be permitted to purchase all the merchandise brought by foreign ships.

10. Samurai are not permitted to purchase any goods originating from foreign ships directly from Chinese merchants in Nagasaki.

11. After a list of merchandise brought by foreign ships is sent to Edo, as before you may order that commercial dealings may take place without waiting for a reply from Edo.

12. After settling the price, all white yarns (raw silk) brought by foreign ships shall be allocated to the five Japanese trading cities and other quarters as stipulated.

13. After settling the price of white yarns (raw silk), other merchandise [brought by foreign ships] may be traded freely between the [licensed] dealers. However, in view of the fact that Chinese ships are small and cannot bring large consignments, you may issue orders of sale at your discretion. Additionally, payment for goods purchased must be made within twenty days after the price is set.

14. The date of departure homeward of foreign ships shall not be later than the twentieth day of the ninth month. Any ships arriving in Japan later than usual shall depart within fifty days of their arrival. As to the departure of Chinese ships, you may use your discretion to order their departure after the departure of the Portuguese *galeota* (galleon).

15. The goods brought by foreign ships which remained unsold may not be deposited or accepted for deposit.

16. The arrival in Nagasaki of representatives of the five trading cities shall not be later than the fifth day of the seventh month. Anyone arriving later than that date shall lose the quota assigned to his city.

17. Ships arriving in Hirado must sell their raw silk at the price set in Nagasaki, and are not permitted to engage in business transactions until after the price is established in Nagasaki.

You are hereby required to act in accordance with the provisions set above. It is so ordered.

Kaga no-kami Hotta Masamori et al., seals.

To: Sakakibara Hida no-kami, Sengoku Yamoto no-kami

III. A CONFUCIAN SCHOLAR SEES CHANGES, CA. 1720

[Ogyu Sorai (1666-1728) was a leading Confucian scholar.]

In olden days, the countryside had hardly any money and all the purchase was made with rice or barley but not with money. This is what I [the author, Ogyū Sorai] experienced while living in the countryside. However, I have heard that from the Genroku period [1688–1704] on, money economy has spread to the countryside, and they now use money to purchase things. . . .

Nowadays [i.e., the Kyōhō period, 1716–1735], samurai are forced to live in castle towns in discharge of their duties. Living away from home, in a manner similar to travelers seeking lodging, requires cash for sustenance. They must sell rice [the stipends that they receive from their lord] for cash, and purchase their daily needs from merchants. In this way, merchants become masters while samurai are relegated to the position of customers, unable to determine prices fixed on different commodities. In olden days when samurai lived on their own lands, they had no need to sell their rice. Merchants came to buy rice, and under such circumstances, samurai remained masters and the merchants their customers. Prices of different commodities were dictated by the samurai class. This is the law that was established by the ancient sage [i.e., Confucius] in his infinite wisdom. It must remain inviolable through the ages. One recommendation I have is to charge an exorbitantly high price for the rice and force the merchants to eat grains other than rice.

IV. A MERCHANT'S OBSERVATIONS, CA. 1730

[Mitsui Takahira (1653–1737), was one of the wealthiest merchant-financiers of his day. His father founded the vast Mitsui business dynasty.]

The world is divided into four classes—samurai, farmers, artisans and merchants. Each man works at his calling, and his descendants carry on the business and establish the family. Merchants in particular, although divided into various lines of business, are all concerned primarily with the profit to be earned on money. In rural areas, merchants pay deference to their respective provincial lords and squires. When they look at their superiors, they see no great splendor and so do not get carried away. Thus most of them work at their business generation after generation. As for the merchants of Kyoto, Edo and Osaka, the founder of the firm, starting either in a country area or as someone's clerk, gradually works his way up, extends his business and, with the idea of leaving a fortune to his descendants, lives frugally all his life, paying no heed to anything but his family business. After he has built up a record of difficulties and sufferings, his son inherits the family business. Having learned from observation of his father's frugality and having passed his formative years while the house was still not so prosperous, he just manages to keep things intact during his lifetime. When it comes to the grandchildren's time, however, having been brought up after the family had already become rich and knowing nothing of physical hardships or of the value of money, they unconsciously pick up the ways of the world, get big ideas, leave their family business to others and pass their time in idleness. With their personal expenses mounting, they gradually grow older. Even if they pay any attention to their business affairs, they do not know how to run them. While letting their expenses rise, they borrow ready money from other people. The usual thing is for them gradually to become saddled with interest payments and to end by ruining their houses. We know from our own observation that notable merchant houses of Kyoto generally are ruined in the second or third generation and disappear from the scene. The old sayings "Some begin well, but few end well" and "When you are in safety, do not forget dangers" are applicable to one who in his own generation sets up a family business and gains wealth. How much more do they apply to one who receives his father's savings by inheritance and has had wealth from his upbringing.

STUDY QUESTIONS

1. What were the goals of the shoguns? How did they try to attain them?
2. Why did the shoguns close off Japan to the wider world?
3. Why does the Confucian scholar oppose the spread of a money economy?
4. How does the merchant's advice illustrate the intertwining of Confucianism and commerce?

VISUAL SOURCE

The Art of the "Floating World"

The Japanese gave the name "floating world" to the vibrant popular culture that emerged in eighteenth-century cities such as Edo, Osaka, and Kyoto. By 1700, each of these great urban centers had a large entertainment district that featured popular theater (performed by both male actors and marionettes), *sumo* wrestling matches, and numerous *geisha* houses.

***Geisha* with Stringed Instrument (*Shamisen*) and text.**
Woodblock print by Kitagawa Utamaro (1754–1806).
(V&A Images / Alamy)

Prosperous merchants were the great patrons of the new entertainment districts. While enjoying their "night on the town," the merchants rubbed shoulders with artisans, apprentices, unskilled workers, peddlers, and even an occasional (and furtive) member of the samurai class.

In the floating world, talent, wealth, beauty, and emotional expressiveness trumped the unusually repressive version of Confucianism promoted by the shoguns. Indeed, the floating world was one of the birthplaces of the modern celebrity entertainer, a development at complete odds with the values of Japan's rulers. "Stardom" for *kabuki* actors, *sumo* wrestlers, and *geisha* was a result, in part, of their depiction in colorful woodblock prints produced in the entertainment districts. The prints sold for no more than the price of a bowl of noodles.

Woodblock prints were the result of collaboration between four types of people: publishers, artists, woodcarvers, and printers. The artists were especially careful in depicting the material culture of the entertainment districts. Although the woodblock method was an import from China, the style of the floating world prints was distinctively Japanese.

STUDY QUESTIONS

1. What aspects of the culture of the floating world are illustrated in the print?
2. How does the print suggest the preparation (education and training) involved in becoming a *geisha*?
3. What is beauty?

ESSAY SUGGESTIONS

A. To what extent were the shoguns Confucians (Chapter 11)?

B. Compare the system of governance in Tokugawa Japan to that in Mughal India (Chapter 10).

13 LATIN AMERICAN CIVILIZATION

ECONOMY AND SOCIETY IN LATIN AMERICA

While Asian societies built on previous developments, an essentially new combination of pre-Columbian, European, and African elements flowed into the creation of Latin American society during the early modern centuries. This was obviously a formative period, involving extensive changes in economic, political, and cultural relationships.

On settling in the Americas, Spanish and Portuguese colonists created new economic systems that tied the New World to European capitalism. By the middle of the sixteenth century, Spaniards discovered large veins of silver north of Mexico City at Zacatecas and in the southern Andes at Potosí. As the great wealth of these discoveries became apparent, Spaniards shaped the other sectors of the American economy to support silver. Colonists formed large estates (*haciendas*) and textile mills (*obrajes*) to supply animals, food, and clothing to mining centers and to growing cities that served as administrative centers as well as commercial and transportation hubs. Although most of the silver was exported to Europe and Asia, either going into the king's treasury or paying for luxury goods, enough minted money stayed in the New World to monetize the economy. In this process, money exchange replaced tribute as the means by which producers transferred goods to consumers. In Portuguese America, a similar process took place, except that the product was sugar, not silver. Sugar plantations, particularly in northeastern Brazil, forged a direct economic link to Europe, spurred the development of ranches and farms, and monetized the economy. Despite boom and bust periods, the economic ties between Europe and America became stronger, and the monetary economy spread ever more widely.

The formation of haciendas, plantations, mills, and mines had dramatic social consequences. To solve their labor needs, Spaniards and Portuguese recruited Native Americans and African blacks. The unequal exploitative relationship between European owner and colored worker, whether Indian, black, or mixed, became the chief characteristic of society. The two passages describing work in the silver mine at Potosí and in a textile mill in Puebla, Mexico, were written by a Carmelite friar who traveled

Selection I from "The Potosí Mine and Indian Forced Labor in Peru," in Antonio Vásquez de Espinosa, *Compendium and Description of the West Indies,* trans. by C. U. Clark (Washington, D.C.: The Smithsonian Institution, 1942), 623–625. Selection II from "A Mexican Textile Factory," in Espinosa's *Compendium,* 133–134. Selection III from L. F. Tollenare, *Notas dominicaes tomadas durante una residencia em Portugal e no Brasil no annos de 1816, 1817 e 1818. Parte relativa a Pernmabuco* (Recife: Empreza do Jornal de Recife, 1905), 78–87, 93–96. Excerpted and translated by Robert Edgar Conrad in *Children of God's Fire, A Documentary History of Black Slavery in Brazil* (Princeton, N.J.: Princeton University Press, 1983), 63–71. Reprinted by permission of the author.

throughout Spanish America between 1612 and 1620. The third passage describing social conditions on a Brazilian sugar plantation was written by a French cotton merchant who resided in Brazil between 1816 and 1818.

LATIN AMERICAN WORKING CONDITIONS

I. THE POTOSÍ MINE AND INDIAN LABOR IN PERU

Continuing to Describe the Magnificence of the Potosí Range; and of the Indians There under Forced Labor (Mita) in Its Operations.

1652. According to his Majesty's warrant, the mine owners on this massive range have a right to the mita of 13,300 Indians in working and exploitation of the mines, both those which have been discovered, those now discovered, and those which shall be discovered. It is the duty of the Corregidor [colonial local official] of Potosí to have them rounded up and to see that they come in from all provinces between Cuzco over the whole of El Collao and as far as the frontiers of Tarija and Tomina; this Potosí Corregidor has power and authority over all the Corregidors in those provinces mentioned; for if they do not fill the Indian mita allotment assigned each one of them in accordance with the capacity of their provinces as indicated to them, he can send them, and does, salaried inspectors to report upon it, and when the remissness is great or remarkable, he can suspend them, notifying the Viceroy of the fact.

These Indians are sent out every year under a captain whom they choose in each village or tribe, for him to take them and oversee them for the year each has to serve; every year they have a new election, for as some go out, others come in. This works out very badly, with great losses and gaps in the quotas of Indians, the villages being depopulated; and this gives rise to great extortions and abuses on the part of the inspectors toward the poor Indians, ruining them and thus depriving the caciques and chief Indians of their property and carrying them off in chains because they do not fill out the mita assignment, which they cannot do, for the reasons given and for others which I do not bring forward.

1653. These 13,330 are divided up every 4 months into 3 mitas, each consisting of 4,433 Indians, to work in the mines on the range and in the 120 smelters in the Potosí and Tarapaya areas; it is a good league between the two. These mita Indians earn each day, or there is paid each one for his labor, 4 reals. Besides these there are others not under obligation, who are mingados or hire themselves out voluntarily: these each get from 12 to 16 reals, and some up to 24, according to their reputation of wielding the pick and knowing how to get the ore out. These mingados will be over 4,000 in number. They and the mita Indians go up every Monday morning to the locality of Guayna Potosí which is at the foot of the range; the Corregidor arrives with all the provincial captains or chiefs who have charge of the Indians assigned them, and he there checks off and reports to each mine and smelter owner the number of Indians assigned him for his mine or smelter; that keeps him busy till 1 p.m., by which time the Indians are already turned over to these mine and smelter owners.

After each has eaten his ration, they climb up the hill, each to his mine, and go in, staying there from that hour until Saturday evening without coming out of the mine; their wives bring them food, but they stay constantly underground, excavating and carrying out the ore from which they get the silver. They all have tallow candles, lighted day and night; that is the light they work with, for as they are underground, they have need of it all the time. The mere cost of these candles used in the mines on this range will amount every year to more than 300,000 pesos, even though tallow is cheap in that country, being abundant; but this is a very great expense, and it is almost incredible, how much is spent for candles in the operation of breaking down and getting out the ore.

These Indians have different functions in the handling of the silver ore; some break it up with bar or pick, and dig down in, following the vein in the mine; others bring it up; others up above keep separating the good and the poor in piles; others are occupied in taking it down from the range to the mills on herds of llamas; every day they bring up more than 8,000 of these native beasts of burden for this task. These teamsters who carry the metal do not belong to the mita, but are mingados—hired.

II. A MEXICAN TEXTILE FACTORY

Continuing the Description of the Features of This City and Diocese, and of Other Cities.

There are in this city [Puebla] large woolen mills in which they weave quantities of fine cloth, serge, and grogram, from which they make handsome profits, this being an important business in this country; and those who run these mills are still heathen (gentiles) in their Christianity. To keep their mills supplied with labor for the production of cloth and grograms they maintain individuals who are engaged and hired to ensnare poor innocents; seeing some Indian who is a stranger to the town, with some trickery or pretext, such as hiring him to carry something, like a porter, and paying him cash, they get him into the mill: once inside, they drop the deception, and the poor fellow never again gets outside that prison until he dies and they carry him out for burial. In this way they have gathered in and duped many married Indians with families, who have passed into oblivion here for 20 years, or longer, or their whole lives, without their wives and children knowing anything about them; for even if they want to get out, they cannot, thanks to the great watchfulness with which the doormen guard the exits. These Indians are occupied in carding, spinning, weaving, and the other operations of making cloth and grograms; and thus the owners make their profits by these unjust and unlawful means.

And although the Royal Council of the Indies, with the holy zeal which animates it for the service of God our Lord, of His Majesty, and of the Indians' welfare, has tried to remedy this evil with warrants and ordinances, which it constantly has sent and keeps sending, for the proper administration and amelioration of this great hardship and enslavement of the Indians, and the Viceroy of New Spain appoints mill inspectors to visit them and remedy such matters, nevertheless, since most of those who set out on such commissions, aim rather at their own enrichment, however much it may weigh upon their consciences, than at the relief of the Indians, and since the mill owners pay them well, they leave the wretched Indians in the same slavery; and even if some of them are fired with holy zeal to remedy such abuses when they visit the mills, the mill owners keep places provided in the mills in which they hide the wretched Indians against their will, so that they do not see or find them, and the poor fellows cannot complain about their wrongs. This is the usual state of affairs in all the mills of this city and jurisdiction, and that of Mexico City; the mill owners and those who have the mills under their supervision, do this without scruple, as if it were not a most serious mortal sin.

III. A BRAZILIAN SUGAR PLANTATION, PERNAMBUCO, LATE COLONIAL ERA: 1816–1818

I will divide the inhabitants of these regions into three classes (I am not speaking of the slaves, who are nothing but cattle). These three classes are:

1. The owners of sugar mills [*senhores de engenho*], the great landowners.
2. The *lavradores,* a type of tenant farmer.
3. The *moradores,* squatters or small cultivators.

The sugar-mill owners are those who early received land grants from the crown, by donation or transfer. These subdivided grants constitute considerable properties even today, as can be seen from the expanses of 7,000 and 10,000 acres of which I spoke earlier; the crown does not have more lands to grant; foreigners should be made aware of this.

There are some sugar-mill owners who interest themselves in the theoretical aspects of agriculture and who make some effort to improve the methods of cultivation and production. I was conscious of their existence, at least, because of the derision of which they were the object. I visited six mills and encountered few notable men.

With bare legs, clad in a shirt and drawers or a dressing gown of printed calico, the sugar-mill owner, armed with a whip and visiting the dependencies of his estate, is a king who has only animals about him: his blacks; his squatters or *moradores,* slaves whom he mistreats; and some hostile vassals who are his tenants or *lavradores.*

The great distances and lack of security on the roads do not encourage contacts with neighbors. Not even in the church are there opportunities to meet, because each mill either has its own chapel, or, what is more frequently the case, there isn't any church and no religious worship is carried on at all.

When a sugar-mill owner visits another one, the ladies do not make their appearance. I spent two days in the house of one of them, a very charming man who overwhelmed me with kindness, and I did not see his family either in the living room or at the dinner table. On a different occasion I arrived unexpectedly after supper at the house of another of them, the splendor of which promised better taste; I noticed on the floor a piece of embroidery which seemed to have been tossed there suddenly. I asked for a glass of water in order to have a chance to go into the next room, but they made me wait for a long time. The lady of the house prepared a choice meal, but I did not see her. Furthermore, the same thing happened to me in a country house near Recife that belonged to a native of Lisbon.

In these houses, where the owners reside for the whole year, one does not observe anything fashioned to make them comfortable; one does not even find the avenue which among [the French] adorn both the simple property and the sumptuous chateau, neither parks, nor gardens, nor walks, nor pavillions. Living in the midst of forests, the inhabitants seem to fear shadows; or more precisely stated, up to the edge of the forest around the mill everything is denuded and scorched to a distance of a quarter of a league. I witnessed at Salgado [a sugar plantation near the town of Cabo] the cutting down for firewood of orange groves which the previous owner had planted near the house, either for his pleasure or his profit.

Luxury consists of a great variety of silverware. When a foreigner is entertained, in order to wash himself he is given splendid vessels made of this metal, of which also the coffee trays used at table, the bridles and stirrups for the horses, and knife hilts are made. Some sugar-mill owners showed me luxurious and expensive English firearms, and I also saw porcelain tea sets from England of the most beautiful type.

I ought to say a few words about meals. Supper consists of an abundant and thick soup, in which garlic abounds, or some other plant of a very pronounced and disagreeable taste which I did not recognize. The first plate is boiled meat which is not very succulent, the tastelessness of which they try to conceal with bacon, which is always a little rancid, and with manioc flour, which each serves himself with his fingers. For a second plate they serve a chicken ragout and rice with pepper. Bread is not seen, although it is much appreciated; they could manufacture it from foreign flour, which Recife is well supplied with, but it is not the custom. The black men or mulatto women (I saw many of the latter serving at table) fill the glasses with wine as soon as they are emptied, but people do not persist in drinking; liqueurs are not served with dessert. . . .

The *lavradores* are tenants without leases. They plant cane, but do not own mills. They send the harvested cane to the mill that they are dependent upon, where it is transformed into sugar. Half of it belongs to the *lavrador* and half to the sugar-mill owner. The latter keeps the molasses, but furnishes the cases for the sugar. Each one pays his tithe separately. The *lavradores* normally possess from six to ten blacks and themselves wield the hoe. They are Brazilians of European descent, little mixed with mulattoes. I counted from two to three *lavradores* per mill.

This class is truly worthy of interest since it possesses some capital and performs some labor. Nevertheless, the law protects it less than it does the mill owners. Since they do not make contracts, once a piece of land becomes productive, the mill owner has the right to expel them without paying compensation. It should be recognized that leases of only a year are not very favorable to agriculture. The *lavrador* builds only a miserable hut, does not try to improve the soil, and makes only temporary fences, because from one year to the next he can be expelled, and then all his labor is lost. He invests his capital in slaves and cattle, which he can always take with him. . . .

If I estimate an average of eight blacks for each *lavrador*, and sugar production at fifty *arrobas* per slave, which is not too much considering the vigilance and labor of the master himself, I can calculate the annual income of each *lavrador* at four hundred *arrobas* of sugar [about 12,800 pounds], which six or seven years ago was sold for about 3,000 francs. Now, this income is clear, since the *lavrador* does not buy anything at all to feed his blacks, and he lives very frugally from the manioc he plants.

I was witness to a rich mill owner's expulsion from his property of *all* the *lavradores* and squatters whom his less wealthy predecessors had allowed to establish themselves there. The number of exiles reached almost 600 persons, the property measuring two square leagues in size [about thirty square miles]. . . .

The *lavradores* are quite proud to receive on a basis of equality the foreigner who comes to visit them. Under the pretext of seeking shelter, I entered the houses of several to speak with them. The women disappeared as in the homes of ladies, though I was always offered sweets. I never managed to get them to accept the little presents of cheap jewelry which I had supplied myself with for the trip. This noble pride caused me to respect the hard-working *lavradores,* a class intermediate between the haughty mill owner and the lazy, subservient, and humble squatter. The *lavrador* has a miserable house, for the reasons I have already mentioned. However, when he abandons the hoe to go to Serinhaem [a nearby town] or to church, he dresses himself up like a city man, rides a good horse, and has stirrups and spurs made of silver.

The *moradores* or squatters are small settlers to whom the sugar-mill owners grant permission to erect a hut in the middle of the forest and to farm a small piece of land. The rent they pay is very small, worth at the most a tenth part of their gross product, without an obligation to pay the royal tithe. Like the *lavradores,* they do not have a contract, and the master can send them away whenever he wishes. As a general rule they are a mixture of mulattoes [mixed-race], free blacks, and Indians, but Indians and pure blacks are rarely encountered among them. This free class comprises the true Brazilian population, an impoverished people because they perform little labor. It would seem logical that from this class a number of salaried workers would emerge, but this does not happen. The squatter refuses work, he plants a little manioc, and lives in idleness. His wife has a small income because, if the manioc crop is good, she can sell a bit of it and buy some clothing. This comprises their entire expense, because their furniture consists of only a few mats and clay pots. Not even a manioc scraper is found in all their houses.

The squatters live isolated, far from civil and religious authority, without comprehending, so to speak, the value of property. They replaced the Brazilian savages but have less value, since the latter at least had some political and national affiliation. The squatters know only their surroundings, and look upon all outsiders practically as enemies. The sugar-mill owners court their women for their pleasure; they flatter them greatly, but from these seductions acts of vengeance as well as stabbings result. Generally speaking, this class is hated and feared. Because they pay them little or badly and often rob them, the sugar-mill owners who have the right to dismiss the squatters fear taking this dangerous step in a country that lacks police. Assassinations are common, but do not result in any pursuit whatsoever. I knew a certain mill owner who did not travel alone a quarter of a league from his house, because of the hostility and treachery of his squatters. He had incurred their wrath, and I had similar reasons to fear them when I entered their huts. . . .

I promised to make a quick survey of the black population. I am not in possession, however, of enough information about the laws that govern them to be able to deal with the matter adequately. Here is what I can say at the moment in respect to them.

The Salgado mill contains about 130 to 140 slaves, including those of all ages, but there is no written list of them. Deducting the children, the sick, and the people employed in domestic service and in the infirmary, there remain only about a hundred people who are fit for agricultural labor. During the four or five months that the sugar harvest lasts, the toil of the mill blacks is most violent; they alternate so as to be able to stay on their feet for eighteen hours. I said earlier that they received for food a pound of manioc flour and seven ounces of meat. Here it is distributed already cooked. There are few properties on which slaves are allowed to plant something for themselves. Passing through the forests I sometimes came upon small clearings where the blacks had come secretly to plant a little manioc. These were certainly not the lazy ones. Nevertheless, Gonçalo [a slave] told me not to speak about it to their master, because this could expose them to punishment.

Upon arrival from Africa, the blacks who have not been baptized in Angola, Mozambique, or another place where there are Portuguese governors, receive baptism upon disembarking; this is nothing but a pointless formality, because they are not given any instruction whatsoever. At certain mills I saw the blacks being married by the priest, but in others they are united only by their whims or inclinations. In either case the master may sell separately the husband and the wife and the children to another buyer, regardless of how young they may be. A black baby is worth 200 francs at birth. Some masters make their slaves hear mass, but others save the cost of a chaplain, claiming that the sacrifice of the mass is a matter too grand for such people. Finally, there are mill owners who are more or less formalistic in matters of religion, and more or less able to appreciate its influence upon the conduct and habits of their slaves. It seems to me that it is in the interest of the masters to maintain family ties.

At the Salgado mill I saw only good slave quarters; everywhere, for that matter, they are of stone and lime and well roofed. Those of Salgado are ten feet wide and fifteen feet in depth, with a small interior division forming almost two rooms. It has a door which can be locked with a key, and a round opening toward the field to provide ventilation. The brick floor is two feet above the level of the adjacent ground, which makes such houses much more healthful than those of many French peasants. Each black is supposed to have his own private room, but love and friendship generally prevent them from living alone.

STUDY QUESTIONS

1. How were mita laborers recruited? Describe the difference between a mingado laborer and a mita laborer. What does this difference suggest about the formation of a new society in Peru?
2. How were workers for obrajes recruited? What was the result of government intervention to improve workers' conditions?

3. Identify the various social groups on the sugar plantation, and describe how they relate to one another. What do these social relationships suggest about the type of society being formed in Brazil?
4. Summarize the French merchant's view of the Brazilian sugar mill owner's lifestyle.
5. How did the French merchant view the living conditions of the slaves? What was his reference point?
6. What were the most important features of Latin American social structure?

ESSAY SUGGESTIONS

A. How do conditions of mine laborers at Potosí; textile workers in Puebla, Mexico; and sugar plantation workers in Brazil compare to those of Russian serfs (Chapter 18) during the late eighteenth century and European factory workers (Chapter 17) during the nineteenth century. In each case, what factors compelled workers to work? How might historians account for differences in the conditions of work?

B. What are the advantages and disadvantages of travelers' accounts of social conditions? Compare the Frenchman's account of plantation life in Brazil to an Englishman's account of plantation life in Yucatan (Chapter 28).

VISUAL SOURCE

Silver Mine at Potosí

The silver mine at Potosí, located in the Andes in southern Bolivia at an altitude of fourteen thousand feet, was the largest and most lucrative silver site in Spanish America during the late sixteenth and early seventeenth centuries. Known as *cerro rico*, or rich mountain, Potosí supplied the silver that fueled the world economy from the Americas to Europe and Asia. Much of the silver stamped and coined at Potosí ended up in China as payment for silk and porcelain. Thousands of Indians, some forced and some voluntarily, worked at the mine site. The drawing, done anonymously, depicts the various jobs and processes associated with the mining and refining of silver. In the background is the *cerro rico* with two veins of silver shown near the summit plus many small entrances into the mountain. Llamas bring the silver ore down to the *ingenio,* or refining location, in the foreground. The aqueduct supplies water to turn the water wheel that powers the stamping machine. The squares (front left) are containers of mercury, which is mixed with silver ore (located in piles along the walls) in the vat in the center of the drawing. Mixing mercury with silver ore yields a new compound, or an "amalgum," of silver and mercury that can be separated from the rest of the ore. Later, the amalgum is heated to extract the pure silver.

(The Granger Collection, NYC — All rights reserved).

This amalgamation process was the technological key to increasing silver production in the late sixteenth century. It was vastly more productive than the old process of silver refining using furnaces.

STUDY QUESTIONS

1. Considering the types of jobs involved in silver mining and that Indians performed nearly all of them, discuss the acculturation of Indians to Spanish ways resulting from this work. Which jobs would lead most quickly to acculturation? Why?
2. Discuss the possible motivations of the anonymous person who drew the picture. What was he or she trying to communicate?

14 BAROQUE CULTURE IN LATIN AMERICA

Baroque culture refers to a European artistic and intellectual movement of the seventeenth and early eighteenth centuries. From Europe, it spread to Latin America. Examples of Baroque architecture include the French king's palace at Versailles and the great plaza in front of St. Peter's Cathedral in Rome, both of which exhibit the "grand scale" of Baroque style. Numerous churches were also built in a Baroque manner that featured ornate, intricate façades and altars. Baroque artists experimented with light and shadow to depict supernatural illusions and religious ecstasy. Poets and scholars also participated in the movement. They mastered intricate wordplay and complex scholarly arguments. This Baroque style spread from Iberia to Spanish and Portuguese America, where architects, poets, and scholars applied it to local conditions. In colonial Mexico, two groups with very little political or economic power—women and Indians—used this elite cultural movement to deal with social conditions over which they had little control.

No person was more influential in this effort than the Jeronymite nun Sister Juana Inez de la Cruz (1651–1695). Like other Baroque poets, she mastered the intricate rules of Baroque style and became adept at wordplay that often obscured meaning. Her cleverness failed to hide a troubled soul. In several poems, she confronted problems encountered by women intellectuals in a male-dominated society. Born to an unmarried mother in a small village outside Mexico City, in her poetry, she rebuked the double standard in sexual relations. Attracted by experimentation to establish truth, she ridiculed the scholastics of the Catholic Church who manipulated biblical texts and the writings of Church fathers to prove anything they wished. Such views conflicted with her status as a woman and a nun. Having vowed obedience to the Church and her religious order, she became increasingly tormented by the jealousy and criticism of her superiors, male and female. Four years before she died, Sister Juana stopped writing, sold all her books to charity, and submitted totally to serving members of her order, many of whom had fallen ill during the pestilence of 1691. One of Sister Juana's poems directly exposed the arrogance and stupidity of men in their relations with women.

Although Baroque culture in Mexico tormented independent thinkers such as Sister Juana, its popular side attracted ordinary people. Commoners could not write, but they could dress up. To contribute to religious celebrations, Indians organized costume parades, or *máscaras*. As described by Carlos de Siguenza y Góngara in 1680, the natives of Querétaro, a grain-producing area north of Mexico City, dedicated their *máscara* to the Virgin of Guadalupe, for whom they had recently built a new church that was officially opened on the day of the parade. The description of the *máscara* shows that the Indians remembered their separate cultural inheritance. It also shows that the Spaniards provided a place for the Indians in society by encouraging cultural blending.

SAMPLINGS OF BAROQUE CULTURE IN LATIN AMERICA

I. SELECTION OF SISTER JUANA INEZ DE LA CRUZ'S POETRY

Ah stupid men, unreasonable
In blaming woman's nature,
Oblivious that your acts incite
The very faults you censure.

If, of unparalleled desire,
At her disdain you batter
With provocation of the flesh,
What should her virtue matter?

Yet once you wear resistance down
You reprimand her, showing
That what you diligently devised
Was all her wanton doing.

With love you feign to be distraught
(How gallant is your lying!
Like children, masked with coconuts.
Their own selves terrifying).

And idiotically would seek
In the same woman's carriage
A Thais for the sport of love,
And a Lucrece for marriage.

What sight more comic than the man,
All decent counsel loathing,
Who breathes upon a mirror's face
Then mourns: "I can see nothing."

Whether rejected or indulged,
You all have the same patter:
Complaining in the former case,
But mocking in the latter.

No woman your esteem can earn,
Though cautious and mistrustful;
You call her cruel, if denied,
And if accepted, lustful.

Inconsequent and variable
Your reason must be reckoned:
You charge the first girl with disdain;
With lickerishness, the second.

How can the lady of your choice
Temper her disposition,
When to be stubborn vexes you,
But you detest submission?

So, what with all the rage and pain
Caused by your greedy nature,
She would be wise who never loved
And hastened her departure.

Let loved ones cage their liberties
Like any captive bird; you
Will violate them none the less,
Apostrophising virtue.

Which has the greater sin when burned
By the same lawless fever:
She who is amorously deceived,
Or he, the sly deceiver?

Or which deserves the sterner blame,
Though each will be a sinner:
She who becomes a whore for pay,
Or he who pays to win her?

Are you surrounded at your faults,
Which could not well be direr?
Then love what you have made her be,
Or, make as you desire her.

I warn you: trouble her no more,
But earn the right to visit
Your righteous wrath on any jade
Who might your lust solicit.

This arrogance of men in truth
Comes armored with all evil—
Sworn promise, please of urgency—
O world, O flesh, O devil!

II. VIRGIN OF GUADALUPE PARADE

If I could present this *máscara* to the ears as it delighted the eyes, I doubt not that I could achieve with my words what the Indians accomplished in it with their adornments. I shall do all that I can, though I know that I shall expose myself to the censure of incredulity. . . .

At three o'clock in the afternoon the masquerade in four sections started to make its appearance on the city streets. The first part was not especially noteworthy as it consisted of a disorganized band of wild Chichimeca Indians who swarmed about the thoroughfares garbed in the very minimum that decency allows. They had daubed their bodies with clay paints of many hues, and their disheveled hair was made even more unsightly by filthy feathers thrust into it in no particular pattern. Like imaginary satyrs and demoniacal furies they whooped, yelled, and howled, waved clubs, and flourished bows and arrows in such a realistic imitation of their warlike practices, that spectators were quite startled and terrified.

More enthusiastic applause greeted the second section, a company of infantrymen formed by one hundred and eight youths marching six abreast, each one bedecked in finest Spanish regalia, with bright-colored plumes fluttering from the crest of helmets and multihued ribbons streaming in the breeze from their shoulders. They presented a noble and inspiring appearance, but nothing amazed me quite as much as the superb precision and perfect rhythm with which they marched, with no other practice or training than that acquired in festive parades and on like occasions. Veterans could not have kept their ranks more evenly, or shown greater dexterity in firing and reloading, or manoeuvered their squads more expertly. . . . This indicates very clearly . . . that these American-born youths are not incapable of discipline should it be necessary to make professional soldiers of them. The rapidity and skill with which the company leader flourished his pike astonished everyone.

Next came four buglers, mounted on well-trained horses barely visible under scarlet trappings and silver trimmings. The clear, shrill notes of their instruments heralded the approach of the most important section of this brilliant *máscara.* This was the part representing the nobility and lords of aboriginal aristocracy which, even though it was pagan and heathenish, must be reckoned as majestic and august inasmuch as it held sway over a vast northern empire in the New World. In taking part in these festivities it is quite unthinkable that these Indians should put on tableaux borrowed from an alien culture when they have such an abundance of themes and subjects for pageantry in the lives of their kings and emperors and in annals of their history. So it was that, on this occasion, they appeared in ancient garbs of their people as portrayed in their hieroglyphic paintings and as still preserved in tribal memory. All were dressed alike with an amazing array of adornments. . . .

Bringing up the rear of this colorful section was a figure representing the august person of the most valiant Emperor Charles V of Spain and the Holy Roman Empire, whose dominions extended from Germany in the north to the western hemisphere of America. He was arrayed in full armor, burnished black and engraved in gold. Like the Indian monarchs preceding him in the procession, he rode behind airy steeds that pranced with grace and stately rhythm as if fully aware of the sublime majesty of the ruler who held the reins. Indeed, these gallant horses, with the rhythmic swaying of plumes and the even gait of their hooves and the carriage gliding like Apollo's chariot across the heavens, made them seem so like Pegasus that onlookers burst into enthusiastic applause. In short, the elegance and splendor of the trappings harmonized completely with the august majesty of the figure represented.

Then came the triumphal float, lovelier than the starry firmament and its twinkling constellations. The base, supported by wheels, was six yards long, about half that width, and from the ground it was raised about a yard and a half. On this ample space rested the form of a large ship plowing through imitation waves of silver and bluish white gauze. The sides covering the underparts of the float bore complex designs of involved spirals, ornate capitals, and decorative emblems, imbuing the whole with an aura of brilliance and splendor. From a large figurehead at the bow of the ship ribbons of scarlet taffeta fell away, intertwined so intricately with the harness traces that they actually seemed to be drawing the conveyance. Above the stern of the simulated vessel rose two exceedingly graceful arches, forming a throne, in the middle of which reposed a large, curved shell, supported from behind by a pair of Persian caryatids [draped female figures supporting an entablature]. Within it was an image of the Virgin of Guadalupe, and from her canopied throne descended a staircase with silken mats. Further embellishing this lovely ensemble were varicolored taffeta streamers, and a plethora of bouquets of many hues. Like an ambulant springtime, it appeared, dedicated to the immortal Queen of the heavenly paradise, and far exceeding in beauty the Hanging Gardens of Babylon which, in their time, were dedicated to Semiramis. At appropriate intervals stood six graceful angels, symbolizing some of the attributes of the most Holy Virgin. Kneeling on the first step of the throne was a lovely child garbed in the native raiment of the Indians, who thus represented the whole of America, particularly this northern part which, in pagan days, was known as Anahuac. One hand held a heart while the other supported an incensor diffusing perfumes and delicate aromas. All about this triumphal float the Indians were dancing one of the famous, royal *toncontines* of the ancient Mexicans. If their costumes in such ceremonial festivities were lavishly colorful in the days of their monarchs, how much more they would be on so auspicious an occasion as this one!

STUDY QUESTIONS

1. In what ways did Sister Juana challenge authority? What did her poetry reveal about a woman's place in colonial Latin American society?
2. Referring to the parade for the Virgin of Guadalupe, indicate the ways Indians remembered their pre-Columbian past. In what ways did the Indians incorporate Spanish beliefs and practices? How did the public celebrations, such as the parade, shape a new culture different from Indian traditions and European models?
3. How would such parades and the celebrations of popular Christianity likely influence the rural and urban workers, such as peasants on haciendas, mine workers, and textile laborers?
4. What political strategy is suggested by the Spanish encouragement of Indian participation in public religious festivals?

ESSAY SUGGESTIONS

A. Compare Sister Juana's life and ideas with those of women in traditional societies of China and postclassical Europe. How were women supposed to relate to traditional authority? Based on her writings, how did Sister Juana try to shape her own life?

B. Given the various cultural currents in early modern Latin America, discuss the relationship between Latin America and Western European intellectual and religious life.

Baroque Church

The Catholic Church in Latin America amassed wealth not only via regular tithe levies but also through donations of land, payments for prayers for deceased relatives, and rents from urban and rural properties. Church officials poured much of this wealth into construction of holy buildings. Built about 170 years after the conquest, between 1690 and 1730, this church, named Santa María and located in the village of Tonantzintla (which in Náhuatl signified "place of our mother"), indicated that the builders still sought to identify preconquest beliefs with the cult of the Virgin. Typically, Indian artisans, following European models but altering them to suit local practices, constructed and decorated such churches.

Exterior and Interior of Baroque Church, Santa María de Tonantzintla, near Cholula, Mexico. The photos are included in the Colonial Mexican Art slide collection at California State University, Los Angeles. (Manuel Aguilar-Moreno, Ph.D)

Study Question

1. What does such a building suggest about the characteristics of the new civilization forming in Latin America?

15 SUB-SAHARAN AFRICA

EAST AFRICA AND PORTUGAL

Like the Americas, Africa was the target of increasing European interactions in the early modern period. This included most obviously the new slave trade with West Africa (see Chapter 21), but it also involved wider trading contacts. The impact on Africa, however, was considerably different from that in the Americas, and this requires analysis in its own right.

The following selection comes from a Portuguese missionary, Gaspar de Santo Bernadino, who visited several parts of the East African coast early in the seventeenth century. He visited present-day Tanzania and Kenya as well as several coastal islands. He dedicated the account of his travels to the Portuguese queen when he published it in 1611. The selection provides opportunities to analyze African-European relations in areas where Europeans, and the Portuguese in particular, had a significant military, trading, and religious presence but where independent African activities and patterns continued as well.

This is a traveler's account, which requires some sense of the particular perspectives of the author, including his attitudes toward Africans and non-Christians. De Santo Bernadino uses the term Moors, for example, to describe African Muslims or people of mixed African-Arabian descent; is this a biased term, in his usage?

East Africa had a rich history of trade and religious exchange well before the arrival of the Portuguese. A number of regional kingdoms and city-states flourished. Portugal's influence did not significantly alter many of these patterns.

Nevertheless, the Portuguese presence was real, and it is important to understand what this presence involved, what consequences it had, and how Africans reacted to it.

GASPAR DE SANTO BERNADINO'S ITINERARIO DA INDIA

Mombasa, the seat of government and the most usual residence of the kings of Malindi, is on the coast of Africa, somewhat removed from the equinoctial line a little more than a degree to the south, and almost adjoining Ethiopia. It is four leagues in circumference and thickly wooded. These woods, sloping towards the river surrounding the town, make the place particularly agreeable, and its pleasantness is increased by the abundance of fish caught in the river in such quantity that

From G. S. P. Freeman-Grenville, *The East African Coast: Select Documents from the First to the Earlier 19th Century* (Oxford University Press, 1962), 156–162.

they are completely valueless. The Portuguese are supplied with flour and wines from Goa [in India] in exchange for a large quantity of ivory from Cafraria, which is shipped from Mombasa to India and to Ormuz. . . . Within a musket-shot away there is a creek or inlet ten fathom deep, where many ships are accustomed to anchor. From this place one may have a good view of the whole of the city of the Portuguese, which consists of a single street, by name *Rapozeira,* of some seventy houses. At the end of the street is the gate of the Fortress known as *Jesus of Mombasa,* in which are always stationed soldiers to guard it all the time, and a sufficient number of officers to command two batteries of heavy artillery, one of which is placed on a level with the sea, and the other is on the square above.

A third of a league away from here upstream is the Court of the King of Malindi, who at the present time is called Sultan Mahamet, a man of middle age and of a pale brown colour, but of pleasing and agreeable countenance. Not less pleasing were his manners and conversation. On several occasions I visited him and his son the Prince, and they always received me and my companion with demonstrations of delight and affection. This same affection was found in him, in his father and grandfather, by the Portuguese from every ship which visited the port from the time when the first ship touched there to the present day. In 1604 our Catholic Majesty, aware of the sultan's good will, rewarded it with royal and excellent gifts, which have made it possible for the sultan to be supreme over all the kings of that coast, and to be in general the most beloved and powerful among them. . . . Whenever we conversed with the king, he sat in a skilfully wrought chair of mother-of-pearl and we in chairs of scarlet velvet embroidered with fine gold thread. When our audience was over and we took our leave, he ordered bugles and trumpets, curved and of ivory, to be sounded, and the mountains and valleys repeated with their echo his pleasure and the affection with which he bade us Godspeed. We afterwards visited the city, the houses of which are lofty and raised from the ground, but are already very ancient. Their inhabitants are Moors who, although formerly rich, now live in utter poverty—their most usual occupation is that of making mats, baskets, and straw hats so perfectly finished that the Portuguese bring them out to wear on feast days.

Well towards the eastern harbour is an Augustinian monastery where not more than six fathers are housed. In the middle of the cloister is a well which is empty at high tide and full at low tide. . . .

So anxious were we to reach Pate that we left at dawn, and six hours later we lowered sail and anchored in the port of that island. As our vessel was the first to direct its course to the island in that year, practically the whole population came to meet us. From the sea we could look at the population scattered along the city walls and on the beach, awaiting us with the greatest excitement; while we ourselves felt not less excited at the prospect of going ashore. As we cast anchor the whole sea front filled with Moors, some merely wishing to ask and learn the news, others intent on seeking out relations and friends. We alone knew no one, and had none to ask for. However, among the noisy crowd I noticed a Moorish prince by name Muynhe Gombe [M'winyi Ngombe], brother of a former king who had been beheaded in 1603 at the command of Dom Fernando Mascarenhas, and deservedly beheaded, because of the great hatred he bore the Portuguese. When the prince noticed our habits and the very different dress of the other Christians, he called our *malemo* [*Mwalimu = pilot*] aside and asked him in his ear if he knew what sort of people we were, or what we wanted. The Moor, to show his fidelity and to relieve us of any suspicion we might have felt concerning the information he was giving, said aloud the words *cassis frangi,* which means: they are priests of the Christians. When the prince heard this, either because he chose to learn from the punishment taken on the head of his brother how to treat us, or because he was moved of his naturally courteous disposition, he threw his arms about our necks, embracing us with a show of pleasure and of affection. This aroused so much surprise among the spectators, and such was the example given to all, that many, who had come merely to behold and scoff, tried to approach and serve us in so far as they were able. On this occasion, indeed, I was finally convinced of the great influence which the actions and examples of princes and prelates have on their subjects and servants.

While the report of our arrival spread through the island, the prince and the governor ordered that houses should be sought out in which we could be entertained, and each came forward to offer his own. I thanked each for his kindness, and accepted the offers of hospitality which gave us the same pleasure to receive as those who offered lodging and company felt in making their offer. As we left the ship together, all well pleased, we saw running towards us two Portuguese, who asked the Moors where the Brothers were. Our recognition of each other aroused that feeling of intense pleasure known only to those who are aware that such emotions are better described by being felt, than felt by being described. Falling at our feet and embracing them, they straightway asked us, still kneeling, for our blessing. These signs of devotion produced a similar feeling among those witnessing the scene—not least of all among the Moors, who stood staring, quite overcome by surprise, as we were by joy; for good works, though practised by few, are nevertheless envied and admired by all.

We arrived at the house of the Portuguese, accompanied by the prince to its threshold, when he courteously took leave of us. The Moors who noticed what had passed on the beach between ourselves and the Christians could hardly wait for the moment to arrive to pass on the news to the rest of the inhabitants. On the one hand they felt obliged to witness our exchange of courtesies, our customs and our manners; on the other hand they greatly desired to earn the largesse which they felt sure would be forthcoming for taking the good news to the Portuguese. Undecided as to which course to take, they lost everything.

We had already been resting for a quarter of an hour when other Portuguese arrived to see us. We were all very happy, and my companion and I told why we had come, and how we had been all but lost in Sao Lourenço. The Portuguese told us they were merchants trading in the island, and how they hoped, if it pleased God, to return shortly to India. . . . While we were talking about this and other matters, a message arrived from the king, brought by one of his own priests. He said that His Highness welcomed our arrival; that in the city there were some eighteen Portuguese (this indeed was the number of those present), and although His Highness was himself not one, he did not deny nevertheless being a vassal of the King of Spain, and therefore a brother of the Portuguese. Moreover we could—so His Highness said—with a goodwill go to see one whose only desire was to serve us.

We all thanked the messenger, and told him that it was only lack of time which had caused us to be so remiss; but we would immediately take time to go and kneel at his feet. At three o'clock in the afternoon the king sent to tell us that he would consider it a favour if we should call on him at any time. We immediately set out, taking the Portuguese with us, all very elegantly dressed.

We found the king seated on the ground in the manner of the Moors, on costly carpets, and robed in white, as is the Moorish fashion. He was surrounded by all the principal persons of the city. He had had placed for us two cushions near him; and for the Portuguese, chairs. He made a sign for us to sit down, and immediately one of his entourage asked us about our arrival and our health. The king said that we were the first of our Order and habit to have been there, and he trusted that God would henceforward give him good fortune, such as had been his so far, and that he had never before had that good fortune which he was at the moment enjoying. He asked us if we would care to accept his hospitality during the days we spent there; and although it was a Moor who made the offer, the spirit in which it was made was Christian. We thanked him kindly, pointing out, however, that as there were so many Portuguese in the town, it was not right for us to leave them. Benegogo—this was the king's name—agreed and said no more, but merely offered us whatever was necessary for our journey back.

This king was about thirty-five years old, of gentle character which everybody praised; and with a merry expression, but serious in his conversation, and modest in his manner. In short, all that was lacking to make him appear a perfect prince was the name of true Christian.

When we returned home, I was told of another city called Ampaza at two leagues distance, in which there was a church administered by an Augustinian. . . . This Augustinian Father sent a message to the king of the city of Ampaza, asking him to be pleased to entertain and receive us when we arrived. . . .

Mubana Mufama Luvale—this was the king's name—was dressed in long trailing robes, and wore on his head a striped turban of damasked silken cloth. His robe was of quilted cotton; while from his left shoulder there was slung gracefully a curved and perfectly finished Turkish scimitar. He was about sixty years old, and had very fine features, although he was rather dark in colour. He had a fine judgement and intelligence, if one may say so of one who does not know God. . . .

Towards evening, three of us, that is, the three Brothers only, went to see the king, whose delight in seeing us at his palace was such that we could not but be pleased to see a heathen prince so attached and devoted to the Christian religion. That he was devoted was clear, since he, a Moor full of grey hairs, old age and troubles, had, at the time of the building of the church, carted and even carried on his shoulders stones and mortar for the church; and had, moreover, given a considerable sum in alms which were spent on its construction. I myself would never have believed this if the Father Rector had not told me the story in the presence of the king himself, who was ashamed because of the small contribution he had made to the task. We thanked him for his outstanding service to our Lord, and placed ourselves—for what we were worth—at his service. He replied: 'Fathers, while I had no Christian church in my city I lived in fear; now, however, I live well content and at peace because in the church I have walls which guard my city; and, in the Fathers, soldiers to defend it.' Well may one raise one's voice at peace because in the church I have walls which guard my city; and, here to remind those Christians who live like Moors to learn from this Moor how to be Christians. . . .

As the island was small and at peace, we decided to return to the city of Pate by land rather than by sea. On our way we entered the city of Şiu where we found neither Christian nor Portuguese, nor anyone who knew about us, with the exception of two heathen merchants, of whom we had heard in Ampaza. These men were natives of the island of Diu where they had seen members of our order, whose monastery had been built with alms which they—the merchants—had given more willingly than when they had contributed to their infamous temples. These took us to the king's palace, and acted as interpreters since they knew Portuguese very well. The king, Mubana Baccar Muncandi, treated us well, inviting us to be his guests and remain with him that day. We excused ourselves, saying that we would describe all that he was pleased to talk about; but that we only craved of him leave to see the interesting sights of the city. The merchants spent a long time with him telling him about the Franciscan way of living in poverty, and of begging alms from door to door, or living in a cloister where the time was spent in praising God. This indeed met with the approval and excited the wonder of the Moors. . . .

When we reached Pate we were informed that some Moors from Arabia had arrived in a small vessel for the purpose of bartering for African boys whom they then carried off to their country. There the boys were made to follow the Moorish religion and treated as slaves for the rest of their lives. Six of them had already been purchased. My companion and I, after thanking those who had given us this information, went at once to the king and expressed our surprise at his giving his consent to the sale, more especially because it was the desire of the King of Spain—whose vassal he was—to save souls and to snatch them from the clutches of the enemy of our salvation. For this reason, we told him, he should have shown especial care and should not have consented to the purchase. The king assured us that he knew nothing about the purchase; and, if his diligence in seeking out the boys should be any proof of his innocence, then we would clearly recognize how truthfully he was speaking. A search was quickly organized throughout the whole city, in which my companion and I and the Portuguese took part. After making inquiries of all, we finally found the boys, sad and tearful, shut up in a house. To our question whether they wished to be Christians, they all answered yes. The Portuguese thereupon bought them, and had them baptized, and I have since seen two of them here in Lisbon.

STUDY QUESTIONS

1. How does the missionary view Africans? Are his attitudes at all surprising in a time of European colonial expansion in Africa? Why or why not? Does he have any definable biases?
2. According to the implications of the account, what was the nature of Portuguese activity and influence in East Africa? What were the motivations of the Portuguese in the area?

3. What were African reactions to the Portuguese? Why were so many African leaders willing to be so accommodating?
4. Besides the new interactions with the Portuguese and Spaniards, what other kinds of interregional contacts affected East Africa?
5. How did Portuguese policies and goals in East Africa compare to European policies and goals in West Africa in the early modern period?
6. Based on this account, would you assume that Portugal caused major changes in East Africa? Why or why not?

ESSAY SUGGESTIONS

A. Using the passage and other readings, discuss the complexities in the attitudes and impacts of Christian missionaries on native peoples in the early modern period.
B. Why was there not more systematic and uniform resistance to new contacts with Europeans in the sixteenth and seventeenth centuries?
C. Compare the European impact on East Africa with its impact in Latin America. What caused the differences?

SECTION II THE LONG NINETEENTH CENTURY: 1750–1914

The long nineteenth century was defined by yet another surge in global contacts. New technologies, such as steam shipping and railroads, fueled this surge. So, more generally, did the advent of the Industrial Revolution, with its capacity to increase goods for exchange and create new divisions of labor and new economic inequalities among major regions.

The framework for world history from the late eighteenth to the early twentieth centuries was heavily influenced by growing European power. This power was based on previous gains in international trade and prior colonization. Now, however, the process was virtually transformed by Europe's growing industrial strength. Industrialization, beginning in the late eighteenth century, generated new goods to sell, new modes of international transportation that facilitated wider market contacts, and new and more lethal weaponry that enhanced Europe's military advantage.

Yet, the long nineteenth century was by no means shaped by European activities alone. Despite the advance of imperialism, most societies could resist European penetration to at least some degree, and several undertook active reform programs designed to enhance independence and the preservation of important values. Latin America freed itself from direct European control early in the nineteenth century, although its economic subordination in many ways intensified. The development of new institutions and social patterns in the United States, Canada, and Australia, although they reflected Western European precedents, added another important source of complexity to modern world history. Finally, the emergence of various kinds of nationalisms and other cultural responses, in many otherwise different societies, reflected the capacity to define distinctive identities combined with the pressing need to innovate. By 1900, reform developments, independence movements, and nationalism were beginning to limit Western European hegemony, although the full reaction would begin to take shape only after 1914.

16 WESTERN CIVILIZATION AND EUROPE

THE FRENCH REVOLUTION AND ITS AFTERMATH

A new period of revolution helped open the long nineteenth century with involvements on both sides of the Atlantic. The French Revolution, starting in 1789, was the centerpiece of the whole movement. It lasted for ten years and was followed by consolidations and conquests under Napoleon's empire. Napoleon's defeat in 1815 led to a rollback of some of the revolutionary measures, but many of these returned during subsequent political changes in the nineteenth century. The Revolution provided something of a blueprint for the constitutions of a modern state.

The Revolution was guided by many of the philosophical ideas developed in the eighteenth-century Enlightenment. The American Revolution and the constitution it engendered were direct inspirations as well. The French Revolution was also a massive social protest, as peasants and workers articulated the grievances they had developed during the Old Regime.

The Revolution happened in France, but it had European and, soon, world impact. French conquests spread many of the principles of the Revolution to most of Western Europe. Wars of independence in Latin America were inspired in part by French revolutionary principles. So was liberal-nationalist agitation in Eastern Europe, for example, in the Balkans against the Ottoman Empire. Revolutionary ideas would show up in other revolutions in the twentieth century and in proclamations of human rights, such as the United Nations charter.

There were vital disagreements within the Revolution, as in all complex events—quite apart from the outright resistance the Revolution generated among conservatives. The first three years of the Revolution emphasized liberal principles, but then the Revolution turned more radical, for example, instituting universal suffrage for all adult males for the first time, although briefly.

Four documents follow. The first three are classics from the Revolution. The Declaration of Rights and the abolition of feudalism emerged quickly in August 1789, as the revolutionary legislature attempted to define basic political and social principles. The Declaration sought to guide a new political structure, while the attacks on feudalism, responding to massive popular protest, unseated the old guard order. The third document, the first two verses of *La Marseillaise* (the French national anthem, the world's first), represents the more radical phase by 1792, when revolutionary leaders were guiding armies to fight opposition at home and abroad.

Selections I, II, and V from James Harvey Robinson, ed., *Readings in European History*, Vol. II (New York: Ginn and Company, 1906), 405–411 and 547–551; Selection III from http://www.elysee.fr/ang/instit/symb1.htm (website of the Republic of France). Selection IV is from *The French Revolution and Human Rights*. Ed. and trans. by Lynn Hunt. Copyright © 1996 by Bedford/St. Martin's.

The Declaration of Rights of Man and the Citizen was a fundamental statement of human rights, inspired in part by American revolutionary documents. It was intended to guide the new political constitution the revolutionary legislature decided was essential. The Declaration invites analysis to determine what its main principles were and why. In the context of the old regime, they were revolutionary. Note that not all the principles were fully followed up by the liberal constitution of 1791, which most notably did not establish universal suffrage.

A final document raises other complexities. This document was written by Olympe de Gouges (Marie Gouze, 1748–1793), a self-educated butcher's daughter who used the French Revolution to call attention to aspects of French society the revolutionaries were leaving untouched. Her work is an example of the extent to which revolutionary ideologies might extend beyond what the revolutionaries themselves wanted. De Gouges was guillotined as a counter-revolutionary and "unnatural" woman, and later legislation actually weakened women's rights within the family.

CLASSIC DOCUMENTS OF THE REVOLUTION

I. DECLARATION OF THE RIGHTS OF MAN AND OF THE CITIZEN

The representatives of the French people, organized as a National Assembly, believing that the ignorance, neglect, or contempt of the rights of man are the sole cause of public calamities and of the corruption of governments, have determined to set forth in a solemn declaration the natural, inalienable, and sacred rights of man, in order that this declaration, being constantly before all the members of the social body, shall remind them continually of their rights and duties; in order that the acts of the legislative power, as well as those of the executive power, may be compared at any moment with the objects and purposes of all political institutions and may thus be more respected; and, lastly, in order that the grievances of the citizens, based hereafter upon simple and incontestable principles, shall tend to the maintenance of the constitution and redound to the happiness of all. Therefore the National Assembly recognizes and proclaims, in the presence and under the auspices of the Supreme Being, the following rights of man and of the citizen:

Article 1. Men are born and remain free and equal in rights. Social distinctions may be founded only upon the general good.

2. The aim of all political association is the preservation of the natural and imprescriptible rights of man. These rights are liberty, property, security, and resistance to oppression.

3. The principle of all sovereignty resides essentially in the nation. No body nor individual may exercise any authority which does not proceed directly from the nation.

4. Liberty consists in the freedom to do everything which injures no one else; hence the exercise of the natural rights of each man has no limits except those which assure to the other members of the society the enjoyment of the same rights. These limits can only be determined by law.

5. Law can only prohibit such actions as are hurtful to society. Nothing may be prevented which is not forbidden by law, and no one may be forced to do anything not provided for by law.

6. Law is the expression of the general will. Every citizen has a right to participate personally, or through his representative, in its formation. It must be the same for all, whether it protects or punishes. All citizens, being equal in the eyes of the law, are equally eligible to all dignities and to all public positions and occupations, according to their abilities, and without distinction except that of their virtues and talents.

7. No person shall be accused, arrested, or imprisoned except in the cases and according to the forms prescribed by law. Any one soliciting, transmitting, executing, or causing to be executed, any arbitrary order, shall be punished. But any citizen summoned or arrested in virtue of the law shall submit without delay, as resistance constitutes an offense.

8. The law shall provide for such punishments only as are strictly and obviously necessary, and no one shall suffer punishment except it be legally inflicted in virtue of a law passed and promulgated before the commission of the offense.

9. As all persons are held innocent until they shall have been declared guilty, if arrest shall be deemed indispensable, all harshness not essential to the securing of the prisoner's person shall be severely repressed by law.

10. No one shall be disquieted on account of his opinions, including his religious views, provided their manifestation does not disturb the public order established by law.

11. The free communication of ideas and opinions is one of the most precious of the rights of man. Every citizen may, accordingly, speak, write, and print with freedom, but shall be responsible for such abuses of this freedom as shall be defined by law.

II. THE DECREE ABOLISHING THE FEUDAL SYSTEM

Article I. The National Assembly hereby completely abolishes the feudal system. It decrees that, among the existing rights and dues, . . . all those originating in or representing real or personal serfdom shall be abolished without indemnification. All other dues are declared redeemable, the terms and mode of redemption to be fixed by the National Assembly. Those of the said dues which are not extinguished by this decree shall continue to be collected until indemnification shall take place.

III. The exclusive right to hunt and to maintain unenclosed warrens is likewise abolished, and every landowner shall have the right to kill, or to have destroyed on his own land, all kinds of game, observing, however, such police regulations as may be established with a view to the safety of the public.

All hunting [preserves] including the royal forests, and all hunting rights under whatever denomination, are likewise abolished. Provision shall be made, however, in a manner compatible with the regard due to property and liberty, for maintaining the personal pleasures of the king.

IV. All manorial courts are hereby suppressed without indemnification. But the magistrates of these courts shall continue to perform their functions until such time as the National Assembly shall provide for the establishment of a new judicial system.

V. Tithes of every description, as well as the dues which have been substituted for them, under whatever denomination they are known or collected (even when compounded for), possessed by secular or regular congregations, . . . are abolished, on condition, however, that some other method be devised to provide for the expenses of divine worship, the support of the officiating clergy, for the assistance of the poor, for repairs and rebuilding of churches and parsonages, and for the maintenance of all institutions, seminaries, schools, academies, asylums, and organizations to which the present funds are devoted. Until such provision shall be made and the former possessors shall enter upon the enjoyment of an income on the new system, the National Assembly decrees that the said tithes shall continue to be collected according to the law and in the customary manner. . . .

IX. Pecuniary privileges, personal or real, in the payment of taxes are abolished forever. Taxes shall be collected from all the citizens, and from all property, in the same manner and in the same form. Plans shall be considered by which the taxes shall be paid proportionally by all, even for the last six months of the current year.

XI. All citizens, without distinction of birth, are eligible to any office or dignity, whether ecclesiastical, civil, or military; and no profession shall imply any derogation.

III. *LA MARSEILLAISE*

1. Arise you children of our motherland,
Oh now is here our glorious day!
Over us the bloodstained banner
Of tyranny holds sway!
Of tyranny holds sway!
Oh, do you hear there in our fields
The roar of those fierce fighting men?
Who came right here into our midst
To slaughter sons, wives and kin.
Your country

To arms, oh citizens!
Form up in serried ranks!
March on, march on!
And drench our fields
With their tainted blood!

2. Supreme devotion to our
Motherland,
Guides and sustains avenging hands
Liberty, oh dearest Liberty,
Come fight with your shielding bands,
Come fight with your shielding bands!
Beneath our banner come, oh Victory,
Run at your soul-stirring cry.
Oh come, come see your foes now die,
Witness your pride and our glory.

To arms, oh citizens!
Form up in serried ranks!
March on, march on!
And drench our fields
With their tainted blood!

IV. THE FEMINIST VARIANT: OLYMPE DE GOUGES

Mothers, daughters, sisters, female representatives of the nation ask to be constituted as a national assembly. Considering that ignorance, neglect, or contempt for the rights of woman are the sole causes of public misfortunes and governmental corruption, they have resolved to set forth in a solemn declaration the natural, inalienable, and sacred rights of woman: so that by being constantly present to all the members of the social body this declaration may always remind them of their rights and duties; so that by being liable at every moment to comparison with the aim of any and all political institutions the acts of women's and men's powers may be the more fully respected; and so that by being founded henceforward on simple and incontestable principles the demands of the cytogeneses may always tend toward maintaining the constitution, good morals, and the general welfare. In consequence, the sex that is superior in beauty as in courage, needed in maternal sufferings, recognizes and declares, in the presence and under the auspices of the Supreme Being, the following rights of woman and the citizeness.

1. Woman is born free and remains equal to man in rights. Social distinctions may be based only on common utility.
2. The purpose of all political association is the preservation of the natural and imprescriptible rights of woman and man. These rights are liberty, property, security, and especially resistance to oppression.
3. The principle of all sovereignty rests essentially in the nation, which is but the reuniting of woman and man. No body and no individual may exercise authority which does not emanate expressly from the nation. . . .
6. The law should be the expression of the general will. All citizenesses and citizens should take part, in person or by their representatives, in its formation. It must be the same for everyone. All citizenesses and citizens, being equal in its eyes, should be equally admissible to all public dignities, offices, and employments, according to their ability, and with no other distinction than that of their virtues and talents. . . .
11. The free communication of thoughts and opinions is one of the most precious of the rights of woman, since this liberty assures the recognition of children by their fathers. Every citizeness may therefore say freely, I am the mother of your child; a barbarous prejudice against unmarried women having children should not force her to hide the truth, so long as responsibility is accepted for any abuse of this liberty in cases determined by the law (women are not allowed to lie about the paternity of their children). . . .
13. For the maintenance of public authority and for expenses of administration, taxation of women and men is equal; she takes part in all forced labor service, in all painful tasks; she must therefore have the same proportion in the distribution of places, employments, offices, dignities, and in industry. . . .
17. Property belongs to both sexes whether united or separated; it is for each of them and inviolable and sacred right, and no one may be deprived of it as a true patrimony of nature, except when public necessity, certified by law, obviously requires it, and then on condition of a just compensation in advance.

Postscript

Women, wake up; the tocsin of reason sounds throughout the universe; recognize your rights. The powerful empire of nature is no longer surrounded by prejudice, fanaticism, superstition, and lies. The torch of truth has dispersed all the clouds of folly and usurpation.

STUDY QUESTIONS

1. What are the main principles of the Declaration of the Rights of Man and the Citizen and the abolition of feudalism? Are the two documents entirely consistent? What was revolutionary about each of the documents?
2. In what sense did the French Revolution translate the principles of the Enlightenment into political life (see Chapter 7)? What principles did it add to mainstream Enlightenment thinking?
3. In what ways did the abolition of feudalism imply an expansion of government functions?
4. What were the implications of both the Declaration and the abolition of feudalism for relations with the Catholic Church?
5. What were the implications of both documents for the lives of ordinary people? Would their lives be "revolutionized"?
6. What were the main themes of *La Marseillaise* verses? What new elements in the Revolution do they suggest? How does *La Marseillaise* suggest the radicalization of the Revolution?
7. Taking the three documents together, what did the Revolution suggest about the nature and meaning of citizenship in a modern state?
8. In what sense was Olympe de Gouges's feminism consistent with the principles of the French Revolution and the Enlightenment? Is her argument no more than an application of these principles to women's conditions, or does it add further elements? What was the relationship, in substance and historical linkage, between French revolutionary feminism and twentieth-century feminism?

ESSAY SUGGESTIONS

A. What were the international implications of French revolutionary principles? Where outside France did revolutionary ideas quickly promote change, and where was impact reduced or delayed?

B. How did the French and American Revolutions compare? Which was more "revolutionary"?

C. How did the global impact of French revolutionary principles compare with the global impact of European imperialism in the nineteenth century? Were the two currents linked in any way?

17 WORK AND WORKERS IN THE INDUSTRIAL REVOLUTION

The Industrial Revolution was one of the great changes in Western and ultimately world history. Taking shape toward the end of the eighteenth century in Great Britain, industrialization dominated the nineteenth century in Western Europe and North America. Based on radically new technologies, including the use of fossil fuels for power, industrialization revolutionized the production and transport of goods. It created growing material abundance, but it also challenged family life by taking work out of the home and redefining the roles of many women and children. It was, in sum, as basic a change in human history as had occurred since the advent of settled agriculture.

One of the many areas altered by industrialization was the nature of work, particularly for those people who labored in the proliferating mines and factories. Some features of industrialization benefited work: machines could lighten labor, factories could provide social stimulation, and some jobs that demanded new technical expertise became unusually interesting. But many workers found industrial working conditions a strain because they challenged a number of traditional values and habits. Certainly, changes in work provide one way of measuring the human impact of the vast industrialization process—some would say, of measuring human degradation.

The following selections focus on three aspects of industrial work during the nineteenth century. The first document comes from a parliamentary inquiry on child labor, conducted in Britain in the early 1830s and ultimately the source of laws restricting child labor. Child labor was not in fact new, so one question to ask is what aspects of the factory system made it seem newly shocking. A second, related feature of industrial work—and one that persisted far longer than child labor—was the attempt to bring new discipline to the labor force. In the second document, shop rules—in this case, from a French factory in the late 1840s—did battle with a number of customary impulses in an effort to make work more predictable and less casual. Finally, new working conditions provoked direct comment by workers through protest and individual statements. The comment offered in the third document, by an unusually sensitive German miner around 1900—among other things, an ardent socialist—is not typical, but it does express some widely shared grievances.

Selection I from *British Sessional Papers, 1831–1832,* House of Commons, Vol. XV, pp. 17–19. Selection II from *The Archives du Haut Rhin* IMI123C1, translated by Peter N. Stearns. Selection III from Adolf Levenstein, *Aus Der Tief, Arbeiterbriefe,* trans. by Gabriela Wettbert (Berlin: 1905), pp. 48, 57, 60.

INDUSTRIAL REVOLUTION DOCUMENTS

I. BRITISH CHILD LABOR INQUIRY (1831–1832)

Mr. Abraham Whitehead

431. What is your business?—A clothier.

432. Where do you reside?—At Scholes, near Holmfirth.

433. Is not that in the centre of very considerable woollen mills? Yes, for a space of three or four miles; I live nearly in the centre of thirty or forty woollen mills. . . .

436. Are there children and young persons of both sexes employed in these mills?—Yes.

437. At how early an age are children employed?—The youngest age at which children are employed is never under five, but some are employed between five and six in woollen mills at piecing.

438. How early have you observed these young children going to their work, speaking for the present in the summer time?—In the summer time I have frequently seen them going to work between five and six in the morning, and I know the general practice is for them to go as early to all the mills. . . .

439. How late in the evening have you seen them at work, or remarked them returning to their homes?—I have seen them at work in the summer season between nine and ten in the evening; they continue to work as long as they can see, and they can see to work in these mills as long as you could see to read. . . .

441. You say that on your own personal knowledge?—I live near to parents who have been sending their children to mills for a great number of years, and I know positively that these children are every morning in the winter seasons called out of bed between five and six, and in some instances between four and five.

442. Your business as a clothier has often led you into these mills?—Frequently. . . .

. . .

460. What has been the treatment which you have observed that these children received at the mills, to keep them attentive for so many hours at such early ages?—They are generally cruelly treated; so cruelly treated, that they dare not hardly for their lives be too late at their work in a morning. . . . My heart has been ready to bleed for them when I have seen them so fatigued, for they appear in such a state of apathy and insensibility as really not to know whether they are doing their work or not. . . .

461. Do they frequently fall into errors and mistakes in piecing when thus fatigued?—Yes; the errors they make when thus fatigued are, that instead of placing the cording in this way [describing it], they are apt to place them obliquely, and that causes a flying, which makes bad yarn; and when the billy-spinner sees that, he takes his strap or the billy-roller, and says, "Damn thee, close it, little devil, close it," and they smite the child with the strap or the billy-roller. . . .

510. You say that the morals of the children are very bad when confined in these mills; what do you consider to be the situation of children who have nothing to do, and are running about such towns as Leeds, with no employment to keep them out of mischief?—Children that are not employed in mills are generally more moral and better behaved than children who are employed in mills.

511. Those in perfect idleness are better behaved than those that are employed?—That is not a common thing; they either employ them in some kind of business at home, or send them to school.

512. Are there no day-schools to which these factory children go?—They have no opportunity of going to school when they are thus employed at the mill.

II. RULES FOR WORKERS IN THE FACTORY OF BENCK AND CO. IN BÜHL, ALSACE (1842)

Article 1. Every worker who accepts employment in any work-site is obligated to read these rules and to submit to them. No one should be unfamiliar with them. If the rules are violated in any work-site, the offenders must pay fines according to the disorder or damage they have caused.

Art. 2. All workers without exception are obligated, after they have worked in the factory for fourteen days, to give a month's notice when they wish to quit. This provision can be waived only for important reasons.

Art. 3. The work day will consist of twelve hours, without counting rest periods. Children under twelve are excepted; they have to work only eight hours a day.

Art. 4. The bell denotes the hours of entry and departure in the factory when it first rings. At the second ring every worker should be at his work. At quitting time the bell will also be sounded when each worker should clean his workplace and his machine (if he has one). It is forbidden under penalty of fines to abandon the workplace before the bell indicates that the work-site is closed.

Art. 5. It is forbidden to smoke tobacco inside the factory. Whoever violates this prohibition is subjected to a heavy fine and can be dismissed. It is also forbidden under penalty of fines to bring beer or brandy into the factory. Any worker who comes to the factory drunk will be sent away and fined.

Art. 6. The porter, whoever he may be, is forbidden to admit anyone after the workday begins. If someone asks for a worker he will make him wait and have the worker called. All workers are forbidden to bring anyone into the factory and the porter is forbidden to admit anyone. The porter is also forbidden to let any workers in or out without the foreman's permission during the hours of work.

Art. 7. Any worker who misses a day without the Director's permission must pay a fine of two francs. The fine is doubled for a second offense. Any worker who is absent several times is dismissed, and if he is a weaver he is not paid for any piece he may have begun unless he can prove he missed work because of illness and should therefore be paid for work he has already done.

Art. 8. All workers in the factory are obligated to be members of the Sickness Fund, to pay their dues, and conduct themselves according to its statutes.

Art. 9. The foreman and the porter are empowered to retain any worker leaving the factory and to search him, as often as the interests of the Director may require. It is also recommended to the foreman to close the work-site himself, give the key to the porter, and to allow no worker inside during meal periods.

Art. 10. Workers should only go in and out of doors where a porter resides, else they will be fined, brought under suspicion, and dismissed. They cannot refuse to surrender any of their belongings at work, for which they will be reimbursed according to the valuation of the Director and the foreman. Workers are also ordered to be obedient to the foreman, who is fully empowered by the Director. Any disobedience will be punished by fines according to the importance of the case. Any offender is responsible for the consequences of his action. It is also forbidden for any worker to seek work in any of the company's work-sites other than the one in which he is employed; anyone encountered in another work-site will be punished.

Art. 11. Every worker is personally responsible for the objects entrusted to him. Any object that cannot be produced at the first request must be paid for. Weavers are obligated to pay careful attention to their cloth when they dry it. They will be fined and held responsible for any damage.

Art. 12. In return for the protection and care which all workers can expect from the Director, they pledge to him loyalty and attachment. They promise immediately to call to his attention anything that threatens good order or the Director's interests. Workers are also put on notice that any unfortunate who commits a theft, however small it may be, will be taken to court and abandoned to his fate.

III. MAX LOTZ, A GERMAN MINER, DESCRIBES HIS WORK (CA. 1900)

A trembling of the pupils forms in the eyes of many miners. At first it is not noticeable but it gradually becomes stronger. Where this eye ailment reaches a certain stage the stricken person becomes unable to work in the pit any longer. The stricken man becomes unsure of his grip, he often misses the desired object by one foot. He has particular difficulties in directing his glance upward. If he fixes but barely on an object his eyes begin to tremble immediately. But this calamity only appears in the mine or in artificial light. Above ground and in daylight it is never present. I know a laborer working quite close to me who takes a quart of liquor daily into the shaft. As soon as the trembling begins he takes a sip and the pupil becomes calm for a short while—so he states. Thus one can become a habitual drunk, too.

But this is not all. Almost all miners are anemic. I do not know what causes this pathological diminution of blood corpuscles in miners, whether this results from a general lack of protein in the blood. I suppose that it is caused mainly by the long, daily stay in bad air combined with the absence of sun or day light. I reason that if one places a potted plant in a warm but dark cellar for a long time it will grow significantly more pale and sickly than her beautifully scenting sisters in the rose-colored sunlight. It must be like this for the drudges down there. Anemia renders the miner characteristically pale. . . .

Let's go, shouted Prüfer, who had already picked up a shovel. Four more wagons have to fall. It is almost 12:30 [p.m.] now. All right, I agreed, and we swung the shovels.

Away it goes, commanded Bittner when the wagons were fully loaded. Jump to it, there is plenty of coal. Well, if I were a pickman, mumbled the chief pickman then I'd have myself a drink. And he breathed heavily behind the wagon.

Let's set up the planking until Rheinhold comes back so that things don't look so scruffy, I said to Bittner even though we would rather have stretched out on the pile of coal because we were so tired.

He replied: I don't care, but first I want to wring out my trousers. And standing there naked he started to squeeze the water from the garment. I followed his example. When we had finished, it looked around us as though a bucket full of water had been spilled. I do not exaggerate. In other locations where it was warmer yet, the workers were forced to undergo this procedure several times during their working hours. But let us remain here.

We put our undergarments back on and did not pay attention to the unpleasant feeling which we had doing so. We placed the wooden planks and cleared aside the debris in order to establish good working conditions for the other third which usually did not do the same for us—because they were too fatigued.

The work is becoming increasingly mechanical. No more incentive, no more haste, we muddle along wearily, we are worn out and mindless. There was sufficient coal, Rheinhold could come at any time. My forehead burned like fire. As a consequence of the anemia from which I suffer I occasionally experience a slight dizzy spell. Bittner does not know about it. But in my head it rages and paralyzes me beyond control or without my being able to think. When it becomes unbearable I stop my slow, phlegmatic and energyless working. I then sit on the side wall of the mountain in order to slurp the last remaining coffee. . . .

This is a brief description of one shift in the pit. And this torture, this inhuman haste repeats itself day after day [so] that the various states of exhaustion express themselves mildly or very pronouncedly in the physical state of the individuals. And that is not all; the spirit, too, the conscience of the individual degenerates. And one drudge, grown vacuous through his work, is put beside another one, and another one and finally this "modern" circle has closed in on the entire working force. And he who says that primarily the professional group of the miners is the rudest, least educated and spiritually lowest class of men does not lie. Of course, there are exceptions here, too. But these exceptions are supposed to validate the rule according to a simple type of logic. In any event, it truly takes spiritual magnitude to occupy still oneself with belletristic, scientific and thought-provoking materials after a completed shift. When I come home in that condition I still have to cope with other necessary heavy work around the house. And finally there only remains the evening hours for the writing tasks which I deem noble.

STUDY QUESTIONS

1. What features of child labor seemed newly objectionable in the context of factory industry?
2. What were the main goals of factory work rules? What problems did they address? What innovations did they particularly suggest, compared with more traditional work patterns?

3. What does Max Lotz see as the primary problems of mine work? Were work conditions getting better or worse by 1900 in highly industrialized societies like Germany? Why might some workers disagree with Lotz's assessment?
4. Do problems of work in nineteenth-century Europe suggest that industrialization deteriorated the quality of human life? What other factors need to be taken into account? How did workers and others deal with the issues identified in these documents?

ESSAY SUGGESTIONS

A. How did European factory conditions relate to working conditions in other parts of the world during the nineteenth century? What were other major changes in work systems during the period, and how did they relate to industrial standards?

B. Did similar changes in work occur when industrialization spread to other countries, from the later nineteenth century until today? What were the main similarities and differences in work experiences between early (European) and more recent industrial revolutions?

18 RUSSIAN PEASANTS: SERFDOM AND EMANCIPATION

More than most Eurasian societies, Russia long remained a land of small cities with limited manufacturing. Not only a majority but a vast majority of its people were peasants well into the nineteenth century. Numbers alone, however, do not account for the omnipresence of peasant issues in Russian history. From a once-held position of substantial freedom and control of village lands, Russian peasants had been subjected to increasingly rigorous serfdom—by the state or by noble landlords—from the fifteenth century onward. This trend thus reversed that of Western Europe, where serfdom on the whole lessened over time. The Russian economy relied on agricultural exports forced from peasant labor on the large estates, and Russian politics and society, which traded noble control over their peasants for docility to the Russian tsar, relied heavily on the subjection of the serfs.

Yet, the peasants' condition created increasingly visible problems. It violated standards of justice felt keenly by many Russians, including those open to Western ideas during the eighteenth and nineteenth centuries. Serfs rioted frequently, for peasants were quite aware of their own servitude (see Chapter 8). Furthermore, tight control of peasant labor limited Russia's economic flexibility, making it hard to recruit urban labor and, at least in the eyes of some observers, reducing productivity on the land as well. Finally, prodded by its loss in the Crimean War, the Russian government took the step of emancipation, ending serfdom while trying to preserve the noble-dominated social hierarchy. This move redefined the peasant question but did not remove it.

The following selections stem from two sources. The first document is an account by an early Russian intellectual, Aleksandr Radishchev (1749–1802), who wrote about the peasants' condition in the book *A Journey from St. Petersburg to Moscow* (1790), which was repressed by the government until 1905. His account reveals peasants' suffering and reactions and also the reformist zeal of a segment of the educated upper class. The second document presents excerpts from the emancipation decree of 1861. It reveals how a new tsar, Alexander II, tried to juggle reform interests with noble resistance. The document invites appraisal in terms of how much was changed and why peasants were so widely disappointed with the results.

RUSSIAN DOCUMENTS

I. RADISHCHEV'S JOURNEY (1790)

I suppose it is all the same to you whether I traveled in winter or in summer. Maybe both in winter and in summer. It is not unusual for travelers to set out in sleighs and to return in carriages. The corduroy road tortured my body; I climbed out of the carriage and went on foot. While I had been lying back in the carriage, my thoughts had turned to the immeasurable vastness of the world. By spiritually leaving the earth I thought I might more easily bear the jolting of the carriage. But spiritual exercises do not always distract us from our physical selves; and so, to save my body, I got out and walked. A few steps from the road I saw a peasant ploughing a field. The weather was hot. I looked at my watch. It was twenty minutes before one. I had set out on Saturday. It was now Sunday. The ploughing peasant, of course, belonged to a landed proprietor, who would not let him pay a commutation tax [*obrok*]. The peasant was ploughing very carefully. The field, of course, was not part of his master's land. He turned the plough with astonishing ease.

"God help you," I said, walking up to the ploughman, who, without stopping, was finishing the furrow he had started. "God help you," I repeated.

"Thank you, sir," the ploughman said to me, shaking the earth off the ploughshare and transferring it to a new furrow.

"You must be a Dissenter, since you plough on a Sunday."

"No, sir, I make the true sign of the cross," he said, showing me the three fingers together. "And God is merciful and does not bid us starve to death, so long as we have strength and a family."

"Have you no time to work during the week, then, and can you not have any rest on Sundays, in the hottest part of the day, at that?"

"In a week, sir, there are six days, and we go six times a week to work on the master's fields; in the evening, if the weather is good, we haul to the master's house the hay that is left in the woods; and on holidays the women and girls go walking in the woods, looking for mushrooms and berries. God grant," he continued, making the sign of the cross, "that it rains this evening. If you have peasants of your own, sir, they are praying to God for the same thing."

"My friend, I have no peasants, and so nobody curses me. Do you have a large family?"

"Three sons and three daughters. The eldest is nine years old."

"But how do you manage to get food enough, if you have only the holidays free?"

"Not only the holidays: the nights are ours, too. If a fellow isn't lazy, he won't starve to death. You see, one horse is resting; and when this one gets tired, I'll take the other; so the work gets done."

"Do you work the same way for your master?"

"No, Sir, it would be a sin to work the same way. On his fields there are a hundred hands for one mouth, while I have two for seven mouths: you can figure it out for yourself. No matter how hard you work for the master, no one will thank you for it. The master will not pay our head tax; but, though he doesn't pay it, he doesn't demand one sheep, one hen, or any linen or butter the less. The peasants are much better off where the landlord lets them pay a commutation tax without the interference of the steward. It is true that sometimes even good masters take more than three rubles a man; but even that's better than having to work on the master's fields. Nowadays it's getting to be the custom to let villages to tenants, as they call it. But we call it putting our heads in a noose. A landless tenant skins us peasants alive; even the best ones don't leave us any time for ourselves. In the winter he won't let us do any carting of goods and won't let us go into town to work; all our work has to be for him, because he pays our head tax. It is an invention of the Devil to turn your peasants over to work for a stranger. You can make a complaint against a bad steward, but to whom can you complain against a bad tenant?"

"My friend, you are mistaken; the laws forbid them to torture people."

"Torture? That's true; but all the same, sir, you would not want to be in my hide." Meanwhile the ploughman hitched up the other horse to the plough and bade me goodbye as he began a new furrow.

The words of this peasant awakened in me a multitude of thoughts. I thought especially of the inequality of treatment within the peasant class. I compared the crown peasants with the manorial peasants. They both live in villages; but the former pay a fixed sum, while the latter must be prepared to pay whatever their master demands. The former are judged by their equals; the latter are dead to the law, except, perhaps, in criminal cases. A member of society becomes known to the government protecting him, only when he breaks the social bonds, when he becomes a criminal! This thought made my blood boil.

Tremble, cruelhearted landlord! on the brow of each of your peasants I see your condemnation written.

II. THE EMANCIPATION MANIFESTO (1861)

By the Grace of God We, Alexander II, Emperor and Autocrat of All Russia, King of Poland, Grand Duke of Finland, etc., make known to all Our faithful subjects:

Called by Divine Providence and by the sacred right of inheritance to the throne of Our Russian ancestors, We vowed in Our heart to respond to the mission which is entrusted to Us and to surround with Our affection and Our Imperial solicitude all Our faithful subjects of every rank and condition, from the soldier who nobly defends the country to the humble artisan who works in industry; from the career official of the state to the plowman who tills the soil.

Examining the condition of classes and professions comprising the state, We became convinced that the present state legislation favors the upper and middle classes, defines their obligations, rights, and privileges, but does not equally favor the serfs, so designated because in part from old laws and in part from custom they have been hereditarily subjected to the authority of landowners, who in turn were obligated to provide for their well being. Rights of nobles have been hitherto very broad and legally ill defined, because they stem from tradition, custom, and the good will of the noblemen. In most cases this has led to the establishment of good patriarchal relations based on the sincere, just concern and benevolence on the part of the nobles, and on affectionate submission on the part of the peasants. Because of the decline of the simplicity of morals, because of an increase in the diversity of relations, because of the weakening of the direct paternal attitude of nobles toward the peasants, and because noble rights fell sometimes into the hands of people exclusively concerned with their personal interests, good relations weakened. The way was opened for an arbitrariness burdensome for the peasants and detrimental to their welfare, causing them to be indifferent to the improvement of their own existence.

These facts had already attracted the attention of Our predecessors of glorious memory, and they had adopted measures aimed at improving the conditions of the peasants; but these measures were ineffective, partly because they depended on the free, generous action of nobles, and partly because they affected only some localities, by virtue of special circumstances or as an experiment. Thus Alexander I issued a decree on free agriculturists, and the late Emperor Nicholas, Our beloved father, promulgated one dealing with the serfs. In the Western *gubernias,* inventory regulations determine the peasant land allotments and their obligations. But decrees on free agriculturists and serfs have been carried out on a limited scale only.

We thus became convinced that the problem of improving the condition of serfs was a sacred inheritance bequeathed to Us by Our predecessors, a mission which, in the course of events, Divine Providence has called upon Us to fulfill.

We have begun this task by expressing Our confidence toward the Russian nobility, which has proven on so many occasions its devotion to the Throne, and its readiness to make sacrifices for the welfare of the country.

We have left to the nobles themselves, in accordance with their own wishes, the task of preparing proposals for the new organization of peasant life—proposals that would limit their rights over the peasants, and the realization of which would inflict on them [the nobles] some material losses. Our confidence was justified. Through members of the *gubernia* committees, who had the trust of the nobles' associations, the nobility voluntarily renounced its right to own serfs. These committees, after collecting the necessary data, have formulated proposals on a new arrangement for serfs and their relationship with the nobles.

These proposals were diverse, because of the nature of the problem. They have been compared, collated, systematized, rectified and finalized in the main committee instituted for that purpose; and these new arrangements dealing with the peasants and domestics of the nobility have been examined in the Governing Council.

Having invoked Divine assistance, We have resolved to execute this task.

On the basis of the above mentioned new arrangements, the serfs will receive in time the full rights of free rural inhabitants.

The nobles, while retaining their property rights on all the lands belonging to them, grant the peasants perpetual use of their domicile in return for a specified obligation; and, to assure their livelihood as well as to guarantee fulfillment of their obligations toward the government, [the nobles] grant them a portion of arable land fixed by the said arrangements, as well as other property.

While enjoying these land allotments, the peasants are obliged, in return, to fulfill obligations to the noblemen fixed by the same arrangements. In this state, which is temporary, the peasants are temporarily bound.

At the same time, they are granted the right to purchase the domicile, and, with the consent of the nobles, they may acquire in full ownership the arable lands and other properties which are allotted them for permanent use. Following such acquisition of full ownership of land, the peasants will be freed from their obligations to the nobles for the land thus purchased and will become free peasant landowners. . . .

We leave it to the nobles to reach a friendly understanding with the peasants and to reach agreements on the extent of the land allotment and the obligations stemming from it, observing, at the same time, the established rules to guarantee the inviolability of such agreements. . . .

What legally belongs to nobles cannot be taken away from them without adequate compensation, or through their voluntary concession; it would be contrary to all justice to use the land of the nobles without assuming responsibility for it.

And now We confidently expect that the freed serfs, on the eve of a new future which is opening to them, will appreciate and recognize the considerable sacrifices which the nobility has made on their behalf.

STUDY QUESTIONS

1. What are Radishchev's main arguments against serfdom? Where did he derive his criteria for judgment? What kind of society would he find preferable to Russia's?
2. Was the emancipation of the serfs a radical move? Why did it provoke renewed discontent among the peasants? How did the arguments and implementation relate to earlier critiques by Westernizers such as Radishchev?
3. What does the emancipation document suggest about the flexibility of Russia's authoritarian political structure?
4. Do these two documents provide clues as to why Russia encountered less social protest than Western Europe did during the first half of the nineteenth century but more fundamental protest movements by the century's end?
5. How does Russian Emancipation compare with the French Revolution's attack on manorialism (Chapter 16)?

ESSAY SUGGESTIONS

A. How did Russia's emancipation move relate to the wider impulses toward abolition of slavery and serfdom in the nineteenth century? What causes were shared with other societies?

B. Assess Russian and American emancipations in the nineteenth century: how do the settlements and the long-term consequences compare?

19 GLOBAL CONTACTS: NEW PATTERNS OF HUMAN MOVEMENT AND IMPERIALISM

WORLD MIGRATIONS IN THE NINETEENTH AND EARLY TWENTIETH CENTURIES

Migrations of peoples during the nineteenth and early twentieth centuries affected nearly every region of the globe, including Europe, North and South America, India, China, and Southeast Asia. The table that follows summarizes the number of people involved, the regions sending and receiving people, and time periods.

WORLD MIGRATION ESTIMATES: OUT OF AFRICA (1650–1880) AND OUT OF EUROPE, INDIA, AND CHINA (1840–1940)

Sending Area	Number Sent	Time Period	Destination	Number Received
Africa	17 million	1650–1880	Caribbean	7 million
			Brazil	4 million
			Middle East	3 million
			Indian Ocean Area	2 million
Europe	56 million	1840–1940	United States	37 million
			South America	10 million
			Siberia and N. Asia	7 million
			Pacific Area	2 million
India	30 million	1840–1940	S.E. Asia	29 million
			Southern Africa and Indian Ocean Area	1 million
China	51 million	1840–1940	N. Asia and Manchuria	30 million
			S.E. Asia	19 million
			N. and S. America	1 million

Source: Table adapted from Patrick Manning, *Migrations in World History* (New York: Routledge, 2005), 146. (The breakdown data for Africa and China are one million short of the total. This shortfall may indicate people going in other directions.)

Selection I found in Jon Gjerde, ed., *Major Problems in American Immigration and Ethnic History* (Boston: Houghton Mifflin, 1998), 172–176, 180–182. Copyright 1998 by Houghton Mifflin Company. Selection II, description of the coffee plantation, found in Pierre Denis, *Brazil*, trans. Bernard Miall (London: T. Fisher Unwin, 1911), 199–208.

The table indicates important aspects about the movement of peoples around the world. It shows that the slave trade from Africa was still strong during the first seven decades of the nineteenth century, primarily due to the expansion of the sugar production in Cuba and coffee production in the Rio de Janeiro area of Brazil. In the second half of the nineteenth century, the British Navy ended the slave trade by force. Without access to African slaves, Cuba and Brazil eventually abolished slavery in the 1880s. As the slave trade and slavery ended, European migration to the Americas vastly expanded. In some areas, such as Brazil, European colonists began replacing Africans as the workforce in plantation agriculture. In other areas, such as the United States, Canada, and Argentina, Europeans filled the frontiers. Also during the nineteenth century, large migrations took place in Asia, particularly Indians and South Chinese moving to Southeast Asia to work in opium and pepper production but also with significant numbers of Chinese and Japanese coming to the Americas.

The above demographic estimates indicate the magnitude, location, and chronology of migrations but not necessarily their significance. To determine significance, the data require context. For example, Western historiography has stressed the formation of new economies and new societies in the Americas, to which immigration contributed greatly. But there has been recurrent disagreement about what happened to immigrants themselves. Did they largely benefit from their move, or were disorientation and problems in their new location more pressing? Answers may vary, of course, depending on the immigrant group and the particular destination. More recent discussion has also focused on the societies that sent people forward: how were they affected by population loss? Did they sacrifice their most venturesome groups? Motivation for immigration also warrants analysis, in terms of factors that pushed immigrants out versus positive attractions of a new destination. The documents that follow relate to the various debates, revealing characteristics about the people who moved, the regions they left, and where they moved. They might be examined in the context of the formation of new societies and in the context of the migrants' impact on the sending society. The first selection on immigrants to the United States indicates their favorable views of America and the potential benefits of moving there in contrast to staying where they were. Often, conditions in America did not meet expectations, but those negative experiences scarcely stemmed the tide of migration. The second selection describes working conditions of Italian migrants on a coffee plantation in Brazil. It offers an example of great labor mobility of the early twentieth century and the economic conditions that spawned it.

I. "COMING TO AMERICA": IMMIGRANTS TELL THEIR STORIES

Chinese Immigrant Recounts Going to and Working in America, 1882

When I was ten years of age I worked on my father's farm, digging, hoeing, manuring, gathering and carrying the crop. We had no horses, as nobody under the rank of an official is allowed to have a horse in China, and horses do not work on farms there, which is the reason why the roads there are so bad. The people cannot use roads as they are used here, and so they do not make them.

I worked on my father's farm till I was about sixteen years of age, when a man of our tribe came back from America and took ground as large as four city blocks and made a paradise of it. He put a large stone wall around and led some streams through and built a palace and summer house and about twenty other structures, with beautiful bridges over the streams and walks and roads. Trees and flowers, singing birds, water fowl and curious animals were within the walls.

The man had gone away from our village a poor boy. Now he returned with unlimited wealth, which he had obtained in the country of the American wizards. After many amazing adventures he had become a merchant in a city called Mott Street, so it was said.

When his palace and grounds were completed he gave a dinner to all the people who assembled to be his guests. One hundred pigs roasted whole were served on the tables, with chickens, ducks, geese and such an abundance of dainties that our villagers even now lick their fingers when they think of it. He had the best actors from Hong Kong performing, and every musician for miles around was playing and singing. At night the blaze of the lanterns could be seen for many miles.

Having made his wealth among the barbarians this man had faithfully returned to pour it out among his tribesmen, and he is living in our village now very happy, and a pillar of strength to the poor.

The wealth of this man filled my mind with the idea that I, too, would like to go to the country of the wizards and gain some of their wealth, and after a long time my father consented, and gave me his blessing, and my mother took leave of me with tears, while my grandfather laid his hand upon my head and told me to remember and live up to the admonitions of the Sages, to avoid gambling, bad women and men of evil minds, and so to govern my conduct that when I died my ancestors might rejoice to welcome me as a guest on high.

My father gave me $100, and I went to Hong Kong with five other boys from our place and we got steerage passage on a steamer, paying $50 each. Everything was new to me. All my life I had been used to sleeping on a board bed with a wooden pillow, and I found the steamer's bunk very uncomfortable, because it was so soft. The food was different from that which I had been used to, and I did not like it at all. I was afraid of the stews, for the thought of what they might be made of by the wicked wizards of the ship made me ill. Of the great power of these people I saw many signs. The engines that moved the ship were wonderful monsters, strong enough to lift mountains. When I got to San Francisco, which was before the passage of the Exclusion act, I was half starved, because I was afraid to eat the provisions of the barbarians, but a few days' living in the Chinese quarter made me happy again. A man got me work as a house servant in an American family, and my start was the same as that of almost all the Chinese in this country.

The Chinese laundryman does not learn his trade in China; there are no laundries in China. The women there do the washing in tubs and have no wash-boards or flat irons. All the Chinese laundrymen here were taught in the first place by American women just as I was taught.

When I went to work for that American family I could not speak a word of English, and I did not know anything about housework. The family consisted of husband, wife, and two children. They were very good to me and paid me $3.50 a week, of which I could save $3.

I did not know how to do anything, and I did not understand what the lady said to me, but she showed me how to cook, wash, iron, sweep, dust, make beds, wash dishes, clean windows, paint and brass, polish the knives and forks, etc., by doing the things herself and then overseeing my efforts to imitate her. She would take my hands and show them how to do things. She and her husband and children laughed at me a great deal, but it was all good natured. I was not confined to the house in the way servants are confined here, but when my work was done in the morning I was allowed to go out till lunch time. People in California are more generous than they are here.

• • •

. . . Men of other nationalities who are jealous of the Chinese, because he is a more faithful worker than one of their people, have raised such a great outcry about Chinese cheap labor that they have shut him out of working on farms or in factories or building railroads or making streets or digging sewers. He cannot practice any trade, and his opportunities to do business are limited to his own countrymen. So he opens a laundry when he quits domestic service.

The treatment of the Chinese in this country is all wrong and mean. It is persisted in merely because China is not a fighting nation. The Americans would not dare to treat Germans, English, Italians or even Japanese as they treat the Chinese, because if they did there would be a war.

There is no reason for the prejudice against the Chinese. The cheap labor cry was always a falsehood. Their labor was never cheap, and is not cheap now. It has always commanded the highest market price. But the trouble is that the Chinese are such excellent and faithful workers that bosses will have no others when they can get them. If you look at men working on the street you will find an overseer for every four or five of them. That watching is not necessary for Chinese. They work as well when left to themselves as they do when some one is looking at them.

It was the jealousy of laboring men of other nationalities—especially the Irish—that raised all the outcry against the Chinese. No one would hire an Irishman, German, Englishman or Italian when he could get a Chinese, because our countrymen are so much more honest, industrious, steady, sober and painstaking. Chinese were persecuted, not for their vices, but for their virtues. There never was any honesty in the pretended fear of leprosy or in the cheap labor scare, and the persecution continues still, because Americans make a mere practice of loving justice. They are all for money making, and they want to be on the strongest side always. They treat you as a friend while you are prosperous, but if you have a misfortune they don't know you. There is nothing substantial in their friendship.

• • •

Irish fill the almshouses and prisons and orphan asylums, Italians are among the most dangerous of men, Jews are unclean and ignorant. Yet they are all let in, while Chinese, who are sober, or duly law abiding, clean, educated and industrious, are shut out. There are few Chinamen in jails and none in the poor houses. There are no Chinese tramps or drunkards. Many Chinese here have become sincere Christians, in spite of the persecution which they have to endure from their heathen countrymen. More than half the Chinese in this country would become citizens if allowed to do so, and would be patriotic Americans. But how can they make this country their home as matters now are! They are not allowed to bring wives here from China, and if they marry American women there is a great outcry.

Eastern Europeans Describe Leaving the "Old Country"

John Lukasavicius

We owned a small tract of land of about five acres in the village and the whole family—my mother, elder brother, and younger sister—all worked the land. My father left for America when I was four years old and used to send us money once in a while so that we managed to get along. He was working in a mine in Pennsylvania.

Until we children grew up so that we were able to help on the land, our mother did most of the farm work with the help of neighbors. When I was about six years old, I started to help by herding the few pigs and other animals we had. Our house was like the rest of those in the village, a log cabin with a thatched roof, dirt floor, one room with a clay stove built in one corner. My brother and I used to sleep outdoors or in the barn when the weather was warm. We only slept in the house in the winter. All summer we worked hard, from dawn to dusk, raising food for ourselves and the animals. With my father sending money occasionally we were able to use that to pay taxes with and were able to keep our food instead of selling part of it in the market.

Most of our meals were black rye bread, soup from vegetables we raised, and milk and cheese. On holidays we had better meals, roast goose or duck, vegetables with sour cream, and perhaps a loaf of wheat bread bought from a baker in the neighboring town. Our clothes were almost all homemade, though my father sent us some from America. He sent me a woolen overcoat, my brother a suit and shoes, and my mother and sister each a velvet dress. We only wore those clothes to church on Sundays and holidays. . . .

My mother was the boss in our house and we all obeyed her orders. If we disobeyed she would give us a good beating. As we grew older my brother and I worked the land and she helped with my sister, when they weren't busy in the house. The only time we did anything different from working and sleeping was when there was a dance at one of the neighbors' houses or a wedding. I never paid much attention to my sister, and my brother was a moody fellow so we didn't do many things together outside of our work.

Michael Daunis

The village I was born in had about 30 houses. My father owned a small farm of about 20 American acres. There were 10 people in my family, 3 boys and 5 girls besides my parents. Everybody in the family went to work on the land as soon as they were able to do something. We had to because our farm was small for such a large family. Most of the year we worked from dawn until dark. In winter we were not so busy because all the crops were harvested.

Our house was like the rest of them in the village. It was a log cabin with a thatched roof, two rooms and only one of them had a wooden floor. Our furniture was homemade and for light we had a kerosene lamp. Like the rest of the houses we had a clay stove in one corner of the kitchen. The floor was hard-packed dirt. My mother used to clean it by sweeping and then covering the dirt with white sand.

We raised everything we ate and wore. Most of the time we ate black rye bread and soup. Three times a week we had a little fat pork for meat. On holidays of course we ate a little better. Those were the only times that we had a goose or chicken for our own table. Any other time we killed animals it was for market, because the only time we had any money was when we sold some of the things we raised. Our clothes were made from cloth that my mother and sisters weaved from wool or flax we raised on the farm. I never wore any other clothes until I came to this country. . . .

A year before I came to this country, a cousin of mine had come here. He wrote once in a while and told of how he was earning a lot of money and how everybody in America lived like princes. Other people in the village had relatives here, too, and they used to talk over the letters that were sent. All the letters said how big wages were paid for easy work and how wonderful it was in America. I wrote my cousin and begged him to send me a ticket to America. I thought that I could come and work hard and get enough money to buy a big farm in Lithuania for myself. I didn't want to stay on my father's farm because I knew that when he died my older brother would own the farm and I would have to depend on his good will to make a living.

When my cousin sent me a ticket, everybody was happy at my good fortune. I left home two days after it came. I crossed the border with six other fellows who came from nearby villages and started my journey to America. I expected that when I came back in a few years I would be able to own the biggest farm in the village.

Maru Strokonos

When I get to be about 22, 23, I think all the time I come to America. Landlord's daughter come to America, then, two, three years come back to see family. Tell big stories about America. She had American clothes and nice things; she bring big blue teapot to mother. I listen to stories like baby listen to stories at bedtime, you know. I think I go to America too, have same things as she has.

My people do not like me to go when I tell them, so I play like fox and no say anything more about plans. Every time I go to market I keep little money for trip. Three, four years ago, then one market day I don't go back home. I walk long time, then farmer give me ride on hay wagon. Ride all night, fall asleep on soft hay. In morning farmer shake me awake and tell me I am in city. What city? I can't think of name now.

I go down to where trains are and I ask the man how much it cost to go to America. He laugh and say you can't ride train all the way to America. But he nice man, he put me on train and I finally get to town where I take boat. Where do I get boat? I think in Germany, maybe Berlin. I can't read or write, so I can't tell. I get to boatman after long time in town. When I told him I wanted to get boat for America, he ask for my money. Then he take some, put some in bag and give it back to me, and tell me I need this in America.

When boat sail I am downstairs in boat. Many, many people down there, very crowded. Everybody very sick. I am so sick I cry and cry, I think I die, then I wish I back on farm. On boat is a young farmer from near town I come from. I lonesome and he is nice to talk to.

After boat rock like cradle back and forth we stop at island. Doctor come in and see if anybody sick, then he let everybody out on island. We wait long time, then we get to America. I get scared when I see so many people and buildings. I walk along street and I come to a shop they have windows full of cakes and goodies like only rich in old country can have. I go into store, but I can't speak English so I point to man and then to cookies. He put them in paper bag and then I show him money and take one, two pieces. I am very, very lonely and I start to cry and it gets very dark but I don't know where to go. I walk along and then I feel a hand on my shoulder. It is a cop and I think I am going to be put in jail, but he take me to a house where the woman is a Lithuanian. I am so happy I kiss his hand, but he only laughs. The woman gets me a job in hotel doing work, but I don't know American way and I am very dumb; everybody laughs at me. I am very saddened; every night I cry.

One day when I leave the hotel I met Walter Stroknos who I met on boat. I am so happy to see someone I can talk to that I hate to see him leave. I come to America in summer and I marry him in fall. We live in New York for a while, then we come to here to farm. We work for people who own farm. It is so nice! People are nice. We live in shed where chickens live now. Old lady in house give us a bed and table and two chairs and a stove and mirror; she give us pans and dishes too. We very happy. After little Walter and Josie were come, old man die and old lady go to live with son. She sell farm to us for $300. Walter get money from man on paper—you know, he sign his name. After we move into big house, Albert and Mary and Vera and Peter were come.

Now Walter is not so nice and one day he throw stick of wood at me. It hit me and cut my head. He get doctor and he sew it up, then he tell him he send him to jail if he do it another time. I don't like my life no more. I wish I don't marry Walter. He work hard but he very mean, say bad things.

Mary Antin, a Russian Jewish Woman, Envisions the "Promised Land," 1912

The next year or so my father spent in a restless and fruitless search for a permanent position. My mother had another serious illness, and his own health remained precarious. What he earned did not more than half pay the bills in the end, though we were living very humbly now. . . .

Just at this time occurred one of the periodic anti-Semitic movements whereby government officials were wont to clear the forbidden cities of Jews, whom, in the intervals of slack administration of the law, they allowed to maintain an illegal residence in places outside the Pale, on payment of enormous bribes and at the cost of nameless risks and indignities.

It was a little before Passover that the cry of the hunted thrilled the Jewish world with the familiar fear. The wholesale expulsion of Jews from Moscow and its surrounding district at cruelly short notice was the name of this latest disaster. Where would the doom strike next? The Jews who lived illegally without the Pale turned their possessions into cash and slept in their clothes, ready for immediate flight. Those who lived in the comparative security of the Pale trembled for their brothers and sisters without, and opened wide their doors to afford the fugitives refuge. And hundreds of fugitives, preceded by a wail of distress, flocked into the open district, bringing their trouble where trouble was never absent, mingling their tears with the tears that never dried.

The open cities becoming thus suddenly crowded, every man's chance of making a living was diminished in proportion to the number of additional competitors. Hardship, acute distress, ruin for many: thus spread the disaster, ring beyond ring, from the stone thrown by a despotic official into the ever-full river of Jewish persecution.

Passover was celebrated in tears that year. In the story of the Exodus we would have read a chapter of current history, only for us there was no deliverer and no promised land.

But what said some of us at the end of the long service? Not "May we be next year in Jerusalem," but "Next year—in America!" So there was our promised land, and many faces were turned towards the West. And if the waters of the Atlantic did not part for them, the wanderers rode its bitter flood by a miracle as great as any the rod of Moses ever wrought.

My father was carried away by the westward movement, glad of his own deliverance, but sore at heart for us whom he left behind. It was the last chance for all of us. We were so far reduced in circumstances that he had to travel with borrowed money to a German port, whence he was forwarded to Boston, with a host of others, at the expense of an emigrant aid society.

I was about ten years old when my father emigrated. I was used to his going away from home, and "America" did not mean much more to me than "Kherson," or "Odessa," or any other names of distant places. I understood vaguely, from the gravity with which his plans were discussed, and from references to ships, societies, and other unfamiliar things, that this enterprise was different from previous ones; but my excitement and emotion on the morning of my father's departure were mainly vicarious.

I know the day when "America" as a world entirely unlike Polotzk lodged in my brain, to become the centre of all my dreams and speculations. Well I know the day. I was in bed, sharing the measles with some of the other children. Mother brought us a thick letter from father, written just before boarding the ship. The letter was full of excitement. There was something in it besides the description of travel, something besides the pictures of crowds of people, of foreign cities, of a ship ready to put out to sea. My father was travelling at the expense of a charitable organization, without means of his own, without plans, to a strange world where he had no friends; and yet he wrote with the confidence of a well-equipped soldier going into battle. The rhetoric is mine. Father simply wrote that the emigration committee was taking good care of everybody, that the weather was fine, and the ship comfortable. But I heard something, as we read the letter together in the darkened room, that was more than the words seemed to say. There was an elation, a hint of triumph, such as had never been in my father's letters before. I cannot tell how I knew it. I felt a stirring, a straining in my father's letter. It was there, even though my mother stumbled over strange words, even though she cried, as women will when somebody is going away. My father was inspired by a vision. He saw something—he promised us something. It was this "America." And "America" became my dream.

I am sure I made as serious efforts as anybody to prepare myself for life in America on the lines indicated in my father's letters. In America, he wrote, it was no disgrace to work at a trade. Workmen and capitalists were equal. The employer addressed the employee as *you*, not, familiarly, as *thou*. The cobbler and the teacher had the same title, "Mister." And all the children, boys and girls, Jews and Gentiles, went to school! Education would be ours for the asking, and economic independence also, as soon as we were prepared.

. . .

My father's letters warned us to prepare for the summons [to move to America], and we lived in a quiver of expectation.

Not that my father had grown suddenly rich. He was so far from rich that he was going to borrow every cent of the money for our third-class passage; but he had a business in view which he could carry on all the better for having the family with him; and, besides, we were borrowing right and left anyway, and to no definite purpose. With the children, he argued, every year in Russia was a year lost. They should be spending the precious years in school, in learning English, in becoming Americans. United in America, there were ten chances of our getting to our feet again to one chance in our scattered, aimless state.

So at last I was going to America! Really, really going, at last! The boundaries burst. The arch of heaven soared. A million suns shone out for every star. The winds rushed in from outer space, roaring in my ears, "America! America!"

II. ITALIAN LABORERS ON A COFFEE PLANTATION IN BRAZIL, 1911

Each plantation constitutes a little isolated world, which is all but self-sufficient, and from which the immigrants rarely issue; the life is laborious. The coffee is planted in long regular lines in the red soil, abundantly watered by the rains, on which a constant struggle must be maintained against the invasion of noxious weeds. The weeding of the plantation is really the chief labour of the immigrant. It is repeated six times a year. Directly after the harvest, if you ride on horseback along the lines of shrubs, which begin, as early as September, to show signs of their brilliant flowering season, you will find the immigrants, men and women, leaning on their hoes, while the sun, already hot, is drying behind them the heaps of weeds they have uprooted.

In the morning the gangs scatter through the plantation; in the evening they gradually collect on the paths of the *fazenda*, and go home in family groups, tired after the day's work, saving of words, saluting one another by gestures. On Sunday work is interrupted; games are arranged; parties are made up to play *mora*, or Italian card games, with *denari* and *bastoni*. Women hold interminable palavers. Sometimes, on an indifferent nag, borrowed at second or third hand from a neighbour, the colonist will ride as far as the nearest town, to see his relations, exercise his tongue, and pit himself against such hazards of fortune as the world outside the *fazenda* may offer.

The immigrants make their purchases in the nearest town, or, more often, if the *plantation* is of any importance, there is a shop or store—what the Brazilians call a *negocio*—in the neighbourhood of the colonists' houses. Its inventory would defy enumeration; it sells at the same time cotton prints and cooking-salt, agricultural implements and petroleum. An examination of the stock will show one just what the little economic unit called a plantation really is. Although the immigrants are to-day almost always free to make their purchases where they please, the trade of shopkeeper on a plantation is still extremely profitable. The shop is the planter's property; he lets it, and usually at a high rent, which represents not only the value of the premises, but also the commercial privilege which goes with it. It is a sort of indirect commercial tariff levied by the planter on the colonists; a sign of the ever so slightly feudal quality of the organisation of property in San Paolo. The custom that used to obtain, of the planter himself keeping shop for the profit, or rather at the expense of his colonists, has generally disappeared.

One of the most serious of the planter's anxieties is the maintenance of the internal discipline of the plantation. This is a task demanding ability and energy. One must not be too ready to accuse the planters of governing as absolute sovereigns. I myself have never observed any abuse of power on their part, nor have I seen unjustifiable fines imposed. The planter has a double task to perform. He employs his authority not only to ensure regularity in the work accomplished, but also to maintain peace and order among the heterogeneous population over which he rules. He plays the part of a policeman. The public police service cannot ensure the respect of civil law, of the person, or of property. How could the police intervene on the plantation, which is neither village nor commune, but a private estate? It falls to the planter to see that the rights of all are protected. Individually the immigrants are often turbulent and sometimes violent; collectively they have hitherto shown a remarkable docility. On some plantations, however, there have been labour troubles, and actual strikes; but they have always been abortive. The strikes have not lasted, and have never spread. One of the means by which the planters maintain their authority and prevent the colonists from becoming conscious of their strength is the prohibition of all societies or associations. They have had little trouble in making this prohibition respected. Accounts are settled every two months. It often happens, even to-day, that the immigrant is in the planter's debt. The planter has kept up the custom of making advances, and every family newly established in the country is, as a general rule, in debt. But the advances are always small, the colonist possessing so little in the way of securities; he has few animals and next to nothing in the way of furniture. His indebtedness towards the planter is not enough, as it used to be, to tie him down to the plantation; that many of them continue to leave by stealth is due to their desire to save their few personal possessions, which the planter might seize to cover his advances. At the last payment of the year all the immigrants are free; their contract comes to an end after the harvest. Proletarians, whom nothing binds to the soil on which they have dwelt for a year, they do not resume their contracts if they have heard of more advantageous conditions elsewhere, or if their adventurous temperament urges them to try their luck further on.

The instability of agricultural labour is the most striking characteristic of rural life in the State of San Paolo. It is a result of the unusual and even artificial nature of the hasty development of coffee-planting.

The agricultural workers of San Paolo are for the most part of Italian nationality. It is Italy that has furnished the greatest proportion of immigrants. Many *fazendas* are peopled entirely by Italians, and in some municipalities they surpass in number the Brazilians and the immigrants of all other nationalities together. From 1891 to 1897 the Italians formed three-fourths or four-fifths of the total immigration, according to the year.

They are so compact, indeed, that the Paulistas came at last to regard the matter with alarm. The Italian element was increasing with such rapidity that they despaired of ever assimilating it. On various occasions the Government has attempted to limit, in the contracts signed with immigration agents, the proportion of immigrants of Italian blood. But these fears had no foundation. As far as I could discover there is no "Italian peril" in San Paolo. I cannot remember to have remarked, in any Italian established in San Paolo, the slightest tendency to resist assimilation, or the least conscious animosity against Brazil as a nation. All those who are not swallowed up by the plantations, but who settle in the towns, become quickly nationalised, overpowered by an atmosphere in which the Brazilian is naturally dominant. Even those who work on the *fazendas* learn Portuguese rapidly and willingly.

STUDY QUESTIONS

1. Describe the circumstances that motivated individuals to migrate to the United States. How did they form opinions about the United States?
2. Were immigrants largely "pushed" by bad conditions at home or "pulled" by a positive desire to move to a new place? How did immigrants fare after migrating to the United States? Why did some groups fare better than others?
3. Describe the relationship of the workers on the coffee plantation in Brazil with the owner of the plantation. Are the workers proletarians or peasants? Identify the criteria for judging whether a worker is a proletarian or a peasant.
4. What were the similarities and differences between immigrant coffee plantation workers in Brazil and slaves?
5. What were some characteristic problems immigrants faced in dealing with their new society? Were conditions in this regard particularly different in Brazil compared to the United States?
6. What were the main results of the massive immigration waves of the nineteenth century?

ESSAY SUGGESTIONS

A. Describe the similarities and differences between the migrants to the United States and those to Brazil. What themes might be used to determine the significance of these experiences?

B. What were the main factors that caused the increase in the number of immigrants and the sources of immigration in the nineteenth century?

20 EUROPEAN IMPERIALISM

The spread of European imperialism throughout Africa and much of Southeast Asia and the Pacific was the most obvious development in world history during the late nineteenth century. It was fueled by Europe's great advantages in weaponry and industrial productivity. Imperialism brought new political controls, new exposure to European-dominated world markets, and new cultural contacts to the colonies involved, plus new spurs to resistance and definitions of regional identity. For the Europeans, imperialism brought economic opportunities but also additional responsibilities, and it unquestionably heightened militarism and nationalist rivalry.

Analysis of the motives of European imperialists is not the only question imperialism raises—the interactions with conquered peoples are even more complex and important—but it is intriguing. Motivations require assessment of conditions within Europe on the part of governments, imperialist adventurers, and even ordinary people, many of whom supported imperialism enthusiastically. They involved beliefs about economic and military needs but also intellectual developments, such as the rise of social Darwinism with its arguments about racial competition. The result of the various sources of imperialist rhetoric was an array of justifications, not all of which were consistent; here is an obvious challenge to historical interpretation.

Analysis of the causes of imperialism also provides a partial entry into discussions about impact. Imperialists presented several different faces to the people in the colonies, from rank exploitation to humanitarian concern. It is important to consider the policy implications of the various arguments for imperialism and the potential reactions of Africans or Asians to these policies.

The first of the documents that follow is from a book by a British soldier, F. D. Lugard, published in 1893, defending the expansion of the empire in East Africa. The second excerpt is from a speech by Jules Ferry, French prime minister, in 1884. Finally, the third document is a famous poem by British author Rudyard Kipling, first published in *McClure's Magazine* in February 1899.

Selection I from F. D. Lugard, *The Rise of Our East African Empire* (Edinborough, 1983). Selection II excerpt from *Discours et Opinions de Jules Ferry,* ed. by Paul Robiquet and trans. by Ruth Kleinman (Paris: Armand Coli, 1897). Selection III from Rudyard Kipling, "The White Man's Burden," *McClure's Magazine* XII #4 (Feb., 1899), 290–291.

DOCUMENTS BY LUGARD, FERRY, AND KIPLING

I. CAPT. F. D. LUGARD: THE RISE OF OUR EAST AFRICAN EMPIRE

It is sufficient to reiterate here that, as long as our policy is one of free trade, we are compelled to seek new markets; for old ones are being closed to us by hostile tariffs, and our great dependencies, which formerly were the consumers of our goods, are now becoming our commercial rivals. It is inherent in a great colonial and commercial empire like ours that we go forward or go backward. To allow other nations to develop new fields, and to refuse to do so ourselves, is to go backward; and this is the more deplorable, seeing that we have proved ourselves notably capable of dealing with native races and of developing new countries at a less expense than other nations. We owe to the instincts of colonial expansion of our ancestors those vast and noble dependencies which are our pride and the outlets of our trade today; and we are accountable to posterity that opportunities which now present themselves of extending the sphere of our industrial enterprise are not neglected, for the opportunities now offered will never recur again. Lord Rosebery [British prime minister] in his speech at the Royal Colonial Institute expressed this in emphatic language: "We are engaged in 'pegging out claims' for the future. We have to consider, not what we want now, but what we shall want in the future. We have to consider what countries must be developed either by ourselves or some other nation. . . . Remember that the task of the statesman is not merely with the present, but with the future. We have to look forward beyond the chatter of platforms, and the passions of party, to the future of the race of which we are at present the trustees, and we should, in my opinion, grossly fail in the task that has been laid upon us did we shrink from responsibilities, and decline to take our share in a partition of the world which we have not forced on, but which has been forced upon us."

If some initial expense is incurred, is it not justified by the ultimate gain? I have already pointed out what other nations are doing in the way of railway extension. The government is not asked to provide the capital of the railway, but only a guarantee on the subscribed capital. . . . Independently of money spent on railways, the conquest of Algeria alone cost France £150,000,000, and it is estimated that her West Coast colonies cost her half a million yearly. . . . Belgium, besides her heavy expenses for the Congo railway, the capital of which she has advanced without interest, guarantees £80,000 per annum to the Congo state, and is altering her constitution in order to allow her to take over that state as a colonial possession. Germany has spent over a million sterling in East Africa, besides her expenditure on the west and southwest colonies. The parallel is here complete, for the German company failed, and government stepped in to carry out the pledges and obligations incurred. Even Portugal who is content to support a yearly deficit on each of her African possessions, gives heavy subsidies to the mail steamers, and £10,000 per annum to the cable. All these nations are content to incur this yearly cost in the present, confident that in the future these possessions will repay the outlay. . . .

The Zanzibar Gazette, which is in a good position to judge, since the imports and exports from German East Africa can be fairly assessed there, speaking of "the comparatively large sums from the national resources" invested in this country, says, "We think it is only a question of time for such investments, with a careful management of the territory, to show highly profitable returns." Such a view from those on the spot and possessing local knowledge, should be a strong testimony in favor of the far richer British sphere. . . .

A word as to missions in Africa. Beyond doubt I think the most useful missions are the medical and the industrial, in the initial stages of savage development. A combination of the two is, in my opinion, an ideal mission. Such is the work of the Scotch Free Church on Lake Nyasa. The medical missionary begins work with every advantage. Throughout Africa the ideas of the cure of the body and of the soul are closely allied. The "medicine man" is credited, not only with a knowledge of the simples and drugs which may avert or cure disease, but owing to the superstitions of the people, he is also supposed to have a knowledge of the charms and *dawa* which will invoke the aid of the Deity or appease His wrath, and of the witchcraft and magic (*ulu*) by which success in war, immunity from danger, or a supply of rain may be obtained. As the skill of the European in medicine asserts its superiority over the crude methods of the medicine man, so does he in proportion gain an influence in his teaching of the great truths of Christianity. He teaches the savage where knowledge and art cease, how far natural remedies produce their effects, independent of charms or supernatural agencies, and where divine power overrules all human efforts. Such demonstration from a medicine man, whose skill they cannot fail to recognize as superior to their own, has naturally more weight than any mere preaching. A mere preacher is discounted and his zeal is not understood. The medical missionary, moreover, gains an admission to the houses and homes of the natives by virtue of his art, which would not be so readily accorded to another. He becomes their adviser and referee, and his counsels are substituted for the magic and witchcraft which retard development.

The value of the industrial mission, on the other hand, depends, of course, largely on the nature of the tribes among whom it is located. Its value can hardly be overestimated among such people as the Waganda, both on account of their natural aptitude and their eager desire to learn. But even the less advanced and more primitive tribes may be equally benefited, if not only mechanical and artisan work, such as the carpenter's and blacksmith's craft, but also the simpler expedients of agriculture are taught. The sinking of wells, the system of irrigation, the introduction and planting of useful trees, the use of manure, and of domestic animals for agricultural purposes, the improvement of his implements by the introduction of the primitive Indian plough, etc.—all of these, while improving the status of the native, will render his land more productive, and hence, by increasing his surplus products, will enable him to purchase from the trader the cloth which shall add to his decency, and the implements and household utensils which shall produce greater results for his labor and greater comforts in his social life.

In my view, moreover, instruction (religious or secular) is largely wasted upon adults, who are wedded to custom and prejudice. It is the rising generation who should be educated to a higher plane, by the establishment of schools for children. They, in turn, will send their children for instruction; and so a progressive advancement is instituted, which may produce really great results. [Mission] schools were literally thronged with thousands of children, and chiefs of neighboring tribes were eagerly offering to erect schools in their own villages at their own cost. . . .

One word as regards missionaries themselves. The essential point in dealing with Africans is to establish a respect for the European. Upon this—the prestige of the white man—depends his influence, often his very existence, in Africa. If he shows by his surroundings, by his assumption of superiority, that he is far above the native, he will be respected, and his influence will be proportionate to the superiority he assumes and bears out by his higher accomplishments and mode of life. In my opinion—at any rate with reference to Africa—it is the greatest possible mistake to suppose that a European can acquire a greater influence by adopting the mode of the life of the natives. In effect, it is to lower himself to their plane, instead of elevating them to his. The sacrifice involved is wholly unappreciated, and the motive would be held by the savage to be poverty and lack of social status in his own country. The whole influence of the European in Africa is gained by this assertion of a superiority which commands the respect and excites the emulation of the savage. To forgo this vantage ground is to lose influence for good. I may add, that the loss of prestige consequent on what I should term the humiliation of the European affects not merely the missionary himself, but is subversive of all efforts for secular administration, and may even invite insult, which may lead to disaster and bloodshed. To maintain it a missionary must, above all things, be a gentleman; for no one is more quick to recognize a real gentleman than the African savage. He must at all times assert himself, and repel an insolent familiarity, which is a thing entirely apart from friendship born of respect and affection. His dwelling house should be as superior to those of the natives as he is himself superior to them. And this, while adding to his prestige and influence, will simultaneously promote his own health and energy, and so save money spent on invalidings [sick leaves] to England, and replacements due to sickness or death. . . .

I am convinced that the indiscriminate application of such precepts as those contained in the words to turn the other cheek also to the smiter, and to be the servant of all men, is to wholly misunderstand and misapply the teaching of Christ. The African holds the position of a late-born child in the family of nations, and must as yet be schooled in the discipline of the nursery. He is neither the intelligent ideal crying out for instruction, and capable of appreciating the subtle beauties of Christian forbearance and self-sacrifice, which some well-meaning missionary literature would lead us to suppose, nor yet, on the other hand, is he universally a rampant cannibal, predestined by Providence to the yoke of the slave, and fitted for nothing better, as I have elsewhere seen him depicted. . . .

[T]here is in him, like the rest of us, both good and bad, and that the innate good is capable of being developed by culture.

II. JULES FERRY (1832–1893): ON FRENCH COLONIAL EXPANSION

The policy of colonial expansion is a political and economic system . . . that can be connected to three sets of ideas: economic ideas; the most far-reaching ideas of civilization; and ideas of a political and patriotic sort.

In the area of economics, I am placing before you, with the support of some statistics, the considerations that justify the policy of colonial expansion, as seen from the perspective of a need, felt more and more urgently by the industrialized population of Europe and especially the people of our rich and hardworking country of France: the need for outlets [for exports]. Is this a fantasy? Is this a concern [that can wait] for the future? Or is this not a pressing need, one may say a crying need, of our industrial population? I merely express in a general way what each one of you can see for himself in the various parts of France. Yes, what our major industries [textiles, etc.] . . . lack more and more are outlets. Why? Because next door Germany is setting up trade barriers; because across the ocean the United States of America have become protectionists, and extreme protectionists at that; because not only are these great markets . . . shrinking, becoming more and more difficult of access, but these great states are beginning to pour into our own markets products not seen there before. This is true not only for our agriculture, which has been so sorely tried . . . and for which competition is no longer limited to the circle of large European states . . . Today, as you know, competition, the law of supply and demand, freedom of trade, the effects of speculation, all radiate in a circle that reaches to the ends of the earth. . . . That is a great complication, a great economic difficulty; . . . an extremely serious problem. It is so serious, gentlemen, so acute, that the least informed persons must already glimpse, foresee, and take precautions against the time when the great South American market that has, in a manner of speaking, belonged to us forever will be disputed and perhaps taken away from us by North American products. Nothing is more serious; there can be no graver social problem; and these matters are linked intimately to colonial policy.

Gentlemen, we must speak more loudly and more honestly! We must say openly that indeed the higher races have a right over the lower races. . . .

I repeat, that the superior races have a right because they have a duty. They have the duty to civilize the inferior races. . . . In the history of earlier centuries these duties, gentlemen, have often been misunderstood; and certainly when the Spanish soldiers and explorers introduced slavery into Central America, they did not fulfill their duty as men of a higher race. . . . But, in our time, I maintain that European nations acquit themselves with generosity, with grandeur, and with sincerity of this superior civilizing duty.

I say that French colonial policy, the policy of colonial expansion, the policy that has taken us under the Empire [the Second Empire, of Napoleon III, to Saigon, to Indochina (Vietnam)], that has led us to Tunisia, to Madagascar—I say that this policy of colonial expansion was inspired by . . . the fact that a navy such as ours cannot do without safe harbors, defenses, supply centers on the high seas . . . Are you unaware of this? Look at a map of the world.

Gentlemen, these are considerations that merit the full attention of patriots. The conditions of naval warfare have greatly changed. . . . At present, as you know, a warship, however perfect its design, cannot carry more than two weeks' supply of coal; and a vessel without coal is a wreck on the high seas, abandoned to the first occupier. Hence the need to have places of supply, shelters, ports for defense and provisioning. . . . And that is why we needed Tunisia; that is why we needed Saigon and Indochina; that is why we need Madagascar . . . and why we shall never leave them! . . . Gentlemen, in Europe such as it is today, in this competition of the many rivals we see rising up around us, some by military or naval improvements, others by the prodigious development of a constantly growing population; in a Europe, or rather in a universe thus constituted, a policy of withdrawal or abstention is simply the high road to decadence! In our time nations are great only through the activity they deploy; it is not by spreading the peaceable light of their institutions . . . that they are great, in the present day.

Spreading light without acting, without taking part in the affairs of the world, keeping out of all European alliances and seeing as a trap, an adventure, all expansion into Africa or the Orient—for a great nation to live this way, believe me, is to abdicate and, in less time than you may think, to sink from the first rank to the third and fourth.

III. KIPLING'S *THE WHITE MAN'S BURDEN*

Take up the White Man's burden—
Send forth the best ye breed—
Go, bind your sons to exile
To serve your captive's need;
To wait, in heavy harness,
On fluttered folk and wild—
Your new-caught sullen peoples,
Half devil and half child.

Take up the White Man's burden—
The savage wars of peace—
Fill full the mouth of Famine,
And bid the sickness cease;
And when your goal is nearest
(The end for others sought)
Watch sloth and heathen folly
Bring all your hopes to nought.

Take up the White Man's burden—
Ye dare not stoop to less—
Nor call too loud on Freedom
To cloak your weariness.
By all ye will or whisper,
By all ye leave or do,
The silent sullen peoples
Shall weigh your God and you.

STUDY QUESTIONS

1. What are Lugard's main arguments for imperialism? Would they lead to consistent policies?
2. How do Lugard's arguments compare with those by Ferry? Where do they overlap, and where do they differ?
3. What aspects of the European and world economies in the nineteenth century helped provoke imperialism? Was imperialism economically beneficial to the European powers?
4. How do Kipling's arguments compare with those by Lugard and Ferry? What was the "white man's burden"?
5. How important were religious and humanitarian arguments in actually causing imperialism? How important were they in shaping how imperialism worked out in Africa?
6. What kinds of arguments for imperialism would be most popular in Europe itself, and why?
7. What attitudes toward Africans are suggested in the three documents? Are they entirely consistent?
8. What kind of future did the imperialists envision for Africa? How do their implicit forecasts compare with what actually happened in Africa in the twentieth century?
9. Using these documents but also those in Chapter 1 on new maritime systems, what were the changes and continuities in European motivations for overseas expansion between 1500 and 1900?

ESSAY SUGGESTIONS

A. Why did Europeans so easily assume their superiority over Africans by the nineteenth century? When did such assumptions begin to surface?

B. Did the European approaches to imperialism help explain African reactions, including divided responses?

21 SUB-SAHARAN AFRICA

THE DECADES OF IMPERIALISM IN AFRICA

The three selections in this chapter all date from 1875 to 1910. This was the great age of European imperialism in sub-Saharan Africa, when virtually all available territory was swept up by the British, French, Germans, or Belgians. African political and economic life was transformed by the inescapable European presence. African reactions caused changes as well, but in complicated ways because different groups varied in their combinations of resistance and accommodation.

The first document comes from German Southwest Africa. It is unusual in having been written, in Swahili, by an African trader. A prosaic account of theft on a trip to an inland tribal village, the statement shows how some Africans and their new rulers could interact to apparent mutual benefit.

The second document, from 1877, comes from King Ockiya of the Brass region, an enclave on the River Niger delta otherwise controlled by the British; the petition was sent to the British Colonial Secretary. It reflected a complex series of economic changes that had been taking place for several decades, involving European pressures, effective African responses, and then further pressures that would ultimately destroy the local company.

The third document comes from the chiefs of a district in British-controlled Sierra Leone, in 1897, detailing clashes between traditional, tribal ideas of government and the political system the British were imposing. The differences between African and European assumptions here are both obvious and complex.

Collectively, the documents on the imperialist impact raise a number of basic questions. How did the Europeans view Africans at this point? How did imperialist penetration and controls compare with earlier colonial outposts described in Chapter 15? What accounts for the change? Finally, how did Africans perceive the new imperialism, and how might their reactions vary?

Imperialism is recent in African history. Understanding its impact, its limitations, and the responses it provoked is vital to a grasp of African patterns even after imperialism subsided.

AFRICAN AND EUROPEAN REACTIONS

STUDY QUESTIONS

1. Between 1870 and 1914, how did Europeans change the map of Africa?
2. In 1914, what parts of Africa were not under white rule?

I. AN AFRICAN ACCOUNT: THE USES OF COLONIAL GOVERNMENT

We consulted together, saying, "Brothers, hadn't we better get going? We talk, and this pagan does not hear. Perhaps he will change his mind and seek to kill us? Our property is lost, and shall not our souls be lost?" Some said, "Shall we not go to Karema and inform the European, because Chata has robbed us? Now when shall we get out of here? It is no good leaving in the daytime, for perhaps the tribesmen will follow us to get us on the way and kill us; we had better go to the Chief and tell him, We agree to what you say, keep our property safe, and we are going to look for Matumla."

We agreed and went to the Chief and told him what we intended, and he said, "Isn't that just what I wanted? Very well, take a hut and go to rest, do not be afraid; sleep until morning, let us take proper leave of one another, and I will give you food for the way [enough] until you arrive at your place [your destination]." And we sat disconsolately, being sorry for our property which was lost and for our brethren who were dead. It was without any proper reason.

In the morning we reached Karema, and we found the European still in bed. . . . So when the Bwana came, we told him, "Bwana, we have been attacked." And he asked, "Who has attacked you?" We replied, "Chata." And he said to us, "But haven't I said that all traders should first come to me! What did you go to do at the pagan's? But never mind, I will send soldiers to make enquiry why you traders have been robbed. And you provide one person from among you to go along with my soldier, so that he can listen to what my soldier says with Chata, and so that you yourselves may hear about it."

So they set off for Chata's place. The soldiers said to him, "You Chata, so now you have become a man who robs people of their property? Aren't you afraid of government rule?" And he said, "I did not attack them for nothing; I attacked them because of Matumla taking my property, twenty pieces of ivory." The soldiers told him, "Oh no, we don't agree, bring the traders' property, that is what the District Officer told us [you must do]." When he saw their superior strength he took out the stuff and gave it to the soldiers, and they brought it to Karema, all that was left of our goods.

When they reached Karema, the European called us [saying], "You traders, come here, come and look at your property, is this what Chata took?" We looked at it and told him, "Yes, Bwana, some more was lost in the fire." And he said, "Never mind, take this which is left."

II. PETITION OF THE CHIEFS OF BRASS REGARDING TRADE ON THE NIGER, 1877

We the undersigned Kings and Chiefs of Brass, West Coast of Africa, beg and pray that you will take our case into consideration.

Many years ago we used to make our living by selling slaves to Europeans which was stopped by your Government and a Treaty made between you and our country that we discontinue doing so, and that we should enter into a legitimate trade and that if we did so an allowance . . . should be paid us by the traders on all produce bought. This we did and our trade gradually increased. We shipped . . . about 4,500 to 5,000 tons of palm oil per annum.

To do all this we had to open up place[s] on the Niger, trading Stations or markets as we call them. Some years ago the White men began trading on the Niger with the intention of opening up this River; this did us no harm as they went up a long way farther than we could go in their Steamers and also bought a different kind of produce to what we were buying, but lately within the last six years they have begun putting trading Stations at our places and consequently they have stopped our trade completely as well as of those in the Lower part of the River Niger, . . . and formerly when we sent nearly 5,000 tons of [palm] oil away we do not [now] send 1,500 per annum. This means starvation to my people as well as Natives of the Niger under my rule. We have no land where we can grow plantains or yams and if we cannot trade we must starve, and we earnestly beg and pray that you will take our case into consideration. We do not want anything that is not fair, we only want the markets that we and our money have made to be secured to us and that the white men who have had nothing to do with opening up the Palm Oil trade shall not come and reap all our benefits.

One of the steamers has just been up the Niger and the people over whom I have no rule and who are starving have fought with her and the white men now accuse me and my people of having done it although I assure them I have nothing to do with it. I have asked the [British] consul out here two or three times to write home and lay our case before your Lordship and he has promised to do so but I have never received an answer. I can truly say that I have never myself nor have I ever allowed my people to break the treaty we have with England nor will I allow them to do so again [sic]. I beg that you will look into this affair for me and my people. What we want is that the markets we have made between the river and Onitsha should be left to ourselves.

III. THE CHIEFS OF TEMNE TO ACTING GOVERNOR CAULFIELD (REGARDING THE PROTECTORATE ORDINANCE OF JUNE 28, 1897)

The substance of the laws is as follows:

1. That the country is no more your petitioners' [i.e., the Chiefs], it is the Queen's; and that your petitioners have no more power over their lands and property; and that their Chiefs cannot do even so much as to settle matters respecting their common farms. All gold and silver found in the country to be the property of the Government.
2. Your petitioners are to pay for their houses from 5s. to 10s. a year.
3. Your petitioners are not to carry on any trade unless they pay to the Queen £2 a year.
4. No rum is to be sold in any part of the country unless your petitioners pay the £2 a year.
5. Native Chiefs may be deposed and deported at the Governor's pleasure.

6. The country is to be in charge of the District Commissioners, whose decision in all cases, and that by the English laws, is final, against which there is no appeal except by paying a large amount of money.
7. . . . that any Chief hearing any case not belonging to his Court will be punished by fine, imprisonment, and flogging.
8. No slave-dealing of any kind to take place in the country.
9. All cases of witchcraft to be tried by the Government.

These and many others, were the laws interpreted to us . . . but those which have thrown your petitioners into the greatest consternation are the following:

(a) That your petitioners are to have no more power over their country. They are not to hear any cases relating to their lands, farms, and the boundaries of their country; this your petitioners take to mean nothing short of total dispossession of their country . . . your petitioners are not aware that they have done anything to merit such great calamity from their friends and benefactors.

(b) That your petitioners are to pay for their houses and huts. The nature of their houses, built of mud and sticks, and thatched with grass and leaves . . . will show the true condition of your petitioners. The numberless deserted villages to be met with in the country tell of the present unsettled state of the country; your petitioners fear that taxing houses will certainly hinder the return of the poor people to their homes. . . . Chiefs own the villages, and the huts therein are built for them by their retainers, the majority of whom can scarcely save enough to provide a suit of clothes for themselves, their children, and wives for the whole year; the burden of paying the tax must necessarily fall upon the Chiefs, and, failing to pay, the villages must fall to the ground . . . the name of the tax recalls to the minds of your petitioners the dreadful days . . . when, for house tax, men and women were ruthlessly dragged from place to place, plundered, and some flogged almost to death by the tax collectors. . . . They have not the means to pay these taxes, and therefore fall at your Excellency's feet and pray to be saved from so much dreaded misfortune.

(c) That any Chief having any case not in his jurisdiction shall be punished by fine, imprisonment and flogging. Your petitioners regard this as a terrible punishment for a right they had enjoyed from their forefathers, and not for any wrong done to the Government or the community at large . . . your petitioners respectfully beg your Excellency to save them from the serious disgrace and pending scourge of a fine, imprisonment, and flogging, by being allowed to continue their ancient privileges of settling all their cases, subject to an appeal to the District Commissioner. Your petitioners, moreover, pray that in their country they be judged by their native laws so long as they do not affect their loyalty to the Queen or her government. . . .

(d) As regards the question of Slavery, your petitioners beg to assure your Excellency that from so many years' experience they now know something of the mind of the English Government on the subject. To buy and sell slaves is now out of the question. . . . All your petitioners desire is, that the few domestics left to them by their people, and who have become part and parcel of their family, should not be encouraged to leave them . . . few [slaves] it is admitted, run away from ill-treatment, but the greater part of the runaways are those who are lazy and who refuse to work.

STUDY QUESTIONS

1. What gains did Europeans think they were bringing to Africa through imperialism?
2. How did Europeans treat local rulers?
3. What were some of the economic changes imperialism brought to Africa?
4. What were the main African objections to imperialism?
5. What do these documents suggest about the effects of European conquest on Africa and Africans at the end of the nineteenth century?
6. How did the actual imperialist approach to Africa compare to the general imperialist arguments suggested in Chapter 20?

ESSAY SUGGESTIONS

A. According to these documents, what factors, in addition to the huge gap in military power, help explain why Africans found it difficult to develop an effective resistance to European encroachment?

B. How might Europeans interpret African complaints as yet another sign that imperialist rule was essential?

C. How did imperialism change Africa's more traditional roles in world trade?

D. Compare the legacies of slavery in late nineteenth-century Africa and Latin America.

22 ASIA

THE OPIUM WAR: CHINA AND THE WEST

During the early modern period, China was one of the most prosperous and orderly societies in the world. Agricultural output outpaced the country's rapidly growing population. Exports of silk, tea, and porcelain soared, far outweighing imports. Silver from European merchants poured into Chinese coffers. As late as 1800, living standards in China were probably equal to or higher than those in other major world regions. European writers such as Voltaire, relying on informative reports by Jesuit missionaries, praised the rule of the Chinese emperors as models of enlightened despotism.

Around 1800, however, much began to go wrong. Agriculture failed to keep up with continued population growth. Living standards fell and famine emerged as a serious problem. The huge artisan-based cotton industry in the Shanghai area stalled, failing to make the type of transition to factory production then underway in England. Village-based protest movements developed, challenging the emperors' efforts to preserve order.

The country's problems were exacerbated by the actions of the British East India Company and other Western traders who began to smuggle huge quantities of opium into China around 1800. Most of the opium came from India, where it was grown and processed under British supervision. Attempts by the Chinese authorities to halt the illegal trade proved ineffective; addiction to the drug spread. In response, the emperor dispatched one of his most highly regarded officials, Lin Zexu (pronounced zeh shu), to Canton (now Guangzhou) to find a remedy. Lin sent a letter of protest to Queen Victoria (Selection I). He also blockaded Canton harbor and had a large quantity of opium seized and destroyed. The British responded with their own letter (Selection II) and by attacking Canton and several other Chinese ports. Overwhelmed, the Chinese surrendered. By the terms of the 1842 Treaty of Nanjing, they were forced to open several ports to trade, cede the island of Hong Kong, grant extraterritoriality to British subjects residing in China, and make additional humbling concessions (soon extended to other Western governments). For the West, the door to China was now open. For the Chinese, the downward slide accelerated.

The documents illustrate the contrast in Chinese and British thinking about the conflict over opium smuggling. What does Lin's letter—which may never have reached its destination—reveal about how the Chinese saw the dispute while also suggesting reasons why they were easily defeated? How does the letter from Lord Palmerston, the British foreign secretary, shed light on the perspective of the British?

CORRESPONDENCE BETWEEN CHINA AND ENGLAND

I. COMMISSIONER LIN'S LETTER TO QUEEN VICTORIA, 1839

A communication: magnificently our great Emperor soothes and pacifies China and the foreign countries, regarding all with the same kindness. If there is profit, then he shares it with the peoples of the world; if there is harm, then he removes it on behalf of the world. This is because he takes the mind of heaven and earth as his mind.

The kings of your honorable country by a tradition handed down from generation to generation have always been noted for their politeness and submissiveness. We have read your successive tributary memorials saying, "In general our countrymen who go to trade in China have always received His Majesty the Emperor's gracious treatment and equal justice," and so on. Privately we are delighted with the way in which the honorable rulers of your country deeply understand the grand principles and are grateful for the Celestial grace. For this reason the Celestial Court in soothing those from afar has redoubled its polite and kind treatment. The profit from trade has been enjoyed by them continuously for two hundred years. This is the source from which your country has become known for its wealth.

But after a long period of commercial intercourse, there appear among the crowd of barbarians both good persons and bad, unevenly. Consequently there are those who smuggle opium to seduce the Chinese people and so cause the spread of the poison to all provinces. Such persons who only care to profit themselves, and disregard their harm to others, are not tolerated by the laws of heaven and are unanimously hated by human beings. His Majesty the Emperor, upon hearing of this, is in a towering rage. He has especially sent me, his commissioner, to come to Guangdong, and together with the governor-general and governor jointly to investigate and settle this matter.

All those people in China who sell opium or smoke opium should receive the death penalty. If we trace the crime of those barbarians who through the years have been selling opium, then the deep harm they have wrought and the great profit they have usurped should fundamentally justify their execution according to law. We take into consideration, however, the fact that the various barbarians have still known how to repent their crimes and return to their allegiance to us by taking the 20,183 chests of opium from their storeships and petitioning us, through their consular officer [superintendent of trade], Elliot, to receive it. It has been entirely destroyed and this has been faithfully reported to the Throne in several memorials by this commissioner and his colleagues.

Fortunately we have received a specially extended favor from His Majesty the Emperor, who considers that for those who voluntarily surrender there are still some circumstances to palliate their crime, and so for the time being he has magnanimously excused them from punishment. But as for those who again violate the opium prohibition, it is difficult for the law to pardon them repeatedly. Having established new regulations, we presume that the ruler of your honorable country, who takes delight in our culture and whose disposition is inclined towards us, must be able to instruct the various barbarians to observe the law with care. It is only necessary to explain to them the advantages and disadvantages and then they will know that the legal code of the Celestial Court must be absolutely obeyed with awe.

We find that your country is sixty or seventy thousand *li* [three *li* make one mile, ordinarily] from China. Yet there are barbarian ships that strive to come here for trade for the purpose of making a great profit. The wealth of China is used to profit the barbarians. That is to say, the great profit made by barbarians is all taken from the rightful share of China. By what right do they then in return use the poisonous drug to injure the Chinese people? Even though the barbarians may not necessarily intend to do us harm, yet in coveting profit to an extreme, they have no regard for injuring others. Let us ask, where is your conscience? I have heard that the smoking of opium is very strictly forbidden by your country [Lin is misinformed here]; that is because the harm caused by opium is clearly understood. Since it is not permitted to do harm to your own country, then even less should you let it be passed on to the harm of other countries—how much less to China! Of all that China exports to foreign countries, there is not a single thing which is not beneficial to people: they are of benefit when eaten, or of benefit when used, or of benefit when resold: all are beneficial. Is there a single article from China which has done any harm to foreign countries? Take tea and rhubarb, for example; the foreign countries cannot get along for a single day without them. If China cuts off these benefits with no sympathy for those who are to suffer, then what can the barbarians rely upon to keep themselves alive? Moreover the woolens, camlets, and longells [textiles] of foreign countries cannot be woven unless they obtain Chinese silk. If China, again, cuts off this beneficial export, what profit can the barbarians expect to make? As for other foodstuffs, beginning with candy, ginger, cinnamon, and so forth, and articles for use, beginning with silk, satin, chinaware, and so on, all the things that must be had by foreign countries are innumerable. On the other hand, articles coming from the outside to China can only be used as toys. We can take them or get along without them. Since they are not needed by China, what difficulty would there be if we closed the frontier and stopped the trade? Nevertheless our Celestial Court lets tea, silk, and other goods be shipped without limit and circulated everywhere without begrudging it in the slightest. This is for no other reason but to share the benefit with the people of the whole world.

The goods from China carried away by your country not only supply your own consumption and use, but also can be divided up and sold to other countries, producing a triple profit. Even if you do not sell opium, you still have this threefold profit. How can you bear to go further, selling products injurious to others in order to fulfill your insatiable desire?

Suppose there were people from another country who carried opium for sale to England and seduced your people into buying and smoking it; certainly your honorable ruler would deeply hate it and be bitterly aroused. We have heard heretofore that your honorable ruler is kind and benevolent. Naturally you would not wish to give unto others what you yourself do not want. We have also heard that the ships coming to Canton have all had regulations promulgated and given to them in which it is stated that it is not permitted to carry contraband goods. This indicates that the administrative orders of your honorable rule have been originally strict and clear. Only because the trading ships are numerous, heretofore perhaps they have not been examined with care. Now after this communication has been dispatched and you have clearly understood the strictness of the prohibitory laws of the Celestial Court, certainly you will not let your subjects dare again to violate the law.

II. LORD PALMERSTON'S LETTER TO THE CHINESE GOVERNMENT, 1840

For more than a hundred years, commercial intercourse has existed between China and Great Britain; and during that long period of time, British Subjects have been allowed by the Chinese Government to reside within the territory of China for the purpose of carrying on trade therein. Hence it has happened that British Subjects, trusting in the good faith of the Chinese Government, have fixed themselves in Canton as Merchants, and have brought into that city from time to time property to a large amount; while other British Subjects who wished to trade with China, but who could not for various reasons go thither themselves, have sent commodities to Canton, placing those commodities in the care of some of their fellow Countrymen resident in China, with directions that such commodities should be sold in China, and that the produce of the sale thereof should be sent to the Owners in the British Dominions.

Thus there has always been within the territory of The Emperor of China a certain number of British Subjects, and a large amount of British Property; and though no Treaty has existed between the Sovereign of England and the Emperor of China, yet British Subjects have continued to resort to China for purposes of trade, placing full confidence in the justice and good faith of The Emperor.

Moreover, of late years the Sovereign of Great Britain has stationed at Canton an officer of the British Crown, no wise connected with trade, and specially forbidden to trade, but ordered to place himself in direct communication with the local Authorities at Canton in order to afford protection to British Subjects, and to be the organ of communication between the British and the Chinese Governments.

But the British Government has learnt with much regret, and with extreme surprise, that during the last year certain officers, acting under the Authority of The Emperor of China, have committed violent outrages against the British Residents at Canton, who were living peaceably in that City, trusting to the good faith of the Chinese Government; and that those same Chinese officers, forgetting the respect which was due to the British Superintendent in his Character of Agent of the British Crown, have treated that Superintendent also with violence and indignity.

It seems that the course assigned for these proceedings was the contraband trade in Opium, carried on by some British Subjects.

It appeared that the Laws of the Chinese Empire forbid the importation of Opium into China, and declare that all opium which may be brought into the Country is liable to confiscation.

The Queen of England desires that Her Subjects who may go into Foreign Countries should obey the Laws of those Countries; and Her Majesty does not wish to protect them from the just consequences of any offenses which they may commit in foreign parts. But, on the other hand, Her Majesty cannot permit that Her Subjects residing abroad should be treated with violence, and be exposed to insult and injustice; and when wrong is done to them, Her Majesty will see that they obtain redress.

Now if a Government makes a Law which applies both to its own Subjects and to Foreigners, such Government ought to enforce that Law impartially or not at all. If it enforces that Law on Foreigners, it is bound to enforce it also upon its own Subjects; and it has no right to permit its own Subjects to violate the Law with impunity, and then to punish Foreigners for doing the very same thing.

Neither is it just that such a Law should for a great length of time be allowed to sleep as a dead letter, and that both Natives and Foreigners should be taught to consider it as of no effect, and that then suddenly, and without sufficient warning, it should be put in force with the utmost rigor and severity.

Now, although the Law of China declared that the importation of Opium should be forbidden, yet it is notorious that for many years past, that importation has been connived at and permitted by the Chinese Authorities at Canton; nay, more, that those Authorities, from the Governor downwards, have made an annual and considerable profit by taking money from Foreigners for the permission to import Opium: and of late the Chinese Authorities have gone so far in setting this Law at defiance, that Mandarin Boats were employed to bring opium to Canton from the Foreign Ships lying at Lintin.

Did the Imperial Government at Peking know these things?

If it did know these things, it virtually abolished its own Law, by permitting its own officers to act as if no such Law existed. If the Chinese Government says it did not know of these things, if it says that it knew indeed that the Law was violated by Foreigners who brought in opium, but did not know that the Law was violated by its own Officers who assisted in the importation, and received fixed sums of money for permitting it, then may Foreign Governments ask, how it happened that a Government so watchful as that of China should have one eye open to see the transgressions of Foreigners, but should have the other eye shut, and unable to see the transgressions of its own officers. . . .

Now as the distance is great which separated England from China, and as the matter in question is of urgent importance, the British Government cannot wait to know the answer which the Chinese Government may give to these demands, and thus postpone till that answer shall have been received in England, the measures which may be necessary in order to vindicate the honour and dignity of the British Crown, in the event of that answer not being satisfactory.

The British Government therefore has determined at once to send out a Naval and Military Force to the Coast of China to act in support of these demands, and in order to convince the Imperial Government that the British Government attaches the utmost importance to this matter, and that the affair is one which will not admit of delay.

And further, for the purpose of impressing still more strongly upon the Government of Peking the importance which the British Government attaches to this matter, and the urgent necessity which exists for an immediate as well as a satisfactory settlement thereof, the Commander of the Expedition has received orders that, immediately upon his arrival upon the Chinese Coast, he shall proceed to blockade the principal Chinese ports, that he shall intercept and detain and hold in deposit all Chinese ports, that he shall proceed to blockade the principal Chinese ports, that he shall intercept and detain and hold in deposit all Chinese Vessels which he may meet with, and that he shall take possession of some convenient part of the Chinese territory, to be held and occupied by the British Forces until everything shall be concluded and executed to the satisfaction of the British Government.

STUDY QUESTIONS

1. What were Lin's objections to the opium trade? What was his solution to the problem of opium consumption?
2. How well informed was Lin about England and about Chinese relations with England?
3. What does the tone of Lin's letter suggest about how China's leaders understood international relations? What changes in the nineteenth-century world does he seem to have missed?
4. How does Palmerston's letter differ from Lin's? Are there any similarities? Was there any basis for compromise between the two governments?

ESSAY SUGGESTIONS

A. How do the two letters illustrate the radically different ways of thinking characteristic of Chinese and British leaders in the mid-nineteenth century? What explains the differences?

B. How do Lin's ideas compare to the thinking during the Scientific Revolution and the Enlightenment (Chapter 7)? What differences do you see? How do you explain them?

C. How does Lin's letter illustrate the continuing power of Confucian thinking in the mid-nineteenth century (Chapter 11)? What explains this?

23 CREATING A HEAVENLY KINGDOM: THE TAIPING REBELLION IN CHINA

China's defeat in the Opium War accelerated the country's downward spiral that began around 1800 (Chapter 22). Poverty spread more widely in the countryside. Increasing numbers of peasants were forced to make a go of it on micro-plots for which the rents were exorbitant. Banditry gained ground. Distress grew in the increasingly disorderly cities. Opium addiction became more common. Key responsibilities of the imperial government fell victim to corruption. The Grand Canal, the waterway linking north and south China for more than a thousand years, began to silt up because the authorities failed to dredge it. The government's salt monopoly, which had ensured the distribution of a dietary essential at controlled prices for two millennia, began to fall apart. Salt smuggling emerged as a new threat to people's livelihood. Forming a backdrop to this panoply of troubles was the Opium War's blow to the prestige—the very moral legitimacy—of the Qing government.

These circumstances gave rise to the largest armed uprising in the nineteenth-century world, the Taiping (Great Peace) Rebellion, a movement that shook China to its foundations from 1850 until its bloody repression in 1864. A young convert to Christianity named Hong Xiuquan (pronounced Shee-yu-chwen), the son of a poor southern farmer, led the uprising. Hong had aspired to a career as a Confucian scholar/teacher but could not pass the requisite examinations in Canton, failing several times. His hopes for a dream job dashed, Hong converted to Christianity, which he had encountered in Canton via tracts translated into Chinese. For reasons that we can only speculate about, Hong came to believe that he was the younger brother of Jesus and was destined to overthrow the corrupt Qing regime to make way for a new Heavenly Kingdom of justice, equality, and sharing. His message combined aspects of Confucianism, Christianity, and traditional Chinese folk religions (but not socialism, of which he was completely unaware). It spread rapidly during the 1840s among the impoverished peasants. Some of his converts emerged as talented military commanders, leading their ragtag fighters to decisive victories over demoralized Qing troops. By 1853, the Taiping armies controlled much of the south, including the major city of Nanjing where they established their capital. However, disputes among the Taiping leaders, a failure to follow through on plans to address the widespread suffering, and renewed energy in the Qing government brought an end to the Heavenly Kingdom in 1864. Twenty million people may have died in the repression.

Two Taiping documents follow. Hong Xiuquan, known to his followers as the Heavenly King, composed the brief poem around 1847. The second selection features a

Selections I and II from Franz Michael, in collaboration with Chung-li Chang, *The Taiping Rebellion: History and Documents,* Vol. II (Seattle and London: University of Washington Press, 1971), 51, 313–316, 320.

Taiping plan for the allocation of land and also addresses other issues relating to the organization of the Heavenly Kingdom. The proposed land reforms, which were never implemented, were inspired by a legendary system of landholding associated with the founder of the Zhou (pronounced jo) dynasty around 1000 B.C.E. How do the selections suggest the problems facing China in the mid-nineteenth century and illuminate the thinking of the Taipings?

TAIPING DOCUMENTS

I. POEM ON OPIUM

The opium pipe is like a gun, wherewith you wound yourself. How many heroes are stretched dying upon their pillows!

II. PLANS FOR THE HEAVENLY KINGDOM (1853–1854)

The division of land must be according to the number of individuals, whether male or female; calculating upon the number of individuals in a household, if they be numerous, then the amount of land will be larger, and if few, smaller; and it shall be a mixture of the nine classes. If there are six persons in a family, then for three there shall be good land and for three poorer land, and of good and poor each shall have half. All the fields in the empire are to be cultivated by all the people alike. If the land is deficient in one place, then the people must be removed to another, and if the land is deficient in another, then the people must be removed to this place. All the fields throughout the empire, whether of abundant or deficient harvest, shall be taken as a whole: if this place is deficient, then the harvest of that abundant place must be removed to relieve it, and if that place is deficient, then the harvest of this abundant place must be removed in order to relieve the deficient place; thus, all the people in the empire may together enjoy the abundant happiness of the Heavenly Father, Supreme Lord and Great God. There being fields, let all cultivate them; there being food, let all eat; there being clothes, let all be dressed; there being money, let all use it, so that nowhere does inequality exist, and no man is not well fed and clothed.

All men and women, every individual of sixteen years and upwards, shall receive land, twice as much as those of fifteen years of age and under. Thus, those sixteen of years of age and above shall receive a *mou* [1 mou 5 ⅙ acre] of superior land of the first class, and those of fifteen years and under shall receive half that amount, five-tenths of a *mou* of superior land of the first class; again, if those of sixteen years and above receive three *mou* of inferior land of the third class, then those of fifteen years and below shall receive half that amount, one and one-half *mou* of inferior land of the third class.

Throughout the empire the mulberry tree is to be planted close to every wall, so that all women may engage in rearing silkworms, spinning the silk, and making garments. Throughout the empire every family should keep five hens and two sows, which must not be allowed to miss their proper season. At the time of harvest, every sergeant shall direct the corporals to see to it that of the twenty-five families under his charge each individual has a sufficient supply of food, and aside from the new grain each may receive, the remainder must be deposited in the public granary. Of wheat, pulse, hemp, flax, cloth, silk, fowls, dogs, etc., and money, the same is true; for the whole empire is the universal family of our Heavenly Father, the Supreme Lord and Great God. When all the people in the empire will not take anything as their own but submit all things to the Supreme Lord, then the Lord will make use of them, and in the universal family of the empire, every place will be equal and every individual well fed and clothed. This is the intent of our Heavenly Father, the Supreme Lord and Great God, in specially commanding the true Sovereign of Taiping to save the world . . . .

In every circle of twenty-five families, all young boys must go to church every day, where the sergeant is to teach them to read the Old Testament and the New Testament, as well as the book of proclamations of the true ordained Sovereign. Every Sabbath the corporals must lead the men and women to the church, where the males and females are to sit in separate rows. There they will listen to sermons, sing praises, and offer sacrifices to our Heavenly Father, the Supreme Lord and Great God.

In every circle of twenty-five families, the diligent husbandmen will be rewarded and the idle husbandmen punished; should disputes arise among the families, both parties must go to the sergeant. The sergeant will hear the case; if it is not settled, the sergeant must bring both parties before the lieutenant. The lieutenant will hear the case; if it is not settled, the lieutenant will report the case successively to the captain, the colonel, the provost marshal, and the corps general. The corps general, in consultation with the provost marshal, must try to decide the case. Having come to a decision, the corps general must send up a report of the case to the corps superintendent, the corps superintendent must next report it to the corps commandant, the general, the imperial guard, the commander, the senior secretary, and the chancellor. The chancellor must report to the chief of staff, and the chief of staff must memorialize the Tien Wang [Heavenly King]. The Tien Wang will then issue an edict instructing the chief of staff, the chancellor, the senior secretary, the provost marshal, and others, to examine the case carefully; and if there is no discrepancy, then the chief of staff, the chancellor, the senior secretary, the provost marshal, and others shall report the case directly to the Tien Wang for his final decision. The Tien Wang will then issue an edict giving his verdict; and whether it be for life or for death, for giving or for taking, the chief of staff shall, in obedience to the edict, carry out the judgment.

Among all officials and subjects throughout the empire, those who universally keep and obey the Ten Commandments of Heaven and who obey orders and faithfully serve the state shall thus be considered loyal subjects, and shall be raised from a low to a high station, their descendants inheriting their official title. Those officials who break the Ten Commandments of Heaven, disobey orders, receive bribes, or engage in corrupt practices shall thus be considered traitors, and shall be degraded from a high to a low station and reduced to mere husbandry. Those subjects who obey the Commandments and orders and exert themselves in husbandry shall be considered honest and faithful, and either elevated or rewarded; but those subjects who disobey the Commandments and orders and neglect the duties of husbandry shall be considered as evil and vicious, to be either put to death or punished. . . .

Within [the court] and without, all the various officials and people must go every Sabbath to hear the expounding of the Holy Bible, reverently offer their sacrifices, and worship and praise the Heavenly Father, the Supreme Lord and Great God. On every seventh seven, the forty-ninth day, the Sabbath, the colonel, captains, and lieutenants shall go in turn to the churches in which reside the sergeants under their command and expound the Holy books, instruct the people, examine whether they obey the Commandments and orders or disobey the Commandments and orders, and whether they are diligent or slothful. On the first seventh seven, the forty-ninth day, the Sabbath, the colonel shall go to a certain sergeant's church, on the second seventh seven, the forty-ninth day, the Sabbath, the colonel shall then go to another sergeant's church, visiting them all in order, and after having gone the round he must begin again. The captains and lieutenants shall do the same.

Each man throughout the empire who has a wife, sons, and daughters amounting to three or four mouths, or five, six, seven, eight, or nine mouths, must give up one to be a soldier. With regard to the others, the widowers, widows, orphaned, and childless, the disabled and sick, they shall all be exempted from military service and issued provisions from the public granaries for their sustenance.

Throughout the empire all officials must every Sabbath, according to rank and position, reverently present sacrificial animals and offerings, sacrifice and worship, and praise the Heavenly Father, the Supreme Lord and Great God. They must also expound the Holy books; should any dare to neglect this duty, they shall be reduced to husbandmen. Respect this.

STUDY QUESTIONS

1. How did opium smoking relate to traditional Chinese culture (Chapter 11)? Why did addiction spread in China?
2. What were the main features of the society that the Taipings hoped to establish?
3. Were the Taipings communists?
4. What was the relationship between the Taipings, Christianity, and Confucianism (Chapter 11)?
5. Poverty was widespread in the nineteenth-century world. Why did such a massive uprising occur only in China?

ESSAY SUGGESTIONS

A. How do the ideas of the Taipings illustrate both Chinese traditions and international influences?

B. What kind of society did the Taipings envision? How did it differ from the model then emerging in Europe, from movements such as the French and industrial revolutions?

24 THE MEIJI RESTORATION IN JAPAN

Far-reaching changes transformed the lives of the Japanese people during the second half of the nineteenth century. In 1853 and 1854, ships from the United States appeared in Edo (now Tokyo) harbor, pressuring the Tokugawa shoguns to end the policy of isolation they had enforced for more than two centuries. For the next fifteen years, the country was racked by political turmoil and economic crisis, the latter development a result of Japan's sudden plunge into the global economy. Finally, in 1867 and 1868, the *daimyo* (great lords) from two of the largest feudal estates, Satsuma and Choshu, joined forces to overthrow the rule of the shoguns in the name of restoring the full authority of the emperor.

In the midst of the crisis, a new emperor—a teenager—acceded to the throne, choosing the name Meiji (Enlightened Rule) for his reign, which lasted until 1912. Too young to lead the Japanese state, he depended upon a coalition of samurai to rule on his behalf. In an astonishing turnabout, they quickly dismantled the essentials of the Tokugawa system—ending the privileges of their own class—and launched Japan on a course of thoroughgoing modernization.

Between 1871 and 1873, about half of the Meiji leaders went on an extended study tour of the United States, Europe, and Russia, where they spent much time visiting governmental agencies, universities, and factories. Returning home with new knowledge and a host of paid consultants, the Meiji leaders set about establishing modern legal and banking systems, a railway network, a national army and navy, a Western-style system of education, and a framework for constitutional rule. The results were truly amazing. Two brief and victorious wars, against China in 1894 and 1895 and against Russia ten years later, demonstrated that Japan had joined the ranks of the imperialist Great Powers. No other country outside the West so transformed itself in the nineteenth century.

How do the selections illustrate major features of the Meiji Restoration? What explains the distinctiveness of Japan in the nineteenth century?

MEIJI DOCUMENTS

I. A GENTLEMAN'S FIVE PLEASURES

[Sakuma Shozan (1811–1864) was a samurai from northern Japan who argued for an end to the Tokugawa policy of isolation, a view that brought him eight years in prison and death by assassination. Shortly after his release in 1862, Sakuma wrote the book from which the following excerpt comes.]

The gentleman has five pleasures, but wealth and rank are not among them. That his house understands decorum and righteousness and remains free from family rifts—this is one pleasure. That exercising care in giving to and taking from others, he provides for himself honestly, free, internally, from shame before his wife and children, and externally, from disgrace before the public—this is the second pleasure. That he expounds and glorifies the learning of the sages, knows in his heart the great Way, and in all situations contents himself with his duty, in adversity as well as in prosperity—this is the third pleasure. That he is born after the opening of the vistas of science by the Westerners, and can therefore understand principles not known to the sages and wise men of old—this is the fourth pleasure. That he employs the ethics of the East and the scientific technique of the West, neglecting neither the spiritual nor material aspects of life, combining subjective and objective, and thus bringing benefit to the people and serving the nation—this is the fifth pleasure.

II. THE CHARTER OATH, 1868

[On April 8, 1868, the Meiji Emperor issued the following statement of principles drawn up by the samurai who led the overthrow of the Tokugawa regime.]

By this oath we set up as our aim the establishment of the national weal on a broad basis and the framing of a constitution and laws.

1. Deliberative assemblies shall be widely established and all matters decided by public discussion.
2. All classes, high and low, shall unite in vigorously carrying out the administration of affairs of state.
3. The common people, no less than civil and military officials, shall each be allowed to pursue his own calling so that there may be no discontent.
4. Evil customs of the past shall be broken off and everything based on the just laws of Nature.
5. Knowledge shall be sought throughout the world so as to strengthen the foundations of imperial rule.

III. OKUBO TOSHIMICHI: ON THE ROLE OF THE STATE IN INDUSTRIALIZATION, 1874

[Okubo Toshimichi (1830–1878), a samurai from Satsuma domain, was one of the most important leaders of the early Meiji government. He was assassinated in 1878 by advocates of democratic reforms.]

Generally speaking, the strength or weakness of a country is dependent on the wealth or poverty of its people, and the people's wealth or poverty derives from the amount of available products. The diligence of the people is a major factor in determining the amount of products available, but in the final analysis, it can all be traced to the guidance and encouragement given by the government and its officials. . . .

We have come to a point where all the internal conflicts have ceased, and the people can now enjoy peace and can securely engage in their respective callings. This is the most opportune time for the government and its officials to adopt a protective policy which has as its goal the enhancement of people's livelihood. . . .

Anyone who is responsible for a nation or its people must give careful consideration to the matters which enhance the livelihood of the people, including the benefits to be gained from industrial production and the convenience derived from maritime and land transportation. He must set up a system suitable to the country's natural features and convention, taking into account the characteristics and intelligence of its people. Once that system is established it must be made the pivot of the country's administrative policies. Those industries which are already developed must be preserved, and those which are not in existence must be brought into being.

An example can be found in England which is a very small country. However, she is an island nation and has excellent harbors. She is also richly endowed with mineral resources. Her government and its officials have considered it the greatest fulfillment of their duties when they have made full use of their natural advantages, and have brought about maximum [industrial] development. In this endeavor the Queen and her subjects have put together their ingenuity and created an unprecedented maritime law in order to monopolize the maritime transportation of the world and to enhance her national industries. . . .

In this way her industries have prospered, and there has always been a surplus after providing the necessary commodities to her people. . . .

It is true that time, location, natural features and convention are not the same for each country, and one must not always be dazzled by the accomplishments of England and seek to imitate her blindly. . . .

However, our topography and natural conditions show similarities to those of England. What differs most is the feebleness in the temperament of our people. It is the responsibility of those who are in the administrative positions in the government to guide and importune those who are weak in spirit to work diligently in the industries and to endure them. Your subject respectfully recommends that a clear-cut plan be established to find the natural advantages we enjoy, to measure the amount by which production can be increased, and to determine the priorities under which industries may be encouraged [subsidized]. It is further recommended that the characteristics of our people and degree of their intelligence may be taken into account in establishing legislation aimed at encouraging development of industries. Let there not be a person who is derelict in performing his work. Let there not be a fear of anyone unable to have his occupation. If these goals can be attained the people can reach a position of adequate wealth. If the people are adequately wealthy, it follows naturally that the country will become strong and wealthy. . . . If so, it will not be difficult for us to compete effectively against major powers. This has always been your subject's sincere desire. He is even more convinced of the necessity of its implementation today, and is therefore submitting humbly his recommendations for Your Majesty's august decision.

IV. FARMERS, SILK WORKERS, AND MINERS DURING INDUSTRIALIZATION

A. Rural Indebtedness in the 1880s

[High land taxes (the revenue from which financed many of the Meiji reforms) and falling prices for farm products led to a flood of rural bankruptcies in Japan during the 1880s. The following petition, drawn up by a prosperous farmer in Kanagawa prefecture, was presented to the authorities in 1884.]

The 200,000 people of this prefecture are unable to repay their debts because of declining prices and the depressed state of the silkworm business and textile industry in general. They are plagued day and night with worries, sorrow, frustration, and hardship. People are being crushed underfoot by the usurers as if they were ants. The demonstration by the members of the Debtors' Party in this prefecture in mid-1884 proved to be fruitless; all we got was a lecture from the authorities. No leniency or generosity was forthcoming. . . . Under current conditions [the debtors] can find no way to repay their debts. I beg your excellencies to allow sentiments of morality and benevolence to come forth and, even if the letter of the law has to be distorted a little, to adopt measures that would aid the impoverished people.

B. Working Conditions in the Silk Factories, ca. 1900

[Silk cloth produced in modern factories that were staffed largely by women and children was a leading Meiji industry. The passages that follow include the testimony of two silk workers on conditions around 1900 and a portion of a 1906 government report on the silk factories.]

1

From morning, while it was still dark, we worked in the lamplit factory till ten at night. After work, we hardly had the strength to stand on our feet. When we worked late into the night, they occasionally gave us a yam. We then had to do our washing, fix our hair, and so on. By then it would be eleven o'clock. There was no heat even in the winter, and so we had to sleep huddled together. Several of the girls ran back to Hida. I was told that girls who went to work before my time had a harder time. We were not paid the first year. In the second year I got 35 yen, and the following year, 50 yen. I felt that it was not a place for a weak-willed person like me. If we didn't do the job right we were scolded, and, if we did better than others, the others resented it. The life of a woman is really awful.

2

The end of the cocoon fiber is visible, but inexperienced workers and those with poor eyesight had difficulty finding it. So they would use a small brush to scratch the cocoon [to find the end], which often shredded the cocoon fibers, however. If this happened, the workers were bawled out. Also we were instructed to entwine the fibers evenly, but an inexperienced worker would carelessly twine several fibers together, causing the silk thread to be uneven and have knotted spots. Also, when the cocoons were steamed too long, they lost their luster and the fibers tended to break. It really was a difficult task.

3

Q: Do you get scolded?
A: We are taken to a room next to the office and are reprimanded there. We are also beaten. And, until we show a change of heart, we are kept there in the dark for several days.
Q: Are you fed?
A: No.
Q: Are there other forms of punishment?
A: If anyone steals something she is stripped naked and marched around the factory with a flag attached to her shoulders. They then take her to the dining hall and report her misdeed to everybody. . . . This spring a girl in the next room took *geta* [wooden clogs], which her roommate purchased for 70 sen. She was stripped naked, had the *geta* and a red flag bearing the words "*geta* thief" strapped to her shoulders, and was then marched around the factory.
Q: Do youngsters of seven and eight work only during the day or do they work at night, too?
A: They work at night, too. Since the supervisors are strict during the day, the children clean up the plant. But at night things are less closely supervised, so they don't do much cleaning. Even in the winter we wear only one unlined kimono.
Q: Do young workers work through the night?
A: They do but sometimes they say they will not go to work unless they are given some candy. So the officials give them some. But if they ask for candy often, they are not given any. They go to work crying.
Q: Do they fall asleep in the factory?
A: If they fall asleep they are scolded and beaten.
Q: Do they get paid?
A: They are paid 8 sen. Then 7 sen is deducted for food, so they get only 1 sen.
Q: Are children charged 7 sen, too?
A: They are charged the same amount [for food as the adults].
Q: Are there many young children?
A: There are about ten workers who are seven or eight. There are many who are ten years old.

C. Coal Miners

[Coal-mining expanded rapidly during the Meiji era, spurring the growth of modern industry and, like silk cloth, becoming a major source of export earnings. The following report on conditions in the mines is based on the observations of a magazine writer in the 1880s.]

The temperature got hotter the farther down in the mine I went. At the most extreme point it reached 120° to 130° F. The miners have to labor under this heat. Their bodies are constantly covered with pouring sweat. The air is stifling and it is difficult to breathe. The smell of coal makes it almost unbearable. Despite such appalling working conditions, the company rules do not allow even one second of rest. The deputy crew boss patrols the work area, and if he sees a miner slacking his pace even for an instant he beats him with his club. These deputy crew bosses are like monsters and demons. If a miner asks permission to rest because of fatigue, or if he disobeys the crew boss, he is punished as an example to others. His hands are tied behind him and he is strung up by the beam, with his feet slightly above ground. Then he is clubbed while the other miners are forced to watch the beating. If a miner, unable to bear the harsh conditions, tries to escape and is caught and brought back he is then kicked, beaten, strung up, and generally treated in a brutal and cruel fashion by the guards. No human being could behave as atrociously [as these guards]. There is no other way to identify them except to call them devils. I heard that when a cholera epidemic struck this island mine in 1844, half of the 3,000 miners, over 1,500, were struck by the epidemic and died. Whether the victims were dead or not, the day after they contracted cholera they were taken to the beach, and five to ten of them at a time were placed on an iron platform and burned.

V. BASEBALL COMES TO JAPAN

[Japanese boys from elite circles first embraced baseball in the 1890s. They learned the game from expatriate Americans in Yokohama, the port of Tokyo. From the Yokohama Athletic Club, the sport spread to prep schools in Tokyo and other cities. The Japanese boys were quick studies. Around the turn of the century, a team from one Tokyo school defeated an American all-star team from Yokohama eleven times out of twelve, often by lopsided scores. Large crowds attended the games and there was much press coverage. The "Baseball Club Rouser" was written in celebration of the Japanese victories.]

BASEBALL CLUB ROUSER

I

Among literary and martial arts pursued
In the righteous air of the First Higher School
Baseball stands especially high
With its spirit of honor that refuses to die.

II

The crack of the bat echoes to the sky
On cold March mornings when we chase balls on the ice
Year in and year out, through wind and rain
Enduring all hardship, we practice our game.

III

While the years have seen many a foe
Come to our schoolyard where strong winds blow
Upon touching the sleeves of our armoured knights
We turn them away, speechless with fright.

IV

The valorous sailors from the *Detroit*, *Kentucky*, and *Yorktown*
Whose furious batting can intimidate a cyclone
Threw off their helmets, their energies depleted
Behold how pathetically they run away defeated.

V

Courageously, we marched twenty miles south
To fight the Americans in Yokohama
Though they boast of the game as their national sport
Behold the games they have left with no score.

VI

Ah, for the glory of our Baseball Club!
Ah, for the glitter it has cast!
Pray that our martial valor never turns submissive
And that our honor will always shine far across the Pacific.

STUDY QUESTIONS

1. In what ways was the Meiji Restoration both conservative and innovative?
2. What do the documents illustrate about working conditions in the factories and mines during the Meiji era?
3. How does the baseball song suggest both openness to the world and the rise of Japanese nationalism? With which major international events did the writing of the song coincide?
4. What explains the dramatic changes in Japan during the Meiji decades? What hints of future troubles do you find in the selections?

THE MEIJI EMPEROR

One example of the acceleration in global contacts during the long nineteenth century was the worldwide spread of photography. French scientists invented the new process of producing images in the 1820s and 1830s. By the time the first book illustrated with photographs appeared in England in the 1840s, British officials were using cameras in India and a photographer from Edinburgh had set up shop in Hong Kong. Within two or three decades of its invention, photography had gone global.

The two representations of the Meiji emperor, both from when he was in his twenties, provide a striking record of another major aspect of increasing global contacts in the nineteenth century—namely, the changes in dress and hairstyle, especially among urban men, that occurred wherever Western influences were important. In the engraving on the left, the young emperor is dressed and coiffed as his predecessors had been for centuries, while the photo on the right shows him with a Western-style haircut and wearing a Western-style naval uniform.

The Meiji Emperor in Traditional and Western-Style Dress. (Left, engraving, [Bettmann/CORBIS]; right, photograph, [Emperor Mutsuhito (1852–1912) of Japan, c.1880–90 (b/w photo), Japanese Photographer, (19th century) / Archives Larousse, Paris, France / Giraudon]. (The Bridgeman Art Library)

STUDY QUESTIONS

1. In addition to the changes in the emperor's hairstyle and dress, what other differences do you see in the two depictions?
2. Evidence from the Meiji inner circles indicates that the emperor's courtiers were shocked when they first saw him with his new haircut and uniform. Why do you think this was the case?
3. Why have Western hairstyles and ways of dressing conquered most of the world since the mid-nineteenth century? Which regions of the world have been most resistant to Western styles? How do you explain this?

ESSAY SUGGESTIONS

A. Compare the responses of Japan and China (Chapters 22 and 23) to the West during the nineteenth century. What explains the differences?

B. How did working conditions in Meiji Japan compare to those in Europe during the nineteenth century (Chapter 17)?

25 THE 1857 UPRISING IN INDIA

In May 1857, Indian soldiers, known as *sepoys* (from *sipahi*, Persian for soldier), rose in rebellion against their British officers at a garrison near Delhi, the Mughal capital. The uprising was triggered by the distribution of a new muzzle-loading rifle, a weapon that required cartridges that were rumored to be lubricated with a mixture of beef and pork fat to facilitate loading. Using beef in this way was deeply offensive to Hindus, and pork was proscribed for Muslims. When about ninety of the soldiers refused to accept the new bullets, they were immediately court-martialed and sentenced to long terms in prison. The day after the trial, the entire garrison rose in rebellion and marched toward Delhi, the home of the eighty-two-year-old and powerless Mughal emperor, Bahadur Shah Zafar II.

India's effective rulers, the officials of the British East India Company, were surprised and initially confused by the uprising of formerly loyal soldiers. The rebels were able to take control of Delhi and the movement spread to other garrisons, as well as to cities and rural areas across northern India (but not to the southern part of the country). Disaffected princes whose lands had been seized by the East India Company joined the soldiers against the British. The *Rani* (Princess) of Jhansi led her army into the fray. In the summer of 1857, Company officials feared they might be permanently driven out of India. No wonder. They were facing the most significant challenge to British colonial rule since the American Revolution.

But the rebels were an extremely heterogeneous force. Religious affiliation, caste loyalty, class tensions, language differences, and regional ties trumped any sense of national identity among the people of India in the middle of the nineteenth century. Seizing on the rebels' lack of cohesion and drawing on loyal *sepoys,* the British retook northern India in fighting that lasted until the summer of 1858. As they recovered their authority, the British introduced major reforms. Bahadur Shah, who had supported the rebels, was deposed, ending the dynasty founded by Babur in the 1520s (Chapter 10). The East India Company, the *de facto* ruler of India since about 1800, was dissolved. India now came under the direct and somewhat more enlightened authority of the government in London, becoming the brightest jewel in Queen Victoria's imperial crown. The British government remained in charge until 1947.

The selection that follows come from the Azamgarh Proclamation, a statement issued on behalf of a grandson of Bahadur Shah by rebels who seized control of a garrison near Benares (now Varanasi). One of many such manifestos in circulation, it sheds light on the causes of the rebellion and the goals of the insurgents. To what extent does the Indian uprising form part of a larger pattern of Asian response to Western intervention in the long nineteenth century?

THE AZAMGARH PROCLAMATION

25th. August, 1857.

It is well known to all, that in this age the people of Hindoostan [northern India], both Hindoos and Mohammedans, are being ruined under the tyranny and oppression of the infidel and treacherous English. It is therefore the bounden duty of all the wealthy people of India, especially of those who have any sort of connection with any of the Mohammedan royal families, and are considered the pastors and masters of their people, to stake their lives and property for the well being of the public. . . .

Several of the Hindoo and Mussalman chiefs, who have long since quitted their homes for the preservation of their religion, and have been trying their best to root out the English in India, have presented themselves to me, and taken part in the reigning Indian crusade, and it is more than probable that I shall very shortly receive succours from the West. Therefore, for the information of the public, the present *Ishtahar* [proclamation], consisting of several sections, is put in circulation, and it is the imperative duty of all to take it into their careful consideration, and abide by it. Parties anxious to participate in the common cause, but having no means to provide for themselves, shall receive their daily subsistence from me; and be it known to all, that the ancient works, both of the Hindoos and the Mohammedans, the writings of the miracle-workers and the calculations of the astrologers, pundits, and rammals [soothsayers], all agree in asserting that the English will no longer have any footing in India or elsewhere. Therefore it is incumbent on all to give up the hope of the continuation of the British sway, side with me, and deserve the consideration of the Badshahi, or imperial Government, by their individual exertion in promoting the common good, and thus attain their respective ends; otherwise if this golden opportunity slips away, they will have to repent of their folly, as it is very aptly said by a poet in two fine couplets, the drift whereof is "Never let a favourable opportunity slip, for in the field of opportunity you are to meet with the ball of fortune; but if you do not avail yourself of the opportunity that offers itself, you will have to bite your finger through grief."

No person, at the misrepresentation of the well-wishers of the British Government, ought to conclude from the present slight inconveniences usually attendant on revolutions, that similar inconveniences and troubles should continue when the Badshahi Government is established on a firm basis: and parties badly dealt with by any sepoy or plunderer, should come up and represent their grievances to me, and receive redress at my hands; and for whatever property they may lose in the reigning disorder, they will be recompensed from the public treasury when the Badshahi Government is well fixed.

Section I—Regarding Zemindars [landlords]. It is evident, that the British Government in making zemindary settlements have imposed exorbitant *Jumas* [taxes], and have disgraced and ruined several zemindars, by putting up their estates to public auction for arrears of rent, in so much, that on the institution of a suit by a common Ryot [peasant], a maid servant, or a slave, the respectable zemindars are summoned into court, arrested, put in gaol and disgraced. In litigations regarding zemindaries, the immense value of stamps, and other unnecessary expenses of the civil courts, which are pregnant with all sorts of crooked dealings, and the practice of allowing a case to hang on for years, are all calculated to impoverish the litigants. Besides this, the coffers of the zemindars are annually taxed with subscription for schools, hospitals, roads, etc. Such extortions will have no manner of existence in the Badshahi Government; but on the contrary, the *Jumas* will be light, the dignity and honour of the zemindars safe, and every zemindar will have absolute rule in his own zemindary. . . .

Section II—Regarding Merchants. It is plain that the infidel and treacherous British Government have monopolized the trade of all the fine and valuable merchandise, such as indigo, cloth, and other articles of shipping, leaving only the trade of trifles to the people, and even in this they are not without their share of the profits, which they secure by means of customs and stamp fees, etc. in money suits, so that the people have merely a trade in name. Besides this, the profits of the traders are taxed, with postages, tolls, and subscriptions for schools, etc. Notwithstanding all these concessions, the merchants are liable to imprisonment and disgrace at the instance or complaint of a worthless man. When the Badshahi Government is established, all these aforesaid fraudulent practices shall be dispensed with, and the trade of every article, without exception, both by land and water, shall be open to the native merchants of India, who will have the benefit of the Government steam-vessels and steam-carriages for the conveyance of their merchandise gratis; and merchants having no capital of their own shall be assisted from the public treasury. It is therefore the duty of every merchant to take part in the war, and aid the Badshahi Government with his men and money, either secretly or openly, as may be consistent with his position or interest, and forswear his allegiance to the British Government.

Section III—Regarding Public Servants. It is not a secret thing that under the British Government, natives employed in the civil and military services, have little respect, low pay, and no manner of influence; and all the posts of dignity and emolument in both the departments, are exclusively bestowed on Englishmen for natives in the military service, after having devoted the greater part of their lives, attain to the post of soobadar [Indian senior officer] (the very height of their hopes) with a salary of 60r. [rupees] or 70r. per mensem [month]; and those in the civil service obtain the post of Sudder Ala [judge], with a salary of 500r. a month, but no influence. . . .

Therefore, all the natives in the British service ought to be alive to their religion and interest, and, abjuring their loyalty to the English, side with the Badshahi Government, and obtain salaries of 200 or 300 rupees per month for the present, and be entitled to high posts in future. If they, for any reason, cannot at present declare openly against the English, they can heartily wish ill to their cause, and remain passive spectators of passing events, without taking any active share therein. But at the same time they should indirectly assist the Badshahi Government, and try their best to drive the English out of the country. . . .

Section IV—Regarding Artisans. It is evident that the Europeans, by the introduction of English articles into India, have thrown the weavers, the cotton dressers, the carpenters, the blacksmiths, and the shoemakers, etc., out of employ, and have engrossed their occupations, so that every description of native artisan has been reduced to beggary. But under the Badshahi Government the native artisan will exclusively be employed in the services of the kings, the rajahs, and the rich; and this will no doubt ensure their prosperity. Therefore these artisans ought to renounce the English services, and assist the *Majahdeens,* engaged in the war, and thus be entitled both to secular and eternal happiness.

Section V—Regarding Pundits [Brahmin priests], *Fakirs* [Sufi holy men], *and other learned persons.* The pundits and fakirs being the guardians of the Hindoo and Mohammedan religions respectively, and the Europeans being the enemies of both the religions, and as at present a war is raging against the English on account of religion, the pundits and fakirs are bound to present themselves to me, and take their share in the holy war. . . .

Lastly, be it known to all, that whoever, out of the above named classes, shall after the circulation of this Ishtabar, still cling to the British Government, all his estates shall be confiscated, and his property plundered, and he himself, with his whole family, shall be imprisoned, and ultimately put to death.

STUDY QUESTIONS

1. To whom is the proclamation addressed? How would it have been circulated?
2. What grievances against the British are indicated in the proclamation? Are the complaints mainly political, economic, or religious?
3. Which social groups are not addressed in the proclamation?
4. Does the proclamation aim at restoring the pre-British situation, or does it aim at establishing a new set of circumstances? Why?

VISUAL SOURCE

British Images of the Indian Uprising

The fighting in 1857 and 1858 was fierce. Both sides were responsible for numerous atrocities. Unforgettable and unforgivable for many British was the rebels' execution of several hundred British occupants of the fortress at Kanpur, including many women and children, after the victims had surrendered and been guaranteed safe passage. In revenge, as the British soldiers (mainly *sepoys* from outside the rebel zones) retook cities, they killed huge numbers of civilians. In addition, the British executed many suspected rebels without trial, often by hanging; some of the suspects were tied to the barrels of cannons, which were then fired (a punishment that had been used earlier by the Mughals).

London newspapers reported extensively on the uprising. The fighting also led to much debate in Parliament, especially regarding the policies of the East India Company (known colloquially as the "John Company"). *Punch* captured much of the criticism in the cartoon shown here. In the aftermath of the rebellion, hastily constructed gallows, like the one photographed in 1858, lined the ancient highway running from Calcutta to Lahore.

EXECUTION OF "JOHN COMPANY;"
The Blowing up (there ought to be) in Leadenhall Street.

"The Execution of 'John Company.'" (Punch Cartoon and Library Archive).

Photograph of the Execution of Rebels in India, 1858. (Felice Beato / Stringer / Hulton Archive / Getty Images).

STUDY QUESTIONS

1. How does the cartoon indicate criticism of the East India Company? Does the cartoon support the rebels?
2. Who is missing from the photo? For whom was it intended?

ESSAY SUGGESTIONS

A. Compare the Indian uprising to the Taiping rebellion.

B. How does the Indian uprising compare to the French Revolution (Chapter 16)? What is the difference between an uprising and a revolution?

C. How does the 2005 film *Mangal Pandey: The Rising,* directed by Ketan Mehta, add to or detract from an accurate understanding of the uprising?

26 ASIAN RESPONSES TO THE GREAT DIVERGENCE

A series of powerful hammer blows rattled the best minds in Asia during the long nineteenth century. Britain's conquest of India, underway from the 1750s, was one such shock. A second was the French takeover of Egypt in 1798, which, though short-lived, cleared the way for the growing presence of European merchants, officials, military personnel, and Christian missionaries in the Ottoman-controlled Middle East. A third was the British humbling of China in the Opium War of 1839–1842. One modern scholar has named the growing gap between wealth and power in Europe compared to Asia as the "Great Divergence."

Why had this gap developed? What did the rise of the West mean for Asians? In the new era of European dominance, of what relevance were the great systems of thought—Confucianism, Hinduism, and Islam—that had long provided Asians with explanations of how the world worked and how people should conduct their lives? Were these teachings no longer applicable? From the mid-nineteenth century on, across Asia from Japan to the Middle East, sensitive writers wrestled with these questions. They continue to do so today.

The selections in this chapter illustrate three classic responses to the growing asymmetry between Europe and Asia. In the first document, Feng Guifen (1809–1874, pronounced Gwee-fen), a Chinese official and Confucian scholar, ponders the meaning of the Great Divergence in the midst of the Taiping Rebellion (which he opposed). Feng's ideas were the seed of the partially successful "self-strengthening" movement that gained ground among Chinese officials toward the end of the nineteenth century. The second document is by Sayyid Jamal ad-Din "al-Afghani" (1838–1897), a widely traveled and influential Muslim writer. Claiming to have been born in Afghanistan but probably Iranian, Afghani (as he is known) spent time in Istanbul, Cairo, Tehran, Mecca, Bombay, Calcutta, St. Petersburg, and Paris. His travels led him to wonder about the reasons for the very different paths followed by Europe and the Middle East during his lifetime. The passages come from a lecture he gave in Calcutta in 1882.

The final selection comes from Mohandas K. Gandhi's 1906 book, *Hind Swaraj* (Indian Self-Rule). Gandhi (1869–1948) was born to a Hindu family in western India,

Selection I from Wm. Theodore de Bary and Richard Lufrano, compilers, *Sources of Chinese Tradition*, Vol. Two: *From 1600 through the Twentieth Century*, 2nd ed. K.C. Liu, ed, "Moderate Reform and the Self-Strengthening Movement," pp. 237–238, selection translated by Chester Tan. New York: Columbia University Press, 2000. Selection II from Nikki R. Keddie, *An Islamic Response to Imperialism: Political and Religious Writings of Sayyid Jamal ad-Din "al-Afghani"* (Berkeley and Los Angeles: University of California Press, 1968), pp. 102–103, 107. Reprinted by permission of the author. Selection III from Anthony J. Parel, ed., *M.K. Gandhi: Hind Swaraj and Other Writings*, pp. 34–37. New York: Cambridge University Press, 1997.

trained as a lawyer in London, and then spent two decades in the British colony of South Africa where he led a movement seeking civil rights for Indian settlers. In 1914, he returned to India and plunged into the independence movement. Of the three writers in this chapter, Gandhi was the most familiar with Western ways. How do the documents illustrate the gap between Europe and Asia? How do they suggest the dilemmas reformers faced?

ASIAN DOCUMENTS

I. FENG GUIFEN ON THE ADOPTION OF WESTERN LEARNING (1861)

Western books on mathematics, mechanics, optics, light, and chemistry contain the best principles of the natural sciences. In the books on geography, the mountains, rivers, strategic points, customs, and native products of the hundred countries are fully listed. Most of this information is beyond the reach of the Chinese people. . . .

If we wish to use Western knowledge, we should establish official translation bureaus in Guangzhou [Canton] and Shanghai. Brilliant students not over fifteen years of age should be selected from those areas to live and study in these schools on double allowances. Westerners should be appointed to teach them the spoken and written languages of the various nations, and famous Chinese teachers should be engaged to teach them [Chinese] classics, history and other subjects. At the same time they should learn mathematics. (Note: All Western knowledge is derived from mathematics. . . . If we wish to adopt Western knowledge, it is but natural that we should learn mathematics.). . . . China has many brilliant people. There must be some who can learn from the barbarians and surpass them. . . .

It is from learning that the principles of government are derived. In discussing good government, the great historian Sima Qian [145–87 B.C.E.] said . . . "Take the latter-day kings as your models." This was because they were nearer in time; their customs had changed from the past and were more similar to the present; and their ideas were not so lofty as to be impracticable. It is my opinion that today we should also take the foreign nations as our examples. They live at the same time and in the same world with us; they have attained prosperity and power by their own efforts. Is it not fully clear that they are similar to us and that their methods can easily be put into practice? If we let Chinese ethics and Confucian teachings serve as the foundation, and let them be supplemented by the methods used by the various nations for the attainment of prosperity and power, would it not be the best of all solutions?

Moreover, during the past twenty years since the opening of trade, a great number of foreign chiefs have learned our written and spoken language, and the best of them can even read our classics and histories. They are generally able to speak on our dynastic regulations and civil administration, on our geography and on the conditions of our people. On the other hand, our officials from the governors on down are completely ignorant of foreign countries. In comparison, should we not feel ashamed?

II. AFGHANI ON SCIENCE AND ISLAM (1882)

The Europeans have now put their hands on every part of the world. The English have reached Afghanistan; the French have seized Tunisia. In reality this usurpation, aggression, and conquest has not come from the French or the English. Rather it is science that everywhere manifests its greatness and power. Ignorance had no alternative to prostrating itself humbly before science and acknowledging its submission.

In reality, sovereignty has never left the abode of science. However, this true ruler, which is science, is continually changing capitals. Sometimes it has moved from East to West, and other times from West to East. More than this, if we study the riches of the world we learn that wealth is the result of commerce, industry, and agriculture. Agriculture is achieved only with agricultural science, botanical chemistry, and geometry. Industry is produced only with physics, chemistry, mechanics, geometry, and mathematics; and commerce is based on agriculture and industry.

Thus it is evident that all wealth and riches are the result of science. There are no riches in the world without science, and there is no wealth in the world other than science. In sum, the whole world of humanity is an industrial world, meaning that the world is a world of science. If science were removed from the human sphere, no man would continue to remain in the world.

Since it is thus, science makes one man have the strength of ten, one hundred, one thousand, and ten thousand persons. The acquisitions of men for themselves and their governments are proportional to their science. Thus, every government for its own benefit must strive to lay the foundation of the sciences and to disseminate knowledge. Just as an individual who has an orchard must, for his own profit, work to level the ground and improve its trees and plants according to the laws of agronomy, just so rulers, for their own benefit, must strive for the dissemination of the sciences. Just as, if the owner of an orchard neglects to tend it according to the laws of agronomy, the loss will revert to him, so, if a ruler neglects the dissemination of the sciences among his subjects, the harm will revert to that government. . . .

The strangest thing of all is that our ulama [learned men, Islamic clergy] these days have divided science into two parts. One they call Muslim science, and one European science. Because of this they forbid others to teach some of the useful sciences. They have not understood that science is that noble thing that has no connection with any nation, and is not distinguished by anything but itself. Rather, everything that is known is known by science, and every nation that becomes renowned becomes renowned through science. Men must be related to science, not science to men.

How very strange it is that the Muslims study those sciences that are ascribed to Aristotle with the greatest delight, as if Aristotle were one of the pillars of the Muslims. However, if the discussion relates to Galileo, Newton, and Kepler, they consider them infidels. The father and mother of science is proof, and proof is neither Aristotle nor Galileo. The truth is where there is proof, and those who forbid science and knowledge in the belief that they are safeguarding the Islamic religion are really the enemies of that religion. The Islamic religion is the closest of religions to science and knowledge and there is no incompatibility between science and knowledge and the foundation of the Islamic faith.

III. A CONTRARY VIEW: GANDHI ON THE MEANING OF CIVILIZATION (1906)

READER: Now you will have to explain what you mean by civilization . . . .

EDITOR [Gandhi]: Let us first what state of things is described by the word "civilization." Its true test lies in the fact that people living in it make bodily welfare the object of life. We will take some examples. The people of Europe today live in better built houses than they did a hundred years ago. This is considered an emblem of civilization, and this is also a matter to promote bodily happiness. Formerly, they wore skins, and used as their weapons spears. Now, they wear long trousers, and, for embellishing their bodies, they wear a variety of clothing, and, instead of spears they carry with them revolvers containing five or more chambers. If people of a certain country, who have hitherto not been in the habit of wearing much clothing, boots, etc., adopt European clothing, they are supposed to have become civilized out of savagery. Formerly, in Europe, people ploughed their lands mainly by manual labour. Now, one man can plough a vast tract by steam-engines, and can thus amass great wealth. This is called a sign of civilization. Formerly, the fewest men wrote books that were most valuable. Now, anybody writes and prints anything he likes and poison people's minds. Formerly, men travelled in wagons; now they fly through the air in trains at the rate of four hundred and more miles per day. This is considered the height of civilization. It has been stated that, as men progress, they shall be able to travel in airships and reach any part of the world in a few hours. Men will not need the use of their hands and feet. They will press a button and they will have their clothing by their side. They will press another button and they will have their newspaper. A third, and a motorcar will be waiting for them. They will have a variety of delicately dished-up food. Everything will be done by machinery. Formerly, when people wanted to fight with one another, they measured between them their bodily strength; now it is possible to take away thousands of lives by one man working behind a gun from a hill. This is civilization. Formerly, men worked in the open air only so much as they liked. Now, thousands of workmen meet together and for the sake of maintenance work in factories and mines. Their condition is worse than that of beasts. They are obliged to work, at the risk of their lives, at most dangerous occupations, for the sake of millionaires. Formerly, men were made slaves under physical compulsion, now they are enslaved by temptation of money and of the luxuries that money can buy. . . . This civilization takes note neither of morality nor of religion. Its votaries calmly state that their business is not to teach religion. Some even consider it to be a superstitious growth. Others put on the cloak of religion, and prate about morality. But, after twenty years experience, I have come to the conclusion that immorality is often taught in the name of morality. Even a child can understand that in all I have described above there can be no inducement to morality. Civilization seeks to increase bodily comforts, and it fails miserably even in doing so.

STUDY QUESTIONS

1. Which branches of Western learning does Feng think are most important? How should the Chinese respond? What should become of Confucianism?
2. According to Afghani, what is the key to Western power and wealth? What are the implications of the rise of the West for Islam?
3. What is Gandhi's objection to civilization? What seems to be his vision for India's future?
4. What do the three writers have in common? Where do they diverge?
5. Does modern science and technology destroy morality, as Gandhi argued, or not, as Feng and Afghani thought? Explain your answer.

ESSAY SUGGESTIONS

A. Which of the writers in this chapter come closest to the thinking undergirding the Meiji Restoration (Chapter 24)?

B. Was Gandhi opposed to modern industrial society? Why or why not?

27 LATIN AMERICA

INDEPENDENCE AND CONSOLIDATION OF NEW STATES (1791–1910)

The wars of independence (1791–1825), the unstable aftermath of independence (1825–1870), and national consolidation (1870–1910) marked the political transformation of Latin America during the long nineteenth century. The wars of independence led to the political separation of most Latin American countries from their former colonial rulers: Spain, Portugal, and France. Often described as civil wars because they involved violent class and racial conflict, the wars of independence resulted not only in the formation of seventeen independent states, but also widespread economic devastation, social disruption, and decades of political instability. From the 1820s to the 1870s, the generals who led the struggle for independence recruited personal armies and fought with one another incessantly over who should rule. By the 1870s, instability gradually ended and national consolidation began. Emerging from the American-born upper class, newly wealthy oligarchs, associated with the export economy (coffee, metals, oil, wheat, and beef) and foreign capital, overthrew the old-style *caudillos* and established new regimes. Based on "democracy for the few," the oligarchs, during the last quarter of the nineteenth century, centralized governmental functions and formed national armies and police forces that solidified their control.

The wars of the French Revolution and Napoleon precipitated Latin America's independence movement. This was particularly true of the Haitian slave revolt from 1791 to 1804. When news of the Declaration of Rights of Man and the Citizen spread to the French sugar plantation colony of St. Domingo, the mulatto population (20,000) sought equality with whites (24,000). But mulatto demands prompted a rebellion for freedom among the slaves (408,000). On January 1, 1804, after thirteen years of war, the former slaves officially declared independence. Black army leaders, Toussaint Loverture and Jean Jaques Desallines, defeated in succession the French colonial regime, a British invasion force, and a Napoleonic invasion. The loss of life during Haiti's struggle for independence was far greater than in the other parts of the Americas. More than one-third of the black population died. Of the 400,000 former slaves, only 250,000 remained. Black armies killed or drove out the white population and many of the mulattoes.

Selection I from Marcus Rainsford, *An Historical Account of the Black Empire of Hayti Comprehending a View of the Principal Transactions in the Revolution of Saint-Domingo; with Its Ancient and Modern State* (London, 1805), 431–439. Selection II from Simón Bolivar to the Congress of Angostura in 1819, in Vicente Lecuna and Harold A. Bierck Jr., eds., *Selected Writings of Bolivar* (New York: Colonial Press, 1951), pp. 175–176, 183, 185–190. Selection III from Porfirio Diaz interview, 1908, Carlos B. Gill, ed., *The Age of Porfirio Diaz: Selected Readings* (Albuquerque: University of New Mexico Press, 1977), pp. 78–81. Reprinted by permission of Carlos B. Gill.

Latin America at Independence.

STUDY QUESTIONS

1. Identify the areas that by 1850 had divided into smaller national units. What does this division suggest about the direction of Latin American political development?
2. Which area in Latin America remained territorially united from the colonial period to the present? How might one account for this territorial unity?

British and French invaders each lost approximately 50,000 men, who succumbed to the violence of war and to yellow fever. Revolutionary leaders also perished. Loverture died in a French prison in 1803, and Desallines was assassinated in 1806. In the first selection, General Desallines "informally" announced independence on November 29, 1803, the day that Napoleon's army withdrew. He reveals the animosities generated by slavery and thirteen years of racial war and hatred.

In Spanish America, Napoleon presented a different problem. By imprisoning the Spanish king in 1808, Napoleon undermined the legitimacy of the Spanish colonial government. As the Spanish American upper class argued over who had the right to rule, lower-class rebellions of Indians, mestizos, and mulattoes, especially in Mexico and Venezuela, shaped the political future of Spanish America. Upper-class Creoles, the descendants of Spaniards born in America, organized armies that accomplished two purposes: they smashed lower-class rebellions by 1815 and eventually achieved independence by 1825.

Simón Bolivar, the liberator of northern South America, Peru, and Bolivia, came from this Creole class. His political ideas clearly expressed the biases of his social origins. He mistrusted the lower classes and advocated elite-run governments. In the second selection, these prejudices are clearly shown in Bolivar's advice to the legislators gathered at Angostura in 1819 to discuss the proposed constitution for the new state of Venezuela.

Mexican president Porfirio Diaz, who governed with an iron hand from 1876 to 1910, exemplified the transition to oligarchic rule that occurred in many now independent Latin American states. Although he was a rough *mestizo* military leader, Diaz enjoyed the support of the Mexican oligarchs and their articulate spokesmen. With the oligarchy's help, he ended fifty years of civil war. Through concessions to foreign investors, particularly in mining, railroads, and oil, Diaz presided over an impressive economic boom in exports to the United States. To maintain economic growth, the oligarchy sought stability, and Diaz provided it. The third selection is from an interview given by Porfirio Diaz in 1908 to the American reporter James Creelman. Diaz candidly revealed how he achieved order.

DOCUMENTS BY JEAN JACQUES DESSALLINES, SIMÓN BOLIVAR, AND PORFIRIO DIAZ

I. JEAN JAQUES DESSALLINES ANNOUNCEMENT OF INDEPENDENCE OF ST. DOMINGO (HAITI), NOVEMBER 29, 1803

In the name of the Black People, and Men of Color of St. Domingo:

The Independence of St. Domingo is proclaimed. Restored to our primitive dignity, we have asserted our rights; we swear never to yield them to any power on earth; the frightful veil of prejudice is torn to pieces, be it so forever. Woe be to them who would dare to put together its bloody tatters.

Oh! Landholders of St. Domingo, wandering in foreign countries by proclaiming our independence, we do not forbid you, indiscriminately, from returning to your property; far be it from us this unjust idea. We are not ignorant that there are some among you that have renounced their former errors, abjured the injustice of their exorbitant pretensions, and acknowledged the lawfulness of the cause for which we have been spilling our blood these twelve years. Toward those men who do us justice, we will act as brothers; let them rely for ever on our esteem and friendship; let them return among us. The God who protects us, the God of Freemen, bids us to stretch out towards them our conquering arms. (ed. note. A large number of whites returned. They were all killed beginning in March 1804.) But as for those, who, intoxicated with foolish pride, interested slaves of a guilty pretension, are blinded so much as to believe themselves the essence of human nature, and assert that they are destined by heaven to be our masters and our tyrants, let them never come near the land of St. Domingo: if they come hither, they will only meet with chains or deportation; then let them stay where they are; tormented by their well-deserved misery, and the frowns of the just men whom they have too long mocked, let them still continue to move, unpitied and unnoticed by all.

We have sworn not to listen with clemency towards all those who would dare to speak to us of slavery; we will be inexorable, perhaps even cruel, towards all troops who, themselves forgetting the object for which they have not ceased fighting since 1780, should come from Europe to bring among us death and servitude. Nothing is too dear, and all means are lawful to men from whom it is wished to tear the first of all blessings. Were they to cause rivers and torrents of blood to run; were they, in order to maintain their liberty, to conflagrate seven-eighths of the globe, they are innocent before the tribunal of Providence, that never created men, to see them groaning under so harsh and shameful a servitude.

In the various commotions that took place, some inhabitants against whom we had not to complain, have been victims by the cruelty of a few soldiers or cultivators, too much blinded by the remembrance of their past sufferings to be able to distinguish the good and humane landowners from those that were unfeeling and cruel, we lament with all feeling souls so deplorable an end, and declare to the world, whatever may be said to the contrary by wicked people, that the murders were committed contrary to the wishes of our hearts. It was impossible, especially in the crisis in which the colony was, to be able to prevent or stop those horrors. They who are in the least acquainted with history, know that a people, when assailed by civil dissentions, though they may be the most polished on earth, give themselves up to every species of excess, and the authority of the chiefs, at that time not firmly supported, in a time of revolution cannot punish all that are guilty, without meeting with new difficulties. But now a-days the Aurora of peace hails us, with the glimpse of a less stormy time; now that the calm of victory has succeeded to the trouble of a dreadful war, every thing in St. Domingo ought to assume a new face, and its government henceforward be that of justice.

II. SIMÓN BOLIVAR'S ADVICE TO THE CONGRESS OF ANGOSTURA, 1819

We are not Europeans; we are not Indians; we are but a mixed species of aborigines and Spaniards. Americans by birth and Europeans by law, we find ourselves engaged in a dual conflict: we are disputing with the natives for titles of ownership, and at the same time we are struggling to maintain ourselves in the country that gave us birth against the opposition of the invaders.

Subject to the threefold yoke of ignorance, tyranny, and vice, the American people have been unable to acquire knowledge, power, or [civic] virtue. The lessons we received and the models we studied, as pupils of such pernicious teachers, were most destructive. We have been ruled more by deceit than by force, and we have been degraded more by vice than by superstition.

Venezuela had, has, and should have a republican government. Its principles should be the sovereignty of the people, division of powers, civil liberty, proscription of slavery, and the abolition of monarchy and privileges. We need equality to recast, so to speak, into a unified nation, the classes of men, political opinions, and public customs.

Like the North Americans, we have divided national representation into two chambers: that of Representatives and the Senate. The first is very wisely constituted. It enjoys all its proper functions, and it requires no essential revision, because the Constitution, in creating it, gave it the form and powers which the people deemed necessary in order that they might be legally and properly represented. If the Senate were hereditary rather than elective, it would, in my opinion, be the basis, the tie, the very soul of our republic. In political storms this body would arrest the thunderbolts of the government and would repel any violent popular reaction. Devoted to the government because of a natural interest in its own preservation, a hereditary senate would always oppose any attempt on the part of the people to infringe upon the jurisdiction and authority of their magistrates. It must be confessed that most men are unaware of their best interests and that they constantly endeavor to assail them in the hands of their custodians—the individual clashes with the mass, and the mass with authority. It is necessary, therefore, that in all governments there be a neutral body to protect the injured and disarm the offender. To be neutral, this body must not owe its origin to appointment by the government or to election by the people, if it is to enjoy a full measure of independence which neither fears nor expects anything from these two sources of authority. The hereditary senate, as a part of the people, shares its interests, its sentiments, and its spirit. For this reason it should not be presumed that a hereditary senate would ignore the interests of the people or forget its legislative duties. The senators in Rome and in the House of Lords in London have been the strongest pillars upon which the edifice of political and civil liberty has rested.

The creation of a hereditary senate would in no way be a violation of political equality. I do not solicit the establishment of a nobility, for, as a celebrated republican has said, that would simultaneously destroy equality and liberty. What I propose is an office for which the candidates must prepare themselves, an office that demands great knowledge and the ability to acquire such knowledge. All should not be left to chance and the outcome of elections. The people are more easily deceived than is Nature perfected by art; and, although these senators, it is true, would not be bred in an environment that is all virtue, it is equally true that they would be raised in an atmosphere of enlightened education. Furthermore, the liberators of Venezuela are entitled to occupy forever a high rank in the Republic that they have brought into existence. I believe that posterity would view with regret the effacement of the illustrious names of its first benefactors. I say, moreover, that it is a matter of public interest and national honor, of gratitude on Venezuela's part, to honor gloriously, until the end of time, a race of virtuous, prudent, and persevering men who, overcoming every obstacle, have founded the Republic at the price of the most heroic sacrifices. And if the people of Venezuela do not applaud the elevation of their benefactors, then they are unworthy to be free, and they will never be free.

A hereditary senate, I repeat, will be the fundamental basis of the legislative power, and therefore the foundation of the entire government. It will also serve as a counterweight to both government and people; and as a neutral power it will weaken the mutual attacks of these two eternally rival powers. In all conflicts the calm reasoning of a third party will serve as the means of reconciliation. Thus the Venezuelan senate will give strength to this delicate political structure, so sensitive to violent repercussions; it will be the mediator that will lull the storms and it will maintain harmony between the head and the other parts of this political body.

III. INTERVIEW WITH PORFIRIO DIAZ, 1908

I received this Government from the hands of a victorious army at a time when the people were divided and unprepared for the exercise of the extreme principles of democratic government. To have thrown upon the masses the whole responsibility of government at once would have produced conditions that might have discredited the cause of free government.

Yet, although I got power at first from the army, an election was held as soon as possible and then my authority came from the people. I have tried to leave the Presidency several times, but it has been pressed upon me and I remained in office for the sake of the nation which trusted me. The fact that the price of Mexican securities dropped eleven points when I was ill in Cuernavaca indicates the kind of evidence that persuaded me to overcome my personal inclination to retire from private life.

We preserved the republican and democratic form of government. We defended the theory and kept it intact. Yet we adopted a patriarchal policy in the administration of the nation's affairs, guiding the restraining popular tendencies, with full faith that an enforced peace would allow education, industry and commerce to develop elements of stability and unity in a naturally intelligent, gentle and affectionate people.

I have waited patiently for the day when the people of the Mexican Republic would be prepared to choose and change their government at every election without danger of armed revolutions and without injury to the national credit or interference with national progress. I believe the day has come.

• • •

The principles of democracy have not been planted very deeply in our people, I fear. But the nation has grown and it loves liberty. Our difficulty has been that the people do not concern themselves enough about public matters for a democracy. The individual Mexican as a rule thinks much about his own rights and is always ready to assert them. But he does not think so much about the rights of others. He thinks of his privileges, but not of his duties. Capacity for self-restraint is the basis of democratic government, and self-restraint is possible only to those who recognize the rights of their neighbors.

The Indians, who are more than half of our population, care little for politics. They are accustomed to looking to those in authority for leadership instead of thinking for themselves. That is a tendency they inherited from the Spanish, who taught them to refrain from meddling in public affairs and rely on the Government for guidance.

Yet I firmly believe that the principles of democracy have grown and will grow in Mexico.

. . .

It is enough for me that I have seen Mexico rise among the peaceful and useful nations. I have no desire to continue in the Presidency. This nation is ready for her ultimate life of freedom. At the age of seventy-seven years I am satisfied with robust health. That is one thing which neither law nor force can create. I would not exchange it for all the millions of your American oil king.

. . .

The railway has played a great part in the peace of Mexico. . . . When I became President at first there were only two small lines, one connecting the capital with Vera Cruz, the other connecting it with Querétaro. Now we have more than 19,000 miles of railways. Then we had a slow and costly mail service, carried on by stage coaches, and the mail coach between the capital and Puebla would be stopped by highwaymen two or three times in a trip, the last robbers to attack it generally finding nothing left to steal. Now we have a cheap, safe and fairly rapid mail service throughout the country with more than twenty-two hundred post offices. Telegraphing was a difficult thing in those times. Today we have more than forty-five thousand miles of telegraph wires in operation.

We began by making robbery punishable by death and compelling the execution of offenders within a few hours after they were caught and condemned. We ordered that wherever telegraph wires were cut and the chief officer of the district did not catch the criminal, *he should himself suffer;* and in the case the cutting occurred on a plantation *the proprietor* who failed *to prevent it should be hanged* to the nearest telegraph pole [emphasis added]. These were military orders, remember.

We were harsh. Sometimes we were harsh to the point of cruelty. But it was all necessary then to the life and progress of the nation. If there was cruelty, results have justified it.

. . .

It was better that a little blood should be shed that much blood should be saved. The blood that was shed was bad blood; the blood that was saved was good blood.

Peace was necessary, even an enforced peace, that the nation might have time to think and work. Education and industry have carried on the task begun by the army.

. . .

I want to see education throughout the Republic carried on by the national Government. I hope to see it before I die. It is important that all citizens of a republic should receive the same training, so that their ideals and methods may be harmonized and the national unity intensified. When men read alike and think alike they are more likely to act alike.

STUDY QUESTIONS

1. Desallines claimed that cruelty is sometimes necessary to achieve important political ends. What is your view of this proposition? Is it a universal claim crossing all cultures?
2. What is Bolivar's view of the common people of Venezuela? What types of institutions does he recommend to rule these people? Why are these types needed?
3. What role should the liberators (the leaders of the independence armies) play in the new government proposed by Bolivar?
4. In what way did Porfirio Diaz, as ruler of Mexico, fulfill the ideas of Bolivar? How did Diaz view the common people? What kind of government did he establish? In what ways did his policies relate to the economy? What was Diaz's goal for education?

ESSAY SUGGESTIONS

A. Discuss the relationship between the Haitian revolution and the principles of the French Revolution of 1789. In what ways did the political ideas and events in France affect Haiti? Were these principles also related to Bolivar's independence movement? Were these political changes part of a single age of Atlantic revolution?

B. Using these documents together: What were some of the key issues in Latin American politics in the nineteenth century? How were they resolved?

C. Discuss the role and limitations of democracy in nineteenth-century Latin America.

28 ECONOMY AND SOCIETY OF LATIN AMERICA

From 1870 to 1914, many regions of Latin America became fully integrated into the world economy. Exports of raw materials, including minerals, oil, food products, and fibers, bound Latin America to the industrialized nations. Latin American nations became dependent on the industrial world's manufactured goods, markets for the export of raw materials, transportation, and credit.

The development of these economies altered patterns of work in the areas they affected. In Cuba, sugar plantations expanded production to supply the growing populations of Europe and North America. Although processing and transportation became mechanized, planting and harvesting sugar remained handwork. The first selection, taken from the transcription of an oral history of a runaway slave, reveals the social conditions among the workers on the Cuban sugar plantations after the abolition of slavery in 1886. The Spanish government granted abolition after a violent upheaval in Cuba known as the Ten Years War (1868–1878), followed by intense pressure from foreign powers, especially Great Britain and the United States.

The second selection describes conditions on the henequen plantations of Yucatan. Demand for henequen (a cactus-like plant) fibers was directly related to the mechanization of agriculture in the United States. In 1878, Cyrus McCormick added a new knotting mechanism for grain binding to his mechanical reaper. The subsequent search for a strong binder twine led directly to henequen in Yucatan. McCormick imported hundreds of thousands of tons of henequen during the late nineteenth century. Exports from Yucatan increased from forty thousand bales in 1875 to six hundred thousand in 1910. In 1902, the same year that McCormick merged with other harvesting machine companies to form International Harvester, he also secretly negotiated lower prices for henequen with the governor of Yucatan in return for steady purchases from the governor's export companies. With that agreement, International Harvester established its "informal empire" in Yucatan. The company neither needed to own its own land nor produce henequen directly. Production was left in the hands of local landowners and merchants, who became fabulously wealthy and who also controlled the Yucatecan state government.

The expansion of henequen production also affected land tenure and labor relations. When henequen became king, new plantations absorbed Indian communal land and imposed on their workers a much stricter regime of work. Seedlings and young plants required constant attention until they matured in seven years, and harvesting the leaves was done by hand. The need for labor on henequen left little time for traditional cultivation of the Mayan workers' plots of corn (*milpas*). Labor shortages also resulted in the importation of Yaqui Indians captured in Northern Mexico and Puerto Rican and Korean workers. But most of all, owners relied on the local Mayan *campesinos,* whether or not they wanted to work on the plantation.

PLANTATION LIFE IN CUBA AND YUCATAN

I. FORMER SLAVE'S LIFE ON A SUGAR PLANTATION AFTER ABOLITION: 1880s CUBA

After all this time in the forest I had become half savage. I didn't want to work anywhere, and I was afraid they would shut me up again. I knew quite well that slavery had not ended completely. A lot of people asked me what I was doing and where I came from. Sometimes I told them, 'My name is Stephen and I was a runaway slave.' Other times I said I had been working on a certain plantation and could not find my relations. I must have been about twenty at the time. This was before I came across my relations. That happened later.

Since I did not know anyone I walked from village to village for several months. I did not suffer from hunger because people gave me food. You only had to say you were out of work and someone would always help you out. But you can't carry on like that for ever. I began to realise that work had to be done in order to sleep in a barracoon [slave quarter] at least. By the time I decided to cut cane, I had already covered quite a bit of ground. I know all the part north of Las Villas well. It is the prettiest part of Cuba. That was where I started work.

The first plantation I worked on was called Purio. I turned up there one day in the rags I stood in and a hat I had collected on the way. I went in and asked the overseer if there was work for me. He said yes. I remember he was Spanish, with moustaches, and his name was Pepe. There were overseers in these parts until quite recently, the difference being that they didn't lay about them as they used to do under slavery. But they were men of the same breed, harsh, overbearing. There were still barracoons after Abolition, the same as before. Many of them were newly built of masonry, the old ones having collapsed under the rain and storms. The barracoon at Purio was strong and looked as if it had been recently completed. They told me to go and live there. I soon made myself at home, for it wasn't too bad. They had taken the bolts off the doors and the workers themselves had cut holes in the walls for ventilation. They no longer had to worry about escapes or anything like that, for the Negroes were free now, or so they said. But I could not help noticing that bad things still went on. There were bosses who still believed that the blacks were created for locks and bolts and whips, and treated them as before. It struck me that many Negroes did not know that things had changed, because they went on saying, 'Give me your blessing, my master.'

Those ones never left the plantation at all. I was different in that I disliked having anything to do with the whites. They believed they were the lords of creation. At Purio I lived alone most of the time. I might have a concubine from Easter to San Juan's day; but women have always been selfish, and there wasn't a Christian soul alive who could support a black woman in those days. Though I do say that women are the greatest thing there is. I was never short of a black woman to say, 'I want to live with you.'

The work was exhausting. You spent hours in the fields and it seemed as if the work would never end. It went on and on until you were worn out. The overseers were always bothering you. Any worker who knocked off for long was taken off the job. I worked from six in the morning. The early hour did not bother me since in the forest it had been impossible to sleep late because of the cocks crowing. There was a break at eleven for lunch, which had to be eaten in the workers' canteen, usually standing because of the crowd of people squashed in. At one everyone went back to the fields. This was the worst and hottest time. Work ended at six in the afternoon. Then I would take myself off to the river, bathe for a while and go back to get something to eat. I had to hurry because the kitchen did not work at night.

Food cost around six pesos a month. They gave good portions, but it never varied: rice with black or white beans, or chick peas and jerked beef.

The Negroes who worked at Purio had almost all been slaves; they were so used to the life in the barracoon they did not even go out to eat. When lunch-time came they shut themselves up in their rooms to eat and the same with dinner. They did not go out at night. They were afraid of people, and they said they would get lost if they did, they were convinced of this. I wasn't like that—if I got lost I always found myself again. When I think of the times I got lost in the forest and couldn't find a river!

On Sundays all the workers who wanted to could work overtime. This meant that instead of resting you went to the fields and cleared, cleaned or cut cane. Or if not that, you stayed in, cleaning out the troughs or scraping the boilers. This would only be in the morning. As there was nothing special to do that day, all the workers used to go and earn themselves extra money. Money is a very evil thing. A person who gets used to earning a lot is on the road to ruination. I earned the same as the rest. The pay worked out at around twenty-four pesos, including food. Some plantations paid twenty-five.

There were still plenty of taverns around to spend one's cash in. There were two or three at Purio. I used to go into them for a drink now and then, and I also went there if I wanted to buy something. To tell the truth, the taverns weren't very nice places. Almost every day fights would break out because of rivalries or jealousy over women. At night there were fiestas, and anyone who wanted could go. They were held in the mill compound. There was enough room to dance, and the Negroes themselves sang the rumbas. The fun was in dancing and shouting and drinking.

In those days you could get either permanent or temporary work on the plantations. Those employed on a permanent basis had to keep to a time-table. This way they would live in the barracoons and did not need to leave the plantations for anything. I preferred being a permanent worker myself, because the other life was too troublesome. A man who decided to freelance would simply go along to a cane-field and, according to the amount of cane there, agree on a price. . . . Those freelance workers were very sharp. They could rest whenever they felt like it, get a drink of water, and even took their women along to the cane-fields to lie with them. . . . Then the overseer came back and, if he was satisfied, they would go off with their money to the towns to wait till the cane grew again. If their money ran out quickly, they would find some way of getting work on another plantation. They lived like tramps, bedding in the smaller rooms of the barracoons. They hardly ever took their women to their rooms, but used to see them at night because they were allowed out after a day's work.

With us fixed-rate workers things were different. We couldn't go out at night because at nine o'clock we had to be ready for the silence bell.

The barracoons were a bit damp, but all the same they were safer than the forest. There were no snakes and all the workers slept in hammocks which were very comfortable, and one could wrap up well in the cold. Many of the barracoons were made of sacking. The one tiresome thing about them was the fleas; they didn't hurt, but you had to be up all night scaring them off with Spanish broom, which gets rid of fleas and ticks.

At Purio, as on all plantations, there were Africans of various countries, but the Congolese were in the majority. It's not for nothing they call all the region in the north of Las Villas 'the Congo.' At that time there were Filipinos, Chinese, Canary Islanders, and an increasing number of Creoles there as well. They all worked on the cane, clearing the ground with spades and machetes and earthing up. Earthing up means ploughing with a bullock and a tree-trunk on a chain to turn over the soil, just as under slavery.

Relations between the groups remained unchanged. The Filipinos were as criminal as before. The Canary Islanders did not speak; the only thing that existed for them was work, and they were as arrogant as ever. They took against me because I wouldn't make friends with them. One had to be careful of the Islanders, because they knew a lot of magic and they would do anyone a bad turn. I think they earned more than the Negroes, although they always used to say that everyone earned the same amount.

[Relations with Women and Children]

I felt better then than I do now. I had my youth. Now I still have my concubine from time to time, but it is not the same. A woman is a wonderful thing. Women, to tell the truth, are what I have got most pleasure from in my life. In the old days, when I was at Purio, I used to get up and go to the village on Sundays, always in the afternoons so as not to miss the morning's overtime, and sometimes I found myself a woman before even reaching the village.

This thing of going to the cane-fields to screw was a common practice, the people made use of the wagon track between the mill and the cane-fields. In those days you grabbed any woman and took her into the cane. There wasn't all the courtship there is now. If a woman went with a man she knew she would have to get down on her back. . . .

Casual relationships were more convenient. The women were free and they didn't have to get along with their parents. They worked in the fields, helping in the hoeing and sowing, and they went with a man when they felt like it. The easy-going fellows always went in for this kind of arrangement, one woman one day, another woman the next. I think this is the better way myself. I stayed free and didn't marry till I was old; I was a bachelor in many places. I knew women of all colours, proud women and kind ones.

If I count up all the women I had it seems that I must have had any number of children, but the strange thing is that I never knew of a single one. At least, none of the women who lived with me in the barracoon ever had any. The others, the women I took into the woods, used to come and say 'This boy is yours,' but how could you ever be certain with them? Besides, children were a big problem in those days. You couldn't educate them because there weren't any schools like there are now.

Little boys . . . were brought up wild and uneducated. The only thing they were taught was raising vegetables and hoeing; but no learning. They were often beaten, and if they went on being naughty they were made to kneel on grains of rice or corn. A whipping was the most common punishment. The parents came and then the boy was beaten with a birch or piece of braided rope until the blood ran. The cane was a green switch which never broke even when it was wielded violently enough to flay the skin. I believe I had sons, maybe many or maybe not, but I don't think I would ever have punished them like that.

Children were always playing truant. They would come scavenging round the houses to get out of work, and they often used to hide to escape from punishments their parents threatened them with.

II. WORK ON THE HENEQUEN PLANTATIONS OF YUCATAN

The Yucatecans have a cruel proverb, *"Los Indios no oigan sino por las nalgas"* ("The Indians can hear only with their backs"). The Spanish half-breeds have taken a race once noble enough and broken them on the wheel of tyranny so brutal that the heart of them is dead. The relation between the two peoples is ostensibly that of master and servant; but Yucatan is rotten with a foul slavery—the fouler and blacker because of its hypocrisy and pretence.

The peonage system of Spanish America, as specious and treacherous a plan as was ever devised for race-degradation, is that by which a farm labourer is legally bound to work for the land-owner, if in debt to him, until that debt is paid. Nothing could sound fairer: nothing could lend itself better to the blackest abuse. In Yucatan every Indian peon is in debt to his Yucatecan master. Why? Because every Indian is a spendthrift? Not at all; but because the master's interest is to get him and keep him in debt. This is done in two ways. The plantation-slave must buy the necessaries of his humble life at the plantation store, where care is taken to charge such prices as are beyond his humble earnings of sixpence a day. Thus he is always in debt to the farm; and if an Indian is discovered to be scraping together the few dollars he owes, the books of the hacienda are "cooked"—yes, deliberately "cooked"—and when he presents himself before the magistrate to pay his debt, say, of twenty dollars (£2) the haciendado can show scored against him a debt of fifty dollars. The Indian pleads he does not owe it. The haciendado-court smiles. The word of an Indian cannot prevail against the Señor's books, it murmurs sweetly, and back to his slave-work the miserable peon must go, first to be cruelly flogged to teach him that freedom is not for such as he, and that struggle as he may he will never escape the cruel master who under law as at present administered in Yucatan has as complete a disposal of his body as one of the pigs which root around in the hacienda yard.

Henequen (Spanish *jeniquen* or *geniquen*) is a fibre commercially known as Sisal hemp, from the fact that it is obtained from a species of cactus, the *Agave Sisalensis,* first cultivated around the tiny port of Sisal in the Yucatan. The older Indian name for the plant is *Agave Ixtli.* From its fleshy leaves is crushed out a fine fibre which, from the fact that it resists damp better than ordinary hemp, is valuable for making ships' cables, but the real wealth-producing use of which is so bizarre that no one in a hundred guesses would hit on it. It is used in the myriad corn-binding machines in America and Canada. They cannot use wire, and cheap string is too easily broken. Henequen is at once strong enough and cheap enough. Hence the piles of money heaping up to the credit of Yucatecans in the banks of Merida. . . .

[At the mill] three or four Indians set to work to arrange the leaves so that their black-pointed ends are all in one direction. Next these thorny points are severed by a machete and in small bundles of six or eight the leaves are handed to men who are feeding a sliding belt-like platform about a yard wide, and on this they are conveyed to the machine. Before they enter its great blunt-toothed, gaping jaws, they are finally arranged, as the sliding belt goes its unending round, so that they do not enter more than one at a time. Woe betide the Indian who has the misfortune to get his fingers in these revolving jaws of the gigantic crusher, and many indeed are there fingerless, handless, and armless from this cause. . . .

For there is money for everyone who touches the magic fibre except the miserable Indian, by whose never-ending labours the purse-proud monopolists of the Peninsula are enabled to be ever adding to their ill-gotten gold. There are in Yucatan to-day some 400 henequen plantations of from 25 to 20,000 acres, making the total acreage under cultivation some 140,000 acres. The cost of production, including shipping expenses, export duties, etc., is now about 7 pesos (14s.) per 100 kilogrammes. The average market price of henequen is 28 pesos per 100 kilogrammes, so the planter gets a return of 400 per cent. All this is obviously only possible as long as he can get slave-labour and the hideous truth about the exploitation of the Mayans is kept dark. The Indian gets a wage of 50 centavos for cutting a thousand leaves, and if he is to earn this in a day he must work ten hours. Near the big towns, 75 centavos are paid, but practically, on many haciendas, it is so managed that the labour is paid for by his bare keep.

STUDY QUESTIONS

1. How did the Cuban plantation workers' conditions change (or stay the same) after the abolition of slavery in 1886?
2. Identify the different types of workers on the sugar plantation. What were the relations among them?
3. What do the narrator's attitudes toward women and children suggest about family life on the plantation?

4. What are the ties that bound the peon to the henequen hacienda in Yucatan?
5. When and why did henequen become a valuable export product?
6. Describe the moral tone expressed by the Englishmen who wrote the document on Yucatan. What does this suggest about their attitudes toward Latin American civilization in general?

ESSAY SUGGESTIONS

A. Do Cuba's and Yucatan's places in the world economy and their social conditions qualify as imperialism? In answering this question, review the causes and consequences of European imperialism as depicted in Chapter 21 on Africa.

B. How did labor conditions in Latin America compare with those in other parts of the world in the nineteenth century? How did they compare with conditions of Russian peasants after emancipation? With conditions in European industrial factories?

29 GLOBAL CONTACTS: NEW CONNECTIONS AND TENSIONS

RACISM IN WORLD HISTORY: GANDHI AND DU BOIS

Fear and hatred of "other" people probably go back to the emergence of *Homo sapiens sapiens* many millennia ago. But most historians think that racism is much more recent than age-old xenophobia. If we define racism as (1) the belief that races exist as facts of nature (a view that contradicts the findings of modern biologists and geneticists) and (2) the claim that some races are better than others, then we may assert that this way of thinking first began to take shape in Europe during the early modern period.

Slavery based on skin color, a new twist on a very old institution, was central to the emergence of the new racialized thinking. From 1500 to 1800, European merchants purchased millions of captured Africans, packed them into the dirty holds of cargo vessels, transported them in harrowing journeys across the Atlantic, and then sold them to the owners of plantations from Maryland and Virginia to Brazil (Chapter 3). When challenged that these practices were contrary to Christian teaching, proponents searched the Bible for evidence "proving" otherwise. They "found" it in a passage in Genesis about Noah's son Ham who, along with all his descendants, was cursed by God and condemned to eternal servitude. The clincher? Ham, many Christians and Muslims wrongly believed, was the ancestor of all Africans. Slavery based on skin color now had God's sanction.

During the nineteenth century, slavery mostly ended, but racism did not. On the contrary, it grew stronger and was increasingly justified on secular grounds. Physical anthropologists argued that humankind was made up of three or four or five races (the number varied according to the scholar) and that whites were the best of the lot while people of color were inferior. Social Darwinists asserted that there was no real alternative to the establishment of European colonial regimes in Africa and Asia; white rule over people of color was the inevitable working out of the "survival of the fittest." Similar arguments were invoked to undergird racial segregation in the United States in the decades following the Civil War. Racism now had a basis in science.

The selections illustrate the rise of racism in two countries governed by people of European descent. In the first group of passages, Mohandas K. Gandhi (1869–1948) remembers the injustice he faced as a young lawyer in British South Africa. The second document comes from the writings of W. E. B. Du Bois (1868–1963; pronounced Due Boyss), the

Selection I from Mohandas K. Gandhi, *An Autobiography: The Story of My Experiments With Truth*, translated by Mahadev Desai (Boston: Beacon Press, 1957), pp. 111–117. Reprinted by permission of Navajivan Trust, Gujarat, India. Selection II from *The Oxford W. E. B. Du Bois Reader*, edited by Eric J. Sundquist (New York: Oxford University Press, 1996), pp. 497–499.

African American scholar and opponent of racism. Du Bois's 1913 essay, "The Souls of White Folk," is especially interesting for its discussion of the emergence of "personal whiteness."

How do the selections illustrate the power of racism in two countries ruled by whites? What other chapters provide evidence for the rise of racism at roughly the same time?

MOHANDAS K. GHANDI AND W. E. B. DUBOIS

I. FROM GANDHI'S *AUTOBIOGRAPHY* [1927]: A TRIP FROM DURBAN TO JOHANNESBURG IN 1893

On the seventh or eighth day after my arrival [in South Africa], I left Durban. A first class seat was booked for me. It was usual there to pay five shillings extra, if one needed a bedding. Abdulla Sheth insisted that I should book one bedding but, out of obstinacy and pride and with a view to saving five shillings, I declined. Abdulla Sheth warned me. 'Look, now,' said he, 'this is a different country from India. Thank God, we have enough and to spare. Please do not stint yourself in anything that you may need.'

I thanked him and asked him not to be anxious.

The train reached Maritzburg, the capital of Natal, at about 9 p.m. Beddings used to be provided at this station. A railway servant came and asked me if I wanted one. 'No,' said I, 'I have one with me.' He went away. But a passenger came next, and looked me up and down. He saw that I was a 'coloured' man. This disturbed him. Out he went and came in again with one or two officials. They all kept quiet, when another official came to me and said, 'Come along, you must go to the van compartment.'

'But I have a first class ticket,' said I.

'That doesn't matter,' rejoined the other. 'I tell you, you must go to the van compartment.'

'I tell you, I was permitted to travel in this compartment at Durban, and I insist on going on in it.'

'No, you won't,' said the official. 'You must leave this compartment, or else I shall have to call a police constable to push you out.'

'Yes, you may. I refuse to get out voluntarily.'

The constable came. He took me by the hand and pushed me out. My luggage was also taken out. I refused to go to the other compartment and the train steamed away. I went and sat in the waiting room, keeping my hand-bag with me, and leaving the other luggage where it was. The railway authorities had taken charge of it.

It was winter, and winter in the higher regions of South Africa is severely cold. Maritzburg being at a high altitude, the cold was extremely bitter. My over-coat was in my luggage, but I did not dare to ask for it lest I should be insulted again, so I sat and shivered. There was no light in the room. A passenger came in at about midnight and possibly wanted to talk to me. But I was in no mood to talk.

I began to think of my duty. Should I fight for my rights or go back to India, or should I go on to Pretoria without minding the insults, and return to India after finishing the case? It would be cowardice to run back to India without fulfilling my obligation. The hardship to which I was subjected was superficial—only a symptom of the deep disease of colour prejudice. I should try, if possible, to root out the disease and suffer hardships in the process. Redress for wrongs I should seek only to the extent that would be necessary for the removal of the colour prejudice.

So I decided to take the next available train to Pretoria.

The following morning I sent a long telegram to the General Manager of the Railway and also informed Abdulla Sheth, who immediately met the General Manager. The Manager justified the conduct of the railway authorities, but informed him that he had already instructed the Station Master to see that I reached my destination safely. Abdulla Sheth wired to the Indian merchants in Maritzburg and to friends in other places to meet me and look after me. The merchants came to see me at the station and tried to comfort me by narrating their own hardships and explaining that what had happened to me was nothing unusual. They also said that Indians travelling first or second class had to expect trouble from railway officials and white passengers. The day was thus spent in listening to these tales of woe. The evening train arrived. There was a reserved berth for me. I now purchased at Maritzburg the bedding ticket I had refused to book at Durban.

The train took me to Charlestown.

The train reached Charlestown in the morning. There was no railway, in those days, between Charlestown and Johannesburg, but only a stage-coach, which halted at Standerton for the night *en route.* I possessed a ticket for the coach, which was not cancelled by the break of the journey at Maritzburg for a day; besides, Abdulla Sheth had sent a wire to the coach agent at Charlestown.

But the agent only needed a pretext for putting me off, and so, when he discovered me to be a stranger, he said, 'Your ticket is cancelled.' I gave him the proper reply. The reason at the back of his mind was not want of accommodation, but quite another. Passengers had to be accommodated inside the coach, but as I was regarded as a 'coolie' and looked a stranger, it would be proper, thought the 'leader', as the white man in charge of the coach was called, not to seat me with the white passengers. There were seats on either side of the coachbox. The leader sat on one of these as a rule. Today he sat inside and gave me his seat. I knew it was sheer injustice and an insult, but I thought it better to pocket it. I could not have forced myself inside, and if I had raised a protest, the coach would have gone off without me. This would have meant the loss of another day, and Heaven only knows what would have happened the next day. So, much as I fretted within myself, I prudently sat next the coachman.

At about three o'clock the coach reached Pardekoph. Now the leader desired to sit where I was seated, as he wanted to smoke and possibly to have some fresh air. So he took a piece of dirty sack-cloth from the driver, spread it on the footboard and, addressing me said, '*Sami,* you sit on this, I want to sit near the driver.' The insult was more than I could bear. In fear and trembling I said to him, 'It was you who seated me here, though I should have been accommodated inside. I put up with the insult. Now that you want to sit outside and smoke, you would have me sit at your feet. I will not do so, but I am prepared to sit inside.'

As I was struggling through these sentences, the man came down upon me and began heavily to box my ears. He seized me by the arm and tried to drag me down. I clung to the brass rails of the coachbox and was determined to keep my hold even at the risk of breaking my wristbones. The passengers were witnessing the scene—the man swearing at me, dragging and belabouring me, and I remaining still. He was strong and I was weak. Some of the passengers were moved to pity and exclaimed: 'Man, let him alone. Don't beat him. He is not to blame. He is right. If he can't stay there, let him come and sit with us.' 'No fear,' cried the man, but he seemed somewhat crestfallen and stopped beating me. He let go my arm, swore at me a little more, and asking the Hottentot servant who was sitting on the other side of the coachbox to sit on the footboard, took the seat so vacated.

The passengers took their seats and, the whistle given, the coach rattled away. My heart was beating fast within my breast, and I was wondering whether I should ever reach my destination alive. The man cast an angry look at me now and then and, pointing his finger at me, growled: 'Take care, let me once get to Standerton and I shall show you what I do.' I sat speechless and prayed to God to help me.

After dark we reached Standerton and I heaved a sigh of relief on seeing some Indian faces. As soon as I got down, these friends said: 'We are here to receive you and take you to Isa Sheth's shop. We have had a telegram from Dada Abdulla.' I was very glad, and we went to Sheth Isa Haji Sumar's shop. The Sheth and his clerks gathered round me. I told them all that I had gone through. They were very sorry to hear it and comforted me by relating to me their own bitter experiences.

I wanted to inform the agent of the Coach Company of the whole affair. So I wrote him a letter, narrating everything that had happened, and drawing his attention to the threat his man had held out. I also asked for an assurance that he would accommodate me with the other passengers inside the coach when we started the next morning. To which the agent replied to this effect: 'From Standerton we have a bigger coach with different men in charge. The man complained of will not be there tomorrow, and you will have a seat with the other passengers.' This somewhat relieved me. I had, of course, no intention of proceeding against the man who had assaulted me, and so the chapter of the assault closed there.

In the morning Isa Sheth's man took me to the coach, I got a good seat and reached Johannesburg quite safely that night.

II. FROM DU BOIS: "THE SOULS OF WHITE FOLK"

High in the tower, where I sit above the loud complaining of the human sea, I know many souls that toss and whirl and pass, but none there are that intrigue me more than the Souls of White Folk.

Of them I am singularly clairvoyant. I see in and through them. I view them from unusual points of vantage. Not as a foreigner do I come, for I am native, not foreign, bone of their thought and flesh of their language. Mine is not the knowledge of the traveler or the colonial composite of dear memories, words and wonder. Nor yet is my knowledge that which servants have of masters, or mass of class, or capitalist of artisan. Rather I see these souls undressed and from the back and side. I see the working of their entrails. I know their thoughts and they know that I know. This knowledge makes them now embarrassed, now furious. They deny my right to live and be and call me misbirth! My word is to them mere bitterness and my soul, pessimism. And yet as they preach and strut and shout and threaten, crouching as they clutch at rags of facts and fancies to hide their nakedness, they go twisting, flying by my tired eyes and I see them ever stripped,—ugly, human.

The discovery of personal whiteness among the world's peoples is a very modern thing,—a nineteenth and twentieth century matter, indeed. The ancient world would have laughed at such a distinction. The Middle Age regarded skin color with mild curiosity; and even up into the eighteenth century we were hammering our national manikins into one, great, Universal Man, with fine frenzy which ignored color and race even more than birth. Today we have changed all that, and the world in a sudden, emotional conversion has discovered that it is white and by that token, wonderful!

This assumption that of all the hues of God whiteness alone is inherently and obviously better than brownness or tan leads to curious acts; even the sweeter souls of the dominant world as they discourse with me on weather, weal, and woe are continually playing above their actual words an obligato of tune and tone, saying:

"My poor, un-white thing! Weep not nor rage. I know, too well, that the curse of God lies heavy on you. Why? That is not for me to say, but be brave! Do your work in your lowly sphere, praying the good Lord that into heaven above, where all is love, you may, one day, be born—white!"

I do not laugh. I am quite straight-faced as I ask soberly:

"But what on earth is whiteness that one should so desire it?" Then always, somehow, some way, silently but clearly, I am given to understand that whiteness is the ownership of the earth forever and ever, Amen!

Now what is the effect on a man or a nation when it comes passionately to believe such an extraordinary dictum as this? That nations are coming to believe it is manifest daily. Wave on wave, each with increasing virulence, is dashing this new religion of whiteness on the shores of our time. Its first effects are funny: the strut of the Southerner, the arrogance of the Englishman amuck, the whoop of the hoodlum who vicariously leads your mob. Next it appears dampening generous enthusiasm in what we once counted glorious; to free the slave is discovered to be tolerable only in so far as it freed his master! Do we sense somnolent writhings in black Africa or angry groans in India or triumphant banzais in Japan? "To your tents, O Israel!" These nations are not white!

After the more comic manifestations and the chilling of generous enthusiasm come subtler, darker deeds. Everything considered, the title to the universe claimed by White Folk is faulty. It ought, at least, to look plausible. How easy, then, by emphasis and omission to make children believe that every great soul the world ever saw was a white man's soul; that every great thought the world ever knew was a white man's thought; that every great deed the world ever did was a white man's deed; that every great dream the world ever sang was a white man's dream. In fine, that if from the world were dropped everything that could not fairly be attributed to White Folk, the world would, if anything, be even greater, truer, better than now. And if all this be a lie, is it not a lie in a great cause?

Here it is that the comedy verges to tragedy. The first minor note is struck, all unconsciously, by those worthy souls in whom consciousness of high descent brings burning desire to spread the gift abroad,—the obligation of nobility to the ignoble. Such sense of duty assumes two things: a real possession of the heritage and its frank appreciation by the humble-born. So long, then, as humble black folk, voluble with thanks, receive barrels of old clothes from lordly and generous whites, there is much mental peace and moral satisfaction. But when the black man begins to dispute the white man's title to certain alleged bequests of the Fathers in wage and position, authority and training; and when his attitude toward charity is sullen anger rather than humble jollity; when he insists on his human right to swagger and swear and waste,—then the spell is suddenly broken and the philanthropist is ready to believe that Negroes are impudent, that the South is right, and that Japan wants to fight America.

After this the descent to Hell is easy. On the pale, white faces which the great billows whirl upward to my tower I see again and again, often and still more often, a writing of human hatred, a deep and passionate hatred, vast by the very vagueness of its expressions. Down through the green waters, on the bottom of the world, where men move to and fro, I have seen a man—an educated gentleman—grow livid with anger because a little, silent, black woman was sitting by herself in a Pullman car. He was a white man. I have seen a great, grown man curse a little child, who had wandered into the wrong waiting-room, searching for its mother: "Here, you damned black——" He was white. In Central Park I have seen the upper lip of a quiet, peaceful man curl back in a tigerish snarl of rage because black folk rode by in a motor car. He was a white man. We have seen, you and I, city after city drunk and furious with ungovernable lust of blood; mad with murder, destroying, killing, and cursing; torturing human victims because somebody accused of crime happened to be of the same color as the mob's innocent victims and because that color was not white! We have seen,—Merciful God! in these wild days and in the name of Civilization, Justice, and Motherhood,—what have we not seen, right here in America, of orgy, cruelty, barbarism, and murder done to men and women of Negro descent.

Up through the foam of green and weltering waters wells this great mass of hatred, in wilder, fiercer violence, until I look down and know that today to the millions of my people no misfortune could happen,—of death and pestilence, failure and defeat—that would not make the hearts of millions of their fellows beat with fierce, vindictive joy! Do you doubt it? Ask your own soul what it would say if the next census were to report that half of black America was dead and the other half dying.

STUDY QUESTIONS

1. How does Gandhi's experience shed light on racism in colonial South Africa? Why did ordinary white people enforce the racist laws?
2. When and where did the idea of "personal whiteness" first become important? What explains this new source of group identity?
3. What does Du Bois imply about the strength of racism in the United States in 1913?

4. Was it presumptuous of Du Bois to try to enter into the thinking of whites? Was Du Bois a racist?
5. In addition to the white racism illustrated in this chapter, are there other types of racism?

ESSAY SUGGESTIONS

A. In 1903, Du Bois wrote, "The problem of the twentieth century is the problem of the color line." Was this also true of the nineteenth century?

B. How might Gandhi have responded to Kipling's poem, "The White Man's Burden" (Chapter 20)?

THE TWENTIETH AND EARLY TWENTY-FIRST CENTURIES

Growing challenges to Western world dominance, sparked by growing nationalism and by divisions within the West, produced new expressions of diversity in the major world civilizations. At the same time, international contacts increased in many ways. New technologies sped exchange; so did heightened trade, new alliance systems, and multinational companies spreading production and products literally around the globe. Much of world history since 1914 involves oscillating tensions between interchange and a growing desire and capacity to define separate systems and identities. A variety of new global and regional conflicts reflected these tensions.

Within this general framework, a number of more specific changes occurred, also reflecting the twentieth century's role as a transition toward a new, but not fully defined, period of world history. Religion declined in some societies but was reasserted in others. Political structures varied from liberal-democratic to authoritarian to communist, as new nations or revolutions yielded different patterns in different parts of the globe. A number of changes occurred in women's conditions, but there were also new reactions against change. But amid renewed diversity, including widely varying levels of economic well-being, there were some common themes. Many civilizations sought ways to modify earlier political traditions—very few regimes in place in 1914 still survived by the early twenty-first century. The shifts in the outlook and conditions of women marked fundamental social and personal upheaval. Hardly uniform, the twentieth-century world also shared a need to come to terms with some basic forces of innovation in the areas of technology, ideas, and social forms.

The 1990s and early 2000s were marked by additional transitions, many quite striking. The Cold War between communism and capitalism largely ended. This plus new technologies heighted the pace of global contacts. At the same time, new tensions arose, particularly those involving new levels of terrorism and new assertions of U.S. power. These contemporary developments became an important part of world history in the making, and they invite analysis based on wider historical perspective as well.

By the early twenty-first century, it seemed possible the accelerating pattern of global contacts—now involving not only trade but also cultural influences, new political relationships, and even environmental change—would be the dominant theme of the most recent world history period. Technologies underwrote this pattern of globalization but so did policy decisions by key actors, such as China and Russia, to reverse earlier impulses toward isolation in favor of greater openness. In this sense, this period, like its predecessors, rested on shifts in international interactions. But these shifts were fragile, as

the isolationist tendencies of the earlier twentieth century—from Stalinism, to Nazism, to narrow nationalism in other areas—had already suggested. The contemporary period in world history opened new opportunities for unprecedented contact, but it had not yet guaranteed that these would be uniformly accepted.

30 FRAMEWORKS FOR THE CONTEMPORARY WORLD

THE EXPERIENCE OF WORLD WAR I

The following three chapters deal with three developments that in many ways provided the basic framework for world history in the twentieth century: World War I, World War II, and then the Cold War. European history was profoundly altered by the experience of two world wars. World War I also spilled over into other parts of the world, with particularly deep influence in the Middle East and East Asia; World War II was even more obviously important on a global scale. The Cold War, though focused on the competition between the United States and the Soviet Union, was a global struggle as well. Developments in many key regions—discussed in subsequent sections—were deeply affected by these three contests. Global power balances, the importance of violence, and economic relationships were three areas in which the impacts clearly showed through. The end of the Cold War (Chapter 31) ushered in a new, and as yet not completely defined, framework. How much influence from the world wars and Cold War still shapes global relationships?

*****

World War I (1914–1918) was an unprecedented conflict in many ways. It involved much of the globe, although the centers of major fighting were in Europe and the Middle East. It showed the power of industrial technology and organization to deepen conflict, causing immense casualties and also extensive economic and political disruption. And it was an agonizing human experience.

These two documents deal with the military experience in the trenches shared by all the combatants. The first selection, from a memoir by Austrian musician Fritz Kreisler, offers an overview of the early stages, suggesting initial excitement, followed by deadening conflict. Kreisler also notes the confusing impact on memory itself.

The second selection is from the war's most famous novel, *All Quiet on the Western Front,* by Erich Maria Remarque. Remarque had served in the German army. He wrote vividly about the nature of trench warfare and the physical and mental burdens it imposed.

Selection I from Fritz Kreisler, *Four Weeks in the Trenches* (Boston: Houghton Mifflin, 1915), pp. 2, 6–8, 65–66, 69; Selection II from Erich Maria Remarque, *All Quiet on the Western Front,* A. W. Wheen, tr. (Boston: Little, Brown and Company, 1929), pp. 90–93, 109–110, 113–114.

The war permanently changed Europe's position in the world and greatly affected European politics—leading, for example, to the rise of fascism and Nazism. It also colored the life of a whole generation that found its expectations and rhythms totally shattered. The analytical challenge is to recapture this experience, at least in part, and discuss how it related to the larger changes the war produced.

FOUR WEEKS IN THE TRENCHES

I. FRITZ KREISLER

In trying to recall my impressions during my short war duty as an officer in the Austrian Army, I find that my recollections of this period are very uneven and confused. . . . This curious indifference of the memory to values of time and space may be due to the extraordinary physical and mental stress under which the impressions I am trying to chronicle were received. The same state of mind I find is rather characteristic of most people I have met who were in the war. It should not be forgotten, too, that the gigantic upheaval which changed the fundamental condition of life overnight and threatened the very existence of nations naturally dwarfed the individual into nothingness, and the existing interest in the common welfare left practically no room for personal considerations. Then again, at the front, the extreme uncertainty of the morrow tended to lessen the interest in the details of to-day; consequently I may have missed a great many interesting happenings alongside of me which I would have wanted to note under other circumstances. One gets into a strange psychological, almost hypnotic, state of mind while on the firing line which probably prevents the mind's eye from observing and noticing things in a normal way. This accounts, perhaps, for some blank spaces in my memory. . . .

I saw the crowds stop officers of high rank and well-known members of the aristocracy and clergy, also state officials and court functionaries of high rank, in quest of information, which was imparted cheerfully and patiently. The imperial princes could frequently be seen on the Ring Strasse [in Vienna] surrounded by cheering crowds or mingling with the public unceremoniously at the cafes, talking to everybody. Of course, the army was idolized. Wherever the troops marched the public broke into cheers and every uniform was the center of an ovation.

While coming from the station I saw two young reservists, to all appearances brothers, as they hurried to the barracks, carrying their small belongings in a valise. Along with them walked a little old lady crying, presumably their mother. They passed a general in full uniform. Up went their hands to their caps in military salute, whereupon the old general threw his arms wide open and embraced them both, saying: "Go on, my boys, do your duty bravely and stand firm for your emperor and your country. God willing, you will come back to your old mother." The old lady smiled through her tears. A shout went up, and the crowds surrounding the general cheered him. Long after I had left I could hear them shouting.

A few streets farther on I saw in an open cafe a young couple, a reservist in field uniform and a young girl, his bride or sweetheart. They sat there, hands linked, utterly oblivious of their surroundings and of the world at large. When somebody in the crowd espied them, a great shout went up, the public rushing to the table and surrounding them, then breaking into applause and waving hats and handkerchiefs. At first the young couple seemed to be utterly taken aback and only slowly did they realize that the ovation was meant for them. They seemed confused, the young girl blushing and hiding her face in her hands, the young man rising to his feet, saluting and bowing. More cheers and applause. He opened his mouth as if wanting to speak. There was a sudden silence. He was vainly struggling for expression, but then his face lit up as if by inspiration. Standing erect, hand at his cap, in a pose of military salute, he intoned the Austrian national hymn. In a second every head in that throng was bared. All traffic suddenly stopped, everybody, passengers as well as conductors of the cars, joining in the anthem. The neighboring windows soon filled with people, and soon it was a chorus of thousands of voices. The volume of tone and the intensity of feeling seemed to raise the inspiring anthem to the uttermost heights of sublime majesty. We were then on our way to the station, and long afterwards we could hear the singing, swelling like a human organ. . . .

We were all looking like shaggy, lean wolves, from the necessity of subsisting on next to nothing. I remember having gone for more than three days at a time without any food whatsoever, and many a time we had to lick the dew from the grass for want of water. A certain fierceness arises in you, an absolute indifference to anything the world holds except your duty of fighting. You are eating a crust of bread, and a man is shot dead in the trench next to you. You look calmly at him for a moment, and then go on eating your bread. Why not? There is nothing to be done. In the end you talk of your own death with as little excitement as you would of a luncheon engagement. There is nothing left in your mind but the fact that hordes of men to whom you belong are fighting against other hordes, and your side must win. . . .

It was there and then that I made a curious observation. After the second day we had almost grown to know each other. The Russians would laughingly call over to us, and the Austrians would answer. The salient feature of these three days' fighting was the extraordinary lack of hatred. In fact, it is astonishing how little actual hatred exists between fighting men. One fights fiercely and passionately, mass against mass, but as soon as the mass crystallizes itself into human individuals whose features one actually can recognize, hatred almost ceases. Of course, fighting continues, but somehow it loses its fierceness and takes more the form of a sport, each side being eager to get the best of the other. One still shoots at his opponent, but almost regrets when he sees him drop.

ALL QUIET ON THE WESTERN FRONT

II. ERICH MARIA REMARQUE

We must look out for our bread. The rats have become much more numerous lately because the trenches are no longer in good condition. Detering says it is a sure sign of a coming bombardment.

The rats here are particularly repulsive, they are so fat—the kind we call corpse-rats. They have shocking, evil, naked faces, and it is nauseating to see their long, nude tails.

They seem to be mighty hungry. Almost every man has had his bread gnawed. Kropp wrapped his in his waterproof sheet and put it under his head, but he cannot sleep because they run over his face to get it. Detering meant to outwit them: he fastened a thin wire to the roof and suspended his bread from it. During the night when he switched on his pocket-torch he saw the wire swing to and fro. On the bread was riding a fat rat.

At last we put a stop to it. We cannot afford to throw the bread away, because then we should have nothing left to eat in the morning, so we carefully cut off the bits of bread that the animals have gnawed.

The slices we cut off are heaped together in the middle of the floor. Each man takes out his spade and lies down prepared to strike. Detering, Kropp, and Kat hold their pocket-torches ready.

After a few minutes we hear the first shuffling and tugging. It grows, now it is the sound of many little feet. Then the torches switch on and every man strikes at the heap, which scatters with a rush. The result is good. We toss the bits of rat over the parapet and again lie in wait.

Several times we repeat the process. At last the beasts get wise to it, or perhaps have scented the blood. They return no more. Nevertheless, before morning the remainder of the bread on the floor has been carried off.

In the adjoining sector they attacked two large cats and a dog, bit them to death and devoured them.

Next day there was an issue of Edamer cheese. Each man gets almost a quarter of a cheese. In one way that is all to the good, for Edamer is tasty—but in another way it is vile, because the fat red balls have long been a sign of a bad time coming. Our forebodings increase as rum is served out. We drink it of course; but are not greatly comforted. . . .

At night they send over gas. We expect the attack to follow and lie with our masks on, ready to tear them off as soon as the first shadow appears.

Dawn approaches without anything happening—only the everlasting, nerve-wracking roll behind the enemy lines, trains, trains, lorries [trucks], lorries; but what are they concentrating? Our artillery fires on it continually, but still it does not cease.

We have tired faces and avoid each other's eyes. "It will be like the Somme," says Kat gloomily. "There we were shelled steadily for seven days and nights." Kat has lost all his fun since we have been here, which is bad, for Kat is an old front-hog, and can smell what is coming. Only Tjaden seems pleased with the good rations and the rum; he thinks we might even go back to rest without anything happening at all.

It almost looks like it. Day after day passes. At night I squat in the listening-post. Above me the rockets and parachute-lights shoot up and float down again. I am cautious and tense, my heart thumps. My eyes turn again and again to the luminous dial of my watch; the hands will not budge. Sleep hangs on my eyelids, I work my toes in my boots in order to keep awake. Nothing happens till I am relieved;—only the everlasting rolling over there. Gradually we grow calmer and play skat and poker continually. Perhaps we will be lucky.

All day the sky is hung with observation balloons. There is a rumour that the enemy are going to put tanks over and use low-flying planes for the attack. But that interests us less than what we hear of the new flame-throwers.

We wake up in the middle of the night. The earth booms. Heavy fire is falling on us. We crouch into corners. We distinguish shells of every calibre.

Each man lays hold of his things and looks again every minute to reassure himself that they are still there. The dug-out heaves, the night roars and flashes. We look at each other in the momentary flashes of light, and with pale faces and pressed lips shake our heads. . . .

The days go by and the incredible hours follow one another as a matter of course. Attacks alternate with counter-attacks and slowly the dead pile up in the field of craters between the trenches. We are able to bring in most of the wounded that do not lie too far off. But many have long to wait and we listen to them dying.

For one of them we search two days in vain. He must be lying on his belly and unable to turn over. Otherwise it is hard to understand why we cannot find him; for it is only when a man has his mouth close to the ground that it is impossible to gauge the direction of his cry.

He must have been badly hit—one of those nasty wounds neither so severe that they exhaust the body at once and a man dreams on in a half-swoon, nor so light that a man endures the pain in the hope of becoming well again. Kat thinks he has either a broken pelvis or a shot through the spine. His chest cannot have been injured otherwise he would not have such strength to cry out. And if it were any other kind of wound it would be possible to see him moving.

He grows gradually hoarser. The voice is so strangely pitched that it seems to be everywhere. The first night some of our fellows go out three times to look for him. But when they think they have located him and crawl across, next time they hear the voice it seems to come from somewhere else altogether.

We search in vain until dawn. We scrutinized the field all day with glasses, but discover nothing. On the second day the calls are fainter; that will be because his lips and mouth have become dry.

Our Company Commander has promised next turn of leave with three days extra to anyone who finds him. That is a powerful inducement, but we would do all that is possible without that for his cry is terrible. Kat and Kropp even go out in the afternoon, and Albert gets the lobe of his ear shot off in consequence. It is to no purpose, they come back without him.

It is easy to understand what he cries. At first he called only for help—the second night he must have had some delirium, he talked to his wife and his children, we often detected the name Elise. Today he merely weeps. By evening the voice dwindles to a croaking. But it persists still through the whole night. We hear it so distinctly because the wind blows toward our line. In the morning when we suppose he must already have long gone to his rest, there comes across to us one last gurgling rattle.

The days are hot and the dead lie unburied. We cannot fetch them all in, if we did we should not know what to do with them. The shells will bury them. Many have their bellies swollen up like balloons. They hiss, belch, and make movements. The gases in them make noises.

The sky is blue and without clouds. In the evening it grows sultry and the heat rises from the earth. When the wind blows toward us it brings the smell of blood, which is very heavy and sweet. This deathly exhalation from the shell-holes seems to be a mixture of chloroform and putrefaction, and fills us with nausea and retching. . . .

• • •

Suddenly the shelling begins to pound again. Soon we are sitting up once more with the rigid tenseness of blank anticipation.

Attack, counter-attack, charge, repulse—these are words, but what things they signify! We have lost a good many men, mostly recruits. Reinforcements have again been sent up to our sector. They are one of the new regiments, composed almost entirely of young fellows just called up. They have had hardly any training, and are sent into the field with only a theoretical knowledge. They do know what a hand-grenade is, it is true, but they have very little idea of cover, and what is most important of all, have no eye for it. A fold in the ground has to be quite eighteen inches high before they can see it.

Although we need reinforcement, the recruits give us almost more trouble than they are worth. They are helpless in this grim fighting area, they fall like flies. Modern trench-warfare demands knowledge and experience; a man must have a feeling for the contours of the ground, an ear for the sound and character of the shells, must be able to decide beforehand where they will drop, how they will burst, and how to shelter from them.

The young recruits of course know none of these things. They get killed simply because they hardly can tell shrapnel from high-explosive, they are mown down because they are listening anxiously to the roar of the big coal-boxes falling in the rear, and miss the light, piping whistle of the low spreading daisy-cutters. They flock together like sheep instead of scattering, and even the wounded are shot down like hares by the airmen.

Their pale turnip faces, their pitiful clenched hands, the fine courage of these poor devils, the desperate charges and attacks made by the poor brave wretches, who are so terrified that they dare not cry out loudly, but with battered chests, with torn bellies, arms and legs only whimper softly for their mothers and cease as soon as one looks at them.

Their sharp, downy, dead faces have the awful expressionlessness of dead children.

It brings a lump into the throat to see how they go over, and run and fall. A man would like to spank them, they are so stupid, and to take them by the arm and lead them away from here where they have no business to be. They wear grey coats and trousers and boots, but for most of them the uniform is far too big, it hangs on their limbs, their shoulders are too narrow, their bodies too slight; no uniform was ever made to these childish measurements.

Between five and ten recruits fall to every old hand.

A surprise gas-attack carries off a lot of them. They have not yet learned what to do. We found one dug-out full of them, with blue heads and black lips. Some of them in a shell hole took off their masks too soon; they did not know that the gas lies longest in the hollows; when they saw others on top without masks they pulled theirs off too and swallowed enough to scorch their lungs. Their condition is hopeless, they choke to death with hemorrhages and suffocation. . . .

STUDY QUESTIONS

1. What was the mood at the outset of the war, and what caused it?
2. What were the main features of trench warfare for the troops involved? What would happen to people who managed to live through this experience?
3. What makes Remarque's writing so powerful? Why would people want to read a war novel of this sort?
4. What was new about warfare as Remarque and Kreisler describe it?
5. What were the wider implications of the fighting, for example for the political values of veterans after the war had ended? Can you see connections with some of the new political and cultural movements of the 1920s? If so, what are they?

ESSAY SUGGESTIONS

A. Was World War I a fundamentally new kind of war? Would its basic features recur in other contemporary wars?

B. How did the experiences and results of World War I affect Europe's relationship with the rest of the world?

C. In what ways did World War I shape major trends in the twentieth century?

31 SOLDIERS AND CIVILIANS IN WORLD WAR II

World War I was shocking to Westerners because of the huge number of casualties; the 1914–1918 war also had some important repercussions outside the West (notably in the Middle East, where it continued into the 1920s). But World War II was far more lethal and was much more genuinely a global conflict (or series of linked conflicts). World War II was a "total war," meaning all citizens were involved with the war effort. Because of this high level of participation, belligerent nations believed that civilians were fair targets for destruction. Only one-third of the casualties in World War II were soldiers; the majority was made up of civilian noncombatants living at home when the war came to them. This erasure of boundaries meant mechanized destruction affected almost everyone, albeit in differing ways.

For soldiers, World War II was much more mobile than it predecessor. In one of the most important battles, the Allies stormed the beaches of Normandy, France, in a surprise amphibious assault on June 6, 1944. A risky gamble, the meticulously planned invasion opened up a second front against the Germans in the European theater. The first selection is from an oral history given by an American soldier. Harold Baumgarten was a nineteen-year-old rifleman with the 116th Infantry who participated in the landing at Normandy.

Another difference between the two wars was the situation in East Asia and the Pacific. There had been no significant fighting in this area during World War I, but, between 1937 and 1945, a bitter "war without mercy," as one leading scholar put it, tore apart the Asia-Pacific region, destroying the lives of millions of Chinese, Japanese, Koreans, and Southeast Asians and leaving their countries in ruins. The second document comes from a collection of Japanese oral histories recorded by two American researchers at the end of the 1980s. Yamaoka Michiko, a high school student in Hiroshima in 1945, recalls the day the atomic bomb hit her city. Her vivid memories of the blast encourage us to ponder the larger meaning of World War II and the cost of total war.

A final document recalls the unspeakable Nazi destruction of Jews, Roma (formerly called Gypsies), Slavs, homosexuals, anti-Nazis, and anyone else deemed unnecessary for Hitler's Third Reich. The Holocaust resulted in the extermination of six million European Jews. Although many went to their deaths peacefully, not realizing what lay ahead of them, others rebelled and resisted. The third document reprints a manifesto of

Selection I from an interview drawn from oral-history project at the Eisenhower Center for American Studies in New Orleans in Douglas Brinkley, "D-Day: What They Saw When They Landed," *Time* 162 no. 22 (May 31, 2004). http://www.time.com/time/subscriber/covers/1101040531/tddbaumgarten.html (accessed May 19, 2010). Selection II from Haruko Taya Cook and Theodore F. Cook, eds., *Japan at War: An Oral History* (New York: New Press, 1992), pp. 384–387. Selection III from "Manifesto of the Jewish Resistance in Vilna" in J. Glatstein, I. Knox, and S. Margoshes, eds., *An Anthology of Holocaust Literature* (Philadelphia: The Jewish Publication Society, 1969), pp. 332–333.

the United Partisan Organization, a Jewish resistance group based in the ghetto in Vilna, Lithuania. After enduring two years of occupation and the deaths of more than 30,000 Jews, the group called for an uprising to avoid the complete liquidation of the ghetto. Ignored by most inhabitants, the group abandoned plans for armed resistance and shepherded hundreds of Jews through city sewers and into nearby forests where they continued to fight the Nazis and their collaborators alongside other partisans.

WORLD WAR II DOCUMENTS

I. HAROLD BAUMGARTEN REMEMBERS D-DAY IN NORMANDY, 1944

Having my college education and a good background in American history and wartime battles, I realized that it was not going to be easy, and I did not expect to come back alive. I wrote such to my sister in New York City—to get the mail before my parents and break the news gently to them when she received the telegram that I was no longer alive. . . .

At about 6:30 a.m., I saw the beach with its huge seawall at the foot of a massive bluff. An 88-mm shell landed right in the middle of the Landing Craft Assault [to] the side of us, and splinters of the boat, equipment and bodies were thrown into the air. Bullets were passing through the thin wooden sides of our vessel. The ramp was lowered, and the inner door was opened. A German machine gun trained on the opening took a heavy toll of lives. Many of my 30 buddies went down as they left the LCA.

I got a bullet through the top of my helmet first, and then as I waded through the deep water, a bullet aimed at my heart hit the receiver of my M-1 rifle. The water was being shot up all around me. Clarius Riggs, who left the assault boat in front of me, went under, shot to death. About 8 or 10 feet to my right, as we reached the dry sand, I heard a hollow thud, and I saw Private Robert Dittmar hold his chest and heard him yell, "I'm hit! I'm hit!" I hit the ground and watched him as he continued to go forward about 10 more yards. He tripped over a tank obstacle, and as he fell, his body made a complete turn, and he lay sprawled on the damp sand with his head facing the Germans, his face looking skyward. He seemed to be suffering from shock and was yelling, "Mother, Mom," as he kept rolling around on the sand.

There were three or four others wounded and dying right near him. Sergeant Clarence Roberson, from my boat team, had a gaping wound on the left side of his forehead. He was walking crazily in the water, without his helmet. Then I saw him get down on his knees and start praying with his rosary beads. At this moment, the Germans cut him in half with their deadly cross fire. I saw the reflection from the helmet of one of the snipers and took aim, and later on, I found out, I got a bull's-eye on him. It was my only time that rifle fired—due to the bullet that hit my rifle. It must have shattered the wood, and the rifle broke in half, and I had to throw it away.

Shells were continually landing all about me in a definite pattern, and when I raised my head up to curse the Germans in the pillbox on our right flank who were continually shooting up the sand in front of me, one of the fragments from an 88-mm shell hit me in my left cheek. It felt like being hit with a baseball bat, only the results were much worse. My upper jaw was shattered; the left cheek was blown open. My upper lip was cut in half. I washed my face out in the cold, dirty Channel water and managed somehow not to pass out. I got rid of most of my equipment. Here I was happy that I did not wear the invasion jacket. I wore a regular Army zippered field jacket, with a Star of David drawn on the back and THE BRONX, NEW YORK written on it. Had I worn the invasion jacket, I probably would have drowned.

The water was rising about an inch a minute as the tide was coming in, so I had to get moving or drown. I had to reach a 15-foot seawall, which appeared to be 200 yards in front of me. Finally, I came to dry sand, and there was only another 100 yards or maybe less to go, and I started across the sand, crawling very fast. The Germans in the pillbox on the right flank were shooting up the sand all about me. I expected a bullet to rip through me at any moment. I reached the stone wall without further injury. I was now safe from the flat-trajectory weapons of the enemy. All I had to fear now were enemy mines and artillery shells.

Things looked pretty black and one-sided until Brigadier General Norman D. Cota rallied us by capturing some men himself and running around the beach with a hand grenade and a pistol in his hand. [He] ran down the beach under fire and sent a call for reinforcements. Every man who could walk and fire a weapon charged up the hill later on in the day toward the enemy. I got hit in the left foot while crawling by a mine.

At the end of June 6, we were only in about half a mile. As the evening progressed, I felt like I was getting very weak, and along the way, I got another bullet through the face again. I was starting to feel very weak from all that bleeding. As it got dark, I became very trigger happy, and anything that moved in front of me, I started to fire at.

About 3 a.m., I found myself lying near a road above the bluffs in the vicinity south of Vierville. I got an ambulance to stop by firing [in its direction], and it stopped, and two men came out and asked if I could sit up in the ambulance. [Later] they took me out and put me in a stretcher, and I saw a huge statue. I think later on, in retrospect, it was a church near the beach, silhouetted in the darkness. The next morning I saw the German prisoners marching by me. The 175th Infantry Regiment apparently landed around that time, and German snipers opened up on the beach, including the wounded. I got shot in my right knee in the stretcher. I had received five individual wounds that day in Normandy. The 1st Battalion of the 116th Infantry was more or less sacrificed to achieve the landing and was completely wiped out. It was a total sacrifice.

II. YAMAOKA MICHIKO REMEMBERS HIROSHIMA, 1945

That year, on August 6, I was in the third year of girls' high school, fifteen years old. I was an operator at the telephone exchange. We had been mobilized from school for various work assignments for more than a year. My assigned place of duty was civilian, but we, too, were expected to protect the nation. We were tied by strong bonds to the country. We'd heard the news about the Tokyo and Osaka bombings, but nothing had dropped on Hiroshima. Japan was winning. So we still believed. We only had to endure. I wasn't particularly afraid when B-29s flew overhead.

That morning I left the house at about 7:45. I heard that the B-29s had already gone home. Mom told me, "Watch out, the B-29s might come again." My house was 1.3 kilometers from the hypocenter. My place of work was 500 meters from the hypocenter. I walked toward the hypocenter in an area where all the houses and buildings had been deliberately demolished for fire breaks. There was no shade. I had on a white shirt and *monpe* [trousers]. As I walked there, I noticed middle-school students pulling down houses at a point about 800 meters away from the hypocenter. I heard the faint sound of planes as I approached the river. The planes were tricky. Sometimes they only pretended to leave. I could still hear the very faint sound of planes. Today, I have no hearing in my left ear because of damage from the blast. I thought, how strange, so I put my right hand above my eyes and looked up to see if I could spot them. The sun was dazzling. That was the moment.

There was no sound. I felt something strong. It was terribly intense. I felt colors. It wasn't heat. You can't really say it was yellow, and it wasn't blue. At that moment I thought I would be the only one who would die. I said to myself, "Goodbye, Mom."

They say temperatures of seven thousand degrees centigrade hit me. You can't really say it washed over me. It's hard to describe. I simply fainted. I remember my body floating in the air. That was probably the blast, but I don't know how far I was blown. When I came to my senses, my surroundings were silent. There was no wind. I saw a slight threadlike light, so I felt I must be alive. I was under stones. I couldn't move my body. I heard voices crying, "Help! Water!" It was then I realized I wasn't the only one. I couldn't really see around me. I tried to say something, but my voice wouldn't come out.

"Fire! Run away! Help! Hurry Up!" They weren't voices but moans of agony and despair. "I have to get help and shout," I thought. The person who rescued me was Mom, although she herself had been buried under our collapsed house. Mom knew the route I'd been taking. She came, calling out to me. I heard her voice and cried for help. Our surroundings were already starting to burn. Fires burst out from just the light itself. It didn't really drop. It just flashed.

It was beyond my mother's ability. She pleaded, "My daughter's buried here, she's been helping you, working for the military." She convinced soldiers nearby to help her and they started to dig me out. The fire was now blazing. "Woman, hurry up, run away from here," soldiers called. From underneath the stones I heard the crackling of flames. I called to her, "It's all right. Don't worry about me. Run away." I really didn't mind dying for the sake of the nation. Then they pulled me out by my legs.

Nobody there looked like human beings. Until that moment I thought incendiary bombs had fallen. Everyone was stupefied. Humans had lost the ability to speak. People couldn't scream, "It hurts!" even when they were on fire. People didn't say, "It's hot!" They just sat catching fire.

My clothes were burnt and so was my skin. I was in rags. I had braided my hair, but now it was like a lion's mane. There were people, barely breathing, trying to push their intestines back in. People with their legs wrenched off. Without heads. Or with faces burned and swollen out of shape. The scene I saw was a living hell.

Mom didn't say anything when she saw my face and I didn't feel any pain. She just squeezed my hand and told me to run. She was going to go rescue my aunt. Large numbers of people were moving away from the flames. My eyes were still able to see, so I made my way towards the mountain, where there was no fire, toward Hijiyama. On this flight I saw a friend of mine from the phone exchange. She'd been inside her house and wasn't burned. I called her name, but she didn't respond. My face was so swollen she couldn't tell who I was. Finally, she recognized my voice. She said, "Miss Yamaoka, you look like a monster!" That's the first time I heard that word. I looked at my hands and saw my own skin hanging down and the red flesh exposed. I didn't realize my face was swollen up because I was unable to see it.

The only medicine was *tempura* oil. I put it on my body myself. I lay on the concrete for hours. My skin was now flat, not puffed up anymore. One or two layers had peeled off. Only now did it become painful. A scorching sky was overhead. The flies swarmed over me and covered my wounds, which were already festering. People were simply left lying around. When their faint breathing became silent, they'd say, "This one's dead," and put the body in a pile of corpses. Some called for water, and if they got it, they died immediately.

Mom came looking for me again. That's why I'm alive today. I couldn't walk anymore. I couldn't see anymore. I was carried on a stretcher as far as Ujina, and then from there to an island where evacuees were taken. On the boat there I heard voices saying, "Let them drink water if they want. They'll die either way." I drank a lot of water.

I spent the next year bedridden. All my hair fell out. When we went to relatives' houses later they wouldn't even let me in because they feared they'd catch the disease. There was neither treatment nor assistance for me. Those people who had money, people who had both parents, people who had houses, they could go to the Red Cross Hospital or the Hiroshima City Hospital. They could get operations. But we didn't have any money. It was just my Mom and I. Keloids covered my face, my neck. I couldn't even move my neck. One eye was hanging down. I was unable to control my drooling because my lip had been burned off. I couldn't get any treatments at a hospital, so my mother gave me massages. Because she did that for me, my keloids aren't as bad as they would have been. My fingers were all stuck together. I couldn't move them. The only thing I could do was sew shorts, since I only needed to sew a straight line. I had to do something to earn money.

The Japanese government just told us we weren't the only victims of the war. There was no support or treatment. It was probably harder for my Mom. Once she told me she tried to choke me to death. If a girl has terrible scars, a face you couldn't be born with, I understand that even a mother could want to kill her child. People threw stones at me and called me Monster. That was before I had my many operations. I only showed this side of my face, the right hand side, when I had to face someone. Like I'm sitting now.

A decade after the bomb, we went to America. I was one of the twenty-five selected by Norman Cousins [a magazine editor] to be brought to America for treatment and plastic surgery. We were called the Hiroshima Maidens. The American government opposed us, arguing that it would be acknowledging a mistake if they admitted us to America, but we were supported by many civilian groups.

We went to Mount Sinai Hospital in New York and spent about a year and a half undergoing treatment. I improved tremendously. I've now had thirty-seven operations, including efforts at skin grafts.

When I went to America I had a deep hatred toward America. I asked myself why they ended the war by a means which destroyed human beings. When I talked about how I suffered, I was often told, "Well, you attacked Pearl Harbor!" I didn't understand much English then, and it's probably just as well. From the American point of view, they dropped that bomb in order to end the war faster, in order to create more damage faster. But it's inexcusable to harm human beings in this way. I wonder what kind of education there is now in America about atomic bombs. They're still making them, aren't they?

III. MANIFESTO OF JEWISH RESISTANCE IN VILNA, 1943

Offer armed resistance! Jews, defend yourselves with arms!

The German and Lithuanian executioners are at the gates of the ghetto. They have come to murder us! Soon they will lead you forth in groups through the ghetto door.

In the same way they carried away hundreds of us on the day of Yom Kippur. In the same way those with white, yellow and pink *Schein* [passes] were deported during the night. In this way our brothers, sisters, mothers, fathers and sons were taken away.

Tens of thousands of us were despatched. But we shall not go! We will not offer our heads to the butcher like sheep.

Jews, defend yourselves with arms!

Do not believe the false promises of the assassins or believe the words of the traitors.

Anyone who passes through the ghetto gate will go to Ponar [a wooded area outside the city where most of the killings had taken place]!

And Ponar means death!

Jews, we have nothing to lose. Death will overtake us in any event. And who can still believe in survival when the murderer exterminates us with so much determination? The hand of the executioner will reach each man and woman. Flight and acts of cowardice will not save our lives.

Active resistance alone can save our lives and our honor.

Brothers! It is better to die in battle in the ghetto than to be carried away to Ponar like sheep. And know this: within the walls of the ghetto there are organized Jewish forces who will resist with weapons.

Support the revolt!

Do not take refuge or hide in the bunkers, for then you will fall into the hands of the murderers like rats.

Jewish people, go out into the squares. Anyone who has no weapons should take an ax, and he who has no ax should take a crowbar or a bludgeon!

For our ancestors!

For our murdered children!

Avenge Ponar!

Attack the murderers!

In every street, in every courtyard, in every house within and without the ghetto, attack these dogs!

Jews, we have nothing to lose! We shall save our lives only if we exterminate our assassins.

Long live liberty! Long live armed resistance! Death to the assassins!

The Commander [of the United Partisan Organization]
Vilna, the Ghetto, September 1, 1943

STUDY QUESTIONS

1. What features of D-Day stand out in Baumgarten's memory? How typical might his experience have been compared with that of others participating in the invasion?
2. What memories of the atomic blast are important to Yamaoka? How does her testimony reveal important aspects of life in wartime Japan?
3. According to Yamaoka, was the dropping of the atomic bombs on Hiroshima and Nagasaki justified by the attack on the military base at Pearl Harbor? Do you agree? Why or why not?
4. What actions did the Jewish resistance leaders in Vilna recommend? Considering the might of the Nazi army and its commitment to exterminate all Jews, what chances did resistance groups have for success? Describe the range of options open to Jews in Nazi-occupied countries.
5. Considering the three sources, construct a definition of *heroism* and think about how to define *victory.* How should people define these key terms when discussing World War II?
6. Using this and the previous chapter, discuss the defining features of *modern* war.

THE ARCHITECTURE OF COMMEMORATION

Remains of the Industrial Promotion Hall, Hiroshima, 1985. (Stephen S. Gosch)

Beginning in 1946, the survivors of the atomic blast over Hiroshima, now known as *hibakusha*, turned to the issue of commemoration. They decided to hold a Peace Memorial Ceremony each August 6. On the first anniversary of the blast, sirens sounded throughout the city and people stood in silence for one minute. Since that time, similar ceremonies have been held annually. The survivors also decided to construct a park dedicated to world peace in the center of the city at approximately ground zero, where, despite the force of the blast, the Hiroshima Industrial Promotion Hall had mostly survived. The park, the Peace Memorial Museum, and several memorials to the victims now surround the stark remains of the Industrial Promotion Hall.

STUDY QUESTIONS

1. How would the reactions of Japanese and American visitors to this site likely differ? What might their responses have in common?
2. How would Chinese and Korean visitors to the site be likely to react to it?
3. What is the difference between a peace memorial and a war memorial?

ESSAY SUGGESTIONS

A. Although each of the selections here comes from a particular individual relating a personal experience, how do the sources work together to create an overall image of the ways World War II was fought and what it was like to live through it? Why are oral histories valuable sources?

B. What were the main similarities and differences between World War I and World War II?

C. Was the Holocaust simply a hideous aberration of Nazi policy, or does it also reflect aspects of the nature of modern war?

D. Considering the destruction of World War II, are there ways to discuss how, and by whom, total war might be limited?

32 THE COLD WAR

In 1946, Winston Churchill, the former prime minister of Britain, delivered a commencement speech at an American college in which he coined the term "iron curtain" to describe the barriers between Communist societies in Europe and what would become known as the "free world." With this speech, the recognition of the emerging Cold War advanced. Joseph Stalin, leader of the Soviet Union, replied to the speech, making counteraccusations.

The Cold War had been building for some time. After the Russian Revolution, countries including Britain and the United States attempted intervention and long opposed the apparent threat of communism. Churchill, as a conservative politician in Britain, was firm in his opposition to the revolutionary regime, although he also warned of the Nazi threat. Western hostility helped persuade Stalin, in 1939, to briefly join with Germany.

Then came Adolf Hitler's attack on Russia, and for several years, the Soviets, British, and Americans were united against the Axis powers. Negotiations toward a postwar settlement, however, revealed increasing differences, with the Soviets eager to extend communism and set up a buffer zone in Eastern Europe and Churchill and the American leaders equally eager to resist. By 1946, Soviets' actions to increase Communist power in the East European countries they occupied, including their zone in Germany, seemed increasingly ominous. Soon, American-led responses, backed by Britain, would seek to bolster the rest of Europe against the Soviet threat. The Cold War was on.

The first two documents in this chapter derive from the Churchill speech, entitled "The Sinews of Peace," and Stalin's reply (which, among other things, reminded Churchill that he had been voted out of office in Britain after his wartime leadership).

The second set of documents comes from a later crisis point in the Cold War, with Dwight Eisenhower as American president and Nikita Khrushchev as Soviet leader. The Soviets had shot down a high-altitude American spy plane that was violating Soviet airspace. The Soviets and the American-led West were still at odds, the Cold War was in many ways as polarized and dangerous as before, but the rhetoric had evolved in interesting ways.

Historians have been debating the nature of the Cold War for several decades. At first, American scholars largely blamed Soviet aggression. But a revisionist school, emerging in the 1960s, wondered if American actions had not been at least as significant in drawing lines and mounting confrontations that were not necessary.

The Cold War divided much of the world for more than 40 years. It led to a massive arms race, whose implications are still important in the world today. It fueled several regional wars, including those in Korea, Vietnam, and, for the Soviets, Afghanistan. It ultimately exhausted the Soviet economy and challenged American vitality, until, with the Soviet collapse in 1989–1991, it drew to a close.

COLD WAR DOCUMENTS

I. THE CHURCHILL SPEECH

I can . . . allow my mind, with the experience of a lifetime, to play over the problems which beset us on the morrow of our absolute victory in arms, and to try to make sure with what strength I have that what has been gained with so much sacrifice and suffering shall be preserved for the future glory and safety of mankind.

The United States stands at this time at the pinnacle of world power. It is a solemn moment for the American Democracy. For with primacy in power is also joined an awe-inspiring accountability to the future. If you look around you, you must feel not only the sense of duty done but also you must feel anxiety lest you fall below the level of achievement. Opportunity is here now, clear and shining for both our countries. To reject it or ignore it or fritter it away will bring upon us all the long reproaches of the after-time. It is necessary that constancy of mind, persistency of purpose, and the grand simplicity of decision shall guide and rule the conduct of the English-speaking peoples in peace as they did in war. We must, and I believe we shall, prove ourselves equal to this severe requirement. . . .

What then is the over-all strategic concept which we should inscribe today? It is nothing less than the safety and welfare, the freedom and progress, of all the homes and families of all the men and women in all the lands. To give security to these countless homes, they must be shielded from the two giant marauders, war and tyranny. We all know the frightful disturbances in which the ordinary family is plunged when the curse of war swoops down upon the bread-winner and those for whom he works and contrives. The awful ruin of Europe, with all its vanished glories, and of large parts of Asia glares us in the eyes. When the designs of wicked men or the aggressive urge of mighty States dissolve over large areas the frame of civilized society, humble folk are confronted with difficulties with which they cannot cope. For them all is distorted, all is broken, even ground to pulp. . . .

Our supreme task and duty is to guard the homes of the common people from the horrors and miseries of another war. We are all agreed on that.

Our American military colleagues, after having proclaimed their "over-all strategic concept" and computed available resources, always proceed to the next step—namely, the method. Here again there is widespread agreement. A world organization has already been erected for the prime purpose of preventing war, UNO [United Nations], the successor of the League of Nations, with the decisive addition of the United States and all that means, is already at work. We must make sure that its work is fruitful, that it is a reality and not a sham, that it is a force for action, and not merely a frothing of words, that it is a true temple of peace in which the shields of many nations can some day be hung up, and not merely a cockpit in a Tower of Babel. Before we cast away the solid assurances of national armaments for self-preservation we must be certain that our temple is built, not upon shifting sands or quagmires, but upon the rock. Anyone can see with his eyes open that our path will be difficult and also long, but if we persevere together as we did in the two world wars—though not, alas, in the interval between them—I cannot doubt that we shall achieve our common purpose in the end. . . .

It would nevertheless be wrong and imprudent to entrust the secret knowledge or experience of the atomic bomb, which the United States, Great Britain, and Canada now share, to the world organization, while it is still in its infancy. It would be criminal madness to cast it adrift in this still agitated and un-united world. No one in any country has slept less well in their beds because this knowledge and the method and the raw materials to apply it, are at present largely retained in American hands. I do not believe we should all have slept so soundly had the positions been reversed and if some Communist or neo-Fascist State monopolized for the time being these dread agencies. The fear of them alone might easily have been used to enforce totalitarian systems upon the free democratic world, with consequences appalling to human imagination. God has willed that this shall not be and we have at least a breathing space to set our house in order before this peril has to be encountered: and even then, if no effort is spared, we should still possess so formidable a superiority as to impose effective deterrents upon its employment, or threat of employment, by others. Ultimately, when the essential brotherhood of man is truly embodied and expressed in a world organization with all the necessary practical safeguards to make it effective, these powers would naturally be confided to that world organization.

Now I come to the second danger of these two marauders which threatens the cottage, the home, and the ordinary people—namely, tyranny. We cannot be blind to the fact that the liberties enjoyed by individual citizens throughout the British Empire are not valid in a considerable number of countries, some of which are very powerful. In these States control is enforced upon the common people by various kinds of all-embracing police governments. The power of the State is exercised without restraint, either by dictators or by compact oligarchies operating through a privileged party and a political police. It is not our duty at this time when difficulties are so numerous to interfere forcibly in the internal affairs of countries which we have not conquered in war. But we must never cease to proclaim in fearless tones the great principles of freedom and the rights of man which are the joint inheritance of the English-speaking world and which through Magna Carta, the Bill of Rights, the Habeas Corpus, trial by jury, and the English common law find their most famous expression in the American Declaration of Independence.

All this means that the people of any country have the right, and should have the power by constitutional action, by free unfettered elections, with secret ballot, to choose or change the character or form of government under which they dwell; that freedom of speech and thought should reign; that courts of justice, independent of the executive, unbiased by any party, should administer laws which have received the broad assent of large majorities or are consecrated by time and custom. Here are the title deeds of freedom which should lie in every cottage home.

Here is the message of the British and American peoples to mankind. Let us preach what we practice—let us practice—what we preach. . . .

A shadow has fallen upon the scenes so lately lighted by the Allied victory. Nobody knows what Soviet Russia and its Communist international organization intends to do in the immediate future, or what are the limits, if any, to their expansive and proselytizing tendencies. I have a strong admiration and regard for the valiant Russian people and for my wartime comrade, Marshal Stalin. There is deep sympathy and goodwill in Britain—and I doubt not here also—towards the peoples of all the Russias and a resolve to persevere through many differences and rebuffs in establishing lasting friendships. We understand the Russian need to be secure on her western frontiers by the removal of all possibility of German aggression. We welcome Russia to her rightful place among the leading nations of the world. We welcome her flag upon the seas. Above all, we welcome constant, frequent and growing contacts between the Russian people and our own people on both sides of the Atlantic. It is my duty however, for I am sure you would wish me to state the facts as I see them to you, to place before you certain facts about the present position in Europe.

From Stettin in the Baltic to Trieste in the Adriatic, an iron curtain has descended across the Continent. Behind that line lie all the capitals of the ancient states of Central and Eastern Europe. Warsaw, Berlin, Prague, Vienna, Budapest, Belgrade, Bucharest and Sofia, all these famous cities and the populations around them lie in what I must call the Soviet sphere, and all are subject in one form or another, not only to Soviet influence but to a very high and, in many cases, increasing measure of control from Moscow. Athens alone—Greece with its immortal glories—is free to decide its future at an election under British, American and French observation. The Russian-dominated Polish Government has been encouraged to make enormous and wrongful inroads upon Germany, and mass expulsions of millions of Germans on a scale grievous and undreamed—of are now taking place. The Communist parties, which were very small in all these Eastern States of Europe, have been raised to pre-eminence and power far beyond their numbers and are seeking everywhere to obtain totalitarian control. Police governments are prevailing in nearly every case, and so far, except in Czechoslovakia, there is no true democracy. Turkey and Persia are both profoundly alarmed and disturbed at the claims which are being made upon them and at the pressure being exerted by the Moscow Government. An attempt is being made by the Russians in Berlin to build up a quasi-Communist party in their zone of Occupied Germany by showing special favors to groups of left-wing German leaders. At the end of the fighting last June, the American and British Armies withdrew westwards, in accordance with an earlier agreement, to a depth at some points of 150 miles upon a front of nearly four hundred miles, in order to allow our Russian allies to occupy this vast expanse of territory which the Western Democracies had conquered.

If now the Soviet Government tries, by separate action, to build up a pro-Communist Germany in their areas, this will cause new serious difficulties in the British and American zones, and will give the defeated Germans the power of putting themselves up to auction between the Soviets and the Western Democracies.

Whatever conclusions may be drawn from these facts—and facts they are—this is certainly not the Liberated Europe we fought to build up. Nor is it one which contains the essentials of permanent peace. . . .

In front of the iron curtain which lies across Europe are other causes for anxiety. In Italy the Communist Party is seriously hampered by having to support the Communist-trained Marshal Tito's claims to former Italian territory at the head of the Adriatic. Nevertheless the future of Italy hangs in the balance. Again one cannot imagine a regenerated Europe without a strong France. All my public life I have worked for a strong France and I never lost faith in her destiny, even in the darkest hours. I will not lose faith now. However, in a great number of countries, far from the Russian frontiers and throughout the world, Communist fifth columns are established and work in complete unity and absolute obedience to the directions they receive from the Communist center. Except in the British Commonwealth and in the United States where Communism is in its infancy, the Communist parties or fifth columns constitute a growing challenge and peril to Christian civilization. These are somber facts for anyone to have to recite on the morrow of a victory gained by so much splendid comradeship in arms and in the cause of freedom and democracy; but we should be most unwise not to face them squarely while time remains. . . .

From what I have seen of our Russian friends and Allies during the war, I am convinced that there is nothing they admire so much as strength, and there is nothing for which they have less respect than for weakness, especially military weakness. For that reason the old doctrine of a balance of power is unsound. We cannot afford, if we can help it, to work on narrow margins, offering temptations to a trial of strength. If the Western Democracies stand together in strict adherence to the principles of the United Nations Charter, their influence for furthering those principles will be immense and no one is likely to molest them. If however they become divided or falter in their duty and if these all-important years are allowed to slip away then indeed the catastrophe may overwhelm us all.

Last time I saw it all coming and cried aloud to my own fellow-countrymen and to the world, but no one paid any attention. Up till the year 1933 or even 1935, Germany might have been saved from the awful fate which has overtaken her and we might all have been spared the miseries Hitler let loose upon mankind. There never was a war in all history easier to prevent by timely action than the one which has just desolated such great areas of the globe. It could have been prevented in my belief without the firing of a single shot, and Germany might be powerful, prosperous and honored to-day; but no one would listen and one by one we were all sucked into the awful whirlpool. We surely must not let that happen again. This can only be achieved by reaching now, in 1946, a good understanding on all points with Russia under the general authority of the United Nations Organization and by the maintenance of that good understanding through many peaceful years, by the world instrument, supported by the whole strength of the English-speaking world and all its connections. There is the solution which I respectfully offer to you in this Address to which I have given the title "The Sinews of Peace."

II. JOSEPH STALIN'S REPLY

In substance, Mr. Churchill now stands in the position of a firebrand of war. And Mr. Churchill is not alone here. He has friends not only in England but also in the United States of America.

In this respect, one is reminded remarkably of Hitler and his friends. Hitler began to set war loose by announcing his racial theory, declaring that only people speaking the German language represent a fully valuable nation. Mr. Churchill begins to set war loose, also by a racial theory, maintaining that only nations speaking the English language are fully valuable nations, called upon to decide the destinies of the entire world.

The German racial theory brought Hitler and his friends to the conclusion that the Germans, as the only fully valuable nation, must rule over other nations. The English racial theory brings Mr. Churchill and his friends to the conclusion that nations speaking the English language, being the only fully valuable nations, should rule over the remaining nations of the world. . . .

As a result of the German invasion, the Soviet Union has irrevocably lost in battles with the Germans, and also during the German occupation and through the expulsion of Soviet citizens to German slave labor camps, about 7,000,000 people. In other words, the Soviet Union has lost in men several times more than Britain and the United States together.

It may be that some quarters are trying to push into oblivion these sacrifices of the Soviet people which ensured the liberation of Europe from the Hitlerite yoke.

But the Soviet Union cannot forget them. One can ask therefore, what can be surprising in the fact that the Soviet Union, in a desire to ensure its security for the future, tries to achieve that these countries should have governments whose relations to the Soviet Union are loyal? How can one, without having lost one's reason, qualify these peaceful aspirations of the Soviet Union as "expansionist tendencies" of our Government?

Mr. Churchill wanders around the truth when he speaks of the growth of the influence of the Communist parties in Eastern Europe. . . . The growth of the influence of communism cannot be considered accidental. It is a normal function. The influence of the Communists grew because during the hard years of the mastery of fascism in Europe, Communists showed themselves to be reliable, daring and self-sacrificing fighters against fascist regimes for the liberty of peoples.

Mr. Churchill sometimes recalls in his speeches the common people from small houses, patting them on the shoulder in a lordly manner and pretending to be their friend. But these people are not so simpleminded as it might appear at first sight. Common people, too, have their opinions and their own politics. And they know how to stand up for themselves.

It is they, millions of these common people, who voted Mr. Churchill and his party out in England, giving their votes to the Labor party. It is they, millions of these common people, who isolated reactionaries in Europe, collaborators with fascism, and gave preference to Left democratic parties.

III. NIKITA KHRUSHCHEV: SUMMIT CONFERENCE STATEMENT, PARIS, MAY 16, 1960

As is generally known, a provocative act by the American air force against the Soviet Union has recently taken place. It consisted in the fact that on May 1 of this year a U.S. military reconnaissance plane intruded into the U.S.S.R. on a definite espionage mission of gathering intelligence about military and industrial installations on Soviet territory. After the aggressive purpose of the plane's flight became clear, it was shot down by a Soviet rocket unit. Unfortunately, this is not the only instance of aggressive and espionage actions by the U.S. air force against the Soviet Union.

Naturally, the Soviet government was obliged to describe these actions by their proper name and show their perfidious character, inconsistent with the elementary requirements of normal peacetime relations between states, to say nothing of their conflicting grossly with the aim of reducing international tension and creating the conditions needed for fruitful work at the Summit conference. This was done both in my speeches at the session of the U.S.S.R. Supreme Soviet and in a special protest note sent to the U.S. government. . . .

It is natural that under these conditions we are unable to work at the conference, unable to work at it because we see from what positions it is desired to talk to us—under threat of aggressive intelligence flights. Everyone knows that spying flights are undertaken for intelligence purposes with a view to starting war. Accordingly, we reject the conditions in which the United States is placing us. We cannot take part in any negotiations, not even in the settlement of questions which are already ripe, because we see that the U.S. has no desire to reach agreement. . . .

We wish to be rightly understood by the peoples of all countries of the globe, by public opinion. The Soviet Union is not abandoning its efforts for agreement, and we are sure that reasonable agreements are possible, but evidently at some other, not this particular time. . . .

The Soviet government is profoundly convinced that if not this U.S. government, then another, and if not another, then a third, will understand that there is no other solution than peaceful co-existence of the two systems, the capitalist and the socialist. It is either peaceful co-existence, or war, which would spell disaster for those now engaging in an aggressive policy. . . .

[W]e firmly believe in the necessity of peaceful co-existence, for to lose faith in peaceful co-existence would mean dooming humanity to war, it would mean accepting that war *IS* inevitable—and everyone knows what calamities war today would spell for all the peoples of the globe. . . .

We regret that this Meeting has been torpedoed by the reactionary element in the United States as the outcome of provocative flights by American military planes over the Soviet Union.

We regret that this meeting has not led to the results which all the peoples of the world expected to follow from it.

Let the shame and blame for it fall on those who have proclaimed a brigand policy in relation to the Soviet Union. . . .

I think that both Mr. Eisenhower and the American people will understand me rightly.

The Soviet government declares that it for its part will continue to do everything in its power to promote the relaxation of international tension and the solution of the problems which today still divide us; in this we shall be guided by the interests of furthering the great cause of peace on the basis of the peaceful co-existence of states with differing social systems.

IV. DWIGHT EISENHOWER: SUMMIT CONFERENCE STATEMENT, PARIS, MAY 16, 1960

In my statement of May 11th and in the statement of Secretary Herter of May 9th the position of the United States was made clear with respect to the distasteful necessity of espionage activities in a world where nations distrust each other's intentions. We pointed out that these activities had no aggressive intent but rather were to assure the safety of the United States and the free world against surprise attack by a power which boasts of its ability to devastate the United States and other countries by missiles armed with atomic warheads. . . .

There is in the Soviet statement an evident misapprehension on one key point. It alleges that the United States has, through official statements, threatened continued over flights. The importance of this alleged threat was emphasized and repeated by Mr. Khrushchev. The United States has made no such threat. Neither I nor my Government has intended any. The actual statements go no further than to say that the United States will not shirk its responsibility to safeguard against surprise attack.

In point of fact, these flights were suspended after the recent incident and are not to be resumed. Accordingly, this cannot be the issue.

I have come to Paris to seek agreements with the Soviet Union which would eliminate the necessity for all forms of espionage, including over flights. I see no reason to use this incident to disrupt the conference.

Should it prove impossible, because of the Soviet attitude, to come to grips here in Paris with this problem and the other vital issues threatening world peace, I am planning in the near future to submit to the United Nations a proposal for the creation of a United Nations aerial surveillance to detect preparations for attack. This plan I had intended to place before this conference. This surveillance system would operate in the territories of all nations prepared to accept such inspection. For its part, the United States is prepared not only to accept United Nations aerial surveillance but to do everything in its power to contribute to the rapid organization and successful operation of such international surveillance.

We of the United States are here to consider in good faith the important problems before this conference. We are prepared either to carry this point no further or to undertake bilateral conversations between the United States and the U.S.S.R. while the main conference proceeds.

Mr. Khrushchev brushed aside all arguments of reason and not only insisted upon this ultimatum but also insisted that he was going to publish his statement in full at the time of his own choosing. It was thus made apparent that he was determined to wreck the Paris conference. . . .

In spite of this serious and adverse development I have no intention whatsoever to diminish my continuing efforts to promote progress toward a peace with Justice. This applies to the remainder of my stay in Paris as well as thereafter.

STUDY QUESTIONS

1. How does Churchill define the iron curtain and the Soviet threat? What does he propose to resist this threat?
2. How did Stalin defend Soviet actions? How would he have explained the growing tension with the West?
3. Judging by the Churchill and Stalin speeches, who was responsible for the Cold War? Was one side more involved than the other? If so, how?
4. What prompted the 1960 crisis? How did both American and Russian leaders avoid outright war?
5. How did Khrushchev's rhetoric compare with that of Stalin? Eisenhower's with that of Churchill? What were the major Cold War issues by this point?
6. How did the experience and results of the two world wars help shape the Cold War?

ESSAY SUGGESTIONS

A. Why and how did some societies seek to avoid engagement in the Cold War?
B. Using these documents and other materials, discuss why the Cold War did not lead to real, all-out war between the two sides.

33 EUROPE AND THE SOVIET UNION

FASCISM AND NAZISM

Political change, worldwide, has been a hallmark of contemporary world history, with the decline of monarchy and the surge of revolutionary and nationalist movements. Several political forms have provided more modern replacements, including, of course, democracy and communism but also new forms of authoritarianism. Of these, fascist regimes may be seen as a particularly extreme example.

Along with the communist state, the rise of the fascist state was one of the most striking political innovations of the twentieth century. Fascism and its Nazi counterpart generated new claims about state power and attacks on the parliamentary tradition. Actual fascist states emerged in parts of western and central Europe where the liberal tradition was relatively weak, and often where the shocks of World War I were particularly great. But the movement had wider appeal, with significant political efforts in places in France. And while fascism was largely eliminated after German and Italian defeats in World War I, some overtones lingered both in Europe and other parts of the world.

The first passage was written by Benito Mussolini (1883–1945) and an intellectual collaborator, Giovanni Gentile, for an encyclopedia entry on fascism, in 1932. Mussolini had formed the fascist movement earlier in the twentieth century, gained significant support after World War I, and came to power in Italy in 1922.

The second passage comes from Adolf Hitler's *Mein Kampf*, his great battle cry written in 1924. Like Mussolini, Hitler gained new attention during the 1920s, but his Nazi, or National Socialist, movement made slower progress, coming to power only after the severe impact of the Great Depression.

MUSSOLINI AND HITLER

I. MUSSOLINI ON FASCISM (1932)

Fascism, the more it considers and observes the future and the development of humanity quite apart from political considerations of the moment, believes neither in the possibility nor the utility of perpetual peace. It thus repudiates the doctrine of Pacifism—born of a renunciation of the struggle and an act of cowardice in the face of sacrifice. War alone brings up to its highest tension all human energy and

Selection I excerpts from *Modern History Sourcebook: Mussolini: What Is Fascism, 1932,* retrieved from *http://www.fordham.edu/halsall/mod/mussolini-fascism.html,* copyright Paul Halsall, August 1997, *halsall@murray.fordham.edu.* Selection II excerpts from *Mein Kampf* by Adolf Hitler, translated by Ralph Manheim.

puts the stamp of nobility upon the peoples who have courage to meet it. All other trials are substitutes, which never really put men into position where they have to make the great decision—the alternative of life or death. . . .

. . . The Fascist accepts life and loves it, knowing nothing of and despising suicide: he rather conceives of life as duty and struggle and conquest, but above all for others—those who are at hand and those who are far distant, contemporaries, and those who will come after. . . .

. . . Fascism [is] the complete opposite of . . . Marxian Socialism, the materialist conception of history of human civilization can be explained simply through the conflict of interests among the various social groups and by the change and development in the means and instruments of production. . . . Fascism, now and always, believes in holiness and in heroism; that is to say, in actions influenced by no economic motive, direct or indirect. And if the economic conception of history be denied, according to which theory men are no more than puppets, carried to and fro by the waves of chance, while the real directing forces are quite out of their control, it follows that the existence of an unchangeable and unchanging class-war is also denied—the natural progeny of the economic conception of history. And above all Fascism denies that class-war can be the preponderant force in the transformation of society. . . .

After Socialism, Fascism combats the whole complex system of democratic ideology, and repudiates it, whether in its theoretical premises or in its practical application. Fascism denies that the majority, by the simple fact that it is a majority, can direct human society; it denies that numbers alone can govern by means of a periodical consultation, and it affirms the immutable, beneficial, and fruitful inequality of mankind, which can never be permanently leveled through the mere operation of a mechanical process such as universal suffrage . . . .

. . . Fascism denies, in democracy, the absur[d] conventional untruth of political equality dressed out in the garb of collective irresponsibility, and the myth of "happiness" and indefinite progress . . . .

. . . Given that the nineteenth century was the century of Socialism, of Liberalism, and of Democracy, it does not necessarily follow that the twentieth century must also be a century of Socialism, Liberalism and Democracy: political doctrines pass, but humanity remains, and it may rather be expected that this will be a century of authority . . . a century of Fascism. For if the nineteenth century was a century of individualism it may be expected that this will be the century of collectivism and hence the century of the State. . . .

The foundation of Fascism is the conception of the State, its character, its duty, and its aim. Fascism conceives of the State as an absolute, in comparison with which all individuals or groups are relative, only to be conceived of in their relation to the State. The conception of the Liberal State is not that of a directing force, guiding the play and development, both material and spiritual, of a collective body, but merely a force limited to the function of recording results: on the other hand, the Fascist State is itself conscious and has itself a will and a personality—thus it may be called the "ethic" State. . . .

. . . The Fascist State organizes the nation, but leaves a sufficient margin of liberty to the individual; the latter is deprived of all useless and possibly harmful freedom, but retains what is essential; the deciding power in this question cannot be the individual, but the State alone. . . .

. . . For Fascism, the growth of empire, that is to say the expansion of the nation, is an essential manifestation of vitality, and its opposite a sign of decadence. Peoples which are rising, or rising again after a period of decadence, are always imperialist; and renunciation is a sign of decay and of death. Fascism is the doctrine best adapted to represent the tendencies and the aspirations of a people, like the people of Italy, who are rising again after many centuries of abasement and foreign servitude. But empire demands discipline, the coordination of all forces and a deeply felt sense of duty and sacrifice: this fact explains many aspects of the practical working of the regime, the character of many forces in the State, and the necessarily severe measures which must be taken against those who would oppose this spontaneous and inevitable movement of Italy in the twentieth century, and would oppose it by recalling the outworn ideology of the nineteenth century—repudiated wheresoever there has been the courage to undertake great experiments of social and political transformation; for never before has the nation stood more in need of authority, of direction and order. If every age has its own characteristic doctrine, there are a thousand signs which point to Fascism as the characteristic doctrine of our time. For if a doctrine must be a living thing, this is proved by the fact that Fascism has created a living faith; and that this faith is very powerful in the minds of men is demonstrated by those who have suffered and died for it.

II. HITLER ON NAZISM (1924)

Anyone who believes today that a folkish National Socialist state must distinguish itself from other states only in a purely mechanical sense, by a superior construction of its economic life—that is, by a better balance between rich and poor, or giving broad sections of the population more right to influence the economic process, or by fairer wages by elimination of excessive wage differentials—has not gone beyond the most superficial aspects of the matter and has not the faintest idea of what we call a philosophy. All the things we have just mentioned offer not the slightest guaranty of continued existence, far less of any claim to greatness. A people which did not go beyond these really superficial reforms would not obtain the least guaranty of victory in the general struggle of nations. A movement which finds the content of its mission only in such a general leveling, assuredly just as it may be, will truly bring about no great and profound, hence real, reform of existing conditions, since its entire activity does not, in the last analysis, go beyond externals, and does not give the people that inner armament which enables it, with almost inevitable certainty I might say, to overcome in the end those weaknesses from which we suffer today. . . .

The folkish state must care for the welfare of its citizens by recognizing in all and everything the importance of the value of personality, thus in all fields preparing the way for that highest measure of productive performance which grants to the individual the highest measure of participation.

And accordingly, the folkish state must free all leadership and especially the highest—that is, the political leadership—entirely from the parliamentary principle of majority rule—in other words, mass rule—and instead absolutely guarantee the right of the personality.

From this the following realization results:

> The best state constitution and state form is that which, with the most unquestioned certainty, raises the best minds in the national community to leading position and leading influence.

But as, in economic life, the able men cannot be appointed from above, but must struggle through for themselves, and just as here the endless schooling, ranging from the smallest business to the largest enterprise, occurs spontaneously, with life alone giving the examinations, obviously political minds cannot be "discovered." Extraordinary geniuses permit of no consideration for normal mankind.

From the smallest community cell to the highest leadership of the entire Reich, the state must have the personality principle anchored in its organization.

There must be no majority decisions, but only responsible persons, and the word "council" must be restored to its original meaning. Surely every man will have advisers by his side, but *the decision will be made by one man.*

The principle which made the Prussian army in its time into the most wonderful instrument of the German people must some day, in a transferred sense, become the principle of the construction of our whole state conception: *authority of every leader downward and responsibility upward.*

Even then it will not be possible to dispense with those corporations which today we designate as parliaments. But their councillors will then actually give counsel; responsibility, however, can and may be borne only by *one* man, and therefore only he alone may possess the authority and right to command.

Parliaments as such are necessary, because in them, above all, personalities to which special responsible tasks can later be entrusted have an opportunity gradually to rise up.

This gives the following picture:

The folkish state, from the township up to the Reich leadership, has no representative body which decides anything by the majority, but only *advisory bodies* which stand at the side of the elected leader, receiving their share of work from him, and in turn if necessary assuming unlimited responsibility in certain fields, just as on a larger scale the leader or chairman of the various corporations himself possesses.

As a matter of principle, the folkish state does not tolerate asking advice or opinions in special matters—say, of an economic nature—of men who, on the basis of their education and activity, can understand nothing of the subject. It, therefore, divides its representative bodies from the start into *political and professional chambers.*

In order to guarantee a profitable cooperation between the two, a special *senate* of the élite always stands above them.

In no chamber and in no senate does a vote ever take place. They are working institutions and not voting machines. The individual member has an advisory, but never a determining, voice. The latter is the exclusive privilege of the responsible chairman.

This principle—absolute responsibility unconditionally combined with absolute authority—will gradually breed an élite of leaders such as today, in this era of irresponsible parliamentarianism, is utterly inconceivable.

Thus, the political form of the nation will be brought into agreement with that law to which it owes its greatness in the cultural and economic field.

. . .

As regards the possibility of putting these ideas into practice, I beg you not to forget that the parliamentary principle of democratic majority rule has by no means always dominated mankind, but on the contrary is to be found only in brief periods of history, which are always epochs of the decay of peoples and states.

But it should not be believed that such a transformation can be accomplished by purely theoretical measures from above, since logically it may not even stop at the state constitution, but must permeate all other legislation, and indeed all civil life. Such a fundamental change can and will only take place through a movement which is itself constructed in the spirit of these ideas and hence bears the future state within itself.

Hence the National Socialist movement should today adapt itself entirely to these ideas and carry them to practical fruition within its own organization, so that some day it may not only show the state these same guiding principles, but can also place the completed body of its own state at its disposal.

STUDY QUESTIONS

1. Why did fascists and Nazis attack democracy and parliamentary rule? What were their basic objections?
2. What were the main similarities between fascist and Nazi ideas of the state? Were there any differences in approach? If so, what were they?
3. What were the military and diplomatic implications of fascism?
4. Both fascism and Nazism came to power in part through manipulations, but both had strong popular followings. What explains the attractiveness of the fascist and Nazi movements?

ESSAY SUGGESTIONS

A. Did fascism have significant roots in Western political ideas, or was it simply a rejection of all Western political traditions?

B. Despite the defeat of fascism in World War II, did the movement leave any subsequent legacy in European or world history?

34 POLITICAL AND SOCIAL CHANGE IN EUROPE

COMMUNIST RULE IN RUSSIA

Chapters in this section cover crucial developments in Europe between the world wars, with implications beyond. The Russian Revolution led to the introduction of a new, Communist-dominated state in Russia itself and a worldwide Communist movement. The rise of fascism, including its Nazi variant in Germany, was another striking political development. Both movements raise questions about the political impact of World War I and the extent to which more traditional political values in Europe were being replaced. Finally, the 1920s also saw a further development of consumerism, which would prove to be one of the strongest global forces in the twentieth century, but also a set of values and behaviors that generated strong criticisms as well as obvious attractions.

This chapter focuses on the upheaval in Russia. The first two selections trace key aspects of the Russian Revolution of 1917 and the consolidation of the Soviet state under the leadership of Lenin and Stalin. Documents issued by Lenin allow assessment of some of the motives of communist revolutionaries and reasons for their appeal but also the evolution of Lenin's emphases once he attained power. Stalin, taking over after Lenin's death, maintained some similar arguments but somewhat altered the focus and justification.

The final document provides a different view of Leninism and Stalinism. It is from 1926: a petition to the Communist Party detailing conditions in a concentration camp for political prisoners. The document suggests a revealing faith in basic revolutionary principles as well as a stinging condemnation of the results of repression. The year 1917 brought momentous change to Russia. The Romanov dynasty and the landlord class, each of which had deep roots in Russian history, were swept away forever. But the victorious Bolshevik revolutionaries did not seek to establish a Western-style, middle-class society. Instead, they proclaimed socialism and communism as their goals.

Lenin (Vladimir Ilych Ulyanov, 1870–1924) was the indefatigable leader of the Bolshevik Party and the first head of the new Soviet regime. His death in 1924 left a huge void at the head of the Soviet government. Gradually, however, over the next several years,

Joseph V. Stalin (1879–1953) emerged as the dominant force in the revolutionary regime. By the late 1920s, Stalin was firmly in charge. The result was a "second revolution" during the following decade. Evidence of Stalin's goals emerge in a speech he made to a conference of Soviet business executives in 1931, as he proclaimed a "revolution from above" and an all-out drive to industrialize the economy and to make agriculture a collective process. His approach also, however, deepened the repressive aspects of the Soviet regime.

LENIN'S WRITINGS, STALIN, AND A BITTER LEGACY

I. LENIN'S WRITINGS

Leading a Revolutionary Movement (1902)

I assert that it is far more difficult to unearth a dozen wise men than a hundred fools. This position I will defend, no matter how much you instigate the masses against me for my "anti-democratic" views, etc. As I have stated repeatedly, by "wise men," in connection with organisation, I mean *professional revolutionaries,* irrespective of whether they have developed from among students or working men. I assert: (1) that no revolutionary movement can endure without a stable organisation of leaders maintaining continuity; (2) that the broader the popular mass drawn spontaneously into the struggle, which forms the basis of the movement and participates in it, the more urgent the need for such an organisation, and the more solid this organisation must be (for it is much easier for all sorts of demagogues to side-track the more backward sections of the masses); (3) that such an organisation must consist chiefly of people professionally engaged in revolutionary activity; (4) that in an autocratic state, the more we *confine* the membership of such an organisation to people who are professionally engaged in revolutionary activity and who have been professionally trained in the art of combating the political police, the more difficult will it be to unearth the organisation; and (5) the *greater* will be the number of people from the working class and from the other social classes who will be able to join the movement and perform active work in it. . . .

Proclaiming the New Soviet Government (November 1917)

Comrades, the workers' and peasants' revolution, the need of which the Bolsheviks have emphasized many times, has come to pass.

What is the significance of this revolution? Its significance is, in the first place, that we shall have a soviet government, without the participation of bourgeoisie of any kind. The oppressed masses will of themselves form a government. The old state machinery will be smashed into bits and in its place will be created a new machinery of government by the soviet organizations. From now on there is a new page in the history of Russia, and the present, third Russian revolution shall in its final result lead to the victory of Socialism.

One of our immediate tasks is to put an end to the war [World War I] at once. But in order to end the war, which is closely bound up with the present capitalistic system, it is necessary to overthrow capitalism itself. In this work we shall have the aid of the world labor movement, which has already begun to develop in Italy, England, and Germany.

In the interior of Russia a very large part of the peasantry has said: Enough playing with the capitalists; we will go with the workers. We shall secure the confidence of the peasants by one decree, which will wipe out the private property of the landowners. The peasants will understand that their own salvation is in union with the workers.

We will establish a real labor control on production.

We have now learned to work together in a friendly manner, as is evident from this revolution. We have the force of mass organization which has conquered all and which will lead the proletariat to world revolution.

We should now occupy ourselves in Russia in building up a proletarian socialist state.

Long live the world-wide socialistic revolution.

Modernizing Russia (1920)

The essential feature of the present political situation is that we are now passing through a crucial period of transition, something of a zigzag transition from war to economic development. This has occurred before, but not on such a wide scale. This should constantly remind us of what the general political tasks of the Soviet government are, and what constitutes the particular feature of this transition. The dictatorship of the proletariat has been successful because it has been able to combine compulsion with persuasion. The dictatorship of the proletariat does not fear any resort to compulsion and to the most severe, decisive and ruthless forms of coercion by the state. The advanced class, the class most oppressed by capitalism, is entitled to use compulsion, because it is doing so in the interests of the working and exploited people, and because it possesses means of compulsion and persuasion such as no former classes ever possessed, although they had incomparably greater material facilities for propaganda and agitation than we have.

. . .

We have, no doubt, learnt politics; here we stand as firm as a rock. But things are bad as far as economic matters are concerned. Henceforth, less politics will be the best politics. Bring more engineers and agronomists to the fore, learn from them, keep an eye on their work, and turn our congresses and conferences, not into propaganda meetings but into bodies that will verify our economic achievements, bodies in which we can really learn the business of economic development.

. . .

While we live in a small-peasant country, there is a firmer economic basis for capitalism in Russia than for communism. That must be borne in mind. Anyone who has carefully observed life in the countryside, as compared with life in the cities, knows that we have not torn up the roots of capitalism and have not undermined the foundation, the basis, of the internal enemy. The latter depends on small-scale production, and there is only one way of undermining it, namely, to place the economy of the country, including agriculture, on a new technical basis, that of modern large-scale production. Only electricity provides that basis.

Communism is Soviet power plus the electrification of the whole country. Otherwise the country will remain a small-peasant country, and we must clearly realise that. We are weaker than capitalism, not only on the world scale, but also within the country. That is common knowledge. We have realised it, and we shall see to it that the economic basis is transformed from a small-peasant basis into a large-scale industrial basis. Only when the country has been electrified, and industry, agriculture and transport have been placed on the technical basis of modern large-scale industry, only then shall we be fully victorious.

•••

I recently had occasion to attend a peasant festival held in Volokolamsk Uyezd, a remote part of Moscow Gubernia, where the peasants have electric lighting. A meeting was arranged in the street, and one of the peasants came forward and began to make a speech welcoming this new event in the lives of the peasants. "We peasants were unenlightened," he said, "and now light has appeared among us, an 'unnatural light, which will light up our peasant darkness.'" For my part, these words did not surprise me. Of course, to the non-Party peasant masses electric light is an "unnatural" light; but what we consider unnatural is that the peasants and workers should have lived for hundreds and thousands of years in such backwardness, poverty and oppression under the yoke of the landowners and the capitalists. You cannot emerge from this darkness very rapidly. What we must now try is to convert every electric power station we build into a stronghold of enlightenment to be used to make the masses electricity-conscious, so to speak.

II. STALIN SPEAKS IN 1931

About ten years ago a slogan was issued: "Since Communists do not yet properly understand the technique of production, since they have yet to learn the art of management, let the old technicians and engineers—the experts—carry on production, and you, Communists, do not interfere with the technique of the business; but, while not interfering, study technique, study the art of management tirelessly, in order, together with the experts who are loyal to us, to become true managers of production, true masters of the business." Such was the slogan. But what actually happened? The second part of this formula was cast aside, for it is harder to study than to sign papers; and the first part of the formula was vulgarised: non-interference was interpreted to mean refraining from studying the technique of production. The result has been nonsense, harmful and dangerous nonsense, which the sooner we discard the better. . . .

It is time, high time that we turned towards technique. It is time to discard the old slogan, the obsolete slogan of non-interference in technique, and ourselves become specialists, experts, complete masters of our economic affairs. . . .

This, of course, is no easy matter; but it can certainly be accomplished. Science, technical experience, knowledge, are all things that can be acquired. We may not have them today, but tomorrow we shall. The main thing is to have the passionate Bolshevik desire to master technique, to master the science of production. Everything can be achieved, everything can be overcome, if there is a passionate desire for it.

It is sometimes asked whether it is not possible to slow down the tempo somewhat, to put a check on the movement. No, comrades, it is not possible! The tempo must not be reduced! On the contrary, we must increase it as much as is within our powers and possibilities. . . .

To slacken the tempo would mean falling behind. And those who fall behind get beaten. But we do not want to be beaten. No, we refuse to be beaten! One feature of the history of old Russia was the continual beatings she suffered because of her backwardness. She was beaten by the Mongol khans. She was beaten by the Turkish boys. She was beaten by the Swedish feudal lords. She was beaten by the Polish and Lithuanian gentry. She was beaten by the British and French capitalists. She was beaten by the Japanese barons. All beat her—because of her backwardness, because of her military backwardness, cultural backwardness, political backwardness, industrial backwardness, agricultural backwardness. They beat her because to do so was profitable and could be done with impunity. You remember the words of the pre-revolutionary poet: "You are poor and abundant, mighty and impotent, Mother Russia." Those gentlemen were quite familiar with the verses of the old poet. They beat her, saying: "You are abundant," so one can enrich oneself at your expense. They beat her, saying: "You are poor and impotent," so you can be beaten and plundered with impunity. Such is the law of the exploiters—to beat the backward and the weak. It is the jungle law of capitalism. You are backward, you are weak—therefore you are wrong; hence you can be beaten and enslaved. You are mighty—therefore you are right; hence we must be wary of you.

That is why we must no longer lag behind.

In the past we had no fatherland, nor could we have had one. But now that we have overthrown capitalism and power is in our hands, in the hands of the people, we have a fatherland, and we will uphold its independence. Do you want our socialist fatherland to be beaten and to lose its independence? If you do not want this, you must put an end to its backwardness in the shortest possible time and develop a genuine Bolshevik tempo in building up its socialist economy. There is no other way. That is why Lenin said on the eve of the October Revolution: "Either perish, or overtake and outstrip the advanced capitalist countries."

We are fifty or a hundred years behind the advanced countries. We must make good this distance in ten years. Either we do it, or we shall go under. . . .

It is said that it is hard to master technique. That is not true! There are no fortresses that Bolsheviks cannot capture. We have solved a number of most difficult problems. We have overthrown capitalism. We have assumed power. We have built up a huge socialist industry. We have transferred the middle peasants on to the path of socialism. We have already accomplished what is most important from the point of view of construction. What remains to be done is not so much: to study technique, to master science. And when we have done that we shall develop a tempo of which we dare not even dream at present.

And we shall do it if we really want to.

III. A BITTER LEGACY: LEADERS' LETTER TO BOLSHEVIK

Petition to the Presidium of the Central Executive Committee of the All-Union Communist Party (Bolshevik), 1926

We appeal to you, asking you to pay a minimum of attention to our request.

We are prisoners who are returning from the Solovetsky concentration camp because of our poor health. We went there full of energy and good health, and now we are returning as invalids, broken and crippled emotionally and physically. We are asking you to draw your attention to the arbitrary use of power and the violence that reign at the Solovetsky concentration camp in Kemi and in all sections of the concentration camp. It is difficult for a human being even to imagine such terror, tyranny, violence, and lawlessness. When we went there, we could not conceive of such a horror, and now we, crippled ourselves, together with several thousands who are still there, appeal to the ruling center of the Soviet state to curb the terror that reigns there. As though it weren't enough that the Unified State Political Directorate [OGPU] without oversight and due process sends workers and peasants there who are by and large innocent (we are not talking about criminals who deserve to be punished), the former tsarist penal servitude system in comparison to Solovky had 99% more humanity, fairness, and legality. [. . .]

People die like flies, i.e., they die a slow and painful death; we repeat that all this torment and suffering is placed only on the shoulders of the proletariat without money, i.e., on workers who, we repeat, were unfortunate to find themselves in the period of hunger and destruction accompanying the events of the October Revolution, and who committed crimes only to save themselves and their families from death by starvation; they have already borne the punishment for these crimes, and the vast majority of them subsequently chose the path of honest labor. Now because of their past, for whose crime they have already paid, they are fired from their jobs. Yet, the main thing is that the entire weight of this scandalous abuse of power, brute violence, and lawlessness that reign at Solovky and other sections of the OGPU concentration camp is placed on the shoulders of workers and peasants; others, such as counterrevolutionaries, profiteers and so on, have full wallets and have set themselves up and live in clover in the Soviet State, while next to them, in the literal meaning of the word, the penniless proletariat dies from hunger, cold, and back-breaking 14–16 hour days under the tyranny and lawlessness of inmates who are the agents and collaborators of the State Political Directorate [GPU].

If you complain or write anything ("Heaven forbid"), they will frame you for an attempted escape or for something else, and they will shoot you like a dog. They line us up naked and barefoot at 22 degrees below zero and keep us outside for up to an hour. It is difficult to describe all the chaos and terror that is going on in Kemi, Solovky, and the other sections of the concentrations camp. All annual inspections uncover a lot of abuses. But what they discover in comparison to what actually exists is only a part of the horror and abuse of power, which the inspection accidently uncovers.

We are sure and we hope that in the All-Union Communist Party there are people, as we have been told, who are humane and sympathetic; it is possible, that you might think that it is our imagination, but we swear to you all, by everything that is sacred to us, that this is only one small part of the nightmarish truth, because it makes no sense to make this up. We repeat, and will repeat 100 times, that yes, indeed there are some guilty people, but the majority suffers innocently, as is described above. The word law, according to the law of the GPU concentration camps, does not exist; what does exist is only the autocratic power of petty tyrants, i.e., collaborators, serving time, who have power over life and death.

STUDY QUESTIONS

1. What were Lenin's organizational contributions to revolutionary Marxism? How did his methods before the revolution help shape the new Soviet state?
2. What specific issues did Lenin face as leader of Communist Russia? How did they relate to Marxist goals? How and why did Lenin approach the task of industrial and technological development?
3. Do these documents provide evidence about Lenin's qualities as a leader? Do they help explain why he played such a decisive role in Russian history?
4. What were Stalin's main goals? What do they have to do with Marxism? What other ideologies did he reflect?
5. How did Stalin's goals for a revolutionary Russia compare with Lenin's? What are the main similarities and differences?
6. Why was Stalin so insistent on Communist mastery of technique and science? What problems was he addressing? What results did this approach have in the actual framework for Soviet industrialization and research?
7. Why did the Russian Revolution produce such severe repression of political dissidents? What do the 1926 complaint and Yevtushenko's retrospective have in common? What kind of expectations of communism do the complaints about repression suggest?
8. What were the main differences between communism and fascism? Were there any similarities?
9. What was the relationship between communism and fascism, on the one hand, and World War I?

ESSAY SUGGESTIONS

A. How did the policies of the Soviet state compare to those of other revolutionary regimes in the twentieth century, such as those in China, Mexico, or Iran?

B. Why were leaders in many societies in Asia, Africa, and Latin America attracted to Soviet goals and achievements?

C. Using these documents and those in the Cold War chapter (Chapter 32), was Soviet society doomed by its very principles, or should other factors be explored in explaining why the Soviet Union ultimately collapsed?

D. What was the relationship between Stalinist and Leninist goals and the political repression that occurred from the 1920s into the 1950s? How can revolutionary achievements and the repression be combined in an assessment of the result of Russian communism?

35 CONSUMERISM

Modern consumerism began in Western Europe in the eighteenth century. It involved a growing emphasis on acquiring material goods by a wide range of social groups and not just the elite. Many historians argue that as consumerism spread and solidified, it represented one of the most profound changes in human values experienced in modern world history. Ultimately, consumerism spread well beyond the West to affect almost all parts of the globe.

Consumerism was not an event, and it is not easy to document its ascent. Changes in distribution—such as the rise of the department store, from the 1830s onward—and the development of modern advertising can be traced fairly readily. But how did ordinary people redefine their lives around consumerism? What were the impacts on other cultural values, including religion and politics?

The following documents involve comments on consumerism in Germany in the 1920s under the Weimar Republic. This was a shaky time in German history, after the nation's defeat in World War I. Not surprisingly, there were many concerns about consumerism as a distraction from proper values. But consumerism gained ground nevertheless. These selections suggest some aspects of what consumerism entailed and why it prompted criticism.

The main concept to explore is consumerism itself. Important aspects, such as claims of special involvements of women, were common in critiques throughout Western society; they were not unique to Germany. But there are some specific German features addressed, including some of the political implications. Consumerism would become one of the targets of Nazi attacks, in the name of German nationalism and subordination of individual interests to those of the state.

The first document was a call for a boycott of French fashions during the French occupation of the Ruhr in 1923—part of the postwar tension between the two nations. A second criticism was more general, from a Berlin newspaper in 1925. But the third document, from 1926, appeared in a more professional journal for advertisers, urging embrace of consumerism, with an eye to manipulation and sales. The final selection is from the first issue of a new car magazine in 1928.

Selection I from "Boykott franzoesicher Modewaren," *Styl Blaetter des Verbandes der deutschen Modeindutrie* 2 #1 (Feb. 1923), pp. 52–53. Selection II from "Nun aber genug! Gegen die Vermaennliching der Frau," *Berliner Illustrierte Zeitschrift des Verbandes deutscher Reklamefachleute* (March 29, 1925), p. 389. Selection III from Hanns Kropff, "Frauen als Käuferinnen," *Die Reklame. Zeitschrift des Verbandes deutscher Reklamefachleute* (July 1926), pp. 649–50. Selection IV from "Zum Geleit," *Auto-magazin*, No. 1 (Jan. 1928), 1. All selections from Anton Kaes, Martin Jay, and Edward Dimendberg, eds., *The Weimar Republic Sourcebook* (Berkeley: University of California Press, 1994).

WEIMAR ARTICLES

I. BOYCOTT OF FRENCH FASHION GOODS

The daily and professional press has made it widely known that the German fashion industry has decided to speak out for a boycott of French fashion goods. This decision is frequently misunderstood, and it is therefore best that a few words be said about it.

We in fashion are fully aware of our dependence on Paris to provide us with the taste of worldwide fashion. It is better to say these things directly than to talk around the issue. We also know that we harm ourselves in multiple ways if we do not travel to Paris. The exporting businesses clearly suffer disadvantages from this step; likewise the fashion salons with foreign retail customers will have to sacrifice this or that sale, for among their customers quite a few specifically want to see patterns from Paris.

In order not to increase damage to ourselves, the Association has no objection if someone wants to travel to Holland, Switzerland, or Vienna to view fashion developments and perhaps purchase copies from houses that were in Paris so that we might supplement our collections with what we would otherwise have lacked. It should be noted here that in these countries too the purchase of original patterns from Paris or any sort of fashion goods originally from France is not permitted.

It was not easy for the men whose inspiration it was to recommend this resolution. It has been seriously and amply considered. Political circumstances were more powerful than any more reasonable considerations and, as so often happens these days, action must be taken under the force of these circumstances.

It is not a question of advantage and disadvantage, not a question of the interests, greater or smaller, of individuals, and not in this case a question of the interests of the industry involved. Rather this time it is a question of the whole, a matter of life and death. We took this step aware that it will put us at a disadvantage, thus we have made a willing sacrifice. We would have found it abominable if fashion representatives had traveled to Paris and made purchases there in a moment when our countrymen in the Ruhr valley, from the simplest workers to the largest industrialists and highest officials, are being harassed and mistreated to the point of bloodshed. It was no longer possible for us to turn our eyes from the fact that the French are doing absolutely everything conceivable to ruin us. In such a moment it is not a question of business, but for everyone who still possesses a spark of national feeling or a spark of the feeling of self-respect there is something natural in self-defense against such humiliation. Those who have no feeling for this have relinquished their right to demand to be respected as a German inside the country or out; neither can they have retained any self-respect, for they betray their national and personal honor for the sake of material interest. . . .

Let us make no secret of our position. Let us say openly to our customers in and outside of Germany: we were not in Paris; have a look at our things and judge whether they are good or bad. And we will see that our customers will also understand us. Most countries possess enough national feeling of their own that they will respect those who say they were not in Paris.

Inside Germany everyone must help us to put the resolution completely and thoroughly into practice and lend to the spirit of the resolution their most emphatic support.

II. ENOUGH IS ENOUGH! AGAINST THE MASCULINIZATION OF WOMEN

What started as a playful game in women's fashion is gradually becoming a distressing aberration. At first it was like a charming novelty: that gently, delicate women cut their long tresses and bobbed their hair; that the dresses they wore hung down in an almost perfectly straight line, denying the contours of the female body, the curve of the hips; that they shortened their skirts, exposing their slender legs up to calf level. Even the most traditional of men were not scandalized by this. A creature like this could have been warmly greeted with the now obsolete pet name *my angel*—for angels are asexual, yet they have always been represented in a pre-adolescent female form, even the archangel Gabriel. But the male sensibility began to take offense at this as the fashion that was so becoming to young girls and their delicate figures was adopted by all women. It did an aesthetic disservice to stately and full-figured women. But the trend went even further; women no longer wanted to appear asexual; rather fashion was increasingly calculated to make women's outward appearance more masculine. The practice of wearing men's nightclothes became increasingly widespread among women, even to the point of wearing them whenever possible for daytime lounging.

And we observe more often now that the bobbed haircut with its curls is disappearing, to be replaced by the modern, masculine hairstyle: sleek and brushed straight back. The new fashion in women's coats is also decidedly masculine: it would scarcely be noticed this spring if a woman absentmindedly put on her husband's coat. Fashion is like a pendulum swinging back and forth. With the hoop skirt the dictates of fashion brought the accentuation of the female form to an extreme, and now things are moving in the completely opposite direction. It is high time that sound male judgment take a stand against these odious fashions, the excesses of which have been transplanted here from America. In the theater we might enjoy, one time, seeing an actress playing a man's part if she is suitable for the role; but not every woman should venture to display herself in pants or shorts, be it on stage or at sporting events. And the masculinization of the female face replaces its natural allure with, at best, an unnatural one: the look of a sickeningly sweet boy is detested by every real boy or man.

III. WOMEN AS SHOPPERS

Seventy-five percent of all things are bought by women. Women buy for themselves, for their children, for their homes, and also very often for their husbands. Most money spent passes through the hands of women. For this reason you should check carefully whether your goods are not also purchased by women. The tie that a man buys because his wife likes it has in reality been purchased by her.

Women tend to think in strongly personal terms. Nevertheless they are easy to influence. Their first question will always be: is there a use or advantage in it for me? They relate everything directly to their appearance, their happiness, their sympathies. General facts, logical reasons, abstract considerations, and technical details do not say much to them. Statistics and politics leave them cold in the moment of a purchase. They demand instead that their smaller desires be understood. They are pleased by easily understood explanations of the use of an item or about the reasons it is better.

Women love a simple and personal language, however modern they might be in their professions and progressive in their opinions. With things that touch them personally, they are first of all women. And, once again, that is the reason they perceive everything personally.

Only in the rarest of cases will women analyze their feelings or actions. Their sensations, decisions, affections, and rejections are thoroughly emotional and irrevocable.

The majority of marketers find it very difficult to write advertisements for women. They think in terms that are too complicated, too masculine. The love they have for the products they sell is colored by their own perspective. They frequently use expressions that mean something entirely different to women, that lead to misunderstandings, indeed, that often offend them. An idea that is good in itself is often spoiled by an incorrect expression.

Consider the fact that women love their homes, be they ever so simple, and that they are proud of certain pieces of furniture and keepsakes. Do not insult them with sarcastic disparagement. Never use ridicule in your texts and never be skeptical. You might cause a few to laugh, but many will be irritated.

Shopping is a serious matter for all people, but most especially for women. Do not attempt to make advertisements humorous, for firstly there are only a few really humorous ads and secondly to women humor is neither generally understood, nor congenial, nor persuasive.

Women regard life as a shockingly serious business which must be endured if necessary with clenched teeth. They wash, they iron, they sweep, they cook, they sew, they attend to the children, they make the beds . . . a woman's work is never done. Not only do they have their own language in which they think and discuss these things, but they also have a whole set of very particular feelings for them, which an advertiser must know and may never overlook.

Consider the fact that women are experienced in the care and treatment of children. If you give them advice in this area, then do so in a way that does not offend the views they learned from their mothers. Women are generally conservative. They find sudden innovations unpleasant—with the exception of those in fashion. Their education in new thoughts must proceed slowly and carefully. Convince the women that your offerings represent an easily understood advantage for them or their children and half the battle is already won.

Speak to housewives of the "small amenities of the item," of the work it saves. Give her suggestions on how to procure and prepare meals with less trouble. Speak with her about new methods for simplifying housework. Inform mothers of new advances in the area of hygiene and nutrition.

Do not speak of slavery but offer the woman a hand to gain more time for herself. She will be grateful to you.

The woman with a profession, unburdened by crude household worries and in possession of more money that she can dispose of freely, wants simply to be a woman in her leisure time. She does not think so much of the price if you convince her that your goods will make her life easier, more pleasant, and nicer. Like the housewife her first question in regard to a fashion advertisement is: does it become me? And like the former, she is interested only in the one pictured, and not in the dozen presented in the text. She strives for new knowledge in order to advance herself, but learning by being entertained is most congenial to her. Women politicians and parliamentarians are captivated by a pretty and skillful speech, even if the calculation is wrong, even if the statistical figures do not add up and even if after the third word all the men are already shaking their heads. In short, having a profession has not changed her in her heart of hearts. She remains a woman.

You see that it is not easy for men to write texts for women. It is even harder to illustrate such texts. Give your drafts, pictures, and texts to women to evaluate—not your wife or your daughter or a lady who knows what is at issue but a complete outsider. A woman's judgment is quickly influenced when she knows why she is supposed to give it.

Everything that has been said already applies to an even greater extent to illustrations. If a good picture is worth a thousand words, then ten thousand good words will not induce any woman to look at an ugly or false picture. The effect of the ad stands and falls with the picture. They look first of all at the picture, and if it appeals to them, they read the text. Something incorrect in fashion, a badly arranged kitchen, or a false step in the care of the children, everything that is ridiculous, impossible, or horrible to women occasions them to pass over the ad immediately in scorn and irritation.

Without a doubt the majority of women would rather look at a pretty, appetizing girl than an ugly one. But the ever-cheerful "sweet girl" performing the dirty chores in the public toilet wearing elegant evening gloves is even more ridiculous for women than for men.

Pure text ads, be they ever so clear and aesthetically pleasing, do not interest women. Mere text is too cold and structural for them. Not even trimmings and borders help matters. On the other hand, many women, out of curiosity and the desire for sensation, read the personal ads and the announcements of weddings and engagements, carefully. A clever ad in close proximity to these generally succeeds.

Let us summarize: ads for women must be as personal as possible. They must take into account the typical female characteristic: to agree without reservation, or to repudiate absolutely. Women see things with their eyes—nothing can move them to read an ad that, for some reason or other, does not appeal to them on first sight.

The young women of the postwar period distinguish themselves in some things very clearly from their sisters of 1914. Their bodies, freed from the corset, reasonably dressed, and athletically trained, have become more natural and prettier. Their minds, steeled by need and the worries of war and sharpened by the business of work, are freer and clearer. Their demeanor, although more tomboyish, is easier and less forced than it was in the times when it was thought that the solution to the problem of the erotic was solved by hushing it up. The fellowship of young men and women, often slandered and abused, has become a fact in many parts of Europe.

A new race of women is growing up in Europe, consciously demanding the rights from which they have been barred by the slavery to convention of earlier times.

IV. AUTO-MAGAZIN (A CAR MAGAZINE)

Editorial Statement

With the enormous upswing that automobilism in Germany has experienced in recent years, the desire for a magazine devoted, alongside the technical periodicals, to the automobile grew as well. There is scarcely any industry that is faster growing than the automobile industry. The young people of today already possess an educational background in automobile technology. Girls and women understand something about the automobile, and fathers are able in the long run to ignore the expertise their families have acquired just as little as they can escape the slow but sure arrival of the day when they purchase an automobile. In Germany today there are approximately three-quarters of a million automobiles on the streets. In just a few years this number will have doubled, so the need for an automobile magazine is obvious. Our task is to report about the automobile here at home and abroad, to illustrate innovations, to report on sporting events, to show automobile fashions just as much as to publish the latest photographs of automobile races, to convey data, ideas, and expert advice, to depict automobile travel, and to collect automotive caricatures from all over the world—in short, to unreel month by month the entire repertoire conjured by the magical word *automobile.*

The *Auto-Magazin* will do justice to all of these desires. Every month in these pages interest in the automobile will be reinvigorated in amusing form, and soon there will not be a single automobilist who can do without the *Auto-Magazin.* This, in a few brief words, is the goal we have set ourselves. To achieve it we need the cooperation of our readers—in particular we should like to receive abundant photographic material.

STUDY QUESTIONS

1. What were some of the objections to consumerism? Which kinds of objections were particular to 1920s Germany, and which were more common as consumerism spread?
2. Does consumerism involve a special role for women? How did German men perceive women's interests? How did discussions of consumerism build on gender stereotypes? Has that relationship changed in contemporary society?
3. What was the relationship between consumerism and nationalism? Has that relationship changed in contemporary society?

36 ASIA AND THE MIDDLE EAST

THE MAKING OF MODERN TURKEY

The chapters in this section cover Asia, including the Middle East, in the tumultuous twentieth and early twenty-first centuries. Leading developments involve the rise of nationalism, with the collapse of the Ottoman Empire, and the resultant new states plus India's independence, Japan's experience in World War II, China's revolutionary upheaval, and varied patterns of economic and religious development. Comparative opportunities most obviously highlight differences, but there are some common features in social change and political restructuring as well.

The unraveling of the Ottoman Empire in the Balkans and North Africa during the long nineteenth century cleared the way for the emergence of the modern nation state of Turkey. In 1908, an uprising of junior officers in the Ottoman army known as Young Turks ended the effective rule of the sultan. They immediately embarked on a course of modernizing reforms while attempting to hold the remaining Ottoman lands together. However, their decision to join in the carnage of World War I on the side of the Central Powers led to disaster. Crushing military defeat and resulting economic chaos destroyed what remained of the empire established by Babur and Akbar (Chapter 10). Because of a fiercely contested "postwar war" with the Greeks, the fighting did not end for the Turks until 1922. By that time, they controlled only Anatolia.

In 1923, Mustapha Kemal (1881–1938), a general who had been one of the Young Turks and had won victories against the Greeks in the postwar war, proclaimed the founding of the Turkish Republic. Later named "Ataturk" (Father Turk), Kemal was one of the first authoritarian modernizers of the twentieth century. He vigorously promoted industrialization and secularism. Polygamy was abolished and women obtained the right to vote. The Islamic caliphate, the office that Sunni Muslims everywhere looked to for leadership, was abolished. Islamic schools were replaced by an expanded state system of education. Islamic law courts were closed. In 1928, Islam was disestablished as the state religion in Turkey.

The following selections come from two writers closely associated with Ataturk and from Ataturk himself. Ziya Gokalp (1876–1924) was one of the most creative and best-known writers of the early republican period. His newspaper essays were widely discussed and influenced governmental policy during the Ataturk years. Halide Edib was

Selection I from *Turkish Nationalism and Western Civilization: Selected Essays of Ziya Gokalp,* translated and edited by Niyazi Berkes (New York: Columbia University Press, 1959), pp. 276–277, 310–311. Reprinted by permission of the publisher. Selection II from Halide Edib [Adivar], "Dictatorship and Reforms in Turkey," *Yale Review* 19 (September 1929), pp. 34–38. Used by permission of Blackwell Publishing. Selection III from Bernard Lewis, *The Emergence of Modern Turkey,* 2nd ed. (London and New York: Oxford University Press, 1968), p. 278.

4. On the basis of these documents, how can consumerism be best define
is the relationship between consumerism and fads/fashions?
5. What was the role of advertising in spreading consumerism? Did adver
shape tastes or did they simply use tastes that had already developed?

ESSAY SUGGESTIONS

A. What was new about consumerism in Western and world history by the nineteenth and twentieth centuries?

B. Is the use of modern consumerism a significant topic for world history? What are the key arguments for or against?

C. How did consumerism relate to political innovations such as fascism and communism?

a novelist and close friend of Ataturk but broke with him in 1925 over his autocratic policies. She and her husband fled into exile and remained abroad until Ataturk's death. Her commentary on the Ataturk reforms of family law and the role of Islam was written for American readers. The selection by Ataturk comes from one of his speeches. How do the documents capture the dilemmas facing the Turks in the 1920s? Were the challenges in Turkey following World War I comparable to those facing other countries?

TURKISH DOCUMENTS

I. ZIYA GOKALP (1923)

A. Toward Western Civilization

There is only one road to salvation: To advance in order to reach—that is, in order to be equal to—Europeans in the sciences and industry as well as in military and judicial institutions. And there is only one means to achieve this: to adapt ourselves to Western civilization completely!

In the past, the makers of *Tanzimat* [reforms introduced by Ottoman sultans, 1830s to 1870s] recognized this and set about to introduce European civilization. However, whatever they wanted to take from Europe, they always took not fully but by half. They created, for example, neither a real university nor a uniform judicial organization. Before they took measures to modernize national production, they wanted to change the habits of consuming, clothing, eating, building, and furniture. On the other hand, not even a nucleus of industry on European standards was built because the policy makers of *Tanzimat* attempted their reforms without studying conditions and without putting forth definite aims and plans. They were always taking only half-measures in whatever they attempted to do.

Another great mistake committed by the leaders of *Tanzimat* was their attempt to create a mental amalgam made up of a mixture of East and West. They failed to see that the two, with their diametrically opposed principles, could not be reconciled. The still existing dichotomy in our political structure, the dual court system, the two types of schools, the two systems of taxation, two budgets, the two sets of laws, are all products of this mistake. The dichotomies are almost endless. Religious and secular schools were not only two different institutions of education, but within each there was again the same dichotomy. Only in military and medical schools was education carried out exclusively along European lines. We owe to these institutions the generals and doctors who today save the life of the nation and the lives of the citizens. The training of specialists within these fields, in a way equal to their European colleagues, was made possible only because of the immunity of these two institutions from dichotomy. If the methods of warfare of the Janissaries or the medical practices of the old-fashioned surgeons were mixed into these modern institutions, we would not have our celebrated generals and doctors today. These two institutions of learning must be models for the educational revolution that has to materialize. Any attempt to reconcile East and West means carrying medieval conditions to the modern age and trying to keep them alive. Just as it was impossible to reconcile Janissary methods with a modern military system, just as it was futile to synchronize old-fashioned medicine with scientific medicine, so it is hopeless to carry the old and the new conceptions of law, the modern and the traditional conceptions of science, the old and the new standards of ethics, side by side. Unfortunately, only in the military arts and medicine was Janissaryism abolished. It is still surviving in other professions as a ghost of medievalism. A few months ago, a new society was founded in Istanbul in order to bring Turkey into the League of Nations. What will be the use of it as long as Turkey does not enter definitely into European civilization? A nation condemned to every political interference by Capitulations is meant to be a nation outside of European civilization. Japan is accepted as a European power, but we are still regarded as an Asiatic nation. This is due to nothing but our non-acceptance of European civilization in a true sense. The Japanese have been able to take the Western civilization without losing their religion and national identity; they have been able to reach the level of Europeans in every respect. Did they lose their religion and national culture? Not at all! Why, then, should we still hesitate? Can't we accept Western civilization definitely and still be Turks and Muslims? . . .

B. On the Need for a National Industry

The modern state is based on large-scale industry. New Turkey, to be a modern state, must, above all, develop a national industry. What should we do to realize this?

The New Turkey, which has to introduce the latest and most developed techniques of Europe, cannot afford to wait for the spontaneous rise of the spirit of enterprise among individuals in order to industrialize. As we have done in the field of military techniques, we have to reach European levels in industry through a national effort. We have to start by utilizing the latest developments in European techniques, without necessarily following the stages of gradual evolution. The starting-point, for example, should be electrification. We must utilize the hydraulic power of the country and put it into an electric network. The people of Turkey, who have been able to adopt European military techniques in all their details, can learn and master the most modern industrial inventions and discoveries. Military techniques, however, were not introduced by the private initiative of individuals. This was accomplished through the state. Our medicine, which is equally advanced, was also initiated through state action. Therefore, only the state can achieve the task of introducing large-scale industry in every field. The Turkish state has the power to be an independent [national] state. Turks are temperamentally *étatists*. They expect the state to take the initiative in everything new and progressive. Even social changes are introduced through the state in Turkey, and it has been the state which has safeguarded social changes against the force of reaction.

In order that the state itself may become competent in economic enterprises, it must become an economic state. The statesmen and government employees should have economic experience and knowledge. The modern state, selecting its personnel with this point in view, is like a big business concern. . . . By following the same line, our state will, at the same time, perform a moral service because the rise of a new class of speculators will be prevented. The ambitions manifested in the Peace Conference clearly showed what a criminal people these capitalists, as they are called in Europe, are! Present-day European imperialism is based on private capitalism. If we accept the system of state capitalism, we will be able to prevent the rise of those insatiable and predatory capitalists in our country.

II. HALIDE EDIB [ADIVAR] (1929)

In 1926 the new law following the Swiss [family] code was passed. It can be termed, perhaps, one of the two most significant and important changes that have taken place during the dictatorial régime. This particular law will mean the final social unification of the Turks with the European nations, since it gives the Turkish family that kind of stability which constitutes the Western ideal of the family. The decision to adopt the Swiss law, which is entirely Western, instead of to revise and alter the old Islamic family law, which could have made marriage a freer if a less stable institution and brought it nearer to the present Russian [i.e. Soviet] law, was one more triumph in Turkey of the Western ideal over the Eastern ideal, and one of more importance for the future than is at present realized.

The educational rights that Turkish women have gained are no longer questioned even by the smallest minority, and the sphere of their work has been constantly widening. It is perhaps a blessing that they have not obtained the vote [granted in 1934]. Thus they have been protected from the danger of being identified with party politics, and their activities outside the political world could not be stopped for political reasons.

In the Turkish home, women continue to be the ruling spirit, more so, perhaps, because the majority contribute to the upkeep by their labors. At the present time, offices, factories, and shops are filled with women workers in the cities; and in addition to their breadwinning jobs, and sometimes in connection with them, women have interested themselves in child welfare and hygiene, and in organizing small associations to teach poor women embroidery, sewing, weaving, and so on. The favorite profession of Turkish women to-day, after teaching, is medicine. All this is the city aspect of the situation. In the rural districts, women still continue to live their old life with its old drudgery, and will continue to live under these conditions until a more up-to-date agricultural system is adopted and the rudiments of education can be taught them. It would not be an underestimate to say that something like ninety percent of the Turkish women are very hard workers; the question is not how to provide more work for them but how to train them better for their work and to give them more leisure. The small percentage of the idle rich (much smaller in Turkey than elsewhere) do on a miniature scale what the idle rich of other countries do. Unfortunately, Turkey is judged by the life and attitude of these idlers, who are conspicuous to the eyes of the traveller, rather than by the hard-working majority.

On the whole, within the last twenty years women in Turkey as elsewhere have profited by changes more than men. It has been a good thing for Turkey that its emancipation of women was the result of an all-party programme rather than a sex struggle. The contribution of the Republic to women's social emancipation in the introduction of the new civil code has brought the movement to its highest and historically its most important stage. But a generation at least must pass before its full effects can be seen. The general criticism that with Westernization a great deal of evil and Western immorality have penetrated into Turkish customs is not very important. The evil affects a small number of the idle, while the good penetrates into the majority, although more slowly.

In 1928 the clause in the Turkish constitution which declared Islam the state religion was abolished. . . .

In the foreign press this act of the dictatorship was criticised very severely on the ground that it amounted to the abolition of religion in Turkey. The criticism was not only superficial but inaccurate. If religion, in the best sense, is in danger of losing its hold on the people in Turkey, this is due not to the lack of governmental interference in its favor but to governmental interference against it. The men who sponsored this measure, may or may not have been atheists, but the measure itself does not do away with religion. No secular state can logically have an established state religion. The removal of this clause from the Turkish constitution was therefore in true and necessary accord with the nature of the new Turkish state at its last stage of secularization. "Render therefore unto Caesar the things that are Caesar's, and unto God the things that are God's." The Turks have at last rendered up the things that were Caesar's or the state's. On the other hand, Caesar, or the states, still keeps things which belong to God. Unless the Presidency of Religious Affairs is made free, unless it ceases to be controlled by the office of the Prime Minister as it is now controlled, it will always be a governmental instrument. In this respect, the Moslem community in Turkey is to-day less privileged and less independent than are the Christian Patriarchates. These are free institutions, which decide upon all questions of dogma and religion according to the desires of their particular group. The Islamic community is, however, chained to the policy of the government. This situation is a serious impediment to the spiritual growth of Islam in Turkey, and there is danger in it of the use of religion for political ends. Now that the state has rid itself entirely of religious control, it should, in turn, leave Islam alone. Not only should it declare, "Every adult Turkish citizen is free to adopt the religion he (or she) wishes to adopt," but it should also allow the Moslem community to teach its religion to its youth. Now that the schools give no religious instruction, and the religious institutions have been abolished, the Islamic community, if it is going to last as a religious community, must create its own means of religious teaching, its own moral and spiritual sanctions.

III. ATATURK (1928)

My friends, our rich and harmonious language will now be able to display itself with new [Latin-style] Turkish letters. We must free ourselves from these incomprehensible [Arabic] signs, that for centuries have held our minds in an iron vice. You must learn the new Turkish letters quickly. Teach them to your compatriots, to women and to men, to porters and to boatmen. Regard it as a patriotic and national duty . . . and when you perform that duty, bear in mind that for a nation to consist of 10 or 20 percent of literates and 80 or 90 percent of illiterates is shameful. . . . The fault is not ours; it is of those who failed to understand the character of the Turk and bound his mind in chains. Now is the time to eradicate the errors of the past. We shall repair these errors, and in doing so I want the participation of all our compatriots. . . . Our nation will show, with its script and with its mind, that its place is with the civilized world.

STUDY QUESTIONS

1. Why did Gokalp think that Turkey should embrace Western civilization? How did he think the Turkish economy should be organized?
2. According to Edib, what was the significance of the 1926 family code? What problems did she see in making the new law effective?
3. What was Edib's view of the 1928 law on Islam? Were her views consistent with Islamic teaching?
4. Edib thought Ataturk's 1928 language reform was as significant as the new family law. After reading his speech, what do you think? What losses were there as a result of this policy?
5. From the vantage point of the early twenty-first century, what was problematic about Ataturk's policies toward Islam?

ESSAY SUGGESTIONS

A. How do the changes in Turkey during the 1920s and 1930s compare to those introduced in Russia after 1917 (Chapter 34)? In which country were the changes more revolutionary? Why?

B. How do Ataturk's reforms compare to those introduced in Japan during the Meiji Restoration (Chapter 24)?

C. What was lost by the collapse of the Ottoman Empire?

37

ISRAELIS AND PALESTINIANS IN CONFLICT

The Israeli-Palestinian conflict is rooted in two powerful and contradictory claims to the same territory. Each side invokes history in defense of its goals. Beginning in the 1890s, European Jews responded to the emergence of modern political anti-Semitism by organizing the Zionist movement to promote emigration to Palestine, then part of the Ottoman Empire and inhabited largely by Arab Muslims. Following World War I, when the British ruled Palestine as a League of Nations mandate, intensified anti-Semitism across much of Europe increased the migration of Jews to Palestine—a process that accelerated after World War II because of the Holocaust. The simultaneous end of the mandate and the establishment of the state of Israel in May 1948 seemingly made real the Zionist dream of a homeland for Jews.

Palestine, however, had been a part of the Arab Muslim world since the seventh century. Palestinians resented the coming of the Jewish colonists and opposed the founding of the new Israeli state, as did most other Arabs in the region. Escalating violence led to war in 1947 and 1948, forcing more than 700,000 Palestinians into exile. Most fled to makeshift camps in Gaza, Lebanon, and Jordan, where they still live. Subsequent wars between Israel and neighboring Arab states in 1956, 1967, 1973, 1978, and 1982 increased the amount of territory—and the number of Palestinians—subject to Israeli authority, most notably in the region west of the Jordan River known as the West Bank and in the Gaza Strip.

Determined to regain their homeland and to establish an independent Palestinian state, in 1964 Palestinian leaders founded the Palestine Liberation Organization (PLO). For the next four decades or so, the secular-oriented PLO led the Palestinian struggle. Fatah, its leading faction, currently exercises some governmental authority in the West Bank region. Since the late 1980s, however, Hamas (the Islamic Resistance Movement) has emerged as a serious rival. Unlike the PLO, Hamas aims at establishing a Palestinian state based on Islamic law (*shariah*). It runs an influential network of schools and social welfare agencies in the West Bank and Gaza. In the latter area, Hamas's victory in elections conducted in 2007 enabled it to take over some governmental functions.

Hamas has also carried out a variety of violent actions, including rocket attacks and suicide bombings, aimed at Israelis. In response, Israeli repression has been quite harsh. Each side believes its use of violence is justified by the wrongs committed by the other.

Selection I from *The Amos Oz Reader,* selected and edited by Nitza Ben-Dov. Boston: Houghton Mifflin, 2009, pp. 236–239. Selection II from *The Disinherited: Journal of a Palestinian Exile.* New York: Monthly Review Press, 1972, by Fawaz Turki, pp. 43–45, 47–48, 54.

The selections provide two perspectives on the conflict. In the first one, Amos Oz, Israel's leading writer, explains why he is a Zionist. The second, by the Palestinian writer Fawaz Turki, is a memoir of dispossession, flight, and life in a refugee camp. Two maps that help clarify the territorial changes from the 1940s onward conclude the chapter. Do the documents and the maps point a way toward peace?

ZIONIST AND PALESTINIAN VOICES

I. AMOS OZ (1967)

Anyone who believes in the power of words must be careful how he uses them. I never use the word *shoah* ("catastrophe") when I want to refer to the murder of the Jews of Europe. The word *shoah* falsifies the true nature of what happened. A shoah is a natural event, an outbreak of forces beyond human control. An earthquake, a flood, a typhoon, an epidemic is a shoah. The murder of European Jews was no shoah. It was the ultimate logical outcome of the status of the Jew in Western civilization. The Jew in Europe, in Christendom, in the paganism within Christendom is not a "national minority," a "religious minority," or a "problem of status." For thousands of years the Jew has been perceived as the symbol of something inhuman. Like the steeple and the cross, like the devil, like the Messiah, so the Jew is part of the infrastructure of the Western mind. If all the Jews had been assimilated among the peoples of Europe the *Jew* would have continued to be present. Someone had to fill his role to exist as an archetype in the dungeon of the Christian soul. To shine and repel, to suffer and swindle, to be fated to be a genius and an abomination. Therefore, being a Jew in the diaspora means that Auschwitz is meant for you. It is meant for you because you are a symbol, not an individual. The symbol of the justly persecuted vampire, or the symbol of the unjustly persecuted innocent victim—but always and everywhere, you are not an individual, not yourself, but a fragment of a symbol.

I am a Zionist because I do not want to exist as a fragment of a symbol in the consciousness of others. Neither the symbol of the shrewd, gifted, repulsive vampire, nor the symbol of the sympathetic victim who deserves compensation and atonement. That is why my place is in the land of the Jews. This does not make me circumvent my responsibilities as a Jew, but it saves me from the nightmare of being a symbol in the minds of strangers, day and night.

The land of the Jews, I said. The land of the Jews could not have come into being and could not have existed anywhere but here. Not in Uganda, not in Ararat, and not in Birobidjan. Because this is the place Jews have always looked to throughout their history. Because there is no other territory to which Jews would have come in their masses to establish a Jewish homeland. On this point I commit myself to a severe, remorseless distinction between the *inner motives* of the return to Zion and its *justification to others.* The age-old longings are a motive, but not a justification. Political Zionism has made political, national use of religious, messianic yearnings. And rightly so. But our justification vis a vis the Arab inhabitants of the country cannot be based on our age-old longings. What are our longings to them? The Zionist enterprise has no other objective justification than the right of a drowning man to grasp the only plank that can save him. And that is justification enough. (Here I must anticipate something I shall return to later: there is a vast difference between a drowning man who grasps a plank and makes room for himself by pushing others who are sitting on it to one side, even by force, and the drowning man who grabs the whole plank for himself and pushes the others into the sea. This is the moral argument that lies behind our repeated agreement in principle to the partition of the Land. This is the difference between making Jaffa and Nazareth Jewish, and making Ramallah and Nablus Jewish.)....

I do not regard myself as a Jew by virtue of "race" or as a "Hebrew" because I was born in the land of Canaan. I *choose* to be a Jew, that is, to participate in the collective experience of my ancestors and fellow Jews down the ages. Albeit a selective participation: I do not approve of everything they approved of, not am I prepared to continue to live obediently the kind of life they lived. As a Jew, I do not want to live among strangers who see me as some kind of stereotype, but in a State of Jews. Such a state could only have come to being in the Land of Israel. That is as far as my Zionism goes.

II. FAWAZ TURKI (1972)

A breeze began to blow as we moved slowly along the coast road, heading to the Lebanese border—my mother and father, my two sisters, my brother and I. Behind us lay the city of Haifa, long the scene of bombing, sniper fire, ambushes, raids, and bitter fighting between Palestinians and Zionists. Before us lay the city of Sidon [Lebanon] and indefinite exile. Around us the waters of the Mediterranean sparkled in the sun. Above us eternity moved on unconcerned, as if God in his heavens watched the agonies of men, as they walked on crutches, and smiled. And our world had burst, like a bubble, a bubble that had engulfed us within its warmth. From then on I would know only crazy sorrow and watch the glazed eyes of my fellow Palestinians burdened by loss and devastated by pain.

April 1948. And so it was the cruelest month of the year; but there were crueler months, then years....

After a few months in Sidon, we moved again, a Palestinian family of six heading to a refugee camp in Beirut, impotent with hunger, frustration, and incomprehension. But there we encountered other families equally helpless, equally baffled, who like us never had enough to eat, never enough to offer books and education to their children, never enough to face an imminent winter. In later years, when we left the camp and found better housing and a better life outside and grew up into our early teens, we would complain about not having this or that and would be told by our mothers: "You are well off, boy! Think of those still living there in the camps. Just think of them and stop making demands." We would look out the window and see the rain falling and hear the thunder. And we would remember. We would understand. We would relent as we thought "of those still living there."

Man adapts. We adapted, the first few months, to life in a refugee camp. In the adaptation we were also reduced as men, as women, as children, as human beings. At times we dreamed. Reduced dreams. Distorted ambitions. One day, we hoped, our parents would succeed in buying two beds for me and my sister to save us the agonies of asthma, intensified from sleeping on blankets on the cold floor. One day, we hoped, there would be enough to buy a few pounds of pears or apples as we had done on those special occasions when we fought and sulked and complained because one of us was given a smaller piece of fruit than the others. One day soon, we hoped, it would be the end of the month when the UNRWA [United Nations Relief and Works Agency] rations arrived and there was enough to eat for a week. One day soon, we argued, we would be back in our homeland.

The days stretched into months and those into a year and yet another. Kids would play in the mud of the winters and the dust of the summers, while "our problem" was debated at the UN and moths died around the kerosene lamps. A job had been found for me in a factory not far from the camp, where I worked for six months. I felt pride in the fact that I was a bread earner and was thus eligible to throw my weight around the house, legitimately demand an extra spoonful of sugar in my tea, and have my own money to spend on comic books and an occasional orange on the side. I had even started saving to buy my own bed, but I was fired soon after that.

A kid at work had called me a two-bit Palestinian and a fist fight ensued. The supervisor, an obese man with three chins and a green stubble that covered most of his face and reached under his eyes, came over to stop the fight. He decided I had started it all, slapped me hard twice, deducted three lira from my wages for causing trouble (I earned seven lira a week), paid me the rest, called me a two-bit Palestinian, and, pointing to my blond hair, suggested I had a whore mother and shoved me out the door.

I went to the river and sat on the grass to eat my lunch. I was shaken more by the two-bit Palestinian epithet than by the plight of being unemployed. At home and around the camp, we had unconsciously learned to be proud of where we came from and to continue remembering that we were Palestinians. If this was stigmatic outside, there it was an identity to be known, perpetuated, embraced. My father, reproaching us for an ignoble offense of some kind, would say: "You are a Palestinian." He would mean: as a Palestinian one is not expected to stoop that low and betray his tradition. If we came home affecting a Lebanese accent, our mother would say: "Hey, what's wrong with your own accent? You're too good for your own people or something? You want to sound like a foreigner when we return to Haifa? What's wrong with you, hey?"

• • •

Our Palestinian consciousness, instead of dissipating, was enhanced and acquired a subtle nuance and a new dimension. It was buoyed by two concepts: the preservation of our memory of Palestine and our acquisition of education. We persisted in refusing the houses and monetary compensation offered by the UN to settle us in our host countries. We wanted nothing short of returning to our homeland. And from Syria, Lebanon, and Jordan, we would see, a few miles, a few yards, across the border, a land where we had been born, where we had lived, and where we felt the earth. "This is my land," we would shout, or cry, or sing, or plead, or reason. And to that land a people had come, a foreign community of colonizers, aided by a Western world in a hurry to rid itself of guilt and shame, demanding independence from history, from heaven, and from us.

STUDY QUESTIONS

1. How does Oz define his type of Zionism? What other definitions are there?
2. Does the "drowning man" metaphor hold up when applied to the conflict?
3. What is life like in the refugee camps? How have people in the host countries received the refugees?
4. How does Turki explain the rise of Palestinian nationalism? In what ways are Western countries partly responsible for the conflict?
5. Should Palestinian refugees be allowed to return to their former homes in Israel? Why? If not, should they be compensated for their losses? How?

VISUAL SOURCE

THE CARTOGRAPHY OF CONFLICT

The map on the left illustrates the 1947 proposal of the United Nations for the creation of a Jewish and a Palestinian state from the British mandate. This plan was a casualty of the fighting that erupted from 1947 to 1949 when the Palestinians and the Arab states

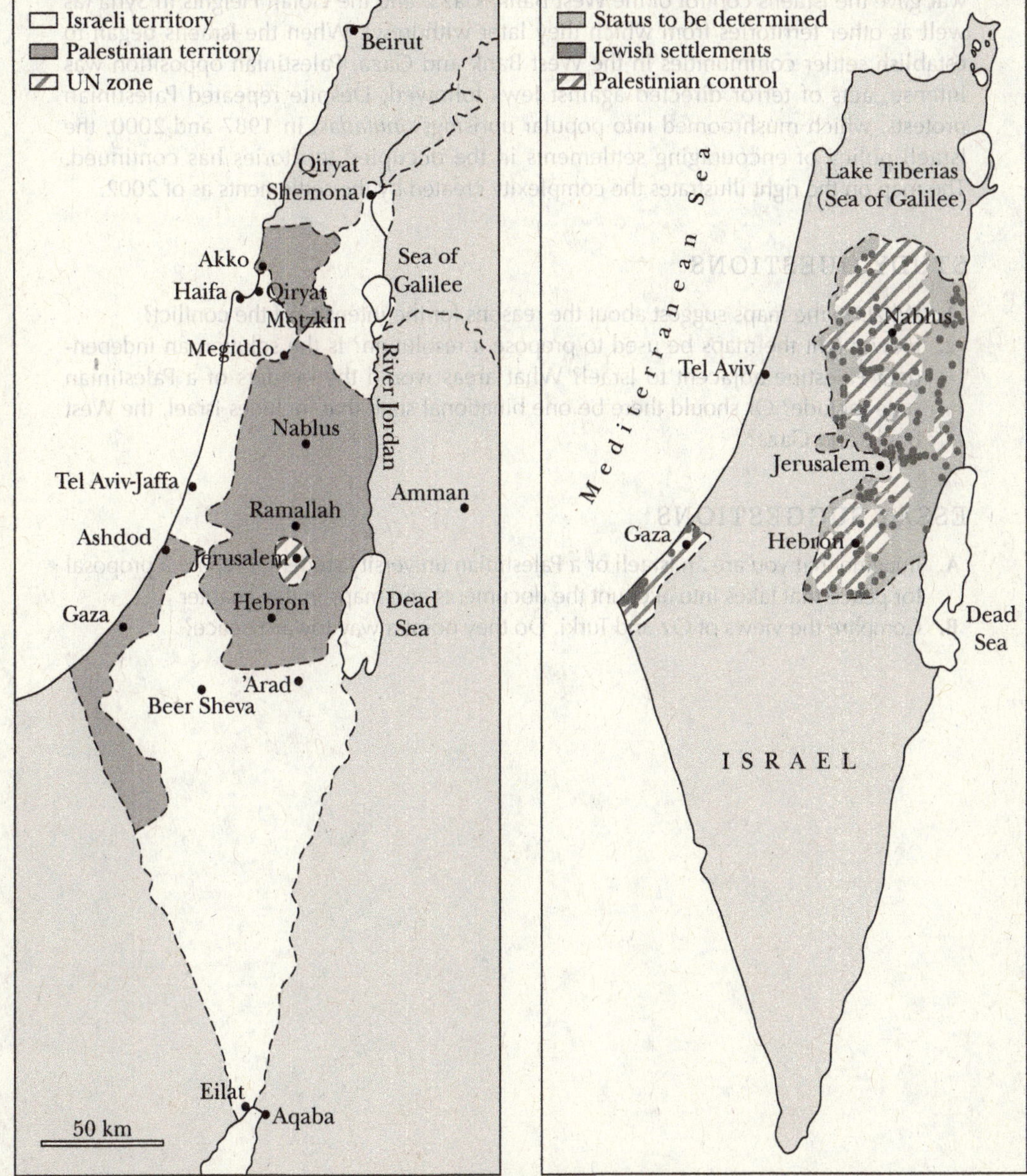

From the UN Plan of 1947 to the Territorial Situation in 2002.

attempted to block the establishment of Israel. Victorious in 1948 and 1949, the Israelis took control of lands well beyond those called for in the UN proposal. The West Bank went to Jordan and the Gaza Strip to Egypt. As for the Palestinians, 700,000 of them fled their homes in the former mandate for refugee camps in Jordan, Gaza, Lebanon, and other Arab states.

The next major turning point in the conflict came in June 1967. In a brief war, Israel decisively defeated the combined armies of Egypt, Jordan, and Syria. Victory in the June war gave the Israelis control of the West Bank, Gaza, and the Golan Heights in Syria (as well as other territories from which they later withdrew). When the Israelis began to establish settler communities in the West Bank and Gaza, Palestinian opposition was intense; acts of terror directed against Jews followed. Despite repeated Palestinian protests, which mushroomed into popular uprisings (*intifadas*) in 1987 and 2000, the Israeli policy of encouraging settlements in the occupied territories has continued. The map on the right illustrates the complexity created by the settlements as of 2002.

STUDY QUESTIONS

1. What do the maps suggest about the reasons for the intensity of the conflict?
2. How might the maps be used to propose a resolution? Is the solution an independent Palestine adjacent to Israel? What areas would the borders of a Palestinian state include? Or should there be one binational state that includes Israel, the West Bank, and Gaza?

ESSAY SUGGESTIONS

A. Imagine that you are an Israeli or a Palestinian university student. Prepare a proposal for peace that takes into account the documents and maps in this chapter.
B. Compare the views of Oz and Turki. Do they point a way toward peace?

38 THE RENEWAL OF ISLAM

One of the most important developments during the past several decades has been the deepening of piety among Muslims worldwide. It began in the Middle East and North Africa and subsequently spread to places wherever Muslims reside. Mosque attendance has shot up, the number of pilgrims to Mecca has reached an all-time high, traditional dress for women has spread, men have grown out their beards, Muslim student organizations have become important on university campuses, and the work of Islamic grassroots organizations has greatly expanded.

Especially noteworthy has been the growth of political activism by Muslims, who—like believers in all the great world religions—interpret the teachings of their faith in various ways. Four signposts: (1) In 1979, Shiite clerics in Iran, led by the charismatic Ayatollah Ruhollah Khomeini (1902–1989), rode to power on a massive wave of popular discontent, replacing the autocratic and secularist Pahlavi shah (a close ally of the United States) with a regime based on a strict understanding of *shariah* (Islamic law). (2) Two years later, Muslim militants in the Egyptian army assassinated Anwar el-Sadat, the secularist head of state who had recently normalized relations with Israel. (3) During the 1980s, Muslim *jihadists* from many countries joined the fight to drive Soviet forces from Afghanistan, a conflict that culminated in the rise of the fundamentalist Taliban during the 1990s and beyond. (4) For Americans, of course, the most shocking example of Muslim political activism was the September 11, 2001, attack on the World Trade Center and the Pentagon.

The documents in this chapter illustrate two very different aspects of the renewed vitality in Islam. In the first one, Ayatollah Khomeini, in a major speech in March 1980, advances the idea of political Islam as a "straight path" between international communism and Western imperialism. The second selection takes us far from politics and into the universe of "women's Islam." The author, Leila Ahmed, grew up in Egypt during the 1940s and 1950s in an upper-class family. She obtained her university education in England and currently teaches at the Harvard Divinity School. How do the documents suggest the diversity of beliefs and practice in present-day Islam?

Selection I from Bernard Lewis, ed., *A Middle East Mosaic: Fragments of Life, Letters and History* (New York: Random House, 2000), 260–261; this selection originally appeared in *Islam and Revolution I: Writings and Declarations of Imam Khomeini (1941–1980)*, trans. and anno. Hamid Algar (Berkeley: Mizan Press, 1981), pages unknown. Selection II from Leila Ahmed, *A Border Passage: From Cairo to America—A Woman's Journey*. Copyright 1999 by Leila Ahmed. Reprinted by permission of Farrar, Straus, & Giroux. pp. 120–125.

ISLAMIC DOCUMENTS

I. AYATOLLAH RUHOLLAH KHOMEINI (1980)

God Almighty has willed—and all thanks are due to Him—that this noble nation be delivered from the oppression and crimes inflicted on it by a tyrannical government and from the domination of the oppressive powers, especially America, the global plunderer, and that the flag of Islamic justice wave over our beloved land. It is our duty to stand firm against the superpowers, as we are indeed able to do, on condition that the intellectuals stop following and imitating either the West or the East, and adhere instead to the straight path of Islam and the nation. We are at war with international communism no less than we are struggling against the global plunderers of the West, headed by America, Zionism and Israel.

Dear friends! Be fully aware that the danger represented by the communist powers is no less than that of America; the danger that America poses is so great that if you commit the smallest oversight, you will be destroyed. Both superpowers are intent on destroying the oppressed nations of the world, and it is our duty to defend those nations.

We must strive to export our Revolution throughout the world, and must abandon all idea of not doing so, for not only does Islam refuse to recognize any difference between Muslim countries, it is the champion of all oppressed people. Moreover, all the powers are intent on destroying us, and if we remain surrounded in a closed circle, we shall certainly be defeated. We must make plain our stance toward the powers and the superpowers and demonstrate to them that despite the arduous problems that burden us, our attitude to the world is dictated by our beliefs.

Beloved youths, it is in you that I place my hopes. With the Qur'ān in one hand and a gun in the other, defend your dignity and honor so well that your adversaries will be unable even to think of conspiring against you. At the same time, be so compassionate toward your friends that you will not hesitate to sacrifice everything you possess for their sake. Know well that the world today belongs to the oppressed, and sooner or later they will triumph. They will inherit the earth and build the government of God.

Once again, I declare my support for all movements and groups that are fighting to gain liberation from the superpowers of the left and the right. I declare my support for the people of Occupied Palestine and Lebanon. I vehemently condemn once more the savage occupation of Afghanistan by the aggressive plunderers of the East, and I hope that the noble Muslim people of Afghanistan will achieve victory and true independence as soon as possible, and be delivered from the clutches of the so-called champions of the working class. . . .

I see that satanic counterrevolutionary conspiracies, aiming at promoting the interests of the East and the West, are on the rise; it is the God-given human and national duty of both the government and the people to frustrate those conspiracies with all the powers at their command.

II. LEILA AHMED (1999)

It is easy to see now that our lives in the Alexandria house, and even at Zatoun, were lived in women's time, women's space. And in women's culture.

And the women had, too, I now believe, their own understanding of Islam, an understanding that was different from men's Islam, "official" Islam. For although in those days it was only Grandmother who performed all the regular formal prayers, for all the women of the house, religion was an essential part of how they made sense of and understood their own lives. It was through religion that one pondered the things that happened, why they had happened, and what one should make of them, how one should take them.

Islam, as I got it from them, was gentle, generous, pacifist, inclusive, somewhat mystical—just as they themselves were. Mother's pacifism was entirely of a piece with their sense of the religion. Being Muslim was about believing in a world in which life was meaningful and in which all events and happenings were permeated (although not always transparently to us) with meaning. Religion was above all about inner things. The outward signs of religiousness, such as prayer and fasting, might be signs of a true religiousness but equally well might not. They were certainly not what was important about being Muslim. What was important was how you conducted yourself and how you were in yourself and in your attitude toward others and in your heart.

What it was to be Muslim was passed on not, of course, wordlessly but without elaborate sets of injunctions or threats or decrees or dictates as to what we should do and be and believe. What was passed on, besides the very general basic beliefs and moral ethos of Islam, which are also those of its sister monotheisms, was a way of being in the world. A way of holding oneself in the world—in relation to God, to existence, to other human beings. This the women passed on to us most of all through how they were and by their being and presence, by the way *they* were in the world, conveying their beliefs, ways, thoughts, and how we should be in the world by a touch, a glance, a word—prohibiting, for instance, or approving. Their mere responses in this or that situation—a word, a shrug, even just their posture—passed on to us, in the way that women (and also men) have forever passed on to their young, how we should be. And all of these ways of passing on attitudes, morals, beliefs, knowledge—through touch and the body and in words spoken in the living moment—are by their very nature subtle and evanescent. They profoundly shape the next generation, but they do not leave a record in the way that someone writing a text about how to live or what to believe leaves a record. Nevertheless, they leave a far more important and, literally, more vital, living record. Beliefs, morals, attitudes passed on to and impressed on us through those fleeting words and gestures are written into our very lives, our bodies, our selves, even into our physical cells and into how we live out the script of our lives.

It was Grandmother who taught me the *fat-ha* (the opening verse of the Quran and the equivalent of the Christian Lord's Prayer) and who taught me two or three other short suras (Quranic verses). When she took me up onto the roof of the Alexandria house to watch for angels on the night of the twenty-seventh of Ramadan, she recited the sura about that special night, a sura that was also by implication about the miraculousness of night itself. Even now I remember its loveliness. It is still my favorite sura.

I remember receiving little other direct religious instruction, either from Grandmother or from anyone else. I have already described the most memorable exchange with my mother on the subject of religion—when, sitting in her room, the windows open behind her onto the garden, the curtain billowing, she quoted to me the verse in the Quran that she believed summed up the essence of Islam: "He who kills one being [*nafs*, self, from the root *nafas*, breath] kills all of humanity, and he who revives, or gives life to, one being revives all of humanity." It was a verse that she quoted often, that came up in any important conversation about God, religion, those sorts of things. It represented for her the essence of Islam.

• • •

I happened to be reading, when I was thinking about all this, the autobiography of Zeinab al-Ghazali, one of the most prominent Muslim women leaders of our day. Al-Ghazali founded a Muslim Women's Society that she eventually merged with the Muslim Brotherhood, the "fundamentalist" association that was particularly active in the forties and fifties. Throughout her life she openly espoused a belief in the legitimacy of using violence in the cause of Islam. In her memoir, she writes of how in her childhood her father told her stories of the heroic women of early Islam who had written poetry eulogizing Muslim warriors and who themselves had gone to war on the battlefields of Islam and gained renown as fearless fighters. Musing about all this and about the difference between al-Ghazali's Islam and my mother's pacifist understanding of it, I found myself falling into a meditation on the seemingly trivial detail that I, unlike al-Ghazali, had never heard as a child or a young girl stories about the women of early Islam, heroic or otherwise. And it was then that I suddenly realized the difference between al-Ghazali and my mother and between al-Ghazali's Islam and my mother's.

The reason I had not heard such stories as a child was quite simply that those sorts of stories (when I was young, anyway) were to be found only in the ancient classical texts of Islam, texts that only men who had studied the classical Islamic literary heritage could understand and decipher. The entire training at Islamic universities—the training, for example, that al-Ghazali's father, who had attended al-Azhar University, had received—consisted precisely in studying those texts. Al-Ghazali had been initiated into Islam and had got her notions as to what a Muslim was from her father, whereas I had received my Islam from the mothers, as had my mother. So there are two quite different Islams, an Islam that is in some sense a women's Islam and an official, textual Islam, a "men's" Islam.

And indeed it is obvious that a far greater gulf must separate men's and women's ways of knowing, and the different ways in which men and women understand religion, in the segregated societies of the Middle East than in other societies—and we know that there are differences between women's and men's ways of knowing even in non-segregated societies such as America. For, beside the fact that women often could not read (or, if they were literate, could not decipher the Islamic texts, which require years of specialist training), women in Muslim societies did not attend mosques. Mosque going was not part of the tradition for women at any class level (that is, attending mosque for congregational prayers, was not part of the tradition, as distinct from visiting mosques privately and informally to offer personal prayers, which women have always done). Women therefore did not hear the sermons that men heard. And they did not get the official (male, of course) orthodox interpretations of religion that men (or some men) got every Friday. They did not have a man trained in the orthodox (male) literary heritage of Islam telling them week by week and month by month what it meant to be a Muslim, what the correct interpretation of this or that was, and what was or was not the essential message of Islam.

Rather they figured these things out among themselves and in two ways. They figured them out as they tried to understand their own lives and how to behave and how to live, talking them over together among themselves, interacting with their men, and returning to talk them over in their communities of women. And they figured them out as they listened to the Quran and talked among themselves about what they heard. For this was a culture, at all levels of society and throughout most of the history of Islamic civilization, not of reading but of the common recitation of the Quran. It was recited by professional reciters, women as well as men, and listened to on all kinds of occasions—at funerals and births and celebratory events, in illness, and in ordinary life. There was merit in having the Quran chanted in your house and in listening to it being chanted wherever it was chanted, whereas for women there was no merit attached to attending mosque, an activity indeed prohibited to women for most of history. It was from these together, their own lives and from hearing the words of the Quran, that they formed their sense of the essence of Islam.

Nor did they feel, the women I knew, that they were missing anything by not hearing the exhortations of sheikhs, nor did they believe that the sheikhs had an understanding of Islam superior to theirs. On the contrary. They had little regard, the women I knew, for the reported views and opinions of most sheikhs. Although occasionally there might be a sheikh who was regarded as a man of genuine insight and wisdom, the women I knew ordinarily dismissed the views and opinions of the common run of sheikhs as mere superstition and bigotry. And these, I emphasize, were not Westernized women. Grandmother, who spoke only Arabic and Turkish, almost never set foot outside her home and never even listened to the radio. The dictum that "there is no priesthood in Islam"—meaning that there is no intermediary or interpreter, and no need for an intermediary or interpreter, between God and each individual Muslim and how that Muslim understands his or her religion—was something these women and many other Muslims took seriously and held on to as a declaration of their right to their own understanding of Islam.

No doubt particular backgrounds and subcultures give their own specific flavors and inflections and ways of seeing to their understanding of religion, and I expect that the Islam I received from the women among whom I lived was therefore part of their particular subculture. In this sense, then, there are not just two or three different kinds of Islam but many, many different ways of understanding and of being Muslim. But what is striking to me now is not how different or rare the Islam in which I was raised is but how ordinary and typical it seems to be in its base and fundamentals. Now, after a lifetime of meeting and talking with Muslims from all over the world, I find that this Islam is one of the common varieties—perhaps even *the* common or garden variety—of the religion. It is the Islam not only of women but of ordinary folk generally, as opposed to the Islam of sheikhs, ayatollahs, mullahs, and clerics. It is an Islam that may or may not place emphasis on ritual and formal religious practice but that certainly pays little or no attention to the utterances and exhortations of sheikhs or any sort of official figures. Rather it is an Islam that stresses moral conduct and emphasizes Islam as a broad ethos and ethical code and as a way of understanding and reflecting on the meaning of one's life and of human life more generally.

This variety of Islam (or, more exactly perhaps, these familial varieties of Islam, existing in a continuum across the Muslim world) consists above all of Islam as essentially an aural and oral heritage and a way of living and being—and not a textual, written heritage, not something studied in books or learned from men who studied books.

STUDY QUESTIONS

1. Why is the Iranian leader hostile to the United States, Israel, and communism? What Iranian group seems to worry him? Why?
2. How does Ahmed define "women's Islam"? Is there a counterpart to women's Islam in other world religions, or is Islam distinctive in this way? Explain your answer.
3. For whom was Khomeini's speech intended? To whom was Ahmed writing? Is one of them truer to the core teachings of Islam? If so, how?

EGYPTIAN PILGRIM MURALS

Islam is the one world religion that requires its members to go on a pilgrimage. In traveling to the holy city of Mecca to visit the *Kaaba* and other holy sites, Muslims follow the example set by Muhammad and also reenact events in the lives of Abraham, his wife Hagar, and their son Ishmael.

One indication of the resurgence of Islam in recent decades is the sharp increase in the number of Muslim pilgrims. In 1940, about one hundred thousand pilgrims from outside of Saudi Arabia journeyed to Mecca for the annual holy rites. Since that time, the number has steadily increased. In recent years, the number of pilgrims from foreign countries has been approximately one million. Another one million have come from within Saudi Arabia.

Although the Quran urges pilgrimage on all the faithful, only about 10 percent of Muslims ever make the sacred journey. Many of those who do so require contributions from family members and neighbors in order to pay for the trip. Thus, when pilgrims return home, their pride is genuine and their standing among their coreligionists is much enhanced. In Egypt, many pilgrims have murals painted on the walls of their houses commemorating their visit to the holy places. The two examples are from the town of Farafra in western Egypt.

Murals on the Sides of the Houses of Two Egyptian Pilgrims to Mecca, ca. 2003. (Photos by David W. Tschanz/Saudi Aramco World/SAWDIA).

STUDY QUESTIONS

1. What features of Muslim pilgrimage are illustrated in the murals?
2. How do the murals suggest aspects of the renewal of Islam?

ESSAY SUGGESTIONS

A. What does it mean to be both Muslim and modern? Is there a fit?
B. What explains the renewal of Islam?

39 EAST ASIA

CHINESE REVOLUTIONARIES: SUN YAT-SEN AND MAO ZEDONG

The first half of the twentieth century was catastrophic for China. A Gordian knot of internal disarray and external pressures finished off the tottering Qing dynasty in 1911 and 1912. Although a republic was immediately established, continuing battles between rival warlords prolonged and deepened the crisis. In the midst of the chaos, Sun Yat-sen (1866–1925), a Western-educated physician, founded China's first modern political party, the Nationalist Party (Guomindang), and became enormously popular as its leader. At the time of Sun's death, however, China's problems were far from resolved.

In 1927, Chiang Kai-shek (1888–1975), Sun's successor as head of the Nationalists, was able to impose a kind of unity on China from his capital in Nanjing. Chiang remained the nominal head of state in China until 1949, but his regime was corrupt and ineffective. When Japan invaded eastern China in 1937, the Nationalist government was unable to muster much of a defense. Chiang moved his capital deep into the interior and became increasingly dependent on aid from Britain and the United States.

In contrast to Chiang's ineffectiveness, China's rural-based Communist Party, led by Mao Zedong (1891–1976), organized strong opposition to the Japanese. By the end of World War II, the Communist Party claimed millions of members, had its own large and battle-tested army, and controlled much of northern China. Attempts by the United States to reconcile the Communists and the Nationalists in 1945 and 1946 quickly broke down. The result was a full-scale civil war. In 1949, the Communists swept to power—moving from the countryside to the cities and from north to south—and they have been in charge ever since.

The first selection is a series of passages taken from lectures Sun Yat-sen gave to Nationalist activists in 1924. An important speech by Mao Zedong, made just prior to the defeat of the Nationalists in 1949, follows. How do the ideas of the two leaders shed light on the conflicts that shook China during the first half of the twentieth century? Which other counties suffered comparably?

Selection I from *Sources of Chinese Tradition,* Vol. II, edited by Theodore de Bary, Wing-tsit Chan, and Burton Watson (New York: Columbia University Press, 1960), pp. 768–771. Selection II from *Selected Works of Mao Tsetung,* Vol. 5, pp. 16–18. Beijing: Foreign Languages Press, 1977.

TWO REVOLUTIONARY LEADERS

I. SUN YAT-SEN: THE THREE PEOPLE'S PRINCIPLES (1924)

[China as a Heap of Loose Sand].

For the most part the four hundred million people of China can be spoken of as completely Han Chinese. With common customs and habits, we are completely of one race. But in the world today what position do we occupy? Compared to the other peoples of the world we have the greatest population and our civilization is four thousand years old; we should therefore be advancing in the front rank with the nations of Europe and America. But the Chinese people have only family and clan [lineage] solidarity; they do not have national spirit. Therefore even though we have four hundred million people gathered together in one China, in reality they are just a heap of loose sand. Today we are the poorest and weakest nation in the world, and occupy the lowest position in international affairs. Other men are the carving knife and serving dish; we are the fish and the meat. Our position at this time is most perilous. If we do not earnestly espouse nationalism and weld together our four hundred million people into a strong nation, there is danger of China's being lost and our people being destroyed. If we wish to avert this catastrophe, we must espouse nationalism and bring this national spirit to the salvation of the country. . . .

[China as a "Hypo-Colony"].

Since the Chinese Revolution [of 1911], the foreign powers have found that it was much less easy to use political force in carving up China. A people who had experienced Manchu [Qing] oppression and learned to overthrow it, would now, if the powers used political force to oppress it, be certain to resist, and thus make things difficult for them. For this reason they are letting up in their efforts to control China by political force and instead are using economic pressure to keep us down . . . . As regards political oppression people are readily aware of their suffering, but when it comes to economic oppression most often they are hardly conscious of it. China has already experienced several decades of economic oppression by the foreign powers, and so far the nation has for the most part shown no sense of irritation. As a consequence China is being transformed everywhere into a colony of the foreign powers.

Our people keep thinking that China is only a "semi-colony"—a term by which they seek to comfort themselves. Yet in reality the economic oppression we have endured is not just that of a "semi-colony" but greater even than that of a full colony. . . . Of what nation then is China a colony? It is the colony of every nation with which it has concluded treaties; each of them is China's master. Therefore China is not just the colony of one country; it is the colony of many countries. We are not just the slaves of one country, but the slaves of many countries. In the event of natural disasters like flood and drought, a nation which is sole master appropriates funds for relief and distributes them, thinking this its own duty; and the people who are its slaves regard this relief work as something to which their masters are obligated. But when North China suffered drought several years ago, the foreign powers did not regard it as their responsibility to appropriate funds and distribute relief; only those foreigners resident in China raised funds for the drought victims, whereupon Chinese observers remarked on the great generosity of the foreigners who bore no responsibility to help. . . .

From this we can see that China is not so well off as Annam [Vietnam under French rule] and Korea [under Japanese rule]. Being the slaves of one country represents a far higher status than being the slaves of many, and is far more advantageous. Therefore, to call China a "semi-colony" is quite incorrect. If I may coin a phrase, we should be called a "hypo-colony." This is a term that comes from chemistry, as in "hypo-phosphite." Among chemicals there are some belonging to the class of phosphorous compounds but of lower grade, which are called phosphites. Still another grade lower, and they are called hypo-phosphites. . . . The Chinese people, believing they were a semi-colony, thought it shame enough; they did not realize that they were lower even than Annam or Korea. Therefore we cannot call ourselves a "semi-colony" but only a "hypo-colony." . . .

[Nationalism and Traditional Morality].

If today we want to restore the standing of our people, we must first restore our national spirit. . . . If in the past our people have survived despite the fall of the state [to foreign conquerors], and not only survived themselves but been able to assimilate these foreign conquerors, it is because of the high level of our traditional morality. Therefore, if we go to the root of the matter, besides arousing a sense of national solidarity uniting all our people, we must recover and restore our characteristic, traditional morality. Only thus can we hope to attain again the distinctive position of our people.

This characteristic morality the Chinese people today have still not forgotten. First comes loyalty and filial piety, then humanity and love, faithfulness and duty, harmony and peace. Of these traditional virtues, the Chinese people still speak, but now, under foreign oppression, we have been invaded by a new culture, the force of which is felt all across the nation. Men wholly intoxicated by this new culture have thus begun to attack the traditional morality, saying that with the adoption of the new culture, we no longer have need of the old morality. . . . They say that when we formerly spoke of loyalty, it was loyalty to princes, but now in our democracy there are no princes, so loyalty is unnecessary and can be dispensed with. This kind of reasoning is certainly mistaken. In our country princes can be dispensed with, but not loyalty. If they say loyalty can be dispensed with, then I ask: "Do we, or do we not, have a nation? Can we, or can we not, make loyalty serve the nation? If indeed we can no longer speak of loyalty to princes, can we not, however, speak of loyalty to our people?"

II. MAO ZEDONG: THE CHINESE PEOPLE HAVE STOOD UP! (SEPTEMBER 21, 1949)

Fellow Delegates,

We are all convinced that our work will go down in the history of mankind, demonstrating that the Chinese people, comprising one quarter of humanity, have now stood up. The Chinese have always been a great, courageous and industrious nation; it is only in modern times that they have fallen behind. And that was due entirely to oppression and exploitation by foreign imperialism and domestic reactionary governments. For over a century our forefathers never stopped waging unyielding struggles against domestic and foreign oppressors, including the Revolution of 1911 led by Dr. Sun Zhongshan [Sun Yat-sen], our great forerunner in the Chinese revolution. Our forefathers enjoined us to carry out their unfulfilled will. And we have acted accordingly. We have closed our ranks and defeated both domestic and foreign oppressors through the People's War of Liberation and the great people's revolution, and now we are proclaiming the founding of the People's Republic of China. From now on our nation will belong to the community of the peace-loving and freedom-loving nations of the world and work courageously and industriously to foster its own civilization and well-being and at the same time to promote world peace and freedom. Ours will no longer be a nation subject to insult and humiliation. We have stood up. Our revolution has won the sympathy and acclaim of the people of all countries. We have friends all over the world.

Our revolutionary work is not completed, the People's War of Liberation and the people's revolutionary movement are still forging ahead and we must keep up our efforts. The imperialists and the domestic reactionaries will certainly not take their defeat lying down; they will fight to the last ditch. After there is peace and order throughout the country, they are sure to engage in sabotage and create disturbances by one means or another and every day and every minute they will try to stage a come-back. This is inevitable and beyond all doubt, and under no circumstances must we relax our vigilance.

Our state system, the people's democratic dictatorship, is a powerful weapon for safeguarding the fruits of victory of the people's revolution and for thwarting the plots of domestic and foreign enemies for restoration, and this weapon we must firmly grasp. Internationally, we must unite with all peace-loving and freedom-loving countries and peoples, and first of all with the Soviet Union and the New Democracies [in eastern Europe], so that we shall not stand alone in our struggle to safe-guard these fruits of victory and to thwart the plots of domestic and foreign enemies for restoration. As long as we persist in the people's democratic dictatorship and unite with our foreign friends, we shall always be victorious.

The people's democratic dictatorship and solidarity with our foreign friends will enable us to accomplish our work of construction rapidly. We are already confronted with the task of nation-wide economic construction. We have very favourable conditions: a population of 475 million people and a territory of 9,600,000 square kilometres. There are indeed difficulties ahead, and a great many too. But we firmly believe that by heroic struggle the people of the country will surmount them all. The Chinese people have rich experience in overcoming difficulties. If our forefathers, and we also, could weather long years of extreme difficulty and defeat powerful domestic and foreign reactionaries, why can't we now, after victory, build a prosperous and flourishing country? As long as we keep to our style of plain living and hard struggle, as long as we stand united and as long as we persist in the people's democratic dictatorship and unite with our foreign friends, we shall be able to win speedy victory on the economic front.

An upsurge in economic construction is bound to be followed by an upsurge of construction in the cultural sphere. The era in which the Chinese people were regarded as uncivilized is now ended. We shall emerge in the world as a nation with an advanced culture.

Our national defence will be consolidated and no imperialists will ever again be allowed to invade our land. Our people's armed forces must be maintained and developed with the heroic and steeled People's Liberation Army as the foundation. We will have not only a powerful army but also a powerful air force and a powerful navy.

Let the domestic and foreign reactionaries tremble before us! Let them say we are no good at this and no good at that. By our own indomitable efforts we the Chinese people will unswervingly reach our goal.

The heroes of the people who laid down their lives in the People's War of Liberation and the people's revolution shall live for ever in our memory!

Hail the victory of the People's War of Liberation and the people's revolution!

Hail the founding of the People's Republic of China!

Hail the triumph of the Chinese People's Political Consultative Conference!

STUDY QUESTIONS

1. According to Sun Yat-sen, what were China's greatest problems? How did he propose to solve them?
2. What was Sun's relationship to Confucianism?
3. How does Mao's address illustrate his understanding of Chinese history? What is a "people's democratic dictatorship"? Is this term an oxymoron?
4. Which theme seems more important in Mao's speech: nationalism or communism? Why?
5. What similarities and differences do you see in the ideas of Sun and Mao? Did they have a common understanding of China's modern history?

ESSAY SUGGESTIONS

A. How were the ideas of Sun Yat-sen and Mao Zedong shaped by China's modern history (Chapters 22 and 23)?

B. Compare Mao's 1949 speech with the one given by Ayatollah Khomeini in 1980 (Chapter 38).

C. Is Robert Wise's 1966 film *The Sand Pebbles* accurate in its depiction of China during the 1920s?

D. How does Bernardo Bertolucci's 1987 film *The Last Emperor* add to or detract from an understanding of China's difficulties during the first half of the twentieth century?

40 COMMUNIST RULE IN CHINA: TWO VIEWS

What has been the impact of six decades of Communist rule on China? What are communism's future prospects? The two documents in this chapter address these questions without, of course, providing definitive answers. In the first selection, a piece of oral history recorded by an American scholar between 1987 and 1994, Wang Fucheng (1923–1995), a Communist official from an impoverished north China village, recalls the disastrous years of the Great Leap Forward at the end of the 1950s. Mao's policy during the Great Leap called for a speedup in the collectivization of agriculture, the initiation of industrial production in the countryside, a sharp increase in economic growth, and a more communal way of living. A colossal failure in all respects, the policy led to widespread famine and to the deaths of many millions. Wang Fucheng helps us understand why.

The second document is excerpted from a manuscript written in 1989 by the eminent Chinese astrophysicist Fang Lizhi (b. 1936) in the context of the large student-led movement for political reform in the spring of that year. In April, students from universities in Beijing, inspired in part by Fang's liberal ideas, organized demonstrations following the death of a Communist Party official who had been somewhat sympathetic to the cause of reform. Confused by the demonstrations and frightened by the possibility that the students might find allies among the workers, party leaders dithered. The protests grew and spread to many other cities. In May, thousands of students occupied Tiananmen (Heavenly Peace) Square, the vast space traditionally symbolizing governmental authority and the site of famous student protests on May 4, 1919. In the weeks that followed, the demonstrations mushroomed. Then, on the night of June 3, the authorities called in the army. Hundreds were killed. Fang and his wife, Li Shuxian, immediately took refuge in the U.S. embassy and were subsequently flown to England. He currently teaches at the University of Arizona. How do the selections suggest the challenges China has faced before and after 1949? How do the problems in Communist China compare with those in Russia after 1917?

Selection I from Peter J. Seybolt, *Throwing the Emperor from the Horse: Portrait of a Village Leader in China, 1923–1995* (Boulder, CO: Westview, 1996), pp. 53–55. Reprinted by permission of Westview Press, a member of Perseus Books Group. Selection II from *Bringing Down the Great Wall* by Fang Lizhi, translated by J. Williams, pp. 39–42. Used by permission of Alfred A. Knopf, a division of Random House, Inc.

WANG FUCHENG AND FANG LIZHI

I. WANG FUCHENG

In mid-1958 cadres [Communist Party officials] from the county and township came to the village and took over all farming decisions. This was the beginning of the Great Leap Forward. We worked three shifts a day. We got up at 5 A.M. and worked until breakfast at 8 A.M., then we worked until supper in the evening, and after that we worked at night. We were urged to do two days' work in one day. In the beginning we all supported the cadres and constantly shouted slogans. At times I was so busy I didn't have time to eat. We were afraid of wasting time, so we moved our cooking stoves and pots to the field. Thirty or forty people shared the same pot. Sometimes we slept in the fields at night. We were organized into a military system. The village was a battalion with companies, platoons, and squads under it. I was the battalion political instructor in charge of all Party matters. The village leader was the battalion commander in charge of farming affairs. We used loudspeakers to criticize those who made mistakes and to praise those with merit. I remember a man named Wang Dehui who slept in the field instead of working after we moved our cooking materials there. I severely criticized him at a meeting, saying, "Your thought is not correct. If all are like you, how can we have a happy life?" Wang Dehui had criticized the Great Leap Forward as unreasonable.

Wang Dehong also criticized it, saying, "You support socialism and shout a lot, but I don't see that you raise more crops." His family had been richer than others. I put a high hat [a dunce cap] on him and said: "You are unsatisfied with socialism. If people believe you, how will the poor be able to lead a happy life? They work day and night and think the Great Leap Forward is a good movement."

Village leaders had no right at that time to decide what to plant and what not to plant. The county and township government planned everything. They said to plant corn, sorghum, and especially sweet potatoes. We planted 1000 mu [1 mu = 1/6 acre] of sweet potatoes that year, and they grew very well. About twenty-two villages in this area ate sweet potatoes from our fields. But we didn't even have time to harvest them all because the outside cadres were in such a rush to plant the next crop. They paid little attention to the harvest but mainly concentrated on planting winter wheat. Then they reported to the township and county government how fast they had done their job. If they planted wheat fast, the government would praise them. Otherwise they were criticized. A nearby village, Weihuang, had been told to plant peanuts. At harvest, in their rush to plant the next crop, they just pulled up the stems and leaves and left most of the peanuts in the ground. Then they plowed the land and planted other crops so the cadres could report that their work had been done very fast. Some of our sweet potatoes rotted in the ground for the same reason. What we did dig up, we dried in pieces. To keep them during the winter we buried them in the ground, but they rotted after two months. We distributed them to the villagers, but they didn't want rotten potatoes. They were hungry and dissatisfied.

When we planted the winter wheat we were told to dig deep, one or two chi [1 chi = 1/3 meter]. An animal pulling a plow couldn't dig that deep, so we had to do it with spades. A cadre from outside the village said, "An ox can't dig as much as a human." We all listened to this cadre's words, but we knew that they were nonsense. We were also told to sow forty to fifty jin [1 jin = 1.1 lbs] of wheat seed per mu instead of the usual eighteen jin. In Dongjiang Village next to us they were told to use 120 jin. We had to spread the seed with our spades because the planting box couldn't sow it in that quantity.

I still didn't have any doubts about the Party's general policy, but I knew in my heart that that was not the way to plant crops. Is it right to waste so much seed? Is it right to cut crops at night? I did not argue with the township and county cadres, but sometimes I said what was true: "That is not the way to do farm work."

We worked in the fields day and night, but often we were forced to waste time. For instance, when visiting groups came from different places, sometimes two or three times a day, we had to greet them, shouting slogans and saying, "Welcome! Welcome!" Sometimes when we were working in the east field, we had to go welcome them in the west. Sometimes when we were working in the west, we had to go welcome them in the east. I was the leader of the village, and I showed my dissatisfaction to the outside cadres. They criticized me for rightist tendencies and said I was lagging behind the developing situation. I dared not reply, but I thought, "I have been a farmer for half of my life, and you have just come from the county town. You cannot know farming better than I. You are directing blindly." All of the village cadres and masses were dissatisfied, but they had to follow the outside cadres' orders. This situation lasted for over a year. The movement eventually failed because the masses were dissatisfied.

At harvest time we were under a lot of pressure to exaggerate the amount of grain production. Many cadres made mistakes on this issue. Many villages gave a "Great Leap Forward report" when they reported their harvest. If they harvested 400 jin of grain, they would say 500 or 700 jin. The higher the report, the more praise from the commune cadres. If the report was low, they were criticized. We had meetings almost every day to report output. I was honest—I didn't exaggerate—so I was severely criticized. A cadre said to me, "Why is production in your village so low compared to others? You are the leader. There is a problem with your thought. If the villages don't give grain, how can the country run? We must think first of the nation, then of the village." I replied that I was reporting true figures; I didn't exaggerate.

Did I ever lie? Did I ever report false figures? Yes. I had to tell lies. We all did. When cadres from outside the village held a meeting to struggle against a village cadre, I had to protect him. They wanted us to estimate the production amount for the next harvest. When that harvest came, we reported the real figure. They kept asking us to give a higher figure until they were satisfied. They asked, "Why is the output in your village so low? Is it because you are lazy or the masses are lazy? Why is the situation in other villages so much better than in yours? Where is your grain? Did you hide it? Did the wind blow it away? Did it rot on the threshing ground?" They told us to find the cause for such low production. Under this pressure we all told lies. Actually, the villages were beginning to run short of grain.

After we had reported the grain amount to the outside cadres, each village had to decide how much grain to give to the government. I'll give you an example that is an approximation, not the real figures. If we had a grain output of 30,000 jin, we might keep 20,000 to eat, save 5,000 for various uses in the brigade, and give 5,000 to the government. The government didn't pay us for that amount. We called it "patriotic grain." Villages that reported very high grain production figures had to give a greater amount to the government. Because of false production reports, there was not enough to eat. The masses' enthusiasm fell. Outside cadres said we had enough to eat, but that wasn't true. They said we had a lot of grain in storage, but actually we had almost nothing.

It wasn't the weather that caused this shortage, as some officials said later. It was humans who made the disaster, I remember that there was a flood that affected this village at that time, but it wasn't too serious. Only some fields were flooded. Bad management was the cause of the disaster.

The Great Leap was supposed to be a leap in making steel and digging ditches as well as in agriculture. In late 1958 my wife went to Anyang City to work for a steel plant during a national campaign to make iron and steel. Thirty-four men and sixteen women from our village went to Anyang.

Wang Xianghua continues the story:

I was in Anyang from the eighth month [of the lunar calendar] until three months later. I lived there in a tent. I drank only from muddy ponds and ate corn porridge. We all ate together without food coupons. My job was to break up stones and load them into a furnace. My husband was a cadre, and being his wife, I had to work actively.

Wang Fucheng:

I had a lot of difficulties at that time. I was working too hard and coughed up a lot of blood. We had a two-year-old son. When my wife went to Anyang, we had to send him to live with his maternal grandmother who lives about 100 meters from here. Grandmother was also a Party member and had to go to meetings. She once locked the house and left the child sleeping on the bed. She was gone three hours, and when she came back she couldn't find him. She finally found him naked in a basket that had some cotton in it. He had cried for a long time. There were a lot of tears on his face. She was very upset and cried, too. Another time she went to a meeting and left the door open. The baby fell from the bed and crawled out the door to the outside gate of the courtyard. He couldn't get out, but he sat there and cried. An outside cadre heard him and called a neighbor, who picked him up and tried to dress him.

II. FANG LIZHI

The Beijing Observatory is intimately linked to the introduction of Western science over the last three centuries. Western science made its debut in China with the arrival of Matteo Ricci in 1582. (Ricci's tomb can be found today on the grounds of the Party School of the Beijing municipal government.) Modern science ran into strong resistance from the very start. Leng Shou-zhong and others in the late Ming Dynasty opposed using Western methods for the formulation of the Chinese calendar, insisting it could be based only on the Song Dynasty neo-Confucianist text *Huangji jingshi;* this was the first historical appearance of the theory of "Chinese characteristics." As a result, the court continued to use the old Datong and Islamic calendars.

In 1610 and again in 1629, the traditional methods led to erroneous predictions of solar eclipses, whereas the Catholic Mandarin Paul Xu Guangqi made wholly accurate forecasts using Western methods. At this point the Chongzhen Emperor accepted the use of these methods, and the Chongzhen Calendar was prepared based on them. But because of the opposition of the traditionalist *[shoujiu]* faction, the calendar was never actually used. The scientific treatise on which it was based was published only after the collapse of the Ming, during the reign of the Qing emperor Shunzhi [1644–1662]. Bearing the title "The New Western Calendar," it was used to formulate the official calendar. This was in all likelihood the first time that contemporary Western science had become a part of Chinese life.

But the good times didn't last. As soon as Shunzhi died, antiscience forces came into power once more. The eminent Confucian Yang Guangxian memorialized the throne: "It would be more preferable for China not to have an accurate calendar, than for it to tolerate the presence of Westerners." This expression of antipathy toward both Western people and their methods qualifies as the second time the theory of "Chinese characteristics" was expounded. Once this attitude prevailed at court, Li Zubai and five other people who'd been involved in calculating the calendar according to Western methods were put to death, making them the first people at the Beijing Observatory to sacrifice their lives for the sake of China's modernization. (Throughout history, astronomers have often been punished or executed as a result of official intolerance.)

During Kangxi's reign [1662–1723], the situation improved, and the Imperial Calendar was once again calculated according to Western methods. Of all the emperors, Kangxi was the one most interested in science; as a youth he even studied Western astronomy with the missionary Ferdinand Verbiest. The *Lixiang Kaocheng* and the Kangxi Calendar *(Yongnianli)* were scientific works that set the world standard for their time, and are representative of that enlightened period.

The ascent of the Yongzheng Emperor to the throne [in 1723] marked the beginning of a period of over 100 years in which science would again be shunted aside. China shut its doors to the world, cutting off scientific exchange in the process. The Qing school of textual criticism, which represented the academic mainstream of the day, was concerned only with research into the classics and had no interest whatsoever in science based on observation. As late as the nineteenth century, the leading Confucian scholar Ruan Yuan still refused to accept the theory that the earth revolves around the sun. He wrote: "This theory, which turns things topsy-turvy and confuses movement and stasis, is heretical and rebellious in nature; it must not be taken as the norm." The only norm that Ruan Yuan would accept was one based on the theory of "Chinese characteristics."

After the Opium Wars [in the mid-nineteenth century], this way of thinking fell into decline. The astronomer Li Shanlan refuted Ruan Yuan, saying, "If one neglects to make careful observations, and instead carelessly interprets the classics, devising preposterous theories, it will be a meaningless exercise." In 1868, Li Shanlan took up the post of chief instructor in astronomy at the Tongwenguan [Interpreter's College] in Beijing, and once more China began the systematic introduction of Western astronomy. Yet even still, scientific methods for calculating the calendar were not officially adopted until after the 1911 Revolution and the establishment of the Republic of China. At that point the Imperial Institute of Astronomy was renamed the Central Observatory and assigned the task of working out the calendar. While it was being prepared, the old calendar was used during the first two years of the Republic. Only in the third year was the calendar based completely on contemporary astronomy. It has never changed back. Even when "bourgeois science" was attacked during the Cultural Revolution, bourgeois science remained the basis of the calendar.

In explanatory notes to the first Republican calendar, Gao Lu and Chang Fuyuan wrote, "This calendar has been calculated on the basis of methods current in both the East and the West." The key expression is *"methods current in both the East and the West,"* for this signaled that Chinese society had finally acknowledged that the laws of science were universal; there were no "Chinese characteristics" when it came to scientific laws. This is how the clash between the Chinese tradition and modern science was resolved at the time of the May Fourth Movement. It started and ended at the Beijing Observatory.

This chapter in the history of science can perhaps help us to see the problems of democracy in China today in a longer-term perspective. First of all, there's no need to be overly pessimistic about the future of democracy in China. It's only been seven decades since the May Fourth Movement began, compared to the three centuries that it took for science to be accepted, so there's no call for complete despair. Second, the basic principles and standards of modernization and democratization are like those of science—universally applicable. In this regard there's no Eastern or Western standard, only the difference between "backward" and "advanced," between "correct" and "mistaken." Third, the chief obstacle to the modernization and democratization of Chinese culture lies in the same erroneous idea that kept science out of China for so many years: the theory of China's "unique characteristics," in all its variations.

The Beijing Observatory celebrates its 710th anniversary this year. Since ancient times, China's emperors have governed according to heavenly portents. After the Yuan Dynasty moved its capital to Beijing, the observatory served the successive courts by interpreting the Will of Heaven. It no longer had to serve this function after the May Fourth period, but its long history still has important lessons to teach, especially to those in power. It's my hope that this history will provide a useful reference for our present rulers.

The Beijing Observatory gives us an excellent vantage point from which to observe the affairs of men. From here you can see the movement of the stars and the turning of the Wheel of the Law. The dharma wheel of science has already come rolling into China, and that of democracy is starting to turn as well. The problems we face today are merely the creaking sounds it makes as it begins to roll. This is the basis of my confidence and strength.

STUDY QUESTIONS

1. What was the standard of living for peasants in the 1950s? What problems did they face in addition to material hardship? Why did the Great Leap fail?
2. What are the strengths and possible weaknesses of oral history?
3. When did modern science come to China? Why was its arrival delayed? In Fang's view, what implications does the coming of science to China have for the prospect of democracy?
4. Is democracy, like science, applicable universally, as Fang thinks, or is it merely Western? Why?

ESSAY SUGGESTIONS

A. Compare the Great Leap Forward to the Taiping Rebellion (Chapter 23).

B. Imagine that you are a Chinese peasant during the Great Leap Forward and that you are able to keep a secret diary. Record one day of your life.

C. Compare Communism in China and Russia. What explains the differences?

41 CORPORATE MANAGEMENT AND SEX WORK IN JAPAN

Japan's emergence as a modern industrial society was one of the major developments of the second half of the twentieth century. At the end of World War II, the country was devastated. Rapid economic growth, stimulated in part by U.S. supply orders for the wars in Korea and Vietnam, overcame the destruction. By the mid-1960s, the Japanese economy was four times as productive as it had been in the 1930s. During the following decade, Japanese automobiles, electronic goods, ships, and many other high-end products flooded global markets, edging out long-established producers in the West. Although the rate of growth stalled in the 1990s, Japan remains one of the most advanced industrial societies in the world of the twenty-first century.

Many observers attribute the Japanese economic "miracle" through the 1980s to the establishment of a distinctive corporate culture—one that was almost entirely male and had obvious links to the legacy of Confucianism and the samurai. The two documents in this chapter, dating from the late 1980s, provide insight into the type of management characteristic of Japanese corporations during the boom decades. In the first of them, Morita Akio (1921–1999), one of the founders of the Sony Corporation, discusses the policies that led to Sony's success. What is the "Sony way"? The second selection, by Matsui Yayori (1934–2002), an editor at one of Japan's largest newspapers, comes from a 1988 address she gave in New York at the Conference on International Trafficking in Women. Matsui's speech illustrates how gender structures and global economic patterns contributed to the success of Japanese-style corporate management. What is distinctive about working for a large corporation in Japan?

MORITA AKIO AND MATSUI YAYORI

I. MORITA AKIO: MANAGING A LARGE CORPORATION (1986)

There is no secret ingredient or hidden formula responsible for the success of the best Japanese companies. No theory or plan or government policy will make a business a success; that can only be done by people. The most important mission for a Japanese manager is to develop a healthy relationship with his employees, to create a family-like feeling within the corporation, a feeling that employees and managers

Selection I from "On Management It's All in the Family," from *Made in Japan* by Akio Morita with Edwin M. Reingold and Mitsuko Shimomura, Copyright © 1986 by E.P. Dutton. Used by permission of Dutton, a division of Penguin Books USA, Inc. Selection II from Sandra Buckley, ed., *Broken Silence: Voices of Japanese Feminism* (Berkeley: University of California Press, 1997), pp. 143, 145–148, 152–153; translation by Sandra Buckley with the permission of the author.

share the same fate. Those companies that are most successful in Japan are those that have managed to create a shared sense of fate among all employees, what Americans call labor and management, and the shareholders.

I have not found this simple management system applied anywhere else in the world, and yet we have demonstrated convincingly, I believe, that it works. For others to adopt the Japanese system may not be possible because they may be too tradition-bound, or too timid. . . .The emphasis on people must be genuine and sometimes very bold and daring, and it can even be quite risky. But in the long run—and I emphasize this—no matter how good or successful you are or how clever or crafty, your business and its future are in the hands of the people you hire. To put it a bit more dramatically, the fate of your business is actually in the hands of the youngest recruit on the staff.

That is why I make it a point personally to address all of our incoming college graduates each year. The Japanese school year ends in March, and companies recruit employees in their last semester, so that before the end of the school year they know where they are going. They take up their new jobs in April. I always gather these new recruits together at headquarters in Tokyo, where we have an introductory or orientation ceremony. This year I looked out at more than seven hundred young, eager faces and gave them a lecture, as I have been doing for almost forty years.

"First," I told them, "you should understand the difference between the school and a company. When you go to school, you pay tuition to the school, but now this company is paying tuition to you, and while you are learning your job you are a burden and a load on the company.

"Second, in school if you do well on an exam and score one hundred percent, that is fine, but if you don't write anything at all on your examination paper, you get a zero. In the world of business, you face an examination each day, and you can gain not one hundred points but thousands of points, or only fifty points. But in business, if you make a mistake you do not get a simple zero. If you make a mistake, it is always minus something, and there is no limit to how far down you can go, so this could be a danger to the company."

The new employees are getting their first direct and sobering view of what it will be like in the business world. I tell them what I think is important for them to know about the company and about themselves. I put it this way to the last class of entering employees:

"We did not draft you. This is not the army, so that means you have voluntarily chosen Sony. This is your responsibility, and normally if you join this company we expect that you will stay for the next twenty or thirty years."

[Mr. Morita goes on to discuss the history of lifetime employment in Japan and discusses his relations with Sony employees.]

. . .

The reason we can maintain good relations with our employees is that they know how we feel about them. In the Japanese case, the business does not start out with the entrepreneur organizing his company using the worker as a tool. He starts a company and he hires personnel to realize his idea, but once he hires employees he must regard them as colleagues, who must help him to keep the company alive and he must reward their work. The investor and the employee are in the same position, but sometimes the employee is more important, because he will be there a long time whereas an investor will often get in and out on a whim in order to make a profit. The worker's mission is to contribute to the company's welfare, and his own, every day all of his working life. He is really needed.

Companies have different approaches to this even in Japan, but basically, there has to be mutual respect and a sense that the company is the property of the employees and not of a few top people. But those people at the top of the company have a responsibility to lead that family faithfully and be concerned about the members.

We have a policy that wherever we are in the world we deal with our employees as members of the Sony family, as valued colleagues, and that is why even before we opened our U.K. factory, we brought management people, including engineers, to Tokyo and let them work with us and trained them and treated them just like members of our family, all of whom wear the same jackets and eat in our one-class cafeteria. This way they got to understand that people should not be treated differently; we didn't give a private office to any executive, even to the head of the factory. We urged the management staff to sit down with their office people and share the facilities. On the shop floor every foreman has a short meeting with his colleagues every morning before work and tells them what they have to do today. He gives them a report on yesterday's work, and while he is doing this he looks carefully at the faces of his team members. If someone doesn't look good, the foreman makes it a point to find out if the person is ill, or has some kind of a problem or worry. I think this is important, because if an employee is ill, unhappy, or worried, he cannot function properly.

. . .

A company will get nowhere if all of the thinking is left to management. Everybody in the company must contribute, and for the lower-level employees their contribution must be more than just manual labor. We insist that all our employees contribute their minds. Today we get an average of eight suggestions a year from each of our employees, and most of the suggestions have to do with making their own jobs easier or their work more reliable or a process more efficient. Some people in the West scoff at the suggestion process, saying that it forces people to repeat the obvious, or that it indicates a lack of leadership by management. This attitude shows a lack of understanding. We don't force suggestions, and we take them seriously and implement the best ones. And since the majority of them are directly concerned with a person's work, we find them relevant and useful. After all, who could tell us better how to structure the work than the people who are doing it?

I am reminded of my argument with Chairman Tajima on differences of opinion and confliction ideas. There is no possibility of the world progressing if we do exactly the same things as our superiors have done. I always tell employees that they should not worry too much about what their superiors tell them. I say,

"Go ahead without waiting for instructions." To the managers I say this is an important element in bringing out the ability and creativity of those below them. Young people have flexible and creative minds, so a manager should not try to cram preconceived ideas into them, because it may smother their originality before it gets a chance to bloom.

In Japan, workers who spend a lot of time together develop an atmosphere of self-motivation, and it is the young employees who give the real impetus to this. Management officers, knowing that the company's ordinary business is being done by energetic and enthusiastic younger employees, can devote their time and effort to planning the future of the company. With this in mind, we think it is unwise and unnecessary to define individual responsibility too clearly, because everyone is taught to act like a family member ready to do what is necessary. If something goes wrong it is considered bad taste for management to inquire who made the mistake. That may seem dangerous, if not silly, but it makes sense to us. The important thing in my view is not to pin the blame for a mistake on somebody, but rather to find out what caused the mistake.

II. MATSUI YAYORI: MIGRANT SEX WORKERS (1988)

I am here to make heard the painful cries of victimized Asian women.

I come from Japan, the country that grew rapidly into an economic giant only four decades after the devastation of World War II. On the surface, such rapid economic growth really does look like a miracle. It is little known, however, that this "miracle" was achieved at the expense of countless women both inside and outside Japan. One of Japan's most serious social problems is an expanding sex industry—this is the other, less publicized side of economic prosperity.

In the 1970s, Japan was known as the country that sent men on sex tours to neighboring Asian countries; today it has become the country that receives the largest number of Asian migrant women working as entertainers in the booming sex industry. Some estimate that nearly 100,000 such women come to Japan every year, including both legal female workers with entertainer visas and those who work illegally on tourist visas.

More than 90 percent of these female migrant workers come from only three countries: the Philippines, Thailand, and Taiwan. The number of Filipinas now accounts for 80 percent of that total, although the number of Thai women coming to Japan is also increasing at an alarming rate. Their jobs are concentrated in the sex industry, with most of them working as prostitutes, hostesses, striptease dancers and other sex-service-related entertainers . . . .

The growing number of migrant women who find their way to shelters all over the country also indicates the scope of human rights violations, inhuman humiliating treatment, and sexual abuse. Over the last three years, 1,200 women have sought refuge and assistance after being subjected to physical violence, psychological threats, nonpayment of wages, or forced prostitution. While migrant women suffer from this gross exploitation, traders—including recruiters, promoters, club owners, and pimps—make enormous profits at their expense; the returns from forced prostitution are particularly high.

Exactly why is it, then, that such huge numbers of Asian women are flooding into Japan? Essentially, this phenomenon results from the unjust economic imbalance between the [global] north and the [global] south. In other words, it is a symptom of deep-rooted economic problems on a global scale. . . .

But why does the sex industry flourish in Japan, creating such a high demand for female workers? The answer to this question is an inseparable part of Japan's economic system and reflects the situation of women and men in Japan. Japanese men are forced to work very hard and are virtually enslaved by the companies that employ them. Under the "Japanese-style management system," which is supported by the three pillars of life-long employment, seniority, and cooperative management-labor relations, employees are treated as members of the company family. In return, they are expected to be loyal and to devote their life to the company.

Employees average more than 2,000 working hours per year, compared to 1,600–1,700 hours in Western European countries; they take only nine days of paid holidays. They will even work on Sundays. Seeking relief from these extremely tense work patterns, Japanese business "warriors" frequent entertainment facilities with their colleagues or business customers. The companies themselves often provide their employees and customers opportunities to drink and enjoy entertainment with women. Sometimes the companies organize sex tours abroad for their employees as a reward for hard work or successful business deals.

In the context of such business practices, the role of Japanese women is either, as hostesses, to extend sexual services to men or, as wives and mothers, to take care of husbands and teach children to be future business warriors. Temporary work is another option, yet this is low-paid and unstable.

It cannot be overemphasized that the sharp increase in Asian female migrant workers coming to Japan is fundamentally linked to the very economic system that has brought about Japan's unprecedented rapid economic development. Based on the dehumanization of both Japanese men and women and on imported cheap labor, that development supports a growing sex industry in Japan, estimated at ¥10 trillion.

In addition, there are historically formed cultural and ideological factors that are vitally important in exposing the origins of the incomparable prosperity of Japan's sex industry. Japan has a long history of prostitution culture, based on deeply rooted sexist and patriarchal attitudes that show the influence of Confucian ideology. Within Japanese traditional values, prostitution has long been socially accepted. After Japan's feudal rulers established the public prostitution system in 1528, the *kuruwa,* or officially authorized prostitution areas, increased. There were twenty-five such areas throughout Japan in 1720.

During the feudal period, Japan was ruled by the warrior [*samurai*] class, which followed a strict Confucian ethic. It was considered unethical for a married couple to enjoy sexual pleasure. Women were supposed to follow the Confucian rule of the three obediences: as a daughter, obey the father; as a wife, the husband; and as a mother, the son. The essential role of women was to give birth to a son, a successor to the head of the feudal family [*ie*]. In other words, they were expected only to be breeding machines.

However, there was another type of woman as well. Men were provided with facilities, the *kuruwa,* where they could enjoy sexual pleasure outside the home. In these areas, prostitutes called *yūjo,* (later, *geisha*) were indentured from poor families to serve men sexually. They were used as tools of pleasure for men. We can say that women were divided into those with wombs and those with sexual organs. Both types of women were treated as mere objects, not as human beings or persons with human dignity.

This dichotomy has been carried over into the present day. Women are divided into "good women," or housewives, and "bad women," or prostitutes. It is common thinking in this society that "bad women" are necessary in order to protect the "good women." Men buying prostitutes are never socially condemned, nor is women's acceptance of this behavior condemned. Women often say: "If my husband goes to a 'professional' woman, it's not a problem, but if he is attracted to an ordinary woman, I get hurt and jealous." Such a double standard is still deep-rooted; the Japanese consider prostitutes as a special category of woman and fail to treat them as human beings or to accord them their human rights. . . .

The tidal wave of such sexual exploitation should be stemmed by all available means. What kind of actions should we take? Here I would like to present a brief history of our campaign against sex tours since the mid-1970s. Japanese women were shocked when Korean women protested against Japanese male sex tours in 1973. First, Korean Christian women's groups published a very strong statement condemning the wealthy Japanese men who were dehumanizing their country's women. Then a handful of Korean women students went to Kimpo airport carrying placards stating: "We are against prostitution tourism!" "Don't make our motherland a brothel for Japanese men!" Some of these women were arrested because the dictatorship didn't like such protests.

Responding to the courageous action of these Korean women, we Japanese feminists organized demonstrations at Haneda Airport, distributing leaflets to tourists bound for Seoul. We used strong language, such as "Shame on you!" "Stop your shameful behavior!" and "We will never allow you to repeat your sexual aggression!" During the war, the Japanese Imperial Army forced young Korean women to serve as prostitutes. Hundreds of thousands of them were sent to the battlefields of China and Southeast Asia, and they were abandoned in the jungle when Japanese troops had to withdraw in defeat.

It was during this demonstration against "*Kisaeng* tourism" that I coined a new word for prostitution. In Japanese, prostitution is called *baishun,* written with two Chinese characters meaning "sell spring." I changed the characters so that it meant "buy spring." I wanted to change attitudes toward and concepts of prostitution. Traditionally, women who sold their bodies were blamed, while men who bought their sex were not condemned. Therefore, the word had to be changed. It may seem a rather small thing, but it is revolutionary to shift the responsibility from women to men. Those who buy sex are to be condemned more than those who sell.

We should not look at prostitution from a perspective of moral judgment but rather analyze the problem within the context of the global economic structure.

STUDY QUESTIONS

1. How does Morita try to mesh profit seeking with Japanese cultural traditions?
2. How does the gender ratio in Japanese corporations during the era of the "miracle" raise questions about the appropriateness of the "family model"? Can a corporation be a family?
3. How were women affected by the corporate system in Japan? To what extent were the problems Matsui identifies a legacy of the past?
4. What solutions does Matsui advocate? Would equal gender relations in Japan solve the problems Matsui points to, or are there deeper issues?

ESSAY SUGGESTIONS

A. Compare life in a Japanese corporation to life during the Tokugawa period (Chapter 12).

B. How do Matsui's concerns echo those in the Meiji Restoration (Chapter 24)?

C. What, if any, was the relationship between Japan's experience in World War II and its economic and social development later in the twentieth century?

42 SOUTH ASIA

SPINNING WHEELS, BLACK FLAGS, AND A "TRYST WITH DESTINY": INDIA WINS INDEPENDENCE

In the aftermath of World War I, the Indian National Congress, founded in 1885 as an upper-class organization, morphed into the first mass-based nationalist movement outside the West. Many factors combined to produce this result. The ghastly intra-European bloodletting between 1914 and 1918 demolished the argument that morally superior Westerners had come to Asia and Africa to raise ethical standards. Proclamations by Woodrow Wilson regarding the desirability of national self-determination and by V. I. Lenin on the need to throw off colonial rule inspired many people across India (and elsewhere). British policy in India—a mix of incremental reforms and violent repression—backfired, dramatically increasing the ranks of those seeking national freedom.

Mohandas K. Gandhi, the lawyer and activist who returned to India in 1914 after having spent two decades in South Africa (Chapter 29), led the way in broadening the base of the nationalist movement. Gandhi's greatest strength may have been his ability to persuade the members of the Indian Congress to accept the support of rural and urban poor people in the struggle against the British. His success in this regard produced the mass movement that ultimately compelled the British to depart. Many of Gandhi's admirers also revere him for his commitment to *satyagraya* ("soul force"), that is, nonviolent resistance to oppressive authority.

The two parts of the first selection in this chapter come from the autobiography of an upper-class woman from north India, Manmohini Zutshi Sahgal, who followed her mother and older sisters into the nationalist cause in the 1920s. How does her memoir illustrate the changes that were taking place in India during the 1920s and 1930s? The second selection is the famous speech given by Jawaharlal Nehru, free India's first prime minister, on Independence eve, August 14, 1947. What themes stand out in the speech?

NATIONALIST DOCUMENTS

I. MANMOHINI ZUTSHI SAHGAL

A. Spinning Wheels

Mahatma Gandhi launched the noncooperation movement on August 1, 1920. He advocated the use of cotton *khadi* [handmade cloth], which became the uniform of the Independence Movement. Everyone—man or woman, urbanite or peasant—was expected to spin yarn on the *charka* [spinning wheel], which became not only the symbol of a peaceful revolution, but also a means of *sadhana* [religious discipline] for purification of the people's lives and bringing them nearer to God. For Indians, appeals must have some element of spirituality to be successful. I remember our own *charka* in Lahore. It was beautiful, and colorful as well, painted in soft shades of blue and red, studded with glass bells that would tinkle as the wheel was turned. Even before Gandhiji [a term of respect and affection] had advocated *charka,* spinning used to be a favorite pastime of even affluent ladies in the Punjab. In this part of the country the *charka* was fashioned in different colors to make it a pleasure to work on. The yarn spun was used mostly for making thick and colorful bed covers, either for use by the family or for charitable donation.

As part of the movement, the public were asked to give up their offices, titles, courts, colleges, councils, and services. At the Congress session in December of that year, the attainment of *swaraj* by peaceful and legitimate means had become the country's aim. *Swadeshi* meant wearing hand-spun, hand-woven cloth and using only indigenous goods. The boycott was to cover all foreign goods. Even the visit of the Prince of Wales was boycotted in 1921. Gandhiji had planned a no-tax campaign in Bardoli Subdivision, Bombay Presidency, but this plan had to be given up because of an outbreak of violence at Chauri Chaura in Gorakhpur District, Uttar Pradesh. Twenty-one constables and one subinspector of police were burned alive in the police station where they had taken shelter. This caused Gandhiji, who abhorred violence in any form, to call off the planned civil disobedience movement. Gandhiji said that the British wanted us to fight on their terms, but they had weapons and we did not. Therefore, he said, we had to put the struggle on terms where we did have weapons.

In March 1922 Gandhiji was arrested and sentenced to six years imprisonment. He was released on January 12, 1924, before the expiration of his term. This earlier noncooperation movement was confined largely to men and was less extensive than the *satyagraha* movement of 1930–32. Women were expected to participate in processions and attend all Congress meetings, however, so with Mother and my two older sisters, Chandra and Janak, I used to join all such functions. I would like my readers to visualize the restricted life women led, even in a province so progressive as the Punjab. Women hardly ever ventured beyond the four walls of their homes, except to visit relatives or to attend a religious festival. My mother's aunt always wore a shawl over her sari when she went visiting. I suppose that could be considered as a sort of Hindu *burqa* [garment that covers the head, face and body of the wearer] although her face was left uncovered. In that atmosphere, for the women to leave their homes and walk in a procession was a big step forward. The present footwear, *chappals* [sandals], had just come into fashion, and women unused to walking any distance in a disciplined manner found it extremely difficult to walk in their *chappals*. The *chappals* would come off as the women walked in procession. They could not pause to put them on again and usually continued walking barefoot in the procession. Mother had two Congress volunteers walk behind the women. Their duty was to pick up any odd *chappal* left behind, put it in a cloth bag, and bring it back to the office of the District Congress Committee at Pari Mahal, where the procession usually terminated. The women would reclaim their footwear and then go home. This was the training period. Later, these women would come into their own and storm the citadels of the mighty British Empire.

The main work of the women, as envisaged by the Congress, was to propagate the use of *khadi*. Women appealed to other women to discard foreign cloth. A number of songs were composed to bring this point home. Not all families could afford to throw away their clothes and buy a completely new wardrobe, but all the women had a couple of *khadi* saris, which they wore to all the meetings and processions. It was extremely difficult to forgo buying the lovely materials available; in contrast, *khadi* was coarse and rough and not easily available. Our own textile industry had been completely destroyed by the British. It is said that the Indian muslin was so fine and soft that an entire sari could pass through a ring. All the foreign cloth collected by Congress would be consigned to the flames in a huge bonfire, held on the banks of the river Ravi. I remember one occasion vividly. It was wintertime and the river had receded, leaving a small sandy island in the middle. The bonfire was set there, where it looked dramatic and was good for publicity.

Another incident is very clearly etched in my mind. A public meeting was to be held at Bradlaugh Hall, and Mother, Chandra, Janak, and I were going there in a *tonga* [horse-drawn cart]. We did not know that the hall had been occupied by the police and that the venue of the meeting had been moved to another place in the heart of the city. En route to the meeting, we were accosted by a stranger who informed us in a whisper that the meeting was being held at such and such a place. Instead of proceeding to Bradlaugh Hall, Mother directed the *tonga* driver to take us to this other place. On the way, she kept wondering whether our informant was a reliable friend or a secret service man trying to prevent us from attending the meeting. When we arrived at our destination, we found that our informant had been correct and the meeting was in progress. I have forgotten the name of that place, but it was a sort of miniature Jallianwala *Bagh* [the site of the 1919 Amritsar massacre], surrounded by tall houses and having only one entry. As the meeting progressed, the police walked in armed with metal-tipped *lathis* [long heavy sticks]. They declared the meeting illegal and requested that all women leave. The women understood that the men would be beaten once they left, so they refused to go. The excitement was intense and I was shouting slogans at the top of my voice. Those were the days when the British still remembered their chivalry. The police were not authorized to *lathi*-charge the men for fear of hitting the women. They tried persuasion and finally permitted the organizers to wind up the meeting and disperse. What a triumphant procession we made, parading through the streets of Lahore, celebrating our victory through nonviolence. Slogans were raised all along the route. I was only eleven years old and my excitement knew no bounds.

When I was twelve or thirteen, and Shyama, poor girl, was even younger, we were put in *khadi* saris. We never had ribbons or lace after that. Andhra Pradesh had started producing very fine *khadi,* but it was not enough for the whole country. We were a large family, four girls and Mother, all wearing saris, and it was impossible to get so much *khadi.* The order had to be placed months in advance, as it took a long time to complete. But we were so proud of our dress that we refused to wear anything else. In 1922, when my two cousins got married at Amritsar, Mother had ordinary white *khadi* dyed in different colors and printed in gold or silver so that we would look as dressy as our other girl cousins for such a grand occasion. We never complained that Mother had given all her lovely silk saris to be burned in the bonfires.

Kashmiri women are very simple in their dress. Summer or winter, they usually wear cotton at home. In Allahabad, before Gandhiji started his noncooperation movement, Mother used to wear cotton in summer and her old silk saris in winter. She came in for a lot of criticism by other women in the family for being so fashionable. . . .

B. Black Flags

[In March 1930, Gandhi resumed the noncooperation movement with a shrewdly organized 240-mile march to the shore of the Arabian Sea in protest against the British tax on salt. Newspaper photos and newsreel film of the march brought Gandhi and the nationalist movement to much wider notice, both in India and in countries abroad (including the United States). In the new cycle of strikes, boycotts, and street demonstrations, women played more active roles than they had previously, and the movement spread to the south of India.]

Together with the local Congress leaders, Mother prepared a scheme for picketing the Central Legislative Assembly at Simla [in the mountains north of Delhi] on the opening day. The whole plan was kept a secret. The Simla Congress Committee was given the task of working out the details. Four women from Lahore went: myself as leader, my sister Shyama, and two of our friends, Shakuntala and Avinash. Six women came from Ambala, and the rest were drawn from Simla itself. Altogether, we were twenty-seven women. The resourceful President of the Simla Congress Committee, Dr. N.L. Varma, had organized it so well that we were sent in batches of twos and threes to assemble at the front of the Central Assembly building. We were to wave black flags and shout "Go back, Irwin." Lord Irwin was then the Viceroy of India and was going to inaugurate the monsoon session of the Assembly. Soon we were a goodly number. Dr. Verma came in a ricksha with curtains drawn so that he would not be seen, but so that he could be there to boost our morale.

A few people were loitering about outside, but there were no crowds. It is surprising that the strangeness of a group of women standing there quietly, neither entering the building nor walking away, struck an Indian policeman and not the Anglo-Indian sergeant on duty. The policeman drew the sergeant's attention to this strange phenomenon, and the sergeant came up to inquire what we were doing. On my replying that we were merely standing there, he asked us to move either across the road or to the side of the steps, as the Viceroy, the Commander-in-Chief, and the Governor of the Punjab would all be arriving and that particular space would be needed for parking their cars. I had never been to Simla before and was unaware that, standing as we were, the Viceroy's car would face us and he would be bound to see us. It was sheer stubbornness that made us refuse to move from that spot. Time was very short. It was already 2:45 P.M. and the Viceroy was due to arrive punctually at 3:00 P.M. Our refusal to move was the first inkling the police had that we were not there for pleasure. The Assembly chamber had no extra police, and no car was permitted on the roads, so how could extra police be brought in? They would have to come from the nearest police station on the mall, and it would take at least fifteen minutes. Meanwhile, the Viceroy would have arrived. The police were in a fix. With great difficulty, they were able to muster five policemen, who tried to throw a cordon around us. But how could five men hide a group of twenty-seven women from the Viceroy? The sergeant kept on shouting, "Push them back!" while the Viceroy's car drove up. We promptly drew out the black flags hidden in the folds of our saris and shouted "Irwin, go back." You can imagine the furor it created! Lord Irwin got down from his car and walked up the steps to the Assembly chamber in a dignified manner. He never showed that he had seen or heard us. But there is a window overlooking the main road, and Lord Irwin was only human. He paused for a while on his way up to look down on the demonstration against him.

After he was inside, there was no point to our shouting ourselves hoarse. We formed a small procession and marched to the mall, singing national songs and shouting slogans. Never in the history of the summer capital of the British Empire had a handful of women been able to defy law and order so successfully. It was the first time that a procession had been taken out on the mall. The authorities were stunned and failed to take any action against us. Several inquiries were instituted as to how Congress had been able to plan a successful demonstration against the Viceroy. I am sure a large number of officers must have been transferred. We were, of course, jubilant. Four of us stayed in Simla for ten days and visited the Indian members of the Assembly at their residences and asked them to resign. I do not think it had the slightest effect on those seasoned politicians, but they liked to have four attractive young girls visit them every morning. We were always made welcome and entertained with a cup of tea or breakfast.

II. JAWAHARLAL NEHRU

Long years ago we made a tryst with destiny, and now the time comes when we shall redeem our pledge, not wholly or in full measure, but very substantially. At the stroke of the midnight hour, when the world sleeps, India will awake to life and freedom. A moment comes, which comes but rarely in history, when we step out from the old to the new, when an age ends, and when the soul of a nation, long suppressed, finds utterance. It is fitting that at this solemn moment we take the pledge of dedication to the service of India and her people and to the still larger cause of humanity.

At the dawn of history India started on her unending quest, and trackless centuries are filled with her striving and the grandeur of her success and her failures. Through good and ill fortune alike she has never lost sight of that quest or forgotten the ideals which gave her strength. We end today a period of ill fortune and India discovers herself again. The achievement we celebrate today is but a step, an opening of opportunity, to the greater triumphs and achievements that await us. Are we brave enough and wise enough to grasp this opportunity and accept the challenge of the future?

Freedom and power bring responsibility. The responsibility rests upon this Assembly, a sovereign body representing the sovereign people of India. Before the birth of freedom we have endured all the pains of labour and our hearts are heavy with the memory of this sorrow. Some of those pains continue even now. Nevertheless, the past is over and it is the future that beckons to us now.

That future is not one of ease or resting but of incessant striving so that we may fulfill the pledges we have so often taken and the one we shall take today. The service of India means the service of the millions who suffer. It means the ending of poverty and ignorance and disease and inequality of opportunity. The ambition of the greatest man of our generation has been to wipe every tear from every eye. That may be beyond us, but as long as there are tears and suffering, so long our work will not be over.

And so we have to labour and to work, and work hard, to give reality to our dreams. Those dreams are for India, but they are also for the world, for all the nations and peoples are too closely knit together today for any one of them to imagine that it can live apart. Peace has been said to be indivisible; so is freedom, so is prosperity now, and so also is disaster in this One World that can no longer be split into isolated fragments.

To the people of India, whose representatives we are, we make an appeal to join us with faith and confidence in this great adventure. This is no time for petty and destructive criticism, no time for ill will or blaming others. We have to build the noble mansion of free India where all her children may dwell.

STUDY QUESTIONS

1. What was the strategy of "noncooperation"?
2. What roles did women play in the protests of the early 1920s? How did their roles change by 1930? How do you explain the change?
3. How do the passages by Sahgal reveal the complexity of the Indian social structure in the 1920s and 1930s?
4. Is Nehru's speech more celebratory or cautionary? How do you account for this?
5. How does Nehru's speech relate to the popular nationalist agitation Gandhi had inspired?

VISUAL SOURCE

Responses to the Amritsar Massacre

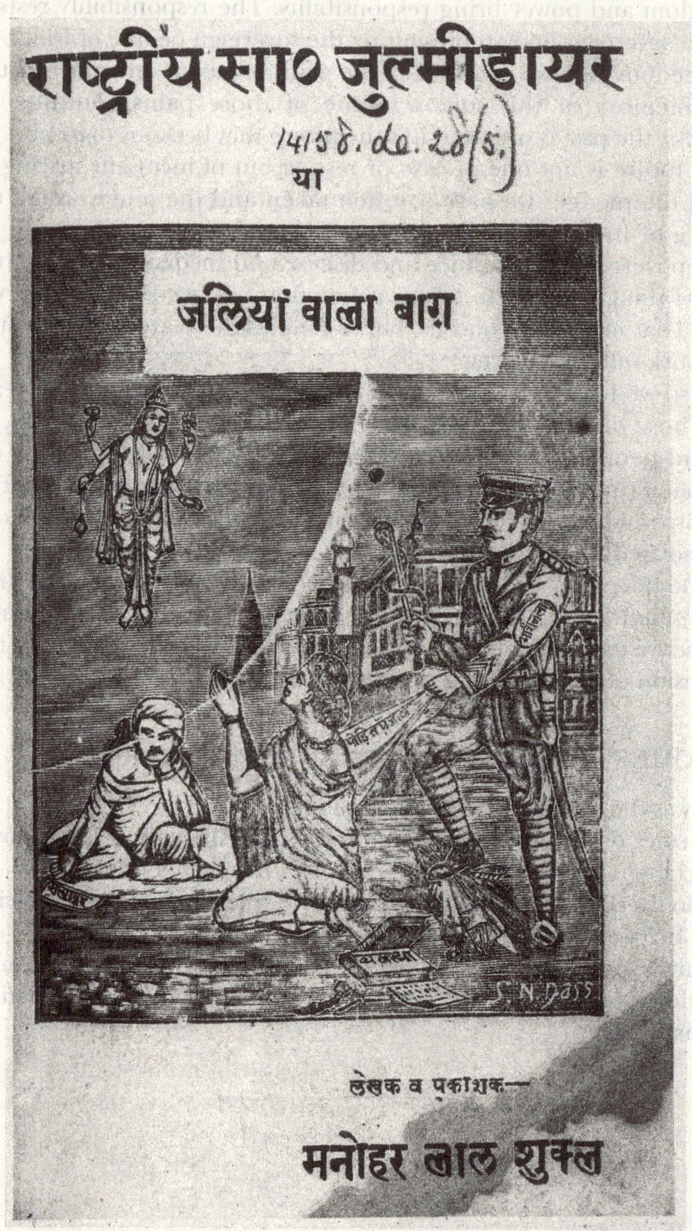

Title Page of *Rashtriya Sangit Julmi Dayar* by Manohar Lal Shukla (Kanpur, 1922).
(The British Library Board)

In April 1919, during widespread protests against British rule, a British general ordered his soldiers, mainly Indian and Gurkha troops, to fire on a peaceful and defenseless crowd of nationalist demonstrators in the northern city of Amritsar. The resulting massacre left several hundred protesters dead and more than a thousand wounded. It was this event that led Gandhi to organize and lead the wave of noncooperation activities that included members of the Zutshi family and millions of others.

The scene depicted here may also be considered a form of protest against the Amritsar massacre. It is the title page of a 1922 Hindi-language play, by Manohar Lal Shukla, that focuses on the massacre. In the center, a kneeling woman represents the Punjab, the region in which Amritsar is located. She prays to the four-armed Hindu deity, Lord Vishnu, who symbolizes security, order, love, and emotion. Standing over the woman is a British policeman, poised to strike a blow with his baton. Seated to the left of these two figures, and slightly to the rear of them, is a troubled Gandhi.

STUDY QUESTIONS

1. How does the scene combine traditional Indian images with a modern political message? How might a Muslim Indian react to this picture?
2. Why do you think the kneeling woman was named Punjabi rather than India? Why is the kneeling figure a female?
3. Given the context, is the depiction of the policeman essentially accurate? Why is Gandhi frowning?
4. What does the scene suggest about how political messages were circulated in a society in which only a minority was literate?
5. Does infusing a work of art with a clear political point of view sometimes strengthen it or, from an artistic point of view, is it a bad strategy?

ESSAY SUGGESTIONS

A. How did the role of women in the Indian national movement change during the 1920s and 1930s?

B. Compare Nehru's speech to the 1857 Azamgarh Proclamation (Chapter 25).

C. Compare Gandhi's strategy with that of the 1857 rebels (Chapter 25). How do you explain the differences?

D. Is the Amritsar massacre sequence in David Lean's 1981 film *Gandhi* historically accurate? Can a British director make a film about Indian nationalism that is good history?

E. Why was India able to maintain democracy after achieving national independence, in contrast to most postcolonial states?

43 UNTOUCHABILITY IN MODERN INDIA

Victory in the long struggle for freedom from British colonial rule opened the way to major changes in India. A vibrant system of political democracy, based on the 1950 Constitution, quickly took root. It has withstood challenges and remains strong today. Economic growth, sluggish through the 1980s, took off in the following decade; the prospects for continued annual growth at levels of 5 percent to 8 percent, high by world standards, look good. A key provision in the Constitution gave women the right to vote. Other legal gains for women followed, though real-life patriarchy, especially in the countryside where most people live, is far from gone. The secular character of the Constitution also provides India's large Muslim minority with important legal guarantees. But here too, everyday life has often belied the laws on the books.

An additional provision of the Constitution outlawed Untouchability, the long-established set of practices (and deeply held beliefs) that relegated one-sixth of the population to the most menial occupations, to dire poverty, to residential segregation, and to countless daily humiliations. As the document in this chapter reveals, *de facto* Untouchability outlived its abolition in law. But two policies adopted during the 1950s—the expansion of educational opportunities and a type of affirmative action—gradually improved the situation. As a result, while today most Untouchables, who now prefer the term *Dalits* (oppressed peoples), remain impoverished and undereducated, some have benefited from the new opportunities and have gone on to become successful professionals, government administrators, elected officials, and businesspersons.

The passages come from *Joothan*, the memoir of Omprakash Valmiki, a *Dalit* writer who was born in a northern Indian village in 1950. Valmiki's book is part of a powerful wave of *Dalit* writing that has been building for the past two decades. The emergence of this literature—poetry, memoirs, short stories, and essays—testifies to the effectiveness, for some, of the expanded educational opportunities and policy of affirmative action.

From Omprakash Valmiki, *Joothan: An Untouchable's Life*, translated by Arun Prabha Muherjee, pp. 8–12. (New York: Columbia University Press, 2003).

FROM *JOOTHAN* (2003)

At harvest time [in the 1950s] all the people in our neighborhood would have to go to the field of the Tagas [upper caste landowners] to reap the crop. Cutting the sheaves of wheat in the midday sun is a very hard and painful task. The sun pours on your head. Fiery-hot ground is beneath you. The roots of the cropped wheat plants pricked our feet like spikes. The roots of mustard and *chana dal* [yellow lentils] hurt even more. The harvesting of these lentils presents an extra difficulty. The leaves are sour and stick all over the body. Even bathing does not get rid of them completely. Most of the reapers were from the untouchable castes of the Chuhras or Chamars [traditionally, the caste of leather workers]. They had clothes on their bodies in name only. There was no question of shoes on their feet. Their bare feet were badly injured by the time the crop was brought in.

The harvesting would often lead to arguments in the fields. Most Tagas were miserly about paying wages. The reapers were helpless. Whatever they got, they took after some protest. After coming back home, they would fret, cursing the Tagas. But their protests died when confronted with hunger. Every year there would be a meeting in the neighborhood at harvest time. People swore to demand one sheaf out of sixteen as wages. But all the resolutions passed at the meeting evaporated into thin air the moment the harvesting began. For wages they got one sheaf for cutting twenty-one sheaves. One sheaf was less than a kilo of grain. Even the heaviest sheaf did not yield a kilo of wheat. That is, a day's wage was not even worth a kilo of wheat. After the harvesting the grain had to be loaded on bullock or buffalo carts and unloaded. Neither money nor grain was given for that work. Sooner or later all of us had to drive the bullocks onto the threshing floor, again without payment. In those days we didn't have threshers for cleaning up the wheat. The bullocks would be taken round and round to break up the sheaves into straw. Then the grain would be separated from the chaff by blowing it in a winnow. It was very long and tiring work, performed mostly by Chamars or Chuhras.

***

Along with these field labors, my mother also cleaned the *baithaks*, the outer room or space that men used as their space for chatting or meeting, and the cattle sheds of eight or ten Tagas, both Hindus and Muslims. My sister, elder *bhabhi*—sister-in-law—and my two brothers, Jasbir and Janesar, helped my mother in this work. My oldest brother, Sukhbir, worked for the Tagas like a permanent servant.

Every Taga would have ten to fifteen animals in his cowshed. We would have to pick up their dung and bring it to the place where *uplas*, or cow-dung cakes were made [for use as fuel]. We would take five to six baskets of dung from every cowshed. During the winter months it was a very painful job. The cows, buffaloes, and bullocks would be tethered in long hallways. The floor would be covered with the dry leaves of cane or straw. The dung and the urine of the animals would spread all over the floor overnight. We would change the matting every ten or fifteen days.

Or sometimes we would add a layer of dry leaves on top of the soiled one. To search for dung in the stinking cowsheds was extremely unpleasant. The stink made one feel faint.

To compensate us for all this work, we got five seers of grain per two animals; that is, about 2.5 kilos of grain. Each Taga household with ten animals gave twenty-five seers of grain a year—about twelve to fifteen kilos; we got a leftover roti [wheaten flat bread] that was specially made by mixing the flour with husks because it was for the Chuhras. Sometimes the *joothan,* the half-eaten scraps, would also be put in the basket with the rotis for us.

During a wedding, when the guests and the *baratis,* those who had accompanied the bridegroom as members of his party, were eating their meals, the Chuhras would sit outside with huge baskets, After the bridegroom's party had eaten, the dirty patals, or leaf plates, were put in the Chuhra's baskets, which they took home, to save the *joothan* that was sticking to them. The little remnants of *pooris,* puffed bread; bits of sweetmeats; and a little bit of vegetable were enough to make them happy. They ate the *joothan* with a lot of relish. They denounced as gluttons the bridegroom's guests who didn't leave enough scraps on their leaf plates. Poor things, they had never enjoyed a wedding feast. So they had licked it all up. During the marriage season, our elders narrated, in thrilled voices, stories of the bridegroom's party that had left several months of *joothan.*

We dried in the sun the pieces of *pooris* that we collected from the leaf plates. We would spread a cloth on a charpai, a rope-string cot, to dry them. Often, I would be placed on guard duty because the drying *pooris* attracted crows, hens, and dogs. Even a moment's lapse and the *pooris* would vanish. Hence one would have to sit near a cot with a stick in hand.

These dried up *pooris* were useful during the hard days of the rainy season. We would soak them in water and then boil them. The boiled *pooris* were delicious with finely ground red chili pepper and salt. Sometimes we mixed them with *gur* [molasses] to make a gruel and ate this dish with great delight.

When I think about those things today, thorns begin to prick my heart. What sort of life was that? After working hard day and night, the price of our sweat was just *joothan.* And yet no one had any grudges. Or shame. Or repentance.

When I was a young boy, I used to go with my parents to help them out. Looking at the food of the Tagas, I would wonder why we never got food like that. When I think of those days today, I feel nauseated.

This past year Sukhdev Singh Tyagi's grandson, Surenda [a Taga], came to my house in connection with some interview. He had obtained my address in the village. He stayed the night with us. My wife fed him a nice meal, and while eating, he said, "Bhabhiji [honorary sister-in-law], you make such delicious food. No one in our family can cook so well." His compliment made my wife happy, but I was deeply disturbed for some time. The incidents of childhood began knocking at my memory's door again.

Surenda had not even been born then. His aunt, that is, Sukhdev Singh Tyagi's daughter was getting married. My mother used to clean their place. For ten to twelve days before the wedding my parents were doing all sorts of work at Sukhdev Singh Tyagi's home. A daughter's wedding meant that the prestige of the whole village was at stake. Everything had to be perfect. My father went from village to village to collect rope-string cots for the guests.

The bridegroom's party was eating. My mother was sitting outside the door with her basket. I and my sister Maya, who was younger than I sat close to my mother in the hope that we too would get a share of the sweets and the gourmet dishes that we could smell cooking inside.

When all the people had left after the feast, my mother said to Sukhdev Singh Tyagi, as he was crossing the courtyard to come to the front door: "Chowdhuriji [Honorable Village Official], all of your guests have eaten and gone. . . . Please put something on a leaf plate for my children. They too have waited for this day."

Sukhdec Singh pointed at the basket full of dirty leaf plates and said, "You are taking a basket of *joothan.* And on top of that you want food for your children? Don't forget your place, Chuhri [a derogatory form of address]. Pick up your basket and get going."

Those words of Sukhdev Singh Tyagi's penetrated my breast like a knife. They continue to singe me to this day.

That night the mother goddess Durga [symbolic of violence and sex] entered my mother's eyes. It was the first time I saw my mother get so angry. She emptied the basket right there. She said to Sukhdev Singh, "Pick it up and put it inside your house. Feed it to the bridegroom's guests tomorrow morning." She gathered me and my sister and left like an arrow. Sukhdev Singh pounced on her to hit her, but my mother had confronted him like a lioness. Without being afraid.

After that day Ma never went back to his door. And after this incident she also stopped taking their *joothan.*

STUDY QUESTIONS

1. What features of Untouchability in the 1950s stand out? What did Valmiki find most painful about his childhood?
2. Who benefited from Untouchability?
3. How does the memoir illuminate broader features of Indian rural life during the 1950s?
4. Does the passage provide evidence of any changes in the lives of *Dalits*?

ESSAY SUGGESTIONS

A. Is Untouchability uniquely Indian, or are there similar patterns or issues in other countries? If so, what are they?

B. Why hasn't there been a Gandhian-style movement of noncooperation among India's Untouchables? Why hasn't there been an armed popular uprising, as in Russia (1917) and China (1949)?

C. How does the emergence of *Dalit* literature mesh with global trends in human rights advocacy?

44 LATIN AMERICA

TWENTIETH-CENTURY LATIN AMERICAN POLITICS: THE REVOLUTIONARY CHALLENGE AND THE TURN TOWARD DEMOCRACY

From the beginning of the twentieth century to the middle of the 1980s, social unrest along with inflexible political regimes led to revolutions and political upheaval in Latin America. Three selections depict episodes during this period. All express some of the basic social grievances that created the unrest.

The first selection comes from the Mexican Revolution of 1910. It was issued by the most radical peasant leader, Emiliano Zapata. Zapata never seized control of the Mexican Revolution, but the radical economic demands of his Plan of Ayala influenced the course of Mexican social development for the next thirty years.

The second selection reflects a new kind of strongman rule that characterized several major Latin states during the twentieth century. In Argentina, Juan Perón resembled revolutionaries in seeking to avoid foreign (in this case almost entirely economic) domination. Perón, a middle-class military man, appealed to working people neglected by earlier civilian governments. The passage shows how union leaders—in this case, the head of the metalworkers' union—had become disenchanted with Communist control and preferred a military ruler who could get things done for the workers. This decision resulted in state control of unions during Perón's presidency (1946–1955), and an enduring attachment of many Argentine workers to an authoritarian, but populist, government.

A new round of revolutionary activity emerged during the 1950s, building on social and economic problems similar to those in Mexico earlier on. The lone successful change came in 1959 with Fidel Castro in Cuba, but his example then spurred other guerrilla movements that, particularly in Central America, have continued to the present day. Later on, it also helped inspire outright revolution in Nicaragua.

Although he became a symbol of Communist insurrection, Castro viewed his revolution as authentically Cuban. Looking back into Cuba's past, Castro saw a deformed nation. At each moment when a true nationalist sought political power, either he was

Selection I from Emiliano Zapata, *The Plan of Ayala* (29 November, 1911). Translated by Erick D. Langer. Reprinted by permission of Dr. Erick D. Langer. Selection II from Angel Perelman, *Como Hicimos el 17 de Octobre* (Buenos Aires: Editorial Coyoacan, 1961), pp. 44–46, translated in *Why Peron Came to Power. The Background to Peronism in Argentine,* edited by Joseph R. Barager (New York: Alfred A. Knopf, 1968), pp. 200–202. Copyright © 1968, Alfred A. Knopf. Reprinted by permission. Selection III from Fidel Castro, *History Will Absolve Me, Moncada Trial Defence Santiago De Cuba* (London: Jonathan Cape, 1958), pp. 40–45. Reprinted by permission. Selection IV from *Business Week,* October 12, 2009, accessed online November 17, 2009. Copyright McGraw-Hill Companies Inc.

blocked by foreign intervention or he betrayed the cause. José Marti, the intellectual spirit of the Cuban independence movement against Spain in 1895, was an authentic Cuban hero. Yet, his political program was never realized because of the intervention of the United States during the Spanish-American War of 1898. From that year until Castro seized power in 1959, the United States dominated Cuba politically and economically, despite Cuba's nominal independence. Presidents of Cuba, such as Fulgencio Batista (1940–1944, 1952–1958), talked of reform but used their office to become wealthy, especially by diverting U.S. loans into their own pockets. Meanwhile, the majority of the Cuban people—the poor—were neglected. For Cuba to take control of its destiny, Castro saw the necessity of revolution. After the failure of his first military operation on July 26, 1953, Castro—while in jail—described why the revolution was being fought and what he would do once in power. In the third selection, one can see that the spirit that animates his program is the same spirit that guides revolutionaries in other parts of Latin America.

During the 1960s and 1970s, except for Cuba and temporarily in Nicaragua, conservative authoritarian governments and outright military dictatorships stamped out most revolutionary factions. Yet these rulers failed to establish legitimate governments based on the ballot. In the early 1980s inability to pay foreign debts and other economic problems further discredited these regimes. Popular demonstrations led to their withdrawal from power and an opening of the political system. Since the 1980s free elections strengthened democratic political parties and, by the first decade of the twenty-first century, led to the election of political leaders who introduced mild socialist programs. Such left leaning political parties reached power in Brazil, Chile, Argentina, Ecuador, Venezuela, and Bolivia.

The fourth selection indicates the goals of one these governments, that in Brazil, during the presidency of Luiz Inacio Lula da Silva. Born in 1945, Lula rose from being a shoeshine boy on the streets of Sao Paulo to press operator in an automobile parts factory to president of the steelworkers' union in 1978 and to founding member of the Workers Party in 1980. Beginning in 1989, Lula ran three times as the Workers Party candidate for the presidency of Brazil. He was elected president in 2002 and again in 2006. In an interview (October 8, 2009) with a reporter from *Business Week*, Lula indicates the direction of his political program in the context of the world economy.

LATIN AMERICAN REVOLUTIONARY DOCUMENTS

I. THE PLAN OF AYALA

The liberating Plan of the sons of the State of Morelos, affiliated with the Insurgent Army which defends the fulfillment of the Plan of San Luis Potosí, with the reforms which they have believed necessary to add for the benefit of the Mexican Fatherland.

We, the subscribers [to this Plan], constituted in a Revolutionary Council . . . declare solemnly before the countenance of the civilized world which judges us and before the Nation to which we belong and love, the principles which we have formulated to terminate the tyranny which oppresses us and redeem the Fatherland from the dictatorships which are imposed on us, which are determined in the following Plan:

1. [Accuses Francisco I. Madero, the leader of the 1910 revolution and President of Mexico, of betraying the Revolution and allying himself with the oppressive old guard in the State of Morelos.]
2. Francisco I. Madero is disavowed as Chief of the Revolution and as President of the Republic, for the above reasons, [and we will] endeavor to overthrow this official.
3. The illustrious General Pascual Orozco, second of the *caudillo* Don Francisco I. Madero, is recognized as Chief of the Liberating Revolution, and in case he does not accept this delicate post, General Emiliano Zapata is recognized as Chief of the Revolution.
4. The Revolutionary Junta of the State of Morelos manifests the following formal points . . . and will make itself the defender of the principles that it will defend until victory or death.
5. The Revolutionary Junta of the State of Morelos will not admit transactions or political compromises until the overthrow of the dictatorial elements of Porfirio Díaz and Francisco I. Madero, since the Nation is tired of false men and traitors who make promises as liberators but once in power, forget them and become tyrants.
6. As an additional part of the Plan which we invoke, we assert that: the fields, woodland, and water which the haciendados [landlords], *científicos* or bosses in the shadow of tyranny and venal justice have usurped, will revert to the possession of the towns or citizens who have their corresponding titles to these properties. [These properties] have been usurped through the bad faith of our oppressors, who maintained all along with arms in hand the above mentioned possession. The usurpers who feel they have the right [to ownership], will demonstrate this before special tribunals which will be established when the Revolution triumphs.
7. In virtue of the fact that the immense majority of the towns and Mexican citizens are not masters of the soil they step upon, suffering horrors of misery without being able to better their social condition at all nor dedicate themselves to industry or agriculture because of the monopoly in a few hands of the land, woodlands, and waters, for this reason [the lands] will be expropriated, with indemnity of the third part of these monopolies to their powerful owners, so that the towns and citizens of Mexico can obtain common lands [*ejidos*], colonies, and legitimate resources for towns or agricultural fields and that above all the lack of prosperity and wellbeing of the Mexican people is improved.
8. The haciendados, *científicos* or bosses who oppose directly or indirectly the present plan, will have their possessions nationalized and two thirds of what they own will be destined for war indemnities, [and] pensions for the widows and orphans of the victims who succumb in the fight for this Plan.

9. To regulate the procedures in regard to the items mentioned above, the laws of disentailment and nationalization will be applied as is appropriate. [The laws] put into effect by the immortal Juarez regarding Church lands will serve as a guide and example, which set a severe example to the despots and conservatives who at all times have tried to impose the ignominious yoke of oppression and backwardness.

10. The insurgent military chiefs of the Republic, who rose up in armed revolt at the behest of Francisco I. Madero to defend the Plan of San Luis Potosí and who now oppose by force the present Plan, are to be judged traitors to the cause they defended and to the Fatherland, given the fact that in actuality many of them to please the tyrants for a handful of coins, or for bribes, are spilling the blood of their brethren who demand the fulfillment of the promises which don Francisco I. Madero made to the Nation.

11–14. [Details the payment of the expenses of war, the administration of the country after the Plan's success, and bids Madero to step down voluntarily.]

15. Mexicans: Consider that the cleverness and the bad faith of one man is spilling blood in a scandalous manner because of his inability to govern; consider that his system of government is putting the Fatherland in chains and by brute force of bayonets trampling under foot our institutions; and as we raised our arms to elevate him to power, today we turn them against him for having gone back on his agreements with the Mexican people and having betrayed the Revolution he initiated; we are not personalists, we are believers in principles, not in men.

People of Mexico: Support with your arms in hand this Plan and you will create prosperity and happiness for the Fatherland.

Justicia y ley. [Justice and Law.]
Ayala, 28 of November, 1911.

II. PERONISM (ARGENTINE METALWORKER RECOLLECTS MEETING WITH PERÓN, MID-1944)

Once the resistance of the [Communist] directors was overcome, we arranged with the Secretariat of Labor to convoke a meeting at which Perón would speak to the metal workers. The date fixed, we calculated that we could fill the assembly hall of the Deliberating Council, where the Secretariat of Labor and Social Welfare was located [Perón headed the Secretariat of Labor].

We had no resources for publicizing this meeting. Until noon of the day of the gathering, we were still sticking together some posters announcing the convocation. It was a great surprise when, by the time of the meeting, the meeting hall was completely filled, and an enormous multitude of nearly 20,000 metal workers was concentrated outside in the Diagonal Roca. The shops they came from were identified by improvised placards and reflected the enormous repercussion the growth of industry was having on the working class at that time. . . .

Colonel Perón, in one of the salient parts of his discourse, told us that he was gratified to see the metal workers enter the house of the workers and that he had assumed that, since they were one of the last unions to come together there, they must be very well paid. But he added that, as a result of the remarks of the comrade who had preceded him on the platform, it appeared that this was not so, and consequently he was urging the metal workers to form a powerful union to defend their rights and the country's sovereignty. At this moment a metal worker interrupted to shout: "Thus speaks a *criollo!*" [true Argentine] Banners and posters fluttered approval of the metal worker's remark. We went out of that meeting with the conviction that the metal workers' union would soon be transformed into a very powerful labor organization. And in effect it was; from a membership of 1,500 we transformed that union "of form" into the present Union of Metal Workers (UOM) with 300,000 workers in the fold. So profound was the need for the country to defend its political independence and economic sovereignty, and for the working class to organize at last its unions on a grade scale, that, faced by the treason of the parties of the left, this need had to be embodied in a military man who had come from the ranks of the Army.

And we came to constitute then that ideological tendency known by many people as the "national left." In our union activities at the end of 1944 we witnessed unbelievable happenings: labor laws neglected in another era were being carried out; one did not need recourse to the courts for the granting of vacations; such other labor dispensations as the recognition of factory delegates, guarantees against being discharged, etc., were immediately and rigorously enforced. The nature of internal relations between the owners and the workers in the factories was completely changed. The internal democratization imposed by the metal workers' union resulted in factory delegates constituting the axis of the entire organization and in the direct expression of the will of the workers in each establishment. The owners were as disconcerted as the workers were astounded and happy. The Secretariat of Labor and Social Welfare was converted into an agency for the organization, development, and support of the workers. It did not function as a state regulator for the top level of the unions; it acted as a state ally of the working class. Such were the practical results that constituted the basis for the political shift of the Argentine masses and that were manifested in the streets on October 17, 1945. [Date when a massive demonstration took place that secured Perón's release from prison.]

III. CASTRO'S PROGRAM (OCTOBER 16,1953)

When we speak of the people we do not mean the comfortable ones, the conservative elements of the nation, who welcome any regime of oppression, any dictatorship, any despotism, prostrating themselves before the master of the moment until they grind their foreheads into the ground. When we speak of struggle, the people means the vast unredeemed masses to whom all make promises and whom all deceive; we mean the people who yearn for a better, more dignified and more just nation; who are moved by ancestral aspirations of justice, for they have suffered injustice and mockery generation after generation; who long for great and wise changes in all aspects of their life; people who, to attain the changes, are ready to give even the very last breath of their lives, when they believe in something or in someone, especially when they believe in themselves. . . . The people we counted on in our struggle were these:

Seven hundred thousand Cubans without work, who desire to earn their daily bread honestly without having to emigrate in search of a livelihood.

Five hundred thousand farm labourers inhabiting miserable shacks (*bohíos*), who work four months of the year and starve during the rest, sharing their misery with their children; who have not an inch of land to till, and whose existence would move any heart not made of stone.

Four hundred thousand industrial labourers and stevedores [workers who load and unload ships] whose retirement funds have been embezzled, whose benefits are being taken away, whose homes are wretched quarters, whose salaries pass from the hands of the boss to those of the money-lender (*garrotero*), whose future is a pay reduction and dismissal, whose life is eternal work and whose only rest is in the tomb.

One hundred thousand small farmers who live and die working on land that is not theirs, looking at it with sadness as Moses looked at the promised land, to die without ever owning it; who, like feudal serfs, have to pay for the use of their parcel of land by giving up a portion of its products: who cannot love it, improve it, beautify it, nor plant a lemon or an orange tree on it, because they never know when a sheriff will come with the rural guard to evict them from it.

Thirty thousand teachers and professors who are so devoted, dedicated and necessary to the better destiny of future generations and who are so badly treated and paid.

Twenty thousand small business men, weighted down by debts, ruined by the crisis and harangued by a plague of grafting and venal officials.

Ten thousand young professionals: doctors, engineers, lawyers, veterinarians, school teachers, dentists, pharmacists, newspapermen, painters, sculptors, etc., who come forth from school with their degrees, anxious to work and full of hope, only to find themselves at a dead end with all doors closed, and where no ear hears their clamour or supplication.

These are the people, the ones who know misfortune and, therefore, are capable of fighting with limitless courage!

To the people whose desperate roads through life have been paved with the bricks of betrayals and false promises, we were not going to say: "We will eventually give you what you need," but rather—"Here you have it, fight for it with all your might, so that liberty and happiness may be yours!"

In the brief of this case, the five revolutionary laws that would have been proclaimed immediately after the capture of the Moncada Barracks and would have been broadcasted to the nation by radio should be recorded. It is possible that Colonel Chaviano may deliberately have destroyed these documents, but even if he has done so I remember them.

The First Revolutionary Law would have returned power to the people and proclaimed the Constitution of 1940 the supreme Law of the State, until such time as the people should decide to modify or change it. And, in order to effect its implementation and punish those who had violated it, there being no organization for holding elections to accomplish this, the revolutionary movement, as the momentous incarnation of this sovereignty, the only source of legitimate power, would have assumed all the faculties inherent in it, except that of modifying the Constitution itself: in other words, it would have assumed the legislative, executive and judicial powers. . . .

The Second Revolutionary Law would have granted property, non-mortgageable and non-transferable, to all planters, non-quota planters, lessees, share-croppers, and squatters who hold parcels of five *caballerías* of land or less, and the State would indemnify the former owners on the basis of the rental which they would have received for these parcels over a period of ten years.

The Third Revolutionary Law would have granted workers and employees the right to share thirty per cent of the profits of all the large industrial, mercantile and mining enterprises, including the sugar mills. The strictly agricultural enterprises would be exempt in consideration of other agrarian laws which would be implemented.

The Fourth Revolutionary Law would have granted all planters the right to share fifty-five per cent of the sugar production and a minimum quota of forty thousand *arrobas* for all small planters who have been established for three or more years.

The Fifth Revolutionary Law would have ordered the confiscation of all holdings and ill-gotten gains of those who had committed frauds during previous regimes, as well as the holdings and ill-gotten gains of all their legatees and heirs. To implement this, special courts with full powers would gain access to all records of all corporations registered or operating in this country, in order to investigate concealed funds of illegal origin, and to request that foreign governments extradite persons and attach holdings rightfully belonging to the Cuban people. Half of the property recovered would be used to subsidize retirement funds for workers and the other half would be used for hospitals, asylums and charitable organizations.

IV. INTERVIEW WITH LUIZ INACIO LULA DA SILVA, PRESIDENT OF BRAZIL, OCTOBER 8, 2009

By Line: By Maria Bartiromo

Section: The Business Week—Facetime Pg. 13 Vol. 4150

As President, Luiz Inacio Lula da Silva has brought to Brazil a blend of capitalism and populism that is taking Latin America's largest economy to new heights. I talked with Lula, as he is popularly known, after the gathering of the U.N. General Assembly and right before the meeting of the G-20 in Pittsburgh.

How Brazil's Lula Sees the Emerging World Order

Maria Bartiromo

What are you looking to achieve at these meetings?

President Luiz Inacio Da Silva

We have an opportunity to do things that we haven't done in the past. There was a time when the world started to believe that the markets didn't need any kind of regulation. Anyone could invest money as they wished. The banks could do whatever they wished. I don't want the president [of a country] or the state managing the economy. But I want the government to drive economies and be a regulator at the same time. One of the reasons for the global economic crisis was the [behavior] of the banks, especially in the U.S. They had no parameters in leveraging their loans. When a bank leverages an amount of money that is many more times its net worth, I say the bank is lending money that it doesn't have. Thank God, in Brazil we have a financial system that is highly regulated. You can only leverage 10% of your net worth. So when the crisis came, Brazil had sound and strong institutions to confront it. Now the G-20 has the opportunity to rethink the role of government. It's very easy to govern when everything is going smoothly. But leaders exist to govern in the face of difficulties.

In Brazil we had no credit to finance used cars. And I told the Bank of Brazil, the state owned bank, to buy a private bank that had expertise in financing used cars. For what reason? We wanted credit to continue flowing. This is the sort of time you need the state. My concern with the G-20 is that the leaders are now becoming [complacent] because the crisis is passing and they won't change anything. We have to change. We have to change the role of the IMF and the World Bank. And we have to control the international financial system so [financial institutions] cannot leverage many more times their net worth. It's difficult because each [leader] has [his or her] own domestic public. But if you're a leader, you have to think what will help solve the world's problems.

But do you worry that we could have too much regulation and too much government ownership of business?

I don't want too much government or minimum government either. Brazil has found a middle path. If a company wants to make an investment in Brazil, [we have discussions] about what region would be [appropriate for] the investment. Why? So we can encourage regional development. That's the role of government. I think we learned a lesson from the global crisis. Remember when oil went up to $150 a barrel. Soy beans also went up. There was a commodity bubble. That was investors getting out of the subprime market and rushing to the futures market for food and oil. Otherwise, there is no explanation for oil going from $30 up to $150 in such a short time. We cannot allow this kind of speculation because this harms the poorest people in the world. It brings damage to job creation. We want the welfare of the society to grow together with the economy. Otherwise the economy grows for only a half a dozen people.

Can you talk about Brazil's strengths, such as agriculture and oil?

Brazil has extraordinary possibilities because we have one of the largest land [masses] in the world available for agriculture. Just to give you an idea, the sugarcane that produces ethanol takes up less than 2% of all the land of Brazil. But we have to be careful that the prices [of agricultural commodities] don't go beyond the purchasing power of the people that need food.

Now, on the oil issue, I believe the price should be stabilized. [The cost of] oil should not strangle countries. Brazil already is self-reliant on oil. We just discovered great deposits of deep-sea oil fields—huge reserves at 7000 meters of depth. The [oil money] will be used to invest in education, science, and technology so we can end poverty and solve chronic problems. We don't want to sell crude oil. We want to sell added-value products. That's why we are building new refineries. We want to sell gasoline.

How is Brazil's economy doing?

We have a lot to do, but Brazil is experiencing a magical economic moment. The global crisis hampered us, and I had to ask the people to buy more because newspaper headlines almost created panic. But the economy grew 0.9% in the second quarter and it can grow around 5% in 2010. We are developing a strong policy of income transfer to the poorest of the population. We made a commitment to build 1 million new houses for low-income [families]. We have almost $359 billion in infrastructure projects. From 1950–1980, Brazil grew at over 7% a year, one year 14%—more than China today. Nevertheless, what happened? There was no income distribution. The rich became even richer. The poor became very poor. Now we have reversed this game. We want to leverage the poor. The better off the poor are, the more we improve the lives of the business community.

STUDY QUESTIONS

1. What are the goals of Zapata's revolution? How much change would take place if they were implemented?
2. How did Perón benefit the workers? Why did they turn toward him? Does this strategy on the part of the union qualify as revolutionary?
3. How do the goals of Perónist workers resemble as well as differ from more explicitly revolutionary currents in Latin America?
4. How radical were Castro's goals? What were the political implications of implementing them? Who would have been harmed by their implementation? Who would have benefited? How do they compare with Zapata's goals?
5. According to Lula da Silva, what should be the role of the government in the economy? By what mechanisms would Lula aid the poor?

ESSAY SUGGESTIONS

A. The documents offer a comparison with earlier grievances when Latin American nations struggled for political independence (Chapter 27). What has changed among the goals and actors on center stage?

B. Do the political programs of Zapata, Perón, Castro, and Lula da Silva align with the general direction of the role of the state in contemporary Europe? Is Latin America following similar trends?

45

SEARCHING FOR THE SOUL OF THE LATIN AMERICAN EXPERIENCE

Essayists and novelists have struggled to capture the uniqueness of Latin America. Although their descriptions are set in specific countries and locations, they tend toward common themes. For example, Mexican essayist Octavio Paz, in search of his identity as well as that of his nation, wrote about the "labyrinth of solitude." Colombian novelist Gabriel García Márquez examined the experiences of a family and a town through "one hundred years of solitude." The common theme of solitude becomes for these two men the chief vehicle for understanding Latin American civilization.

Gabriel García Márquez was awarded the Nobel Prize for literature in 1982. In his acceptance speech, "The Solitude of Latin America," he explained the source of that solitude. To García Márquez, Latin Americans lacked a conventional means of believing their past. Rather, they lived in a world of illusion that produced separation and solitude. This "fantasy reality" could not be understood by outsiders, who were equipped only with their own cultural tools. Europeans, for example, accepted Latin American literature; however, they ridiculed the Latin Americans' attempts at social change. Latin Americans were accepted not as a distinct whole but as an incomplete Western form. García Márquez asserts that Latin America is distinct. Latin Americans will invent their own solutions and utopias. They will affirm their own reality, illusory or not.

The concern about identity in Latin America reflects an important facet of Latin American culture, but this is not unique. Other twentieth-century civilizations worry about identity issues; these Latin American reflections can thus be compared with the issues of identity in societies such as those in sub-Saharan Africa.

LATIN AMERICAN IDENTITY

Antonio Pigafetta, a Florentine navigator who went with Magellan on the first voyage around the world, wrote, upon his passage through our southern lands of America, a strictly accurate account that nonetheless resembles a venture into fantasy. In it he recorded that he had seen hogs with navels on their haunches, clawless birds whose hens laid eggs on the backs of their mates, and others still, resembling tongueless pelicans, with beaks like spoons. He wrote of having seen a misbegotten creature with the

From Gabriel García Márquez, "The Solitude of Latin America" (Nobel Lecture, 1982), translated from the Spanish by Mariana Castaneda in Julio Ortega, *Gabriel García Márquez and the Powers of Fiction* (Austin: University of Texas Press, 1988), pp. 87–91.

head and ears of a mule, a camel's body, the legs of a deer and the whinny of a horse. He described how the first native encountered in Patagonia was confronted with a mirror, whereupon that impassioned giant lost his senses to the terror of his own image.

This short and fascinating book, which even then contained the seeds of our present-day novels, is by no means the most staggering account of our reality in that age. The Chroniclers of the Indies left us countless others. Eldorado, our so avidly sought and illusory land, appeared on numerous maps for many a long year, shifting its place and form to suit the fantasy of cartographers. In his search for the fountain of eternal youth, the mythical Alvar Núñez Cabeza de Vaca explored the north of Mexico for eight years, in a deluded expedition whose members devoured each other and only five of whom returned, of the six hundred who had undertaken it. One of the many unfathomed mysteries of that age is that of the eleven thousand mules, each loaded with one hundred pounds of gold, that left Cuzco one day to pay the ransom of Atahualpa and never reached their destination. Subsequently, in colonial times, hens were sold in Cartagena de Indias, that had been raised on alluvial land and whose gizzards contained tiny lumps of gold. The founders' lust for gold beset us until recently. As late as the last century, a German mission appointed to study the construction of an inter-oceanic railroad across the Isthmus of Panama concluded that the project was feasible on one condition: that the rails not be made of iron, which was scarce in the region, but of gold.

Our independence from Spanish domination did not put us beyond the reach of madness. General Antonio López de Santa Anna, three times dictator of Mexico, held a magnificent funeral for the right leg he had lost in the so-called Pastry War. General Gabriel García Moreno ruled Ecuador for sixteen years as an absolute monarch; at his wake, the corpse was seated on the presidential chair, decked out in full-dress uniform and a protective layer of medals. General Maximiliano Hernández Martínez, the theosophical despot of El Salvador who had thirty thousand peasants slaughtered in a savage massacre, invented a pendulum to detect poison in his food, and had street lamps draped in red paper to defeat an epidemic of scarlet fever. The statue to General Francisco Morazán erected in the main square of Tegucigalpa is actually one of Marshal Ney, purchased at a Paris warehouse of second-hand sculptures.

Eleven years ago, the Chilean Pablo Neruda, one of the outstanding poets of our time, enlightened the audience with his word. Since then, the Europeans of good will—and sometimes those of bad, as well—have been struck, with ever greater force, by the unearthly tidings of Latin America, that boundless realm of haunted men and historic women, whose unending obstinacy blurs into legend. We have not had a moment's rest. A promethean president, entrenched in his burning palace, died fighting an entire army, alone; and two suspicious airplane accidents, yet to be explained, cut short the life of another great-hearted president and that of a democratic soldier who had revived the dignity of his people. There have been five wars and seventeen military coups; there emerged a diabolic dictator who is carrying out, in God's name, the first Latin American ethnocide of our time. In the meantime, twenty million Latin American children died before the age of one—more than have been born in Europe since 1970. Those missing because of repression number nearly one hundred and twenty thousand, which is as if no one could account for all the inhabitants of Upsala. Numerous women arrested while pregnant have given birth in Argentina prisons, yet nobody knows the whereabouts and identity of their children, who were furtively adopted or sent to an orphanage by order of the military authorities. Because they tried to change this state of things, nearly two hundred thousand men and women have died throughout the continent, and over one hundred thousand have lost their lives in three small and ill-fated countries of Central America: Nicaragua, El Salvador, and Guatemala. If this had happened in the United States, the corresponding figure would be that of one million six hundred thousand violent deaths in four years.

One million people have fled Chile, a country with a tradition of hospitality—that is, ten percent of its population. Uruguay, a tiny nation of two and a half million inhabitants which considered itself the continent's most civilized country, has lost to exile one out of every five citizens. Since 1979, the civil war in El Salvador has produced almost one refugee every twenty minutes. The country that could be formed of all the exiles and forced emigrants of Latin America would have a population larger than that of Norway.

I dare to think that it is this outsized reality, and not just its literary expression, that has deserved the attention of the Swedish Academy of Letters. A reality not of paper, but one that lives within us and determines each instant of our countless daily deaths, and that nourishes a source of insatiable creativity, full of sorrow and beauty, of which this roving and nostalgic Colombian is but one cipher more, singled out by fortune. Poets and beggars, musicians and prophets, warriors and scoundrels, all creatures of that unbridled reality, we have had to ask but little of imagination, for our crucial problem has been a lack of conventional means to render our lives believable. This, my friends, is the crux of our solitude.

And if these difficulties, whose essence we share, hinder us, it is understandable that the rational talents on this side of the world, exalted in the contemplation of their own cultures, should have found themselves without a valid means to interpret us. It is only natural that they insist on measuring us with the yardstick that they use for themselves, forgetting that the ravages of life are not the same for all, and that the quest of our own identity is just as arduous and bloody for us as it was for them. The interpretation of our reality through patterns not our own serves only to make us ever more unknown, ever less free, ever more solitary. Venerable Europe would perhaps be more perceptive if it tried to see us in its own past. If only it recalled that London took three hundred years to build its first city wall, and three hundred years more to acquire a bishop; that Rome labored in a gloom of uncertainty for twenty centuries, until an Etruscan king anchored it in history; and that the peaceful Swiss of today, who feast us with their mild cheeses and apathetic watches, bloodied Europe as soldiers of fortune, as late as the 16th century. Even at the height of the Renaissance, twelve thousand lansquenets in the pay of the imperial armies sacked and devastated Rome and put eight thousand of its inhabitants to the sword.

I do not mean to embody the illusions of Tonio Krüger, whose dreams of uniting a chaste north to a passionate south were exalted here, fifty-three years ago, by Thomas Mann. But I do believe that those clear-sighted Europeans who struggle, here as well, for a more just and humane homeland, could help us far better if they reconsidered their way of seeing us. Solidarity with our dreams will not make us feel less alone, as long as it is not translated into concrete acts of legitimate support for all the peoples that assume the illusion of having a life of their own in the distribution of the world.

Latin America neither wants, nor has any reason, to be a pawn without a will of its own; nor is it merely wishful thinking that its quest for independence and originality should become a Western aspiration. However, the navigational advances that have narrowed such distances between our Americas and Europe seem, conversely, to have accentuated our cultural remoteness. Why is the originality so readily granted us in literature so mistrustfully denied us in our difficult attempts at social change? Why think that the social justice sought by progressive Europeans for their own countries cannot also be a goal for Latin America, with different methods for dissimilar conditions? No: the immeasurable violence and pain of our history are the result of age-old inequities and untold bitterness, and not a conspiracy plotted three thousand leagues from our home. But many European leaders and thinkers have thought so, with the childishness of old-timers who have forgotten the fruitful excesses of their youth as if it were impossible to find another destiny than to live at the mercy of the two great masters of the world. This, my friends, is the very scale of our solitude.

In spite of this, to oppression, plundering, and abandonment, we respond with life. Neither floods nor plagues, famines nor cataclysms, not even the eternal wars of century upon century have been able to subdue the persistent advantage of life over death. An advantage that grows and quickens: every year, there are seventy-four million more births than deaths, a sufficient number of new lives to multiply, each year, the population of New York sevenfold. Most of these births occur in the countries of least resources—including, of course, those of Latin America. Conversely, the most prosperous countries have succeeded in accumulating powers of destruction such as to annihilate, a hundred times over, not only all the human beings that have existed to this day, but also the totality of all living beings that have ever drawn breath on this planet of misfortune.

On a day like today, my master William Faulkner said, "I decline to accept the end of man." I would feel unworthy of standing in this place that was his, if I were not fully aware that the colossal tragedy he refused to recognize thirty-two years ago is now, for the first time since the beginning of humanity, nothing more than a simple scientific possibility. Faced with this awesome reality that must have seemed a mere utopia through all of human time, we, the inventors of tales, who will believe anything, feel entitled to believe that it is not yet too late to engage in the creation of the opposite utopia. A new and sweeping utopia of life, where no one will be able to decide for others how they die, where love will prove true and happiness be possible, and where the races condemned to one hundred years of solitude will have, at last and forever, a second opportunity on earth.

STUDY QUESTIONS

1. What occurrences in Latin American history led García Márquez to conclude that the reality of Latin America was "unearthly," "outsized," and "unbridled"?
2. What is the source of "solitude" in Latin America?
3. According to García Márquez, in what ways should Europeans view Latin America?

ESSAY SUGGESTIONS

A. In the same fashion as Latin American writers, sub-Saharan African novelists also worry about identity issues (Chapter 49). Why does the theme of identity echo in both African and Latin American civilizations? Is it in effect the same theme?

B. What is Gabriel García Márquez recommending to Latin Americans and Europeans? How should each group relate to the other? What realities should be taken into account in relating to each other?

46 LATIN AMERICA'S SOCIAL CRISIS IN THE TWENTIETH CENTURY

At the beginning of the twenty-first century, Latin America is undergoing a social crisis of vast proportions. The current conditions of widespread urban and rural poverty resulted from massive social changes over the previous one hundred years. Most conspicuously, population increased ninefold during the twentieth century. For example, Mexico's population has increased from 13.6 million in 1900 to 104.9 million in 2003, Brazil's from 18 million to 182.1 million, and Peru's from 3 million to 28.4 million over the same period. Cities have grown disproportionately faster than rural areas, resulting in the appearance of megacities, such as Mexico City with 28 million residents and São Paulo, Brazil, with 25 million. Poverty, landlessness, and lack of jobs have driven the rural poor to the cities. But job creation in Latin America's industrial cities has not nearly kept pace with population growth. Industrial development has led to the expansion of an urban middle class, but these same zones attracted millions of slum dwellers. They live a precarious, insecure life, surviving in the "informal economy." Many of the poor either pick up odd jobs day by day or sell small items or beg. They have no security, no access to a system of social services. Although population growth rates declined in the 1990s because of birth control campaigns, problems of poverty, insecurity, and sporadic bouts of despair persist. They are encountered in both the city and the countryside. The first selection describes the lives of struggling workers in the urban slum of Chorillos in Lima, Peru. The second is an oral history of a mother in the impoverished rural sugar-producing zone of Pernambuco in northeastern Brazil.

LATIN AMERICAN STRUGGLES

I. CHORILLOS, LIMA, PERU, 1967

Jacinta Vegas

"I come from the district of Piura in northern Peru, and I have lived in Lima for sixteen years, almost half my life. It is difficult living here, but I have got used to it and my children, after all, were born here. I have no money in Lima, but then I wouldn't have any money in Piura either.

Selection I from *The Shadow: Latin America Faces the Seventies,* translated by Keith Bradfield (England: Penguin Books, 1972), pp. 19–22. Reprinted by permission of The Regents of Albert Bonniers Forlag. Selection II from *Death Without Weeping: The Violence in Everyday Brazil,* pp. 348–351. Copyright © 1992 by The Regents of the University of California. Reprinted by permission of The Regents of the University of California for the University of California Press.

"The father of my eldest boy was a good-for-nothing, he denied paternity. But the boy bears my present man's name. We aren't married. We met here in Lima, but he is also from Piura.

"My eldest boy wants to be an engineer or doctor. He'll go to night school, he says. He is twelve years old now, and in the fifth grade. The eldest girl is five, and she goes to kindergarten for a dollar 20 cents a month. She gets food there and they look after her while I work. The two youngest I take with me.

"I work at the Regatta Club down by the beach. It's a very exclusive club. I clean the toilets and work as a cloakroom attendant, looking after people's cases and clothes while they bathe. I work for two days a week, and make two dollars a day. For three months during the summer I have work every day, and on top of that I get an annual bonus of twelve dollars. That's when I buy school things for the boy, he gets a big writing book with over 100 pages.

"We moved to this shed four years ago, and we own the site, it's a good shed, very solid, fresh bamboo mats in the walls. And two rooms! Everything looked fine, but two years ago I got a sore on my foot, and had to stay in bed for a month. Then my man fell sick, and was in bed for six months. And then the boy got appendicitis. The operation cost 120 dollars. We took the money we had saved to build a proper house, and borrowed the rest.

"Three months ago it happened. My man is a driver, he got mixed up in a traffic accident, hit someone in the dark and the police took his papers away. He was supposed to pay 200 dollars in damages, so he had to go underground. He ran away, and I haven't heard from him since. I have to manage on my own. We spend about twenty or forty cents a day. We eat porridge made from pea-meal or oatmeal. On Sundays, we eat porridge made with flour. Sometimes we manage rice and stewed vegetables. Never meat.

"I've never voted. I don't have a birth certificate. I went to the authorities, and asked for dispensation. It cost twelve dollars, I took my annual bonus and paid. But I got a paper that was no good, the signature was wrong and the stamp. My employer went back with me, and the man was sent to prison. But I never got my money back, and I still have no birth certificate. So I've never voted."

Rinaldo Rivas Loude

"I work for Manufactura de Calzado [shoe factory] Glenny, España 211, Chorrillos. I'm the one who sews on the uppers. I get a dollar 30 per dozen and I do a dozen to a dozen and a half a day. I don't get more work than that until Christmas, then I get as much as I want and can work all round the clock.

"I support a wife and four children, and my two brothers, aged fifteen and eight, all with this machine. I had a bit of luck when I picked it up second-hand eight years ago. Then it cost 72 dollars. Today a new one would cost 480 dollars. I also work as guard for the Leasehold Association, which means that I can live in this house for two dollars a month. Of course, this means that one of us—my wife or I—must always be at home. But I sit here all day in any case, at the machine.

"There are fifteen guards here altogether. We have to sound the alarm if there is an invasion. Yes, you see, those who have leases here don't want other people to come and settle and build huts. Four years ago, this was one great rubbish heap.

The Association, they say, paid 4,000 dollars to get the rubbish away, and in the end the members had to come and move it out themselves. Now everything has been cleaned up, and they don't want anyone else moving in.

"I was born in Lima, just near here in Barranco, in 1933. My parents rented a room in a *barriada* [slum town]. I started early as an apprentice, and I have worked for six years since my training ended.

"Better pay? Well, I could take an extra job. Or look for some other job. More than a dollar 30 per dozen? I never thought of it. No, I'm not a union member. It's just not worth it. The factory is owned by Juan García and Victor Glenny. They decide. There are ten of us working for them. The factory provides the leather, I buy my own thread, needles, whetstone and other bits and pieces. It makes a bit of a change to go into Lima on business.

"My eldest brother is in the *primaria,* in fifth grade. I think he can go on to the first or second year of the *secundaria.* I can't support him any longer than that, the secondary school is more expensive. Then he can start in the police school or join the army if he wants to go on studying. But my brothers are not big enough yet to understand what a burden they are to me.

"When did I last eat meat? On Sunday. We have meat on Sundays. Otherwise we have soups and porridge. The worst thing is that the children never get milk. The cinema? I get round to it every other week, I suppose. And every other week some friends come over, and we have a few drinks. Otherwise, I have the transistor here on the machine.

"Yes, I've voted. I voted for the present mayor. I believed in him, he grew up in a *barriada* himself. He has promised water, street lights, sewerage, pavements, everything. So far there's only lighting on the main road over there, it's still a long way to us. But he's got two years to do the job.

"Fidel? I've read the newspapers. He's done some good things. But here in Peru, well, we have Hugo Blanco [Peruvian revolutionary], of course, but I don't think he's the sort of man who could fight a guerrilla war in the hills, like they're doing in Bolivia.

"What I fear most is eviction. What I want most of all is a safe site, where no one can put us out, and a house of sun-dried brick. Also, of course, I can fall sick. I have no insurance, and the factory doesn't do anything for you if you are ill. It should, of course. I must try to find out a bit more about it."

The whole time we are talking, I can hear a whining sound as if from a dog that has been shut in. It comes from a little cubicle by the door. A small boy is lying there, in the rags of the family bed. Lying absolutely silent in the darkness, perfectly still, with fright in his eyes. The new baby is on the earthen floor, smeared with feces. Flies are crawling round his eyes. The whining is from him.

II. A MOTHER'S LIFE IN RURAL PERNAMBUCO, BRAZIL, 1982.

"I never learned to read or write, although Mama and Auntie tried to make me go to school. It was no use. I learned to sign my name, but not very well, because it is a complicated name and it has a lot of parts to it. When I was about five years old Mãe [mother] took me away from Tia [aunt] and gave me to another woman, a woman who lived next to us on the plantation. It was during this time that my aunt found a job as a maid in Recife, and she could take only one child with her. So we got divided up. Mama took Biu, Tia took Antonieta, and I stayed at Bela Vista with my godmother, Dona Graças.

"My *madrinha* was a real mother to me. Dona Graças raised me with care and great sacrifice. In those days food was scarce, and some days all we had to eat was the coarsest manioc flour, *farinha de roça.* I found it hard to swallow because of a sickness that injured my throat when I was a small baby. It made my godmother sad to see me getting skinny, so she begged a few spoonfuls of the finest whitest *farinha* every day from her *patroa* [female landowner] so that she could make me a smooth custard. When there was no other food, Madrinha would take an ear of hard Indian corn, and she would roast it and coax me into eating the dried kernels one by one. I was close to dying more than once, but my godmother fought with me to stay alive. And she won!

"When I was fifteen I married for the first time. I became the legitimate wife of Severino José da Silva. But it was a marriage that wasn't worth much, and it soon fell apart. We lived in a tiny room built onto the side of Tia's house on the Alto do Cruzeiro, so small you could only lie down in it. Severino was miserable the whole time we were together. He never wanted to marry me; it was Mama and Auntie who forced him into it. In those days when a boy ruined a virgin, he was made to marry the girl, and if he refused, the judge could put him behind bars. So when it happened like that to me, Mãe and Tia went to the judge and made a formal complaint against Severino. When he heard what my family was up to, he ran away. But a boy of fifteen doesn't have too many places to hide, and within a week he was back on the Alto staying with friends. José Leiteiro, the old *pai dos santos* (Xangô master), spotted Severino, and he ran down the path, grabbed him, and tied him up good. Then José called Mãe and Tia, and the three of them carried Severino to the judge. Severino refused to have me, and so the judge locked him up. Severino stayed in jail for two weeks until he gave in. When they let him out, I was standing right there in my best dress, and they married us on the spot with two police for witnesses. It was a real *casamento matuto,* a shotgun wedding!

"Even though we didn't have a good start to our marriage, I was determined to make it turn out all right. I worked myself sick. I did everything I could to put food on the table, but all Severino did was lie around and mope. He was lovesick, but not for his bride! You see, all along Severino had promised himself to another woman, and during the time that he was living with me, he was always thinking about *her.* That's why he had put up such a fight not to marry me. Finally, he left me to live with his other woman. By then I was almost glad to be rid of him.

"Well, once Severino was gone, I had to figure out what to do. First I lived with Mãe, then Auntie, and then with our neighbor Beatrice. Bea found me a live-in job as an assistant to a shoemaker and his wife in town. I lived with them for two years, and then I outgrew it. So I left to work outside of town in a ceramic factory, and that's where I met my second husband, Nelson. Nelson's job was firing roof tiles, and he was very skilled at this. I can't really say that Nelson was my 'husband,' though, because I was still legally married to Severino. And I can't even say that we 'lived together' because Nelson was very attached to his old grandmother, and he never stopped living with her the whole time we were together.

"At first Nelson was good to me. Every Saturday he would climb the Alto to visit, and he always brought a basket of groceries for the week. He never once came empty-handed. And so everyone really thought of him as my husband. But after I got pregnant, everything changed. Nelson began to abuse me. It looked like I was going to follow in my mother's footsteps. I was actually glad that my first-born died right away. Things got better for a little bit, and then I was pregnant again. After Zezinho was born, things went from bad to worse. I was living in a hovel without even a roof over my head. It was worse than living in an outhouse. Virgin Mary, goats on the Alto lived better than me! But I clung to Nelson thinking he would change. I had it in my head that he mistreated me only because he was so young and still very attached to his grandmother. But finally I began to see that Nelson was abusing me for the fun of it. It was a kind of sport. He wanted to keep making me pregnant just so he could threaten to leave me again and again. I was young and emotional and so I cried a lot, but once I saw what he was up to, I got stronger, and I put him out for good.

"That was all well and good, but there I was still living in my stick house with my stick baby, Zezinho. What a mess, and I was only eighteen years old! I was my mother's daughter for sure. That's when I decided to go to Ferreiras to find work picking vegetables. I spent three months working in the tomato fields, and that's where I met Milton, my third husband, the one you liked so well and whose tongue was so tied up in his mouth that no one could understand him. They put us working together on the same *quadro,* and he looked over at me, and I looked over at him, and before long nature had its way. I was too afraid to say anything when I got pregnant again because Mama and Tia were losing patience with me. So I tried to hide it, and I never told anyone at all about Milton.

"I was low and dispirited during this time. It was the only time in my life that I didn't have energy for anything. I didn't have any interest in Zezinho, and I never did anything to prepare for the birth of Wagner. That's how it happened that I had to call on you at the last minute to cut the cord. I didn't care about anything. I *wanted* that baby to die and Zezinho, too. But it turned out to be a pretty baby. Still, they were the cause of my misery! I was so unhappy that I didn't pay any attention when you took Zé away to raise him in the creche. You could have taken him and never brought him back, for all it mattered to me then. *Oxente* [expression of surprise], and today that boy is my arms and legs, more than a husband, better than any husband could ever be!

"After Wagner was born there was no reason to hide what was going on. So finally Milton came to visit, carrying a big sack of fresh corn on his head to give as a present to Mãe. He told both Mãe and Tia that he was responsible for the baby. And that's how he became my third husband. Well, with Milton I finally had some luck. It worked out, and I wound up living with him for fourteen years. I was pregnant ten more times with him. I had three miscarriages and seven live births, and of those I managed to raise four. So we didn't do badly. The three of his that died all died quickly. The first one died in his hammock while I was away working. One of the older children killed him. He got too close and yelled in his ear. He just frightened that baby to death. He died of *susto* [fright] in less than a day, and I didn't suffer very much. The other two were weak and sickly from birth. They had no 'knack' for life. The other four came into the world ready to confront [*enfrentar*] hardship and suffering, and so naturally they lived.

"Although things were going along well enough with Milton, I took a fancy to leave him and take up with Seu Jaime, the old widower I live with now. What can I say? First you love one, and then another one comes along, and your heart goes out to him. Isn't it Jesus that made us this way? Didn't he put these feelings into our hearts? If it is wrong, then we will be punished. That I know. Milton accepted it without much of a fuss. He went back to live in the *mata,* [woods] and people say that he has found himself another wife on the Engenho Votas and that he has a new family already. I'll say one thing about Milton: he has never forgotten his own children, and he always sends us produce from his *roçado* [garden plot].

"I have been living with my old man for almost four years now, and it hasn't been easy. Because of our sin, violence entered our lives. The first real trouble came from Jaime's side. A group of his first wife's relatives stoned him one night as he was coming home from work. They left him bleeding and unconscious on the sidewalk. 'My poor old man,' I said, 'what have they done to you all because of me?' How was it their business anyway? Jaime's first wife was dead, and he was free to do what he wanted with the rest of his life, even throw it away on a woman such as me! Jaime's old in-laws were Protestants, and they didn't want to see their family tainted by association with the likes of me. By bringing Seu Jaime down, I was bringing shame on them as well.

"Seu Jaime was so injured that he couldn't go back to work for a long time. I thought that we might have to move back to a shanty on the Alto. But then as luck would have it, my first husband, Severino, died suddenly, and as I was still his legal wife and not the other woman he'd lived with all these years, I was entitled to the widow's pension. So in the end it paid off, and Severino's pension brought a little bit of comfort into our lives. Now I hope that we are entering a period of calm and tranquility and that God has finally forgiven us."

STUDY QUESTIONS

1. What was the slum dweller's relationship to the state?
2. What types of events produced insecurity?
3. What was the purpose of the Leasehold Association? What was the attitude of the Leasehold Association toward people outside its area?
4. Describe the political attitudes of the poor in Chorillos. What did they expect from politicians?
5. What were the mother's attitudes toward marriage, childbearing, and death of children in Bom rural Pernambuco, Brazil?

ESSAY SUGGESTIONS

A. Identify the coping mechanisms of the poor. What do these mechanisms suggest about the political culture of the poor?

B. Compare the attitudes of the women in the slum of Lima, Peru, and the rural town of northeast Brazil to the attitudes expressed by "Kenyan Women Speak Out" in Chapter 49. How do they rate their abilities to change conditions? How do they propose to do so? What are the political implications of the various types of attitudes toward living and working conditions?

47 SUB-SAHARAN AFRICA

AFRICAN NATIONALISM

Nationalism was one of the crucial, although unintended, products of European imperialism. Local leaders—particularly aspiring newcomers often exposed to European education—saw the importance of nationalism in Western society and used it as a vehicle for protesting colonial controls and demanding independence. Nationalism could also be mobilized to elicit loyalty to a newly free state, especially when appeals to tradition could not suffice because the nation combined different cultural groups. Thus, nationalism had the merit of appealing both to past values and to the idea of progress, although the combination could sometimes be uncomfortable.

Nationalism began to blossom in Africa between the world wars. It had several facets, as indicated in the three selections that follow. One nationalist source stemmed from black leaders in the United States and West Indies sincerely concerned about Africa but also eager for the liberation of their own people. Marcus Garvey's black nationalist movement won loyalty on both sides of the Atlantic in the 1920s and helped define a positive African spirit. Jomo Kenyatta, a British-educated Kenyan—ultimately the first president of Kenya after many jail terms as a nationalist agitator under the colonial government—represents African nationalism directly. Writing in 1938, Kenyatta defined a special African agenda of combining tradition with change plus selective borrowing from the West.

The final selection is postcolonial and invites comparison with the earlier nationalist expression: how was nationalism maintained once independence had been achieved, and what changes resulted in tone and purpose? Written by Kwame Nkrumah, an American-educated leader and the first president of Ghana, this nationalist statement reflects a turn away from Africa-in-general to a specific new nation. It also shows some shifts in goals. Once independence was achieved, what targets did African nationalists have? Nkrumah's own career illustrates some of the nationalist dilemma. A brilliant agitator, he proved less successful in running an independent Ghana. The economic problems he defined as next on the nationalist agenda proved more elusive than the earlier goal of independence. Yet, nationalism remained a factor in Africa—a guide to policy and a popular rallying point in the new nations. These three selections, from different decades as well as different inspirations, give a flavor of African nationalism and some indication of its power. They also permit comparison of African with Indian or Arab nationalism. Is nationalism always the same movement?

Selection I from Marcus Garvey, "Redeeming the African Motherland," in *Philosophy and Opinions of Marcus Garvey*, edited by Amy Jacques Garvey (New York: University Publishing House, 1923), pp. 71–74. Selection II from Jomo Kenyatta, *Facing Mount Kenya* (London, 1938). Selection III from Kwame Nkurmah, *Revolutionary Path* (London: Panaf Books Limited, 1973).

AFRICAN NATIONALISM DOCUMENTS

I. MARCUS GARVEY PREACHES AFRICAN REVOLUTION

George Washington was not God Almighty. He was a man like any Negro in this building, and if he and his associates were able to make a free America, we too can make a free Africa. Therefore, let not man, let no power on earth, turn you from this sacred cause of liberty. I prefer to die at this moment rather than not to work for the freedom of Africa. If liberty is good for certain sets of humanity it is good for all. Black men, Colored men, Negroes have as much right to be free as any other race that God Almighty ever created, and we desire freedom that is unfettered, freedom that is unlimited, freedom that will give us a chance and opportunity to rise to the fullest of our ambition and that we cannot get in countries where other men rule and dominate.

We have reached the time when every minute, every second must count for something done, something achieved in the cause of Africa. We need the freedom of Africa now, therefore, we desire the kind of leadership that will give it to us as quickly as possible. You will realize that not only individuals, but governments are using their influence against us. But what do we care about the unrighteous influence of any government? Our cause is based upon righteousness. And anything that is not righteous we have no respect for, because God Almighty is our leader and Jesus Christ our standard bearer. We rely on them for that kind of leadership that will make us free, for it is the same God who inspired the Psalmist to write "Princes shall come out of Egypt and Ethiopia shall stretch out her hands unto God." At this moment methinks I see Ethiopia stretching forth her hands unto God and methinks I see the Angel of God taking up the standard of the Red, the Black and the Green, and saying "Men of the Negro Race, Men of Ethiopia, follow me." Tonight we are following. We are following 400,000,000 strong. We are following with a determination that we must be free before the wreck of matter, before the crash of worlds.

It falls to our lot to tear off the shackles that bind Mother Africa. . . . Climb ye the heights of liberty and cease not in well doing until you have planted the banner of the Red, the Black and the Green on the hilltops of Africa.

II. JOMO KENYATTA DEFINES AMERICAN NATIONALISM

There certainly are some progressive ideas among the Europeans. They include the ideas of material prosperity, of medicine, and hygiene, and literacy which enables people to take part in world culture. But so far the Europeans who visit Africa have not been conspicuously zealous in imparting these parts of their inheritance to the Africans, and seem to think that the only way to do it is by police discipline and armed force. They speak as if it was somehow beneficial to an African to work for them instead of for himself, and to make sure that he will receive this benefit they do their best to take away his land and leave him with no alternative. Along with his land they rob him of his government, condemn his religious ideas, and ignore his fundamental conceptions of justice and morals, all in the name of civilisation and progress.

If Africans were left in peace on their own lands, Europeans would have to offer them the benefits of white civilisation in real earnest before they could obtain the African labour which they want so much. They would have to offer the African a way of life which was really superior to the one his fathers lived before him, and a share in the prosperity given them by their command of science. They would have to let the African choose what parts of European culture could be beneficially transplanted, and how they could be adapted. He would probably not choose the gas bomb or the armed police force, but he might ask for some other things of which he does not get so much today. As it is, by driving him off his ancestral lands, the Europeans have robbed him of the material foundations of his culture, and reduced him to a state of serfdom incompatible with human happiness. The African is conditioned, by the cultural and social institutions of centuries, to a freedom of which Europe has little conception, and it is not in his nature to accept serfdom for ever. He realises that he must fight unceasingly for his own complete emancipation; for without this he is doomed to remain the prey of rival imperialisms, which in every successive year will drive their fangs more deeply into his vitality and strength.

III. ECONOMIC NATIONALISM: KWAME NKRUMAH

Organization presupposes planning, and planning demands a programme for its basis. The Government proposes to launch a Seven-Year Development Plan in January, 1963. The Party, therefore, has a pressing obligation to provide a programme upon which this plan could be formulated.

We must develop Ghana economically, socially, culturally, spiritually, educationally, technologically and otherwise, and produce it as a finished product of a fully integrated life, both exemplary and inspiring.

This programme, which we call a programme for "Work and Happiness," has been drawn up in regard to all our circumstances and conditions, our hopes and aspirations, our advantages and disadvantages and our opportunities or lack of them. Indeed, the programme is drawn up with an eye on reality and provides the building ground for our immediate scientific, technical and industrial progress.

We have embarked upon an intensive socialist reconstruction of our country. Ghana inherited a colonial economy and similar disabilities in most other directions. We cannot rest content until we have demolished this miserable structure and raised in its place an edifice of economic stability, thus creating for ourselves a veritable paradise of abundance and satisfaction. Despite the ideological bankruptcy and moral collapse of a civilization in despair, we must go forward with our preparations for planned economic growth to supplant the poverty, ignorance, disease, illiteracy and degradation left in their wake by discredited colonialism and decaying imperialism.

In the programme which I am today introducing to the country through this broadcast, the Party has put forward many proposals. I want all of you to get copies of this programme, to read and discuss it and to send us any observations or suggestions you may have about it.

Tomorrow, the National Executive Committee of the Party will meet to discuss the Party programme and officially present it to the nation. I feel sure that it will decide in favour of an immediate release of this programme to the people. The Party, however, will take no action on the programme until the masses of the people have had the fullest opportunity of reviewing it.

This programme for "Work and Happiness" is an expression of the evidence of the nation's creative ability, the certainty of the correctness of our Party line and action and the greatest single piece of testimony [to] our national confidence in the future.

Ghana is our country which we must all help to build. This programme gives us the opportunity to make our contributions towards the fulfillment of our national purposes.

As I look at the content of the programme and the matters it covers, such as Tax Reform, Animal Husbandry and Poultry Production, Forest Husbandry, Industrialization, Handicrafts, Banking and Insurance, Foreign Enterprise, Culture and Leisure, I am convinced beyond all doubt that Ghana and Ghanians will travel full steam ahead, conscious of their great responsibilities and fully aware that the materialization of this bright picture of the future is entirely dependent on their active and energetic industry. Remember that it is at the moment merely a draft programme and only your approval will finalize it.

At this present moment, all over Africa, dark clouds of neocolonialism are fast gathering. African States are becoming debtor-nations and client States day in and day out, owing to their adoption of unreal attitudes to world problems, saying "no" when they should have said "yes," and "yes" when they should have said "no." They are seeking economic shelter under colonialist wings, instead of accepting the truth—that their survival lies in the political unification of Africa.

Countrymen, we must draw up a programme of action and later plan details of this programme for the benefit of the whole people. Such a programme is the one that the Party now brings to you, the people of Ghana, in the hope that you will approve it critically and help to make it a success.

We have a rich heritage. Our natural resources are abundant and varied. We have mineral and agricultural wealth and, above all, we have the will to find the means whereby these possessions can be put to the greatest use and advantage. The Party's programme for work and happiness is a pointer to the way ahead, the way leading to a healthier, happier and more prosperous life for us all. When you have examined and accepted this programme, the Government and the people will base on it and initiate our Seven-Year Development Plan, which will guide our action to prosperity.

STUDY QUESTIONS

1. What are Garvey's goals for Africa? How does he justify them? Does he identify crucial African values? Does he suggest what Africa will be once it is free?
2. Was Kenyatta's nationalism similar to Garvey's? Were there any differences?
3. What is Kenyatta's attitude toward Western achievements? What aspects of African tradition does he seek to protect or restore?
4. How do Nkrumah's concerns as a nationalist compare with those of pre-independence leaders such as Kenyatta? What problems is he referring to

under the heading of neocolonialism? What are his main solutions? Do they fit under the heading of nationalism?

5. What are the similarities and differences between African and Turkish nationalism (see Chapter 36)? Between African and Gandhi's Indian nationalism (see Chapter 42)?

ESSAY SUGGESTIONS

A. Compared to other national liberation struggles, what special problems did African nationalist leaders face in defining their goals and tactics?

B. What were the key problems new nations faced—in Africa and elsewhere—after successful decolonization in the second half of the twentieth century?

48 AFRICAN POLITICS

Most sub-Saharan African states obtained freedom from European colonial control in the 1960s and 1970s. Like other new nations, many then faced significant political turmoil. Initial efforts to establish constitutional democracies often failed. Ambitious strongmen or military leaders often seized control, and some states failed altogether.

By the 1990s, democratic forms began to gain ground again, with more than twenty new democracies established. Disputes about political organization continued, however, and the overall future of democracy in the subcontinent remained unclear.

The following documents focus on issues of democracy and state structure in recent African history. The first document, from the period of decolonization, offers the purposes of the newly constituted Organization of African Unity, which continues to play a role in attempting to ensure political stability and independence in the region. Then two documents come from the final stages of the struggle against white-sponsored racial segregation in South Africa—the system known as apartheid. Nelson Mandela, the longtime foe of apartheid, speaks as he was released from long imprisonment in 1990—he would later become the first president of democratic South Africa. Shortly after this, the existing (white) South African leader, F. W. de Klerk, talks about his approach to establishing a new political structure once apartheid is ended. Both leaders speak of democracy, but both identify rather different sets of conditions and problems. The fourth document comes from the Republic of Niger, as a university student writes of democracy shortly after a strongman regime was toppled. The final document features a recent democratic constitution, from Angola, issued in the year 1992 after a period of internal civil war following the end of Portuguese colonial control.

I. CHARTER OF THE ORGANIZATION OF AFRICAN UNITY, 1963

Article I

1. The High Contracting Parties do by the present Charter establish an Organization to be known as the ORGANIZATION OF AFRICAN UNITY.
2. The Organization shall include the Continental African States, Madagascar and other Islands surrounding Africa.

Selection I from Charter of the Organization of African Unity, 1963, retrieved from http://www.africa-union.org/root/au/Documents/Treaties/text/OAU_Charter_1963.pdf. Selection II from Nelson Mandela, Speech on Release from Prison, 1990. Selection III from President Mr. F. W. deKlerk, at the First Session of CODESA, World Trade Centre, Kempton Park, December 20, 1991. Selection IV from Yacouba Saibatou, Transition to Democracy, May 11, 1992. Selection V from Constitution of Angola, Part II, Fundamental Rights and Duties.

PURPOSES

Article II

1. The Organization shall have the following purposes:
   a. To promote the unity and solidarity of the African States;
   b. To coordinate and intensify their cooperation and efforts to achieve a better life for the peoples of Africa;
   c. To defend their sovereignty, their territorial integrity and independence;
   d. To eradicate all forms of colonialism from Africa; and
   e. To promote international cooperation, having due regard to the Charter of the United Nations and the Universal Declaration of Human Rights.
2. To these ends, the Member States shall coordinate and harmonize their general policies, especially in the following fields:
   a. Political and diplomatic cooperation;
   b. Economic cooperation, including transport and communications;
   c. Educational and cultural cooperation;
   d. Health, sanitation and nutritional cooperation;
   e. Scientific and technical cooperation; and
   f. Cooperation for defence and security.

PRINCIPLES

Article III

The Member States, in pursuit of the purposes stated in Article II solemnly affirm and declare their adherence to the following principles:

1. The sovereign equality of all Member States.
2. Non-interference in the internal affairs of States.
3. Respect for the sovereignty and territorial integrity of each State and for its inalienable right to independent existence.
4. Peaceful settlement of disputes by negotiation, mediation, conciliation or arbitration.
5. Unreserved condemnation, in all its forms, of political assassination as well as of subversive activities on the part of neighbouring States or any other States.
6. Absolute dedication to the total emancipation of the African territories which are still dependent.
7. Affirmation of a policy of non-alignment with regard to all blocs.

II. MANDELA, 1990

Comrades and fellow South Africans, I greet you all in the name of peace, democracy and freedom for all. I stand here before you not as a prophet but as a humble servant of you, the people. Your tireless and heroic sacrifices have made it possible for me to be here today. I therefore place the remaining years of my life in your hands.

On this day of my release, I extend my sincere and warmest gratitude to the millions of my compatriots and those in every corner of the globe who have campaigned tirelessly for my release. I extend special greetings to the people of Cape Town, the city which has been my home for three decades. Your mass marches and other forms of struggle have served as a constant source of strength to all political prisoners.

I salute the African National Congress. It has fulfilled our every expectation in its role as leader of the great march to freedom.

I salute combatants of Umkhonto We Sizwe (the ANC's military wing) who paid the ultimate price for the freedom of all South Africans.

I salute the South African Communist Party for its sterling contribution to the struggle for democracy: You have survived 40 years of unrelenting persecution. . . .

The mass campaigns of defiance and other actions of our organizations and people can only culminate in the establishment of democracy.

The apartheid's destruction on our subcontinent is incalculable. The fabric of family life of millions of my people has been shattered. Millions are homeless and unemployed. Our economy lies in ruins and our people are embroiled in political strife.

Our resort to the armed struggle in 1960 with the formation of the military wing of the ANC (Umkhoto We Sizwe) was a purely defensive action against the violence of apartheid. The factors which necessitated the armed struggle still exist today. We have no option but to continue. We express the hope that a climate conducive to a negotiated settlement would be created soon, so that there may no longer be the need for the armed struggle. . . .

It is our belief that the future of our country can only be determined by a body which is democratically elected on a non-racial basis.

Negotiations on the dismantling of apartheid will have to address the overwhelming demands of our people for a democratic, non-racial and unitary South Africa.

There must be an end to white monopoly on political power and a fundamental restructuring of our political and economic systems to ensure that the inequalities of apartheid are addressed, and our society thoroughly democratized.

We have waited too long for our freedom. We can no longer wait. Now is the time to intensify the struggle on all fronts. To relax our efforts now would be a mistake which generations to come will not be able to forgive.

The sight of freedom looming on the horizon should encourage us to redouble our efforts. It is only through disciplined mass action that our victory can be assured.

We call on our white compatriots to join us in the shaping of a new South Africa. The freedom movement is a political home for you, too.

We call on the international community to continue the campaign to isolate the apartheid regime. To lift sanctions now would run the risk of aborting the process toward the complete eradication of apartheid.

Our march toward freedom is irreversible. We must not allow fear to stand in our way.

Universal suffrage on a common voters roll in a united, democratic and non-racial South Africa is the only way to peace and racial harmony.

In conclusion, I wish to go to my own words during my trial in 1964—they are as true today as they were then:

> I have fought against white domination, and I have fought against black domination. I have cherished the ideal of a democratic and free society in which all persons live together in harmony and with equal opportunity. It is an ideal which I hope to live for and to achieve. But, if need be, it is an ideal for which I am prepared to die.

III. DE KLERK, 1991

The eyes of all of South Africa are upon us gathered here today. The future of every man, woman and child, rich or poor, educated or uneducated, will be affected decisively by our success or failure.

Africa is holding its breath in the knowledge that South Africa is an important key to greater stability and prosperity in a large part of the continent. Important African leaders with whom I have met during the past year, have put it to me that they regard South Africa as the locomotive of economic progress on the continent.

The international community is looking with anticipation to the stabilization of our troubled country so that we may begin to play the constructive international role for which we are well suited. The world accepts that the process of change is irreversible and that the pillars of apartheid have been removed. All over the world doors have opened to us.

The stubborn, the malicious and the revolutionaries want us to fail. The vast and silent majority are praying for us to succeed.

On the shoulders of all of us gathered here, there rests an enormous responsibility to realize the hopes of our citizens and friends and to thwart the plans of those who wish to cause chaos.

Our ultimate goal is a new, fair, just, negotiated fully democratic constitution—a constitution that will be able to ensure good and stable government, prevent abuse of power and domination and guarantee equitable participation to all in every sphere of life. . . .

We are convinced that it is in the best interests of South Africa and all its people for us to institute expeditiously, as a first phase, a government, that is broadly representative of the total population. Such a generally representative government will not only see to the administration of the country, but will also be able to take the lead in further constitutional reform.

We are equally convinced that the composition of parliament, too, should be changed during this initial phase already to include the total population in an equitable manner.

In this respect, we are almost ready to table specific proposals which, naturally, will have to be negotiated intensively together with proposals by others.

What we are not prepared to consider is the circumvention or suspension of the present Constitution of the Republic. Any substantive constitutional amendments, even if they are aimed at transitional measures only, will have to be adopted by Parliament after a mandate has been obtained by means of a referendum.

Such a referendum will have to produce, among other things, a positive mandate from the electorates of each of the existing Houses of Parliament. If the proposals in respect of transitional measures are fair to all, the response from every section of the population will be an overwhelming Yes. . . .

To sum up, I wish to state today in clearer terms than ever before that the Government is amenable to a negotiated form of transitional government being implemented expeditiously in a democratic and constitutional manner. A newly constituted Parliament may be part of it. That could produce an entirely new dimension in the debate about a constituent assembly.

From the Government's point of view, there is one major obstacle in the way of rapid progress within CODESA [Convention for a Democratic South Africa]. I regret having to refer to it here, but that is, unfortunately, unavoidable. It has to do with the lack of progress by the ANC [African National Congress] in coming into line with other political parties and movements. It wishes to remain different.

The heart of the problem is the following:

The ANC has not yet terminated what it has itself defined as the 'armed struggle'. In this connection, the ANC has not honoured important undertakings . . . and has resorted to delaying tactics.

Before the Peace Conference on the 14th of September 1991, I considered making the solution of this important problem, which includes disclosure of illegal arms caches within the Republic of South Africa, a pre-condition for signing the Peace Accord. In view of renewed undertakings by ANC, I refrained from doing so.

Unfortunately, this concession did not produce results. As we are gathered here, there still has not been sufficient progress in spite of ongoing efforts on the part of the Government. The stipulation in the Peach Accord that no political party shall have a private army places a question mark over the ANC's participation in a Convention which, essentially, is taking place among political parties.

An organization which remains committed to an armed struggle cannot be trusted completely when it also commits itself to peacefully negotiated solutions. Everything that is happening in the world today proves that violence and peaceful compromise are not compatible. The choice is between peace through negotiation or a power struggle through violence. The ANC and other organizations still sitting on two stools, such as PAC [Pan Africanist Congress], now have to make this choice.

The very stage of negotiation towards a new constitution we have reached . . . now make it imperative that the ANC and others who wish to participate will have to terminate armed struggle before such participants can really enter into binding, legitimate, reliable and credible peaceful agreements.

To achieve a win/win result will require us to face reality. Apparently conflicting demands will have to be reconciled with one another sensibly—conflicting demands such as:

Protection of the established economic interests of investors, landowners, businessmen, professional people and salaried workers against the demand for better living conditions on the part of the less-privileged.

Participation by and protection of minorities from domination, against the demand of a majority—however constituted—for democratically obtained power.

Recognition and accommodation of our diversity of population against the necessity of a single nationhood with a common loyalty.

The need for education linked to language and culture against the necessity of a single educational system. So I could continue. The heart of the challenge lies in all of us having to learn not to propagate only the truth that fits our case, but also in being able to see and understand the truth that may not suit our case—and then together working out a solution that recognizes the whole truth and deals with it sensibly.

IV. YACOUBA SAIBATOU, 1992

The National Conference began ten months ago. The Conference set up the Transitional Government, which is supposed to bring certain changes to Nigeriens. Before this, there was no democracy in Niger. People were ignorant of the reality of the country's government. No one had the right to say what was good or wrong or to give his opinion.

This kind of regime existed during the rule of the former president Seyni Kountche, who is dead now, Indeed, during Kountche's rule, people were arrested for no reason. Today, even a child knows the character of Kountche.

With the second president, Ali Chaibou, there was a clear improvement in the living conditions of Nigeriens. However, there was no democracy: the government accepted the president's decisions without question; and people in the government made themselves rich at the expense of others.

This corruption was revealed during the National Conference: even the food and milk donated by relief organizations and reserved for the poor was diverted, and taken by people in the government.

We Nigeriens should now be happy that all these facts are known. There is nothing that can be done secretly today; moreover anybody can revolt against any kind of law he judges wrong. This is democracy. So now, with the transitional government, there will be no more cheating. However, Nigeriens have a tendency to not see all the benefits of the transitional government. The government's aim is to help the country to face and solve its difficult situations, but meeting this goal requires cooperation from the citizens. However, because there is a new government, everybody builds his own hopes on it. They even hope that old claims will be paid, and stage revolts to support these claims. Where will our country go and search for this money? Has the transitional government told people how little money was in the treasury when it took office? Today, there are more and more demonstrations and revolts, because people believe there is money in the treasury and that their claims for damages and back wages will be paid.

Why doesn't one think of his neighbor? What about people in the countryside who need schools, what about our sisters and mothers who need medical facilities for maternity care? What about food for the sick people at the hospital? What about roads that need to be repaired with the coming of the rainy season?

People must think and put aside selfishness, in order to make the transition not fail. Nowadays, many revolts are caused by so-called intellectuals. The soldiers calling themselves the Troop caused a rebellion, then the workers and students staged their own demonstrations to complain. With all this unrest, which way to democracy?

As the prime minister said and continues to say, the transition to democracy is not the task of an individual, nor the task of the government, but the task of all people. People must think about the consequences of their acts. They must get ready to work, in order to free the country from dependence on outside help.

V. CONSTITUTION OF ANGOLA, 1992

Article 18

1. All citizens shall be equal under the law and shall enjoy the same rights and be subject to the same duties, without distinction as to color, race, ethnic group, sex, place of birth, religion, ideology, level of education or economic or social status.
2. All acts aimed at jeopardizing social harmony or creating discrimination or privileges based on those factors shall be severely punishable by law.

Article 20

The State shall respect and protect the human person and human dignity. Every citizen shall be entitled to the free development of his or her personality, with due respect for the rights of other citizens and the highest interests of the Angolan nation. The life, freedom, personal integrity, good name and reputation of every citizen shall be protected by law.

Article 21

1. The fundamental rights provided for in the present Law shall not exclude others stemming from the laws and applicable rules of international law.
2. Constitutional and legal norms related to fundamental rights shall be interpreted and incorporated in keeping with the Universal Declaration of the Rights of Man, the African Charter on the Rights of Man and Peoples and other international instruments to which Angola has adhered.
3. In the assessment of disputes by Angolan courts, those international instruments shall apply even where not invoked by the parties.

Article 22

1. The State shall respect and protect the life of the human person.
2. The death penalty shall be prohibited.

Article 23

No citizen may be subjected to torture or any other cruel, inhuman or degrading treatment or punishment.

Article 24

1. All citizens shall have the right to live in a healthy and unpolluted environment.
2. The State shall take the requisite measures to protect the environment and national species of flora and fauna throughout the national territory and maintain ecological balance.
3. Acts that damage or directly or indirectly jeopardize conservation of the environment shall be punishable by law.

Article 29

1. The family, the basic nucleus of social organization, shall be protected by the State, whether based on marriage or de facto union.
2. Men and women shall be equal within the family, enjoying the same rights and having the same duties.
3. The family, with special collaboration by the State, shall promote and ensure the all-around education of children and young people.

Article 30

1. Children shall be given absolute priority and shall therefore enjoy special protection from the family, the State and society with a view to their all-around development.
2. The State shall promote the harmonious development of the personality of children and young people and create conditions for their integration and active participation in the life of society.

Article 31

The State, with the collaboration of the family and society, shall promote the harmonious development of the personality of young people and create conditions for fulfillment of the economic, social and cultural rights of the youth, particularly in respect of education, vocational training, culture, access to a first job, labor, social security, physical education, sport and use of leisure time.

Article 32

1. Freedom of expression, assembly, demonstration and all other forms of expression shall be guaranteed.
2. The exercise of the rights set out in the foregoing paragraph shall be regulated by law.
3. Groupings whose aims or activities are contrary to the fundamental principles set out in Article 158 of the Constitutional Law and penal laws, and those that, even indirectly, pursue political objections through organizations of a military, paramilitary or militarized character, secret organizations and those with racist, fascist or tribalist ideologies shall be prohibited.

Article 35

Freedom of the press shall be guaranteed and may not be subject to any censorship, especially political, ideological or artistic. The manner of the exercise of freedom of the press and adequate provisions to prevent and punish any abuse thereof shall be regulated by law.

Article 36

1. No citizen may be arrested or put on trial except in accordance with the law, and all accused shall be guaranteed the right to defense and the right to legal aid and counsel.
2. The State shall make provision to ensure that justice shall not be denied owing to insufficient economic means.
3. No one shall be sentenced for an act not considered a crime at the time when it was committed.
4. The penal law shall apply retroactively only when beneficial to the accused.
5. The accused shall be presumed to be innocent until a judicial decision is taken by the court.

Article 45

Freedom of conscience and belief shall be inviolable. The Angolan State shall recognize freedom of worship and guarantee its exercise, provided it does not conflict with public order and the national interest.

Article 46

1. Work shall be the right and duty of all citizens.
2. Every worker shall have the right to fair pay, rest, holidays, protection, health and security at work, in accordance with the law.
3. Citizens shall have the right freely to choose and exercise an occupation, apart from requirements established by law.

Article 47

1. The State shall promote the measures needed to ensure the right of citizens to medical and health care, as well as child, maternity, disability and old-age care, and care in any situation causing incapacity to work.
2. Private and cooperative enterprise in health, social welfare and social security shall be exercised in accordance with the law.

Article 49

1. The State shall promote access to education, culture and sports for all citizens, guaranteeing participation by various private agents in the provision thereof, in accordance with the law.

2. Private and cooperative enterprise in education shall be practiced in accordance with the law.

Article 52

1. The exercise of the rights, freedoms and guarantees of citizens may be restricted or suspended only in accordance with the law if such Constitute a threat to public order, community interests, individual rights, freedoms and guarantees, or in the event of the declaration, a state of siege or emergency, and such restrictions shall always be limited to necessary and adequate measures to maintain public order, in the interest of the community and the restoration of constitutional normality.
2. On no account shall the declaration of a state of siege or state of emergency affect the right to life, personal integrity, personal identity, civil capacity, citizenship, the non-retroactive nature of penal law, the right of the accused to defense or freedom of conscience and religion.
3. A state of siege and state of emergency shall be regulated by specific law.

STUDY QUESTIONS

1. What were the main goals of the Organization of African Unity? What were the implications concerning the form of government in postcolonial Africa?
2. What were the main disagreements between de Klerk and Mandela about what it would take to establish democracy? Did they mean the same things when they referred to democracy?
3. What were some of the key problems in establishing democracy in the wake of repressive strongman rule in a country such as Niger?
4. Did the constitution of Angola reflect any particular problems or hesitations about democracy? Was it a fully democratic document?
5. What were the main forces encouraging democracy in postindependence or late-twentieth-century Africa?
6. Why did many countries find it difficult to establish or maintain democracy?

ESSAY SUGGESTIONS

A. Compare the specifically African causes with the global causes of the spread of democracy from the 1990s into the twenty-first century.

B. Why do newly independent nations often find it difficult to establish stable political structures? Have the problems been unusually acute in Africa, compared to other postindependence regions?

49 CHANGES IN AFRICAN CULTURE AND SOCIETY

New forces continued to have an impact on the traditional culture of sub-Saharan Africa throughout the twentieth century. Conversions both to Islam and to Christianity increased, although a polytheist minority remained. Whereas in 1900, 80 percent of all sub-Saharan Africans adhered to traditional religions, by 1990, 80 percent were either Muslim or Christian. Conversion brought more than new beliefs about the deity; it also attacked family traditions (such as polygamy, for Christians) and traditional ideas of harmony with nature. Education spread, and with it came not only literacy but, often, knowledge of a European language—another force for change.

The selections that follow deal with missionary activity, urbanization, and changes in family roles as sources of change and tension in twentieth-century African society. European missionary activity, both Catholic and Protestant, increased rapidly from 1890 onward, as various Western teachers and medical personnel worked hard to modify or undermine traditional African religious values, property concepts, and family practices. African reactions to missionary efforts ranged from stark rejection to a combination effort to outright acceptance. (It is important to remember that Islam was also spreading rapidly in the nineteenth and twentieth centuries; Christians were not the only missionaries, and Muslims were sometimes preferred precisely because they were not European.)

Urban growth was another framework for cultural change. African cities, once small, grew rapidly both under colonial administration and with independence. About a quarter of all sub-Saharan Africans lived in cities by the 1970s, and the numbers increased steadily. Urban Africans, although often poor, were usually more educated than their rural counterparts, and they enjoyed the excitement of city life. But they were also confusingly torn from traditional community customs.

The selections in this chapter are divided into two parts: the first two selections deal with successive waves of cultural change affecting parts of Nigeria; they are drawn from the work of a perceptive Nigerian novelist who chronicled what he saw as major and in some ways tragic cultural disruption. The second set of selections involves reactions of African women, drawn to change themselves but with various specific qualifications and hesitations.

The first selection, from a novel by Chinua Achebe, written decades after the setting being described, reflects deep awareness of the complex balance of gain and loss brought by changes away from tradition. Discussing British missionary activity around 1900, Achebe conveys the different types of Africans, the different kinds of motives involved in at least partial religious conversion, and the reasons for resistance (and its failure). The second selection comes from another Achebe novel, depicting an urbanite but from the same village origins, after World War I but before independence. Obi Okonkwo is the first village member to receive higher education in British-run schools. He goes to Lagos, the growing Nigerian capital, to take a civil service job. He finds the glitter of city life there but also a consumerist culture and a pleasure-seeking sexual ethic both influenced by Western standards. The third selection comes from a series of interviews done by a Western anthropologist with women in Kenya, including one group organized in a cooperative to try to compensate for new uncertainties about family ties and support from men. It focuses on new roles for African women even in rural villages when men had left to take urban jobs.

The varied cultural changes and reactions express Africa's growing international contacts but also new uncertainties as older institutions unravel. Africans themselves disagree over whether new opportunity or the erosion of vital traditions should receive the main emphasis. Not surprisingly, important prior values, such as family solidarity, persist as well, as Africans create their own cultural amalgams.

AFRICAN VOICES

I. *THINGS FALL APART*

Although Nwoye had been attracted to the new faith from the very first day, he kept it secret. He dared not go too near the [European] missionaries for fear of his father. But whenever they came to preach in the open marketplace or the village playground, Nwoye was there. And he was already beginning to know some of the simple stories they told.

"We have now built a church," said Mr. Kiaga, the interpreter, who was now in charge of the infant congregation. The white man had gone back to Umuofia, where he built his headquarters and from where he paid regular visits to Mr. Kiaga's congregation at Mbanta.

"We have now built a church," said Mr. Kiaga, "and we want you all to come in every seventh day to worship the true God."

On the following Sunday, Nwoye passed and repassed the little red-earth and thatch building without summoning enough courage to enter. He heard the voice of singing and although it came from a handful of men it was loud and confident. Their church stood on a circular clearing that looked like the open mouth of the Evil Forest. Was it waiting to snap its teeth together?

That week [the missionaries] won a handful more converts. And for the first time they had a woman. Her name was Nneka, the wife of Amadi, who was a prosperous farmer. She was very heavy with child.

Nneka had had four previous pregnancies and childbirths. But each time she had borne twins, and they had been immediately thrown away. Her husband and his family were already becoming highly critical of such a woman and were not unduly perturbed when they found she had fled to join the Christians. It was a good riddance. . . .

"How do you think we can fight when our own brothers have turned against us? The white man is very clever. He came quietly and peaceably with his religion. We were amused at his foolishness and allowed him to stay. Now he has won our brothers, and our clan can no longer act like one. He has put a knife on the things that held us together and we have fallen apart." . . .

There were many men and women in Umuofia [the village] who did not feel as strongly as Okonkwo about the new dispensation. The white man had indeed brought a lunatic religion, but he had also built a trading store and for the first time palm-oil and kernel became things of great price, and much money flowed into Umuofia. . . .

Mr. Brown [the missionary to the Ibo village] learned a good deal about the religion of the clan and he came to the conclusion that a frontal attack on it would not succeed. And so he built a school and a little hospital in Umuofia. He went from family to family begging people to send their children to his school. But at first they only sent their slaves or sometimes their lazy children. Mr. Brown begged and argued and prophesied. He said that the leaders of the land in the future would be men and women who had learned to read and write. If Umuofia failed to send her children to the school, strangers would come from other places to rule them. They could already see that happening in the Native Court, where the D.C. [District Commission] was surrounded by strangers who spoke his tongue. Most of these strangers came from the distant town of Umuru on the bank of the Great River where the white man first went.

In the end Mr. Brown's arguments began to have an effect. More people came to learn in his school, and he encouraged them with gifts of [clothing] and towels. They were not all young, these people who came to learn. Some of them were thirty years old or more. They worked on their farms in the morning and went to school in the afternoon. And it was not long before the people began to say that the white man's medicine was quick in working. Mr. Brown's school produced quick results. A few months in it were enough to make one a court messenger or even a court clerk. Those who stayed longer became teachers; and from Umuofia laborers went forth into the Lord's vineyard. New churches were established in the surrounding villages and a few schools with them. From the very beginning religion and education went hand in hand. . . .

II. *NO LONGER AT EASE*

As a boy in the village of Umuofia he had heard his first stories about Lagos from a soldier home on leave from the war [World War I]. Those soldiers were heroes who had seen the great world . . . .

"There is no darkness in Lagos," [the veteran] told his admiring listeners, "because at night the electric shines like the sun, and people are always walking about, that is, those who want to walk. If you don't want to walk you only have to wave your hand and a pleasure car stops for you." His audience made sounds of wonderment. Then by way of digression he said: "If you see a white man, take off your hat for him. The only thing he cannot do is mold a human being."

For many years afterwards, Lagos was always associated with electric lights and motorcars in Obi's mind. Even after he had at last visited the city and spent a few days there before flying to the United Kingdom his views did not change very much. [His friend] Joseph had so much to tell Obi on his first night in Lagos that it was past three when they slept. He told him about the cinema and the dance halls and about political meetings.

"Dancing is very important nowadays. No girl will look at you if you can't dance. I first met Joy at the dancing school." "Who is Joy?" asked Obi, who was fascinated by what he was learning of this strange and sinful new world. "She was my girl friend for—let's see . . . "—he counted off his fingers—" . . . March, April, May, June, July—for five months. She made these pillowcases for me."

Obi raised himself instinctively to look at the pillow he was lying on. He had taken particular notice of it earlier in the day. It had the strange word *osculate* sewn on it, each letter in a different color.

"She was a nice girl but sometimes very foolish. Sometimes, though, I wish we hadn't broken up. She was simply mad about me; and she was a virgin when I met her, which is very rare here."

On top of it all came his mother's death. He sent all he could find for her funeral, but it was already being said to his eternal shame that a woman who had borne so many children, one of whom was in a European post, deserved a better funeral than she got. One Umuofia man who had been on leave at home when she died brought the news to Lagos to the meeting of the Umuofia Progressive Union.

"It was a thing of shame," he said. Someone else wanted to know, by the way, why that beast [meaning Obi] had not obtained permission to go home. "That is what Lagos can do to a young man. He runs after sweet things, dances breast to breast with women and forgets his home and his people. Do you know what medicine that *osu* woman may have put into his soup to turn his eyes and ears away from his people?" . . .

"Everything you have said is true. But there is one thing I want you to learn. Whatever happens in this world has a meaning. As our people say: 'Wherever something stands, another things stands beside it.' You see this thing called blood. There is nothing like it. That is why when you plant a yam it produces another yam, and if you plant an orange it bears oranges. I have seen many things in my life, but I have never yet seen a banana tree yield a coco yam. Why do I say this? You young men here, I want you to listen because it is from listening to old men that you learn wisdom. I know that when I return to Umuofia I cannot claim to be an old man. But here in this Lagos I am an old man to the rest of you." He paused for effect. "This boy that we are all talking about, what has he done? He was told that his mother died and he did not care. It is a strange and surprising thing."

III. KENYAN WOMEN SPEAK OUT

What we need in this village is teachers to teach women handicrafts and sewing and agricultural skills. We have organized a women's group. I am one of the leaders. We are saving up for a building to meet in. All women are trying to earn money, and we want to have a building for our meetings. It will be called the "adult education building"—with rooms for handicrafts, literacy, and other things.

We also want our children to be educated—so we can have good leaders to keep our country good. I think now it is best to have only four children—so you can take care of them.

It is better to educate a girl than a boy, although one should educate both. Girls are better. They help a lot. See this house? My daughters built it for me. If you don't have any daughters, who will build for you? The boys will marry and take care of their wives—that's all. They don't care about mothers. For example, if my son gets married, the daughter-in-law will say, "Let's take our mothers to live with us." The son will say, "No, we will just have our own family and do our own things." So you are left alone. What do you do? . . .

My mother has eleven children. She is my father's only wife. She works in the fields and grows the food we eat. She plants cabbage, spinach, and corn. She works very hard, but with so many children it is difficult to get enough food or money. All of my sisters and brothers go to school. One is already a teacher, and that is why I am trying to learn a profession. If I can get enough schooling, I can serve the country and my own family. I can also manage to have a life for myself. That is why I came to this school. We have a big family, and I have to help.

My life is very different from my mother's. She just stayed in the family until she married. Life is much more difficult now because everybody is dependent on money. Long ago, money was unheard of. No one needed money. But now you can't even get food without cash. Times are very difficult. That is why the towns are creating day-care centers—so women can work and have their own lives. I have to work, for without it I will not have enough money for today's life.

These are the problems I face and try to think about. How shall I manage to pick up this life so that I can live a better one? You know, we people of Kenya like to serve our parents when they are still alive—to help the family. But first, women have to get an education. Then if you get a large family and don't know how to feed it—if you don't have enough money for food—you can find work and get some cash. That's what I will teach my children: "Get an educa-tion first."

If I had a chance to go to the university, I would learn more about health education. I could help women that way. If I were in a position of authority, I would really try to educate women. Right now, girls are left behind in education. It costs money, and parents think it is more important to educate boys. But I think that if people are intelligent, there is no difference. Girls and boys should be educated the same. I would make rules and teach women who are not educated and who have never been to school. They, too, must understand what today's problems are. If I have any spare time, I want to learn new things. I would like to learn how to manage my life, my future life, and have enough say in things so that my husband and I could understand each other and share life with our family. And I would change the laws so that men would understand women and their needs and not beat them as they do.

I only hope that I will have a mature husband who will understand and discuss things with me. . . .

Most women don't rely on their husbands now. If they get some money, well and good; and if they don't, they just try to get money for themselves—selling vegetables or making and selling handicrafts.

Life is very difficult these days, and men are paying less attention to their wives. You see, men have wrongly just taken advantage of having more money. Instead of using money properly, to improve the lives of their families, they spend it on all the "facilities" available at hotels. Instead of spending nights in their own homes, they fight at home and seek women outside—in the hotels. Many men cheat on their wives now because they are employed and have money. A husband can say, "I have been sent as a driver to Nairobi" (or elsewhere), when he actually spends the money on girls.

So women are fed up. They think now that relying on a man can be a problem. They say, "We should try to do something ourselves. Then, whether we get something from our men or not, we still will be able to raise our children properly." The problem that many women face is that they must become self-supporting. They either have no support from their husbands at all, or very little. And there is no law to protect them.

But women *are* trying to do something for themselves, and if they had the capital they could establish businesses to help them make money. The main problem here is the money problem. Many women are alone. They need to earn for their families.

Women feel very hurt because they think their men don't recognize them as human beings. They are unhappy because of this inequality. I am lucky; my husband is good. He never took another wife. We are still together. . . . My wish would be that men and women could live as two equal people.

STUDY QUESTIONS

1. What were the main disputes over Christianity in the Nigerian region Achebe describes? What kinds of people were most drawn to this religion? Why? What kinds of people most resisted? Why?
2. Given the novel's title, *Things Fall Apart,* does Achebe suggest that it would be best to go back to the traditional values?
3. What are the value dilemmas in the excerpt from *No Longer at Ease*? What are the dominant features of the urban culture of Lagos? How do they relate to traditional culture?
4. What are the main aspirations of the Kenyan women interviewed in the third selection? What is new about them? In what ways do they clearly seek to defend older cultural and social traditions?
5. Are the interviewees feminists? Why or why not?
6. What problems of interpretation do novels raise in trying to get at historical conditions? What kinds of problems does an interview raise, as a source of recent history, even one conducted by a skilled Western scholar?
7. How do the cultural changes discussed in this chapter compare with African nationalist goals and reactions? Would nationalism help deal with some of the cultural issues raised by Achebe and the Kenyan women?

ESSAY SUGGESTIONS

A. Discuss the special problems and opportunities for women's rights advocates in contemporary sub-Saharan Africa.
B. Compare the spread of Christianity and Islam and the spread of consumer values as sources of cultural change in twentieth- to twenty-first-century Africa.
C. Compare issues of cultural identity in Latin America, in the contemporary world history period, with potential identity issues in sub-Sahara Africa.

African Women's Work

This picture portrays economic activities far different from those of industrial societies in the late twentieth century. The focus is on village agriculture and the production of maize. Women are involved rather than the men who traditionally participated in agricultural work. The picture, in other words, shows both highly traditional and dramatically new characteristics, and both invite analysis.

Pictures like this were common parts of magazine articles about African life. This raises questions about the kind of audience the picture was intended for and what impact it was supposed to have. It was not a picture intended as a keepsake for the people involved, who would probably never see it.

African Women's Work. From Kenya, in 2008. (Friedrich Stark / Alamy)

STUDY QUESTIONS

1. What kind of work was being done here?
2. What does this type of work say about women's conditions in contemporary Africa?
3. Why were adult men not pictured here?
4. How do these women's work patterns compare with those in more industrial societies? Aside from the obvious technological differences, are there any similarities?
5. What audience was this picture intended for? What impact was it meant to have?
6. How does this kind of evidence about African women compare to the anthropologists' interviews?

50 GLOBALIZATION AND NEW FORCES OF CHANGE

THE END OF THE COLD WAR AND THE COLLAPSE OF THE SOVIET UNION

Chapters in this section deal with key changes in the framework for contemporary world history. These changes became inescapably evident by the 1990s, although, in fact, many had significant roots earlier. Globalization—the network of varied and intense contacts among different parts of the world, with several regions including but not only the West participating strongly—was the most fundamental force. But the new framework was also facilitated by the end of the Cold War between 1989 and 1991.

This chapter deals with the collapse of the Soviet system, as it had been constructed from the Russian Revolution onward (Chapter 34) and as it had solidified during the Cold War (Chapter 32).

The Soviet collapse emerged between 1985 and 1991, and part of the even older Russian empire fell apart as well. This was one of the signal developments of the late twentieth century. It had repercussions that will almost surely persist for decades, both in terms of the future political and economic systems of Russia and other successor states, and in terms of world diplomatic alignments given the end of Soviet–United States Cold War rivalries.

Change began when Mikhail Gorbachev was named to the top leadership position in the Soviet Union, as first secretary of the Communist Party. Gorbachev was the first leader selected of his generation, and he had a different vantage point from older Bolsheviks. More important, he faced a number of crucial economic problems, after several post–World War II decades in which Soviet industrial growth had seemed quite strong. Workers' motivation was weakening, in part because of the absence of satisfactory consumer goods. Growing alcoholism and massive environmental problems were damaging health. Military expenditures, part of the Cold War competition, were consuming up to a third of the total national product, limiting other kinds of investment and output. Gorbachev was firmly wedded to a socialist vision, but he argued that the Soviet version of this vision required massive transformation. Greater freedom for criticism and commentary was essential—what Gorbachev called *glasnost*—along with a restructuring of management to provide greater flexibility and motivation (*perestroika*), including more participation in the international economy.

Gorbachev's reforms unleashed a massive process of change, although political results accelerated more rapidly than economic shifts. New parties began to compete in elections. Eastern European countries in the Soviet empire began to insist on greater autonomy and then, by 1989, on abolition of the Communist system. Hungary and Poland installed non-Communist governments in 1988, and other countries followed. Then, in 1990 and 1991, regions within the Soviet Union began to press for independence, led by the Baltic States—Latvia, Lithuania, and Estonia—which headed a parade that soon included key areas in Central Asia as well.

Many Soviet leaders were appalled at this process, and in August 1991, several organized a coup that imprisoned Gorbachev in his summer home. Led by a self-styled leader of democracy, Boris Yeltsin, the coup was thwarted; but Gorbachev resigned his position, now as president under a new constitution, at the end of the year. The process of change continued, both in Russia and in the newly independent nations. Market economies gained ground, although often with considerable disruption and hardship, against the old state-run operations. Efforts to revise international relations and internal political arrangements continued as well, with many uncertainties about ultimate outcomes.

Three selections illustrate key aspects of the Soviet crisis. In the first document, from 1986, Gorbachev explains his initial reform policies to a regional Communist Party meeting in the Asian city of Khabarovsk. In the second document, Vladimir Kryuchov, head of the KGB (the secret police), outlines pressing concerns about Soviet stability in a secret memo to Gorbachev in 1991, as the Soviet Union had already begun to break apart. Kryuchov was at this point a Communist conservative, hoping to stem the tide of reform; he would later be a leader of the anti-Gorbachev coup and was arrested and expelled from the KGB after the plot failed. Finally, the third document stems from Gorbachev's resignation speech on December 25, 1991. Following his resignation, the heads of the component Soviet Republics voted to dissolve the USSR and form the much looser Commonwealth of Independent States in its stead, and Boris Yeltsin assumed the leadership of the new Russian state.

The end of the Soviet system was as dramatic as its beginning in the 1917 revolution and as significant in terms of larger world history. Seldom does a structure seemingly so well established unravel so completely. Documents provide crucial insight into how reforms turned into collapse and why the tide could not be turned back.

RUSSIAN DOCUMENTS: THE END OF AN ERA

I. GORBACHEV AND REFORM (1986)

None of us can continue living in the old way. This is obvious. In this sense, we can say that a definite step toward acceleration has been made.

However, there is a danger that the first step will be taken as success, that we will assume that the whole situation has been taken in hand. I said this in Vladivostok. I want to say it again in Khabarovsk. If we were to draw this conclusion, we would be making a big mistake, an error. What has been achieved cannot yet satisfy us in any way. In general, one should never flatter oneself with what has been accomplished. All of us must learn this well. Such are the lessons of the past decades—the last two, at least. And now this is especially dangerous.

No profound qualitative changes that would reinforce the trend toward accelerated growth have taken place as yet. In general, comrades, important and intensive work lies ahead of us. To put it bluntly, the main thing is still to come. Our country's Party, the entire Party, should understand this well. . . .

We should learn as we go along, accomplishing new tasks. And we must not be afraid of advancing boldly, of doing things on the march, in the course of the active accomplishment of economic and social tasks. . . .

Restructuring is a capacious word. I would equate the word restructuring with the word revolution. Our transformations, the reforms mapped out in the decisions of the April plenary session of the Party Central Committee and the 27th CPSU (Communist Party of the Soviet Union) Congress, are a genuine revolution in the entire system of relations in society, in the minds and hearts of people, in the psychology and understanding of the present period and, above all, in the tasks engendered by rapid scientific and technical progress.

There is a common understanding in the CPSU and in the country as a whole—we should look for answers to the questions raised by life not outside of socialism but within the framework of our system, disclosing the potential of a planned economy, socialist democracy and culture and the human factor, and relying on the people's vital creativity.

Some people in the West do not like this. There everyone lies in wait for something that would mean a deviation from socialism, for us to go hat in hand to capitalism, for us to borrow its methods. We are receiving a great deal of "advice" from abroad as to how and where we should proceed. Various kinds of provocative broadcasts are made, and articles are published, aimed at casting aspersions on the changes taking place in our country and at driving a wedge between the Party leadership and the people. Such improper attempts are doomed to failure. The interests of the Party and the people are inseparable, and our choice and political course are firm and unshakable. On this main point, the people and the Party are united.

But we also cannot allow ingrained dogmas to cloud our eyes, to impede our progress and keep us from creatively elaborating theory and applying it in practice, in the given, concrete historical stage through which our society is passing. We cannot allow this, either.

I am saying this also because among us there are still, of course, people who have difficulty in accepting the world "restructuring" [*perestroika*] and who even sometimes can pronounce it only with difficulty. In this process of renewal, they often see not what it in fact contains but all but a shaking of foundations, all but a renunciation of our principles. Our political line is aimed at fully disclosing the potential and advantages of the socialist system, removing all barriers and all obstructions to our progress, and creating scope for factors of social progress.

I want to say something else. The further we advance into restructuring, the more the complexity of this task is revealed, and the more fully the enormous scale and volume of the forthcoming work are brought out. It is becoming clearer to what extent many notions about the economy and management, social questions, statehood and democracy, upbringing and education and moral demands still lag behind today's requirements and tasks, especially the tasks of further development.

We will have to remove layer by layer, the accumulated problems in all spheres of the life of society, freeing ourselves of what has outlived its time and boldly making creative decisions. . . .

Restructuring proposes the creation of an atmosphere in society that will impel people to overcome accumulated inertia and indifference, to rid themselves, in work and in life, of everything that does not correspond to the principles of socialism, to our world views and way of life. Frankly, there is some work to be done here. But in this instance everyone must look first of all at himself, comrades—in the Politburo, in the primary Party organizations—and everyone must make a specific attempt to take himself in hand. In past years, we got used to some things in an atmosphere of insufficient criticism, openness and responsibility, things that do not all correspond to the principles of socialism. I apply this both to rank-and-file personnel and to officials. . . .

In general, comrades, we must change our style of work. It should be permeated with respect for the people and their opinions, with real, unfeigned closeness to them. We must actually go to people, listen to them, meet with them, inform them. And the more difficult things are, the more often we must meet with them and be with them when some task or other is being accomplished. In our country, people are responsive; they are a wonderful people, you can't find another people like them. Our people have the greatest endurance. Our people have the greatest political activeness. And now it is growing. This must be welcomed and encouraged in every way. Let us consider that we have come to an agreement on this in the Khabarovsk Party organization (*Applause*).

In this connection, some words about public openness [*glasnost*]. It is sometimes said: Well, why has the Central Committee launched criticism, self-criticism and openness on such a broad scale? I can tell you that so far we have lost nothing, we have only gained. The people have felt an influx of energy; they have become bolder and more active, both at work and in public life. Furthermore, you know that all those who had been trying to circumvent our laws immediately began to quiet down. Because there is nothing stronger than the force of public opinion, when it can be put into effect. And it can be put into effect only in conditions of criticism, self-criticism and broad public openness. . . .

Incidentally, it looks as if many local newspapers in cities and provinces are keeping quiet. The central newspapers are speaking out in full voice, supporting everything good and criticizing blunders and shortcomings. But the local papers are silent. When a group of editors assembled in the Central Committee's offices, they said bluntly: "Well, you tell this to our secretaries in the city and district Party committees." And indeed, why shouldn't people know what is going on in the district or the city? Why shouldn't they make a judgment on it and, if need be, express their opinion? This is what socialism is, comrades. Are there any editors present? (*A voice:* Yes, we're here.)

I hope that the secretaries of the city and district Party committees will take our talk into account. They are the managers. These are their newspapers. We must not be afraid of openness, comrades. We are strong, and the people are in favor of socialism, the Party's policy, changes and restructuring. In general, it is impermissible to approach openness with the yardsticks of traditional short-term campaigns. Public openness is not a one-shot measure but a norm of present-day Soviet life, a continuous, uninterrupted process during which some tasks are accomplished and new tasks—as a rule, still more complicated ones—arise. (*Applause*).

I could say the same thing about criticism and self-criticism. If we do not criticize and analyze ourselves, what will happen? For us, this is a direct requirement, a vital necessity for purposes of the normal functioning of the Party and of society.

II. A SECRET POLICE REPORT (1991)

On the Political Situation in the Country

The acute political crisis which has enveloped our country threatens the fate of *perestroika,* the processes of democratization, the renewal of society. The possibility of the collapse of the unity of the USSR, the destruction of the sociopolitical and economic system has become real. Provoked by the decisions of a number of Union republics, the "war of sovereignties" has practically nullified efforts to stabilize the economy and has greatly complicated conditions for the signing of a new Union treaty. Under the influence of well-known decisions of the Congress of People's Deputies and the Supreme Soviet, the confrontations between the Center and the Union republics have received a powerful impetus. The head of the Russian parliament, together with certain forces, circles of shady business, have clearly declared their intention to create a "second Center" as a counterweight to the state political leadership of the USSR. Practically all opposition parties and movements have not failed to make use of it to strengthen their positions. National chauvinistic and separatist tendencies have increased in many regions of the country.

Events have confirmed our evaluation that the policy of appeasing the aggressive wing of the "democratic movement" is not able to forestall the spread of destructive processes and, in fact, allows the pseudo-democrats to realize unhindered their plans concerning the usurpation of power and changing the nature of the social system.

The outcome of the political battle in the coming months will depend on who wins the support of the bulk of the toiling population. In turn, active support of the leadership of the country, it would seem, hinges decisively on the extent of its success in averting a drastic decline in the living standard of the population. It is impossible not to take into account the fact that large social groups are poorly protected and are frequently impoverished. There exists no real possibility of improving their well-being at this time.

Taking into consideration the peculiarities of the economic structure of the USSR as well as the misapprehension by a significant portion of the population of even primitive forms of market relations, every step in the transition to a market economy demands circumspection, caution, and verification. The commitment to a forced introduction of market relations might turn out to exact an exorbitantly high price from the country. . . .

Public opinion reacts negatively to the way in which shady businessmen exploit the unfolding situation. The intensifying property stratification evokes an increase in social tensions. The process of enrichment, by its internal logic, draws shady business into the battle for political influence, so that within the framework of privatization it may further broaden the scope for property accumulation. That inevitably leads to the creation of a category of "new bourgeoisie" with all that it entails. . . .

The reality is such that the United States is working towards the collapse of the USSR as a superpower. In political circles of the United States the predominant opinion is that the weakening of the Soviet Union—down to the secession of a series of republics, above all the Baltics—is in the American national interest. The departure of Lithuania, for example, would in turn make the prospect of losing the Kaliningrad oblast quite real.

Taking into account this situation, we can scarcely count on significant financial and economic help from the United States. According to reliable information, the United States is putting pressure on Japan and Western Europe to limit the possible scale of their cooperation with the USSR. One should also be aware of the fact that even extensive help from the West would not, in itself, be sufficient to extricate this country from its economic crisis. . . .

The anti-constitutional forces, acting according to a scenario worked out with the participation of Western experts, view the present moment as favorable for the organization of a frontal attack on the existing governmental and social structures of the Soviet state. The leading role in this belongs to the organizationally formed block of opposition forces "Democratic Russia" (DR), whose political precepts the leadership of the Supreme Soviet of the [Russian Federation] [Boris Yeltsin] is trying to realize.

With the formation of the governing organs of DR, the task of "transforming the soviets on all levels into instruments of the opposition" has moved into the realm of practicality, as is the imminent winning to its side of the vast majority of the population. Measures are being taken for the creation of the cells of DR in industrial enterprises, in state institutions, and colleges. The attention "Democrats" pay to engineering and technical personnel, as well as to the working class as a whole, is growing, inasmuch as expectations of an "elite coup" by the humanitarian [cultural] intelligentsia have not been fulfilled. Opposition leaders have embarked on the formation of a party built on the foundation of DR that would be capable of pushing the CPSU out of the political area. It is assumed that it will be headed by the most prominent leaders among the "Democrats" and will become de facto the leading force in the alignment of political forces both in the Supreme Soviet of the RSFSR and in the soviets of a number of large republican centers. . . .

Supporters of the "Democrats" are taking persistent measures to extend their influence in the army, striving to neutralize it as one of the guarantors of the unity of the USSR and the integrity of the constitutional system. On the other hand, the recent events in the Baltic republics have had a very negative effect on the morale of the troops and have strengthened, especially among the officer corps, doubts about the ability of the country's leadership to keep the situation under control.

The escalation of the propaganda war that is being waged by the anticommunists against their own people, and the increased material means at their disposal (including the drawing in of shady capital), are devastating for the unity of the USSR and for Soviet society. The conquest of one propaganda organ after another is under way, and when that fails, they create new ones. Within just the last month in Russia, more specifically in Moscow, four substantial new publications have begun to appear and two radio stations have begun to broadcast. Western specialists are drawn into the activity in the sphere of psychological warfare. . . .

The interests of the Soviet constitutional system insistently dictate essential state control over the mass media and the inadmissibility of watering down its personnel, much less its transformation into a mouthpiece for antisocialist forces.

An analysis of the unfolding situation demands serious and critical comprehension of the extent to which the concepts of democratization and *glasnost* formulated six years ago have currently been implemented in practice. It is impossible not to see that antisocialist circles have, at a given stage, succeeded in replacing their contents, imposing upon society a vision of *perestroika,* not as the renewal of socialism but as the inexorable return into the "mainstream of world civilization"—capitalism. The thesis of the "illegality of the October Revolution" [of 1917] is being promoted. Democratization and *glasnost* come to be seen as the elimination of any limitations on political insinuations and unbridled slander under the flag of "freedom of speech." The cynical manipulation of public opinion shows with particular clarity in the firmly established "double standards," in accordance with which even the criminal actions of "democratic leaders" (down to the use of bloody coercion in Lithuania, Latvia, and Georgia) are unconditionally justified or hushed up, whereas the actions of the authorities in restoring order and constitutional norms are decried wholesale as illegal and dictatorial.

According to incoming information, an understanding of the dire consequences that the lingering crisis in the CPSU will have for the country is growing among the population. It is clear that the weakening of ideological work in defense of the socialist ideal cannot be made up by any other political force. Although the opposition is able to appeal to the personal interests of the average person, Party propaganda is still fumbling about for ways to conduct mass agitational work.

With all its drama, the current situation can still be turned around, considering the unused arsenal of constructive measures. There is not a great deal of room in which to maneuver, but there is some. One must not fail to consider that, as is everywhere noted, people are tired of the hardships, stress, and social collisions and are losing their faith in the ability of the leadership to restore order. The danger arises that people will follow those who take it upon themselves to restore order.

The Supreme Soviet and the Congress of People's Deputies of the USSR, as the most constructive political institutions, can and must play an essential role in the search for a way out of the unfolding crisis. This requires protecting these organs of popular government from attacks and activating and strengthening their creative potential.

At the same time, considering the depth of the crisis and the probability of a dramatic worsening of circumstances, one cannot exclude the possibility of forming, at the appropriate moment, temporary bodies within the framework of extraordinary measures to be introduced by the President of the Supreme Soviet of the USSR.

Such a step would require powerful propaganda support, a direct address to the nation with an appeal to unity for the preservation of the USSR and the defense of the public order.

III. GORBACHEV'S RESIGNATION SPEECH (1991)

Dear compatriots! Fellow citizens! Due to the situation that has taken shape as a result of the formation of the Commonwealth of Independent States, I am ceasing my activity in the post of President of the USSR. I am making this decision out of considerations of principle.

I have firmly advocated the independence of peoples and the sovereignty of republics. But at the same time I have favored the preservation of the Union state and the integrity of the country.

Events have taken a different path. A policy line aimed at dismembering the country and disuniting the state has prevailed, something that I cannot agree with. . . .

Speaking to you for the last time as President of the USSR, I consider it necessary to express my assessment of the path traversed since 1985. Especially since there are a good many contradictory, superficial and unobjective opinions on this score.

Fate ordained that when I became head of state it was already clear that things were not going well in the country. We have a great deal of everything—land, petroleum, gas and other natural resources—and God has endowed us with intelligence and talent, too, but we live much worse than people in the developed countries do, and we are lagging further and further behind them.

The reason was evident—society was suffocating in the grip of the command-bureaucratic system. Doomed to serve ideology and to bear the terrible burden of the arms race, it had been pushed to the limit of what was possible.

All attempts at partial reforms—and there were a good many of them—failed, one after the other. The country had lost direction. It was impossible to go on living that way. Everything had to be changed fundamentally.

That is why I have never once regretted that I did not take advantage of the position of General Secretary just to "reign" for a few years. I would have considered that irresponsible and immoral.

I realized that to begin reforms on such a scale and in such a society as ours was an extremely difficult and even risky endeavor. But even today I am convinced of the historical correctness of the democratic reforms that were begun in the spring of 1985.

The process of renewing the country and of fundamental changes in the world community proved to be much more complex than could have been surmised. However, what has been accomplished should be appraised on its merits.

Society has received freedom and has been emancipated politically and spiritually. This is the most important gain, one that we have not yet become fully aware of, and for this reason we have not yet learned to make use of freedom.

Nevertheless, work of historic significance has been done:

—The totalitarian system, which for a long time deprived the country of the opportunity to become prosperous and flourishing, has been eliminated.

—A breakthrough has been achieved in the area of democratic transformations. Free elections, freedom of the press, religious freedoms, representative bodies of power and a multiparty system have become a reality. Human rights have been recognized as the highest principle.

—Movement toward a mixed economy has begun, and the equality of all forms of ownership is being established. Within the framework of a land reform, the peasantry has begun to revive, private farming has appeared, and millions of hectares of land are being given to rural and urban people. The economic freedom of the producer has been legalized, and entrepreneurship, the formation of joint-stock companies and privatization have begun to gather momentum.

—In turning the economy toward a market, it is important to remember that this is being done for the sake of human beings. In this difficult time, everything possible must be done for their social protection, and this applies especially to old people and children.

We are living in a new world:

—An end has been put to the cold war, and the arms race and the insane militarization of the country, which disfigured our economy and the public consciousness and morals, have been halted. The threat of a world war has been removed.

I want to emphasize once again that, for my part, during the transitional period I did everything I could to preserve reliable control over nuclear weapons.

—We opened up to the world and renounced interference in the affairs of others and the use of troops outside the country's borders. And in response we received trust, solidarity and respect.

—We have become one of the main bulwarks in the reorganization of present-day civilization on peaceful, democratic principles.

—Peoples and nations have received real freedom in choosing the path of their self-determination. Searches for democratic reforms in the multinational state led us to the threshold of concluding a new Union Treaty.

All these changes required enormous effort and took place in an acute struggle, with mounting resistance from old, obsolete and reactionary forces—both the former Party-state structures and the economic apparatus—and also from our habits, ideological prejudices, and a leveling and parasitic mentality. The changes ran up against our intolerance, low level of political sophistication and fear of change.

For this reason, we lost a great deal of time. The old system collapsed before a new one had time to start working. And the crisis in society became even more exacerbated.

I know about the dissatisfaction with the present grave situation and about the sharp criticism that is being made of the authorities at all levels, and of my personal activity. But I would like to emphasize once again: Fundamental changes in such an enormous country, and one with such a legacy, could not proceed painlessly or without difficulties and upheavals. . . .

It seems vitally important to me to preserve the democratic gains of the past few years. They were achieved through suffering throughout our history and our tragic experience. Under no circumstances and on no pretext can they be given up. Otherwise, all hopes for something better will be buried. . . .

I am grateful to state, political and public figures and the millions of people abroad who understood our plans, supported them, met us halfway, and embarked on sincere cooperation with us.

I am leaving my post with a feeling of anxiety. But also with hope and with faith in you, in your wisdom and strength of spirit. We are the heirs to a great civilization, and its rebirth into a new, up-to-date and fitting life now depends on each and every one of us.

I want to thank from the bottom of my heart those who during these years stood with me for a right and good cause. Certainly some mistakes could have been avoided, and many things could have been done better. But I am sure that sooner or later our common efforts will bear fruit and our peoples will live in a prosperous and democratic society.

I wish all of you the very best.

STUDY QUESTIONS

1. What kinds of reforms did Gorbachev envision in 1986? What problems was he trying to address? What did he mean by "restructuring" and "public openness"?
2. What kinds of threats did the Secret Police highlight in 1991? How does the view of Soviet society implied here compare with Gorbachev's reform intentions? Does the report suggest the basis for Kryuchov's later attempted coup? What kind of state and society does Kryuchov seem to want?
3. What does Gorbachev say caused him to resign? What, by 1991, were his goals for Russian society, and how did they compare with the goals of 1986? How had his outlook toward the West changed?
4. From these documents, how much can be determined about the nature of and reasons for the collapse of the Soviet system? What kinds of disagreements persisted into the 1990s about the appropriate directions for Russian political and economic systems?

ESSAY SUGGESTIONS

A. How do political and economic conditions in Russia today reflect the collapse of the earlier Soviet system and the conditions that caused the collapse? How much fundamental change has occurred?

B. How did the Soviet collapse affect Communist societies in other parts of the world? To what extent did other societies experience similar problems and reform currents?

C. What was the relationship between the end of the Cold War and globalization?

STUDY QUESTIONS

1. Looking at the map on page 361, in what regions of the world is the memory of the struggle against European colonial rule the freshest?
2. How did the collapse of the Soviet Union change the map of Eurasia?
3. What links do you see in the map on page 361 between the decline of communism and the legacy of earlier cultural traditions?

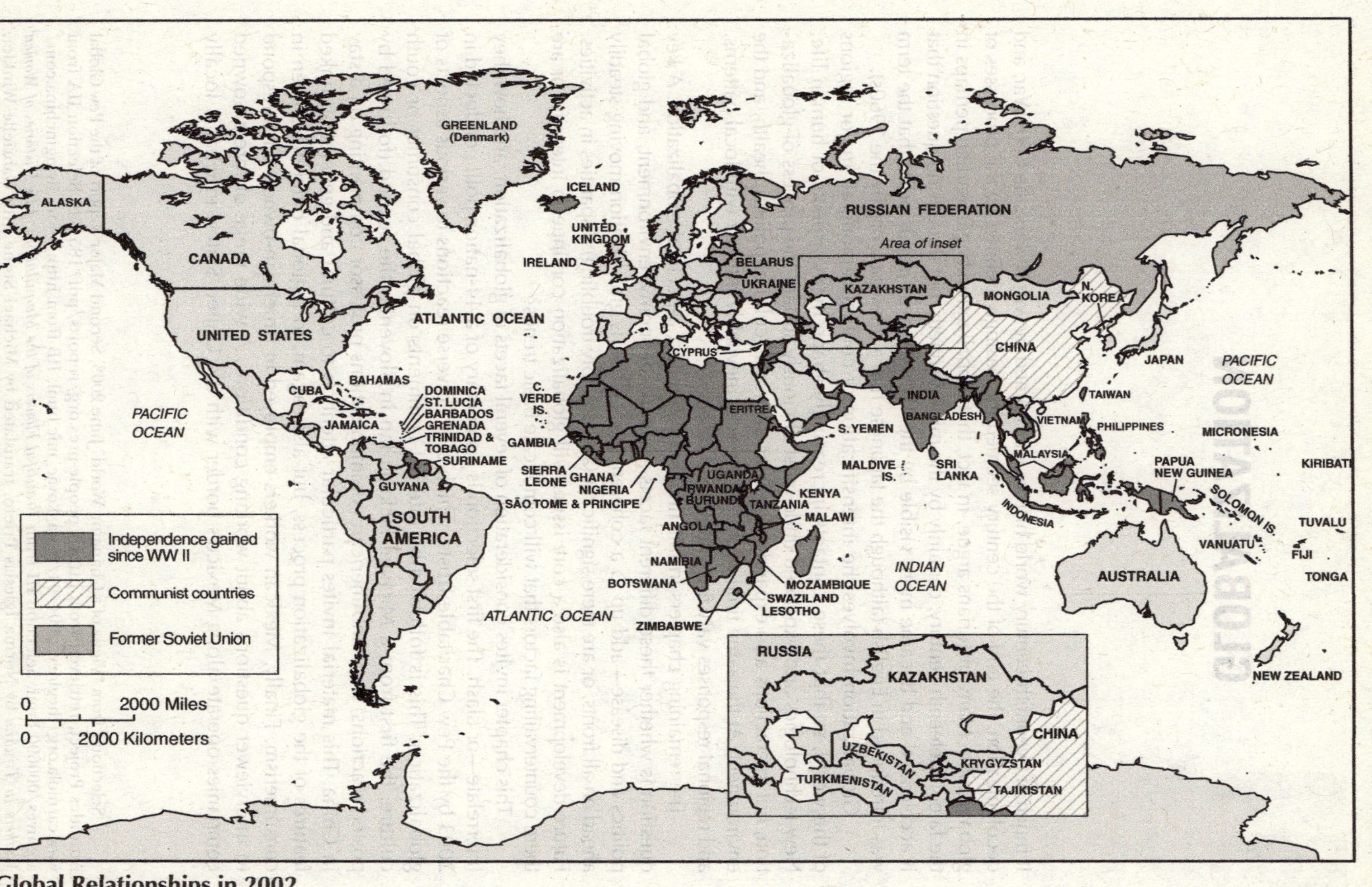

Global Relationships in 2002

51 GLOBALIZATION

If much of twentieth-century world history was framed by world wars, the Cold War, and decolonization, the end of the century seemed increasingly defined by the processes of globalization. Many historians argue, in fact, that globalization began earlier, perhaps in the later nineteenth century, certainly by the mid-twentieth, but there is no question that it accelerated and became more visible by the 1990s. It was at this point that the term was introduced in English (although the Japanese had a relevant word by the 1960s).

Globalization involves the intensification of contacts among all major regions of the world, so that these contacts increasingly shape many aspects of human life. New technologies and expanded trade most obviously sustain the process of globalization, but interactions also expand in areas as diverse as culture, politics, health, and the environment. At the same time, global exchanges inevitably interact with local patterns, and regional responses vary for a number of reasons.

The remaining chapters in this final section reflect aspects of globalization. A key question is whether these different facets—culture, economy, environment, and global politics and disease—add up to a coherent framework. Is globalization moving steadily ahead on all fronts, or are there significant (and possibly troubling) disparities in activities. Future development is also a core issue: will globalization continue to intensify, or are there countervailing factors that will complicate basic trends?

This chapter invites consideration of several facets of globalization, and how they interrelate—or clash. The first selection is a summary of a 44-nation poll, conducted in 2003 by the Pew Charitable Trusts, which offers diverse reactions to various aspects of globalization. This is followed by Internet comments on global consumer or youth culture, the first from a Michael Jackson fan in Slovenia, the second (followed by posted reactions) from an American communications professor commenting on a stay in China. This material invites particular attention to cultural and generation-linked features of the globalization process, but also, again, to regional differences even in consumerism. Finally, Mexican workers employed in American-owned firms respond to interviewer questions about working conditions. A wide range of foreign-owned companies operate along Mexico's border with the United States, in what is locally called the *maquiladora*, or "little flowers" industry, seeking to take advantage of favorable labor costs and regulations; similar operations form part of the contemporary global economy in China and southeast Asia, in Africa, and elsewhere. Figuring out the human and economic impact of this key facet of economic globalization is a crucial interpretive issue.

I. PEW GLOBAL ATTITUDES PROJECT, 2003

Connected World: Impact on Countries

Overwhelming majorities of those surveyed—at least two-thirds of the public in every country except Jordan and Tanzania—think it is a good thing that their countries are becoming more connected with the world through trade and communication. For the most part, however, enthusiasm for the connected world is tempered. In most countries, majorities surveyed think growing connectedness is at least *somewhat* good for their nation, not *very* good.

People in Africa, the poorest continent, stand out for their strong embrace of globalization. Majorities in seven of ten African nations surveyed have very positive views of increased global trade and communication, including 71% in Uganda and roughly two-thirds in Nigeria and Kenya (68%, 67%). In other regions, support for expanding trade and communications is also quite strong in Vietnam (57%), Uzbekistan (54%) and Turkey (50%), which is aspiring to join the European Union.

By comparison, Western Europeans and North Americans take a more moderate view of the impact of globalization on their countries. Roughly nine-in-ten in every country surveyed in these regions believe more trade and faster communication have been at least somewhat good for their countries. But there are differences in the strength of this opinion—nearly half of British respondents (47%) and more than four-in-ten in Canada (43%) believe these trends have been very good for their countries. Fewer respondents in Germany (37%), the U.S. (36%), France (36%) and Italy (25%) agree.

Foreign Culture's Personal Impact

Globally, most respondents have a favorable personal reaction to the opportunity to sample foreign television, movies and music. In France . . . 91% say it is good that they and their families have the opportunity to watch foreign movies and television and listen to music from other parts of the world.

While this view is shared almost everywhere, a few notable exceptions exist. Kenyans are about as negative about the personal impact of foreign culture as they are about increasing foreign trade: 61% of respondents in Kenya say foreign television, movies and music are bad for them and their families. A majority in Pakistan (55%) agrees, while Jordanians are split over the personal impact of foreign culture (50% positive/49% negative). In Bangladesh, another predominantly Muslim country, the public also is divided (49% positive/46% negative).

Generations Divide Over Cultural Imports

In most countries, younger respondents are more positive than older ones about the effect of foreign television, music and movies on their families. In Russia and Bangladesh, these age differences are particularly noteworthy. Fully 85% of Russians under age 30 say the opportunity to watch foreign movies and television programs and listen to foreign music is a good thing for them and their families; just 35% of those 50 and older agree. In Bangladesh, young people are nearly three times more likely than those age 50 and older to view foreign culture favorably (65% – 22%).

Significant generational differences on this issue are apparent in many other countries, across all regions of the world: Senegal, South Korea, Guatemala, Mexico and Uzbekistan. The generational differences over foreign culture are much smaller in Pakistan, where young and old alike are critical of the impact of cultural imports, and in the United States and France, where nearly everyone likes these products.

Globally, Problems Worsen

People's attitudes toward the global changes that are affecting their nations and their families are best understood in the context of whether they think their lives are getting better or worse. For the most part, the people surveyed by the *Pew Global Attitudes Project* think life has deteriorated in many ways over the past five years.

Majorities, in most cases strong majorities, in 34 of 44 nations surveyed think the availability of good paying jobs has gotten worse in the last five years. Even in relatively successful economies such as the U.S. and Canada, most people say the job situation has gotten worse (55% U.S., 52% Canada). The notable exceptions are Vietnam (92%), Philippines (68%) and China (52%), where people generally think job opportunities have improved.

Strong majorities of the public also think that the gap between the rich and the poor has worsened in the last five years. In 30 of 44 countries, at least seven-in-ten people say economic inequality has grown, including 94% of those surveyed in Argentina, 92% in Russia, 91% in the Slovak Republic and 90% in Germany. Such concerns are particularly widespread in Eastern Europe, with the single exception of Ukraine. Roughly half of Ukrainians say economic inequality has decreased over the past five years, while 44% say it has increased.

Most people also believe that diseases spread more rapidly today than they did half a decade ago (the survey was conducted before the SARS outbreak). This is particularly true in Africa and Latin America where, in 16 of the 18 countries surveyed, more than seven-in-ten people think the incidence of disease has gotten worse. These are many of the same societies where AIDS and other infectious diseases are viewed as top national problems. But concern about the spread of disease is not limited to poor nations. Two in three Americans (68%) and more than half of all Western Europeans and Japanese share such fears.

II. GLOBAL YOUTH VOICES

A. A Michael Jackson fan in Slovenia

Tanja Kovac (a 23-year-old financial assistant): The first time I heard a Michael Jackson song was way back in 1987. It was the time when Michael was on his world tour for BAD. I was just 7 years old and I only knew Michael by the way he looks. When I first became his fan I didn't even know that he was a singer. I just came into my sister's room and saw a poster of him on the wall and my eyes immediately turned to him. I remember asking my sister who this man was and my mouth was just wide open. I just couldn't believe that one man could look so beautiful. A week after that I heard the whole BAD album when my sister brought it home so I could hear it. I guess my very first song by Michael was BAD since that's the first song on the album. When I heard it I fell in love with him even more. He just has it all: the looks, the voice and such a wonderful character. I remember being very much in shock over his whole image and music.

TGoC: *What's in your current Michael Jackson collection?*

Tanja: I have a large collection of Michael Jackson memorabilia. There are so many MJ things that people don't even know exist. I have all of his albums, singles, vinyls, picture discs, special edition discs, his rare mixes and tapes, Jackson 5 and The Jacksons albums . . . all about his music. Then I have so many of his books, magazines (from all over the world), song books, calendars, notebooks, PVC bags with MJ on it, puzzles, MJ perfumes, sculptures, badges, stickers, over 1500 of his original photos, over 100 videocasettes of rare footage of Michael Jackson, pillows, posters, promotional posters, tour books, flags, caps, Mystery drink cans, MJ dolls (which sing the Black or White song), T-shirts, Billie Jean glove, hats (one of them was touched by Michael himself), DVDs, concert tickets, original History tour bag, . . . My most special items are two Michael Jackson autographs that I got when I went to see Michael live (Berlin and London). I made a tattoo on my right arm of one of the autographs.

TGoC: *Tell me about the tattoo. Do you have any more—or are you planning on more?*

Tanja: I always wanted to have a MJ tattoo and this dream came true for me just two days after I met Michael in Harrods, London. It was in June 2002. First I wanted to make a tattoo of Michael's face but since I didn't have enough money to do that, I decided it would be best to make a tattoo of a MJ autograph that my boyfriend got from Michael personally just a few days before. Everyone who saw it till this day has said it looks amazing, I've never heard anyone say anything bad about it. Yes, I plan to do more of them. I want a tattoo of Michael's face and I believe I will get it done soon.

TGoC: *Does your boyfriend ever get jealous of your love for Michael Jackson?*

Tanja: No. My boyfriend never gets jealous of my GIGANTIC love for Michael. He was even with me when I got the chance to meet Michael and didn't mind that I kissed Michael's hand. My boyfriend is a Michael Jackson fan as well.

B. McDonald's and Love in China

He ate so little, as the two of them sat knees touching, eyes on each other, oblivious to those who shared their four-foot oval dining table. I sat uncomfortably on the child-sized seat directly across from the lovers, my knees banging against the table with each bite of my big Mac. The 30-something father with his three-year-old son munched noisily through a happy meal, slurping on their drinks, and playing with the Nemo toy. A voyeur, I watched the lovers eat and speak the language of love. A year in China has erased some of my initial discomfort when forced to invade personal space. Ten months ago my eyes would have remained on my food tray, attempting to decipher the symbols and Mandarin characters describing McDonald's newest advertising scheme. On this day, however, I sat transfixed by the scene a mere two feet before me. The university-aged lovers (a word the Chinese apply to boyfriend/girlfriend) shared a small hot tea, which remained capped and unopened, an order of spicy McWings, a fish sandwich, and small fries. The woman was feasting on the chicken wing morsels; the man was feasting on the woman. He frequently stroked her long, dark hair, placing it behind her right shoulder. Both her hands were full of food, his remained free to assist her in opening cartons, peeling the paper from her sandwich. Leaning into each other, they were merely a burger distance apart as he fed her fries . . . . The woman, abandoning the spicy wings and delicately picking up the fish sandwich (careful to keep it encased in its paper wrapper), spoke excitedly about some event. Gesture free, her rich voice, full of inflection, pauses, and excited, high tones caused the young man to maintain sustained eye contact, a thin mouth alternating between a shy smile and despairing frown. I watched him raise his eyebrows in amazement, and, finally, to laugh freely at her completed story. She took the last bite of a shared sandwich that he'd not touched. He picked up a nude French fry, offering it first to her before licking the salt. The tea, apparently forgotten and unattended, was getting cold. Chicken bones lay discarded in a tiny heap next to the crumpled fish wrapper and unused ketchup packages. I found myself part of a threesome. No longer aware of the little boy sitting on the fixed stool next to me making swimming noises with his cheeseburger and Nemo, I was swimming in love. The turquoise scarf she wore shimmered under the fluorescent light. The brown sweater he wore over layers of shirts added strength and maturity to his lean frame. Her petite cell phone hung from a red cord around her neck, resting half-way down her chest. His phone shared table space with their food tray. Neither stopped their look of love to send text messages to anyone. Western university students eat on-the-run at McDonald's. Their Chinese counterparts eat at McDonald's with special friends or lovers—a date place. Expensive, by Chinese standards, western-modern, and food for the soul—not one's health—is the draw. A safe, public place where diners are definitely still part of a crowd, yet easy for two people in love to carve a privacy zone just for their pleasure.

Comments:

Being a chinese boy, I have read the lovely story for three times. I wish same story in my life.

Posted by Fuwei | 03/31/04

A beautiful story. I see a bigger picture involved here. The much needed privacy for young lovers in a eating place. That's quite an achievement. I remember when I was still dating with my wife we had a tough time finding a private place for two young lovers. This was 5–6 years back in Hyderabad, India. Things have changed in India too now, the present crop of young lovers do not care much and there are more of them now so the number of places are increasing. Anyway, thanks for the lovely story. Suhit
Posted by Suhit Anantula | 03/31/04

It's pathetic, man, the whole article reflected how lonely you are!
Posted by 5600hp | 04/04/04

III. MAQUILADORA WORKERS

Ángela on Managers

Ángela paused for a breath: "Really, thank God he switched us back, because it was a killer to work all night and get home just in time to make breakfast and clean the house, before trying to get some sleep with all the daytime racket."

Ángela was grateful to the manager. She associated the North Americans with the good and the humane. At various times she has commented to me that they should replace all the Mexican supervisors with North Americans, because the latter are much better. Many female factory workers shared this notion. In their opinion, the Mexicans were tyrants, good-for-nothings. The women concurred in viewing the North Americans as more responsible, more considerate, and, above all, more appreciative and considerate of women. As one observed, "We have never had North American supervisors, but I know that they're better because those who have been to the factory, the engineers and the coordinators, are very nice people."

The workers at Ángela's plant once proposed to the manager that he replace all the Mexican supervisors with North Americans. He smiled at the flattery of his North American pride. "Let's see what we can do," he responded, but nothing changed. Clearly, the firm has no interest in changing supervisors. It is necessary to maintain the reputation of the considerate North American, but the supervisor, as an intermediary representing the owners' interests, can rarely afford to be considerate. Besides, a North American supervisor would earn a very high salary, paid in dollars. . . .

Alma on Pay and Product

I had been working for six years in a textile maquiladora, where I nearly destroyed my kidneys and my eyes. I never earned a fixed salary. They paid me by the job, on a piecework basis, as they also call it. In this maquiladora here, we work quite differently from the way they do in other textile plants. . . .

The dresses we make are beautiful, for very fashionable women. They're incredibly expensive! They sell them in the best stores in the United States and they cost $200 or $300. And what do we get? We make 45 pesos [about U.S. $1] per dress. Incredible, don't you think? We spend ten hours a day in front of a sewing machine to make a man rich and we don't even know him. And the worst of it is that we continue doing it, some not even making the minimum wage, without complaining, asleep at the wheel, watching time go by, years in front of the sewing machine. I recognize the glares; I know how we protest on the inside because we don't dare say anything to the bosses. We wait for the quitting bell to ring so we can hit the street, believing that it's all a bad dream, and that it's going to change. It's like we put these thoughts aside for a moment and go back to work, without doing anything more about it. At times we forget why the devil we're working, just waiting for a little bit of money so our kids can survive.

You get used to it all, or at least we pretend to. At times we let ourselves be carried away by the noise or the music of the radios we all carry. It helps us forget the fatigue and the back pain we all have working in front of the sewing machine. The moment came when I just couldn't take any more and I quit, knowing that the money my husband makes, together with what our oldest daughter gives us, wasn't going to be enough.

Maria Luisa on Urban Life

I didn't know anything about Tijuana. I had never been in a city. I had never left the village, and the village wasn't very big! So it was quite an experience to go to Mazatlán and take the train. Everything seemed beautiful to me.

I got to Tijuana and I couldn't pronounce a lot of words. I couldn't pronounce "carpet," or "linoleum," or "newspaper." I didn't even know these things existed. The old lady's niece told me, "You don't say it like that! You say it this way." She taught me how to pronounce the words correctly. I was really taken with TV because I had never seen it. I had seen movies, because there was a man who brought them to show in the village. I had only seen movies, that was it. But I had never imagined there could be this little box, you turn it on, and there are people talking. I really liked TV. It's very entertaining! . . .

Ángela on Factory Life Compared with Village Work

It might seem like I exaggerate, but it gave me a great sense of happiness to start working at the maquiladora; I thought I had overcome my past. It was the moment in which God heard my prayers and changed my life. I could forget what was behind me. That part of my life was so very difficult that on one occasion I threw myself in front of a car, and on another I took a bunch of pills. What I wanted was to die.

Gabriela on a Plant Strike

We workers were affected by the devaluation, but for the owners it was a great deal. Here in Tijuana, and generally along the entire border, we have to buy a lot of American products—basic necessities—with prices marked in dollars. Every time there is a devaluation we buy fewer products; every time we poor people become poorer, and the rich become richer.

During the strike the manager tried to bribe the union membership, offering money and better salaries on the condition the people leave the union. After ten days of striking, the Board of Conciliation and Arbitration [Junta de Conciliación y Arbitraje] declared the strike null and void.

The first day of February 1983 they closed the plant permanently. They fooled us good. We were all demoralized: the state government, the American owners, and the Mexican manager had united to do us in. They stopped at nothing to destroy the union. We pressured the Board of Conciliation and Arbitration to secure compensation, and after fighting around the clock, they gave us only 70 percent of what we were owed.

STUDY QUESTIONS

1. What are some of the most important regional disagreements about globalization? How might they be explained?
2. How does globalization relate to social and economic class? How do class differences, in impact and assessment, relate to regional differences? Which are more important? Why?
3. Which aspects of globalization seem most appealing? Why? Which aspects seem most questionable? Why?
4. Are there major problems in using polling data to determine evaluations of globalization? What other evidence would be useful?
5. What are the main characteristics of the global youth culture? What are its limitations?
6. How does economic globalization relate to global consumerism? Do these facets generate different evaluations of the larger globalization process?
7. What is the impact of globalization on poverty (see Chapter 44)?

SUGGESTED ESSAYS

A. Which changes more with contemporary globalization: youth culture or manufacturing work? Be sure to refer to specific parts of the documents, along with any other relevant evidence, in developing your answer.

B. What is the evidence that globalization is a new phenomenon? How far back in time do some of its major features go?

C. Is international support for globalization likely to increase or decrease over time?

52 GLOBALIZATION AND THE ENVIRONMENT

The late twentieth century saw a double first in world history: the globalization of environmental impacts and the globalization of efforts at responses. Human impact on the environment was not new: hunters had sometimes overkilled, reducing animal populations, and agriculture often created regional environmental loss. Industrialization expanded the capacity to affect the environment but still on a regional basis, around factory cities and colonial agricultural estates.

Expanding populations, expanding industry, increasing numbers of automobiles, and expanding demand for resources changed the equation by the late twentieth century, as forested areas rapidly declined and polluting emissions rapidly accelerated. One key result, most relevant scientists increasingly agreed, was a pattern of global warming that portended changes in weather patterns, the survival of some species and agricultural regions, and a rise in sea levels. Growing realization of the issue prompted efforts to formulate international agreements and policies, with several conferences, notably in Rio de Janeiro and Kyoto, pledging pollution restraint. Different groups had different interpretations of the problem and its urgency, of responsibility, and of the nature of effective responses. Among industrial countries, the United States particularly held back, refusing to accept the Kyoto accords on gas emissions developed in 1997. Other nations and environmental groups criticized the U.S. stance but without much immediate effect. Other countries had their own issues about the priority of environment concerns.

The following materials come from President George W. Bush, in June 2001, on the eve of a trip to more environmentally conscious Europe and after he had indicated that the United States would not sign the Kyoto accords; from a statement to a United Nations sustainable development meeting, in 2002, by the Chinese Premier, Zhu Rongji; and from a statement by the U.S. branch of the global environmental group Greenpeace, a leading international nongovernmental organization (NGO).

Selection I from http://www.whitehouse.gov/news/releases/2001/06/21100611-2.html. Selection II from http://www.china-un.ch/eng/qtzz/wtojjwt/t85654.htm. Selection III from http://www.greenpeace.org/ usa/takeaction/the-people-s-ratification-of-t.

ADDRESSING GLOBAL WARMING

I. PRESIDENT BUSH'S NEWS CONFERENCE STATEMENT, JUNE 2001

[Global climate change] is an issue that I know is very important to the nations of Europe, which I will be visiting for the first time as President. The earth's well-being is also an issue important to America. And it's an issue that should be important to every nation in every part of our world.

The issue of climate change respects no border. Its effects cannot be reined in by an army nor advanced by any ideology. Climate change, with its potential to impact every corner of the world, is an issue that must be addressed by the world.

The Kyoto Protocol was fatally flawed in fundamental ways. But the process used to bring nations together to discuss our joint response to climate change is an important one. That is why I am today committing the United States of America to work within the United Nations framework and elsewhere to develop with our friends and allies and nations throughout the world an effective and science-based response to the issue of global warming.

My Cabinet-level working group has met regularly for the last 10 weeks to review the most recent, most accurate, and most comprehensive science. They have heard from scientists offering a wide spectrum of views. They have reviewed the facts, and they have listened to many theories and suppositions. The working group asked the highly respected National Academy of Sciences to provide us the most up-to-date information about what is known and about what is not known on the science of climate change.

First, we know the surface temperature of the earth is warming. It has risen by .6 degrees Celsius over the past 100 years. There was a warming trend from the 1890s to the 1940s. Cooling from the 1940s to the 1970s. And then sharply rising temperatures from the 1970s to today.

There is a natural greenhouse effect that contributes to warming. Greenhouse gases trap heat, and thus warm the earth because they prevent a significant proportion of infrared radiation from escaping into space. Concentrations of greenhouse gases, especially CO_2, have increased substantially since the beginning of the industrial revolution. And the National Academy of Sciences indicates that the increase is due in large part to human activity.

Yet, the Academy's report tells us that we do not know how much effect natural fluctuations in climate may have had on warming. We do not know how much our climate could, or will change in the future. We do not know how fast change will occur, or even how some of our actions could impact it.

Our country, the United States is the world's largest emitter of man-made greenhouse gases. We account for almost 20 percent of the world's man-made greenhouse emissions. We also account for about one-quarter of the world's economic output. We recognize the responsibility to reduce our emissions. We also recognize the other part of the story—that the rest of the world emits 80 percent of all greenhouse gases. And many of those emissions come from developing countries.

This is a challenge that requires a 100 percent effort; ours, and the rest of the world's. The world's second-largest emitter of greenhouse gases is China. Yet, China was entirely exempted from the requirements of the Kyoto Protocol.

Kyoto is, in many ways, unrealistic. Many countries cannot meet their Kyoto targets. The targets themselves were arbitrary and not based upon science. For America, complying with those mandates would have a negative economic impact, with layoffs of workers and price increases for consumers. And when you evaluate all these flaws, most reasonable people will understand that it's not sound public policy.

That's why 95 members of the United States Senate expressed a reluctance to endorse such an approach. Yet, America's unwillingness to embrace a flawed treaty should not be read by our friends and allies as any abdication of responsibility. To the contrary, my administration is committed to a leadership role on the issue of climate change.

Today, I make our investment in science even greater. My administration will establish the U.S. Climate Change Research Initiative to study areas of uncertainty and identify priority areas where investments can make a difference. . . .

Our approach must be flexible to adjust to new information and take advantage of new technology. We must always act to ensure continued economic growth.

And, finally, our approach must be based on global participation, including that of developing countries whose net greenhouse gas emissions now exceed those in the developed countries.

II. STATEMENT BY ZHU RONGJI, 2002

Concerted efforts of all countries are needed in achieving sustainable development. We should take common development as our objective and bring about a new partnership featuring mutual respect, equality and mutual benefit. The principles laid down by the [United Nations Conferences] in Rio, especially the principle of "common but differentiated responsibilities," should be adhered to. The United Nations should play an active role in coordinating the overall international strategy of environment and development, as well as in conducting technology transfer, technical consultation, personnel training and aid programs. Relevant international and regional organizations and agencies should strengthen their cooperation with all countries, especially developing countries. Countries should do a still better job in mobilizing their social groups, enterprises and population to work for sustainable development.

We should strengthen scientific and technological cooperation in achieving sustainable development. Rapid development of science and technology in today's world has increasingly become a powerful engine for human progress. It is essential that we extensively apply the research results, especially those in information, biology and other hi-tech fields, in resources exploitation, environment protection and ecological development. Spread of science and technology should recognize no national boundaries. The international community and national governments should adopt new policies and mechanisms to help reduce clashes between protecting intellectual property rights and promoting wider application of technology so as to facilitate transfer of technology among states.

We should endeavour to create an international economic environment conducive to sustainable development. Global sustainable development requires a fair and equitable new international economic order and a new regime of world trade. Erecting trade barriers with excessive environmental standards will, instead of getting us any closer to solving the environmental issues, seriously hamper the capabilities of the developing countries for sustainable development. The international community should fully understand the difficulties faced by the developing countries in the areas of fund, trade and debts, and take effective steps to remove protective trade practices of one kind or another. The developed countries, in particular, should make their market more accessible by dismantling trade barriers. The developing countries should take an active part in international cooperation and competition with a view to steadily enhancing their capabilities of sustainable development. To this end, we call for a proper handling of the relationship between trade and environment at the new round of multilateral trade negotiations so as to ensure that the two will promote each other. . . .

Mr. President, Since the Rio UNCED, the Chinese Government, acting in a highly responsible manner to discharge its commitment, has taken the lead in formulating China's Agenda 21, mapped out the strategy of rejuvenating the nation through science and technology and the strategy of sustainable development, and identified the key sectors of China's sustainable development for the early years of the new century and relevant programs of action. Having formulated and improved more than 120 laws, rules and regulations concerning population, family planning, environment protection, natural resources management, disaster prevention and relief, China now has an organizational and administrative system operating at various levels that involves multiple agencies of both the central and local governments. At the same time, China has acceded to a series of international conventions and completed the domestic procedure for the approval of the Kyoto Protocol with a view to taking an active part in multilateral environment cooperation. . . .

After years of searching, we have found for ourselves a development model with Chinese characteristics and our sustainable development is holding out a promising prospect. By 2005, the tendency of ecological degradation will be on the whole arrested, and the total discharge of major pollutants will drop by 10% compared with 2000. In 2010, our GDP will double that of 2000 when our people will be much better off, the development of our resources more rational and the quality of our environment more improved, thus presenting a more uplifting picture of harmonious development of the economy, population, resources and environment.

Mr. President, as the world's largest developing country and a major player in environment protection, China is an important force in international environment cooperation. We are deeply aware of the responsibilities on our shoulders. If we do a good job in running China well, it will be a great contribution to the world cause of sustainable development. We are still faced with considerable restraints and difficulties in implementing the sustainable development strategy due to our large population, low per capita resources, vulnerable ecology, uneven regional economic development and inadequate development of our overall economy. We will continue to work hard, unflinchingly shoulder our responsibilities, honor our commitments with deeds, and steadfastly take the road of sustainable development. I firmly believe that this summit will usher in a better implementation of the sustainable development strategy in all countries. We in China will, as always, energetically participate in international environment cooperation and work with all other countries in protecting the global environment and realizing sustainable development throughout the world. We are destined to have an even better future for China and for our entire world.

THE PEOPLE'S RATIFICATION OF THE KYOTO PROTOCOL

III. GREENPEACE STATEMENT, 2005

When faced with a grave threat to a livable future for ourselves, our children and future generations, it is our duty as Americans to respond.

To date, some 140 nations have ratified the Kyoto Protocol, which took effect in February 2005, in order to arrest the intensifying destructiveness of global climate change.

In contrast, the United States, which generates 25 percent of the world's polluting carbon emissions with only five percent of its population, refuses to join in this worldwide effort to keep this planet hospitable to civilization.

We recognize the current goals of the Protocol are too low—and its timetable too long—to effectively halt the escalating instability of the global climate.

We also recognize the Kyoto Protocol is the only existing diplomatic framework through which the entire global community can address this unprecedented challenge.

We further recognize that the Constitution of the United States grants us the ultimate authority of government.

Therefore, as citizens of the United States, we hereby ratify the Kyoto Protocol and demand that you and our elected representatives follow suit.

Additionally, we pledge to support subsequent phases of the Kyoto Protocol to reduce worldwide greenhouse emissions by 70 percent. This global transition to clean energy would address nature's demand for a stable climate even as it generates millions of clean energy jobs.

Finally, we declare, through this act of ratification, our allegiance to the democratic process, our fundamental and mortal relationship with this Earth and our essential solidarity with every other member of the human family.

STUDY QUESTIONS

1. What are the main international disagreements over global warming and appropriate responses?
2. Why was President Bush often accused of dragging his feet on the issues? Did his rhetoric conceal key hesitations, not just over the Kyoto accords but over the whole problem?

3. What distinctive concerns did China bring to the table?
4. Why can an NGO such as Greenpeace feel authorized to participate in the debate over international policy?
5. Is it likely that American concern over global warming will increase in the twenty-first century? Why or why not?
6. How does experience with handling historical documents—dealing with disagreements and with overt and hidden points of view—help in interpreting a contemporary controversy such as that over global warming? Does a more objective analysis of recent debates suggest any ways to promote greater accord on this issue? If so, how?
7. How does the issue of environmental change and global response fit into the larger patterns of globalization in the late twentieth and early twenty-first centuries?

ESSAY SUGGESTIONS

A. China and the United States are now the two biggest atmospheric polluters in the world. Given their current policies, is there much hope of dealing with global warming in the near future? Why do their positions and those of European countries differ so greatly?

B. What other kinds of documents would assist in exploring possible ways to improve international dialogues over global warming?

C. How does the debate over global warming suggest major changes in world history in recent decades?

D. For further research: Has international cooperation on any global issue, over the past half-century, fared better than the responses to global warming? Or does recent history suggest that international political action can never catch up with the generation of new global problems?

53 GLOBAL POLITICS AND DISEASE MANAGEMENT

Human contacts across regions have always had the potential of spreading disease. Major cases involve transmission of epidemic diseases to the Mediterranean and China (probably from India) late in the classical period, the bubonic plague that spread from China westward in the fourteenth century, and the "Columbian exchange" of diseases from the eastern hemisphere to the western in the sixteenth and seventeenth centuries.

Contemporary globalization has introduced new elements into this old equation, however, particularly in terms of changes in the nature of potential transmission and the capacity for international response. Some new diseases have appeared, as well.

Documents in this section reflect the severe acute respiratory disease syndrome (SARS) epidemic in 2003, a disease with significant potential for contagion and fatalities. The disease began in Asia and was not initially clearly recognized or handled by some of the governments involved. International awareness built fairly quickly, prompting policy changes and involving the World Health Organization (WHO), an agency of the United Nations. By 2004, the epidemic was halted, at least for the time being.

The first document is a speech by the Chinese prime minister to the Association of Southeast Asian Nations (ASEAN); the second is from the Canadian health ministry; the third is from a WHO report; and the fourth document offers a retrospective assessment by the Chinese ambassador to Singapore, speaking to a gala concert audience, a year after the crisis had peaked. The final document is even more after-the-fact, a 2009 public statement from a doctor who had warned about SARS (in 2003), and about the Chinese government's first impulse to conceal the problem. The doctor was later disciplined; nevertheless, this document raises some particular problems of interpretation, both about an authoritarian government and its behaviors in a crisis and about evaluating a complainant.

Selection I from Premier Wen Jiabao at the China-ASEAN Leaders Meeting, retrieved from http://losangeles.china-consulate.org/eng/news/topnews/t27622.htm. Selection II retrieved from http:// www.phac-aspc.gc.ca/sars-sras/hc_response04_27-eng.php. Selection III from Fifty-sixth World Health Assembly WHA56.29 Agenda Item 14.16, 28 May 2003. Selection IV retrieved from http:// www.chinaembassy.org.sg/eng/dscz/dscfyi/t165678.htm. Selection V retrieved from http:// hina.blogs.time.com/ 2009/03/13/sars-hero-seeks-apology/.

SEVERE ACUTE RESPIRATORY DISEASE SYNDROME (SARS) EPIDEMIC

I. SPEECH BY PREMIER WEN JIABAO AT THE SPECIAL CHINA-ASEAN LEADERS MEETING ON SARS, 2003

I came to attend this conference in the spirit of candid responsibility, trust and cooperation. I will brief ASEAN leaders on the SARS situation in China, major experience and lessons in the prevention and treatment of SARS, and the measures taken by the Chinese government. I hope that mutual understanding and trust between China and ASEAN countries will be promoted and cooperation between us enhanced through this conference.

The SARS epidemic currently spreading in some countries and regions poses a grave threat to life and health of mankind. SARS is a brand new contagious disease, yet to be fully understood to mankind. There is neither a conclusive method of diagnosis, nor an effective cure, nor a full understanding of how this disease spreads. Given our huge and highly mobile population and our lack of experience with controlling a sudden epidemic, the country is still faced with a serious situation despite a great deal of work. Right now, places like Guangdong, where SARS hit rather early, still see a few new cases. The number of SARS cases in Beijing, Shanxi and Inner Mongolia is rising noticeably. The situation has not been brought fully under control and there is the tendency of spreading to most provinces of China.

The Chinese Government is a highly responsible government, ready to face difficulties squarely and putting the health, safety and life of the people above everything else. We have, and will continue to take resolute steps in an effort to turn the situation around.

First, strengthening prevention across the board to contain the spread of disease. The Chinese Government has made SARS a statutory epidemic under the country's legislation, and established an open and transparent system for epidemic reporting and news briefing. We make daily reports of SARS statistics to the WHO [World Health Organization], and publish it to the communities in the meantime. By ensuring early detection, early reporting, early quarantine and early treatment, we have done everything possible to control infection source. We have imposed strict quarantine and prevention measures in public transit systems, major locations and ports of exit and entry. Guarding against cross infection in all contaminated areas and articles to isolation and prevention measures. People having had close contact with them are quarantined for medical observation. Units and places identifies as epidemic high-risk areas have been isolated in accordance with law. Besides, we have conducted publicity campaigns on disease prevention to increase the citizens' awareness and capability for self-protection so that prevention can be ensured with mass participation.

Second, going all out to treat SARS patients and setting up SARS funds. China's provinces, regions and municipalities have designated special hospitals and enlarged medical facilities to bring timely treatment to SARS patients.

Efforts were made to ensure adequate supply of medicine and improve hospital facilities. The central government has allocated RMB 2 billion yuan for the establishment of a SARS fund, to be used mainly for the treatment of SARS patients from rural backgrounds or needy urban families and for emergency upgrading of county-level hospitals in the poor areas of central and western China and their purchases of SARS-related medical equipment. The localities have also made special funds available for SARS prevention and treatment. We have paid close attention to SARS control in rural areas and taken all necessary measures, including free medical care for rural-based SARS patients and on-spot treatment for farmer patients who hold jobs in cities so as to prevent SARS from spreading to the countryside.

Thirdly, establishing an epidemic contingency mechanism and enhancing the capacity for emergency management. We lost no time in establishing a national public health contingency response mechanism, a disease monitor and data collection network and an ascertaining network of laboratories. The central government has allocated RMB 3.5 billion yuan for infrastructure development of a national disease control system, together with other special expenditures for the construction of the China Center for Disease Control and Prevention.

Fourthly, stepping up critical SARS research and exploring effective methods of diagnosis and treatment. We have mobilized multi-disciplinary experts across the country to look for the cause of the SARS epidemic, and study new methods of diagnosis and treatment. We have developed a fast diagnostic method and are trying to improve it and testing it clinically. Efforts are also made to research and develop drugs and equipment for SARS prevention and treatment. The central government has provided a special fund for SARS research and development.

Fifthly, increasing cooperation with the international community and drawing on others' successful experience. We have worked hard to promote cooperation with the WHO and other international organizations, discussing with them ways to treat SARS patients, control the epidemic and investigate the cause of the disease. We value the useful advice by WHO experts after their field inspections and have acted upon them. We welcome the understanding, support, desires and gestures for cooperation from the international community on China's SARS prevention efforts. We will keep up our cooperation and exchanges with the WHO and other countries.

II. HEALTH CANADA'S RESPONSE TO REPORTS OF SARS CASES IN CHINA, 2004

On April 23rd, the WHO announced that individuals in China met WHO case definitions for probable SARS infections and other individuals were under investigation. The National Institute of Virology in Beijing is being investigated as the originating source of the outbreak. The institute has been engaged in research with the SARS coronavirus, including the development of a vaccine.

Health Canada has alerted clinical, public health and laboratory professionals to heightened the vigilance for SARS detection in patients with severe respiratory illness (fever, cough and radiographic evidence of pneumonia or acute respiratory distress syndrome), who in the 10 days prior to symptom onset:

- Have traveled to mainland China
- Have had close contact with a symptomatic person with a history of travel to mainland China
- Have worked in a laboratory where SARS coronavirus is being handled.

Health professionals are alerted to the importance of collecting a travel and occupation history for symptomatic patients and contacts.

In situations where SARS is suspected:

- Enhanced respiratory and contact precautions are recommended, and appropriate isolation precautions should be used.
- Patients should be promptly investigated and tested for SARS as per the laboratory guidelines.
- Local public health should be notified immediately for case investigation and contact tracing.
- Clinical guidelines are also available for case management.

Regular updates are communicated to our provincial and territorial public health, clinical and laboratory partners on SARS and other emerging severe respiratory illnesses.

Health Canada continues to maintain Quarantine Services at [all] the international airports. Quarantine Officers continue to be at a heightened state of vigilance to respond quickly to a passenger with severe respiratory illness. As is normal procedure, quarantine officers will respond to reports of ill passengers on board.

Health Canada distributes Flu/SARS brochures at the international airport and has begun to proactively disseminate a SARS health alert notice to passengers arriving from East Asia at Vancouver and Toronto Pearson International airports. The notice asks passengers to be on the lookout for symptoms of SARS and gives advice on seeking medical care as necessary.

Health Canada is monitoring this situation very closely and is working with its international partners to verify reports. Regular updates are communicated to our provincial and territorial partners as new information is obtained.

III. FIFTY-SIXTH WORLD HEALTH ASSEMBLY, SEVERE ACUTE RESPIRATORY SYNDROME (SARS) 2003

The 56th World Health Assembly, on the emergence of severe acute respiratory syndrome (SARS) and on the prevention and control of influenza pandemics:

Deeply concerned that SARS, as the first severe infectious disease to emerge in the twenty-first century, poses a serious threat to global health security, the livelihood of populations, the functioning of health systems, and the stability and growth of economies;

Deeply appreciative of the dedication in responding to SARS of health care workers in all countries, including WHO staff member, Dr. Carlo Urbani, who in late February 2003 first brought SARS to the attention of the international community, and died of SARS on 29 March 2003;

Recognizing the need for Member States to take individual and collective actions to implement effective measures to contain the spread of SARS;

Acknowledging that the control of SARS requires intensive regional and global collaboration, effective strategies and additional resources at local, national, regional and international levels;

Appreciating the crucial role of WHO in a worldwide campaign to control and contain the spread of SARS;

Acknowledging the great effort made by affected countries, including those with limited resources, and other Member States in containing SARS;

Acknowledging the willingness of the scientific community, facilitated by WHO, to collaborate urgently, which led to the exceptionally rapid progress in the understanding of a new disease;

Noting, however, that much about the causative agent and the clinical and epidemiological features of SARS remain to be elucidated, and that the future course of the outbreak cannot as yet be predicted;

Noting that national and international experiences with SARS contribute lessons that can improve preparedness for responding to, and mitigating the public health, economic, and social consequences of the next emerging infectious disease, the next influenza pandemic, and the possible use of a biological agent to cause harm;

URGES Member States:

1. To commit fully to controlling SARS and other emerging and re-emerging infectious diseases, through political leadership, the provision of adequate resources, including through international cooperation, intensified multisectoral collaboration and public information;
2. To apply WHO recommended guidelines on surveillance, including case definitions, case management and international travel;
3. To report cases promptly and transparently and to provide requested information to WHO;
4. To enhance collaboration with WHO and other international and regional organizations in order to support epidemiological and laboratory surveillance systems, and to foster effective and rapid responses to contain the disease;
5. To strengthen, to the extent possible, capacity for SARS surveillance and control by developing or enhancing existing national programmes for communicable disease control;
6. To ensure that those with operational responsibilities can be contacted by telephone or through electronic communications at all times;
7. To continue to collaborate with and, when appropriate, provide assistance to WHO's Global Outbreak Alert and Response Network as the operational arm of the global response;

8. To request the support of WHO when appropriate, and particularly when control measures employed are ineffective in halting the spread of disease;
9. To use their experience with SARS preparedness and response to strengthen epidemiological and laboratory capacity as part of preparedness plans for responding to the next emerging infection, the next influenza pandemic, and the possible deliberate use of a biological agent to cause harm;
10. To exchange information and experience on epidemics and the prevention and control of emerging and re-emerging infectious diseases in a timely manner, including among countries sharing land borders;
11. To mitigate the adverse impact of the SARS epidemic on the health of the population, health systems and socioeconomic development;

REQUESTS the Director-General:

1. To further mobilize and sustain global efforts to control the SARS epidemic;
2. To update and standardize guidelines on international travel, in particular those related to aviation, through enhanced collaboration with other international and regional organizations;
3. To update guidelines on surveillance, including case definitions, clinical and laboratory diagnosis, and management, and on effective preventive measures;
4. To review and update, on the basis of epidemiological data and information provided by Member States, the classification of "areas with recent local transmission," through close interactive consultation with the Member States concerned, and in a manner that safeguards the health of populations while minimizing public misunderstanding and negative socioeconomic impact;
5. To mobilize global scientific research to improve understanding of the disease and to develop control tools such as diagnostic tests, drugs and vaccines that are accessible to and affordable by member states, especially developing countries and countries with economies in transition;
6. To collaborate with member States in their efforts to mobilize financial and human resources and technical support in order to develop or enhance national, regional and global systems for epidemiological surveillance and to ensure effective responses to emerging and reemerging diseases, including SARS;
7. To respond appropriately to all requests for WHO's support for surveillance, prevention, and control of SARS in conformity with the WHO Constitution;
8. To strengthen the functions of WHO's Global Outbreak Alert and Response Network;
9. To strengthen the global network of WHO collaborating centres in order to carry out research and training on the management of emerging and re-emerging diseases, including SARS.

IV. AMBASSADOR ZHANG'S SPEECH AT THE CONCERT IN SUPPORT OF SARS FIGHTING IN CHINA, OCTOBER 2004

I am very pleased to attend tonight's performance. In the form of performance, the Singapore Chinese Orchestra and the Chinese Overseas Students Association will show their support to the Chinese and Singaporean medical staffs, who are fighting against SARS at the very frontier, and they will express their deep sympathy and care to their compatriots, who are still suffering from SARS. This remarkable event will transcend the space and time, and join together hearts of both countries' people. Valuable and touching, it will represent the purest passion and greatest philanthropy of human being. I would like to express my heartfelt admiration and gratitude to the students and friends who attend tonight's concert!

SARS came as an unforeseeable catastrophe. Honestly, I should say that at the beginning, China failed to accumulate enough knowledge about SARS, which resulted in a stranded scenario. As the new generation of Chinese leaders took office, they soon recognized the stern situation before they addressed a series of effective measures in the decisive and firm manner. They managed to lead China out of the predicament, actively curb the dangerous tide and in the end, created a better situation. People have obtained information from different sources that the SARS contagion trend has been stabilized and now is under effective control.

China's notable progress in SARS control corresponds with the victorious news that Singapore is removed from list of areas with local SARS transmission. We feel so pleased at the success achieved by the Chinese and Singaporean government. As a matter of fact, the two countries have been maintaining sound cooperation in combating SARS. The Singaporean government has set up a good example for China with its transparency, decisiveness and efficiency of the action. Various Singaporean societies have given valuable material and spiritual support to the Chinese people. On behalf of the Chinese government and the Chinese people, I would like to take this opportunity to convey sincere gratitude to the Singaporean government and people.

The worldwide battle of SARS prevention and control has reached a turning point. The stormy struggle has ended. However, the anti-epidemic war still has a long run. For the next step, two targets should be pursued at the same time. We should still continue our work in preventing SARS spread and keep vigilant against reoccurrence of the epidemic until the last success. On the other hand, no efforts should be spared in fostering the economy and improvement of other fields in order to make up the losses caused by the epidemic in the first half year. How to do a good job in the post-SARS period will become our focus. Both governments of China and Singapore share consensus in this aspect. Since the cooperation at the first stage has exerted a distinctive effect in fighting against SARS, the collaboration of the next stage will be more meaningful to both countries' economic development.

Against different national backgrounds, SARS-caused economic damage in China and Singapore varies in different scales. As far as China is concerned, the negative influence is short lasting, partial and limited, so its economy will continue maintaining a strong expansionist impulse. Many worldwide authoritative economic organizations all share the view that China's economy will grow at the speed no less than 7% this year. After getting rid of the SARS shadow, China will be bathed under the sunshine, with hope and vigour. Still considered a promising land in terms of foreign investment, China is an oasis of safety, lowland of cost, and highland of profit for the foreign investors.

V. DR. JIANG ADDRESSES GENERAL SECRETARY HU JINTAO AND THE MEMBERS OF THE POLITBURO STANDING COMMITTEE, FEBRUARY 2009

As a doctor, my duty is to save people's lives. That is why I sent out a letter of warning about Beijing's SARS epidemic in 2003. It is also why I sent a letter of February 24, 2004 to leaders of the NPC and the Central Committee calling for a reappraisal of June 4 [student democratic demonstrations of 1989] based on what I witnessed as the director of surgery at No. 301 Hospital. My letters were all delivered through proper channels, and my actions were all in line with the Constitution, the Party Charter and army disciplinary rules.

However, on June 1, 2004, my wife and I were kidnapped without any proper procedure or documentation. For the first two weeks, I was purportedly held in an "administrative detention." My wife was kidnapped and detained at the same time but she was only shown an "administrative detention" order a week later, back-dated. . . .

According to the CCP disciplinary rules, article 58: "For creating rumors that demonize the Party and the State, for mild offenses, a warning or a serious warning shall be issued; for serious offenses, probation or a change of position with the party organization shall be issued; for extremely serious offenses, expulsion from the Party shall be issued." The case of Jiang Yanyong should be considered an extremely serious offense. However, because Jaing has admitted to his mistakes and provided a written letter of repentance and a wish for redemption, we hereby issue, with the approval of the Central Military Commission, a two year internal Party probation for Jiang Yanyong.

I immediately complained that the statement was not based on the truth and was therefore unacceptable. . . . Furthermore, it is really outrageous that I have continued to be restricted from visiting family members overseas. I believe all restrictions on me should be removed and the relevant departments should correct their mistakes and issue an apology. Only then will they be in compliance with the ideals of the Party's fourth generation leadership: "rule by law," "the people first" and "harmonious society."

STUDY QUESTIONS

1. In what ways does contemporary globalization promote changes in international disease transmission?
2. Why might different governments respond differently to an epidemic disease threat? What were the differences in Canadian and Chinese responses?
3. How and why did Chinese policies change over time? What particular challenges did China face in dealing with SARS?

4. What is the role of global political institutions in responding to disease? How effective is the response?
5. How do global politics concerning disease compare to global politics concerning the environment? How can the differences best be explained?
6. Judging by these documents, what can be done to improve international disease control?

ESSAY SUGGESTIONS

A. Compare the SARS epidemic to the spread of bubonic plague in the fourteenth century. What accounts for the major differences?
B. What are the most likely future issues in global patterns of, and responses to, disease transmission?
C. Compare the response to SARS with the response to the international spread of the H1N1 influenza virus in 2009–2010. Has global response improved? What new issues have emerged?
D. How do the various facets of globalization—economic, political, cultural, environmental—add up? Can they be embraced in a single definition of globalization and the changes and continuities it represents?